Port Management Strategy for Enhancing Cybersecurity and Resilience

This book provides a comprehensive overview of cybersecurity management in ports, cybersecurity vulnerabilities, and managerial strategies to improve cyber resilience.

Organized into three sections, the book provides an overview of seaport infrastructure and actors and cyber and technological risks. It is written in a non-technical manner, focusing on the intersection of maritime transport and information security.

Key elements of the book include:

- Analysis of 11 publicly reported cyber-attacks, to understand hacker penetration techniques and motivations, as well as the impact on port operations.
- Clear technical explanations of port cybersecurity strategy, including cybersecurity hygiene and the cyber-attack management cycle.
- Step-by-step guidelines for making response, recovery, and mitigation plans for new managers and port officers involved in cybersecurity teams.

This book will appeal to students and researchers of port operations and management, logistics, and supply chain management. Practitioners can also use this book as a guide to improve their knowledge of cyber risk and the measures to address it.

Chalermpong Senarak is an associate professor in the Logistics Management Program, Faculty of Management Sciences, Kasetsart University, Thailand. His research interests include maritime transport, port technology, and management.

Routledge Studies in Transport Analysis

19. **Maritime Ports, Inland Corridors and Logistics**
    Edited by Cyrille Bertelle, Nathan Gouin and Antoine Frémont

20. **Strategies for Sustainable Air Services Development**
    An Airport-Destination Collaborative Approach
    Edited by Kareem Yarde and Chrystal Zhang

21. **Digital Transport Platforms and Urban Mobility**
    Ride Hailing Applications in Southeast Asia
    Edited by Hironori Kato and Saksith Chalermpong

22. **Strategies for Sustainable Air Services Development**
    An Airport-Destination Collaborative Approach
    Edited by Chrystal Zhang and Kareem Yarde

23. **Artificial Intelligence in Shipping**
    The State of Digital Innovation
    Maria Lambrou

24. **Railway Safety Management**
    Systems, Practices, and Emerging Trends
    Katarzyna Chruzik and Marzena Graboń-Chałupczak

25. **Port Management Strategy for Enhancing Cybersecurity and Resilience**
    Learning from Case Studies
    Chalermpong Senarak

For more information about this series, please visit: www.routledge.com/Routledge-Studies-in-Transport-Analysis/book-series/RSTA

Port Management Strategy for Enhancing Cybersecurity and Resilience

Learning from Case Studies

Chalermpong Senarak

Routledge
Taylor & Francis Group
LONDON AND NEW YORK

First published 2026
by Routledge
4 Park Square, Milton Park, Abingdon, Oxon, OX14 4RN

and by Routledge
605 Third Avenue, New York, NY 10158

Routledge is an imprint of the Taylor & Francis Group, an informa business

British Library Cataloguing-in-Publication Data
A catalogue record for this book is available from the British Library

ISBN: 9781032907031 (hbk)
ISBN: 9781032907048 (pbk)
ISBN: 9781003559320 (ebk)

DOI: 10.4324/9781003559320

Typeset in Galliard
by Newgen Publishing UK

Contents

Figures

Preface

In the digital era, ensuring cybersecurity and resilience within seaport operations requires more than technical safeguards; it calls for strategic foresight, integrated management, and cross-sector collaboration. As ports undergo rapid digital transformation, all operational domains become vulnerable to cyber threats, making cybersecurity a shared responsibility across organizational levels.

This book presents a comprehensive framework of strategies and managerial practices aimed at mitigating cyber risks inherent in modern port ecosystems. While grounded in technical realities, it is written to support readers from diverse backgrounds, offering practical insights to enhance both cybersecurity and long-term resilience policies.

Central themes include the structure and functions of seaport infrastructure, the role of PIS in managing cargo and vessel logistics, the nature of emerging cyber risks, and their business implications. The book also explores adaptive strategies for safeguarding critical operations, drawing on case studies, sector-specific standards, and industry best practices. Particular attention is given to advanced tools—such as AI-driven threat detection—and collaborative frameworks that leading ports use to strengthen cyber defense.

Designed as a bridge between technical and managerial domains, this resource serves non-technical staff, operational teams, and executives navigating the complexities of digital port systems. It is equally relevant to researchers and early-career academics seeking to analyze real-world cyber incidents and develop effective mitigation strategies.

Acknowledgments

This book would not have been possible without the support and insights of many individuals and institutions. I am particularly grateful to the anonymous reviewers whose constructive feedback at both the proposal and manuscript stages greatly strengthened the quality and clarity of the final work.

I would also like to express my sincere appreciation to the editorial team at Routledge, an imprint of Informa UK Limited trading as Taylor & Francis Group, for their professionalism and guidance throughout the publishing process. Their support has been instrumental in transforming this manuscript into a finished volume.

Gratitude is also due to the many practitioners, port stakeholders, and researchers whose expertise—whether shared formally or through years of collaboration—has helped inform and shape the practical insights presented in this book.

Finally, I extend heartfelt thanks to my family, whose patience and encouragement provided unwavering support throughout the writing process.

Abbreviations

ACLs	Access Control Lists
AGVs	Automated Guided Vehicles
AI	Artificial Intelligence
AISs	Automatic Identification Systems
APIs	Application Programming Interfaces
APTs	Advanced Persistent Threats
AWS	Amazon Web Services
BAD	Behavioral Anomaly Detection
BCP	Business Continuity Planning
BIA	Business Impact Analysis
BIPVs	Building-Integrated Photovoltaics
BLE	Bluetooth Low Energy
BMSs	Berth Management Systems
CCTV	Closed-Circuit Television
CERTs	Computer Emergency Response Teams
CHSs	Cargo-Handling Systems
CIA	Confidentiality, Integrity, and Availability
CICS	Cybersecurity and Infrastructure Security Agency
CIO	Chief Information Officer
CIRTs	Cyber Incident Response Teams
CISA	Cybersecurity and Infrastructure Security Agency
CISO	Chief Information Security Officer
CMS	Cargo Management System
CO	Cyber Officer
CSA	Cyber Security Agency of Singapore
CSF	Cybersecurity Framework
CSOs	Company Security Officers
CSPs	Collaborative Strategic Partnerships
CSRs	Customer Service Relations
CTI	Cyber Threat Intelligence
CVSS	Common Vulnerability Scoring System
CYREN	Cyber Resilient North Sea Canal Area Network

DASs	Digital Attack Surfaces
DC/DC	Direct Current to Direct Current
DDoS	Distributed Denial-of-Service
DMZs	Demilitarized Zones
DNS	Domain Name System
DoC	Document of Compliance
DOS	Drayage Operation System
EDI	Electronic Data Interchange
EDR	Endpoint Detection and Response
ENISA	European Union Agency for Cybersecurity
FEU	Forty-Foot Equivalent Unit
FIN	Finish
GDPR	General Data Protection Regulation
GHG	Greenhouse Gas
GMS	Gate Management System
GPS	Global Positioning System
GPUs	Graphics Processing Units
HR	Human Resources
HSMs	Hardware Security Modules
IACS	International Association of Classification Societies
IAM	Identity and Access Management
IAPH	International Association of Ports and Harbors
ICMP	Internet Control Message Protocol
ICSs	Industrial Control Systems
IDSs	Intrusion Detection Systems
IEC	International Electrotechnical Commission
IMO	International Maritime Organization
IOCs	Indicators of Compromise
IoTs	Internet of Things
IP	Internet Protocol
IPSs	Intrusion Prevention Systems
IRP	Incident Response Plan
IRR	Incident Response and Recovery
IRRP	Incident Response and Recovery Plan
IRT	Incident Response Team
ISM	International Safety Management
ISMS	Information Security Management Systems
ISO	International Organization for Standardization
ISPS	International Ship and Port Facility Security
IT	Information Technology
KPIs	Key Performance Indicators
LANs	Local Area Networks
LiDAR	Light Detection and Ranging
LNG	Liquefied Natural Gas
LOSs	Landside Operating Systems

LPG	Liquefied Petroleum Gas
MFA	Multi-factor Authentication
ML	Machine Learning
MPA	Maritime and Port Authority
MPPT	Maximum Power Point Tracking
MSSPs	Managed Security Service Providers
NFV	Network Function Virtualization
NIST	National Institute of Standards and Technology
OSINT	Open-Source Intelligence
OT	Operational Technology
PASs	Physical Attack Surfaces
PCSs	Port Community Systems
PCT	Port Cybersecurity Team
PDPA	Personal Data Protection Act
PDS	Position Detection System
PFSA	Port Facility Security Assessment
PFSOs	Port Facility Security Officers
PFSPs	Port Facility Security Plans
PII	Personally Identifiable Information
PISs	Port Information Systems
PLCs	Programmable Logic Controllers
PNI	Port Network Integration
PNS	Port Network Segmentation
PRM	Proactive Risk Management
PV	Photovoltaic
RATs	Remote Access Tools
RBAC	Role-Based Access Control
RDP	Remote Desktop Protocol
RFID	Radio-Frequency Identification
RGETs	Renewable and Green Energy Technologies
Ro-Ro	Roll-on/Roll-off
RPOs	Recovery Point Objectives
RTLSs	Real-Time Locating Systems
RTOs	Recovery Time Objectives
SACS	Security and Access Control System
SCADA	Supervisory Control and Data Acquisition
SDN	Software Defined Networking
SEA	Social Engineering Attacks
SGOs	Strategies, Goals, and Objectives
SIEM	Security Information and Event Management
SLA	Service Level Agreement
SMSs	Safety Management Systems
SNMP	Simple Network Management Protocol
SOAR	Security Orchestration, Automation, and Response
SOCs	Security Operations Centers

SOLAS	International Convention for the Safety of Life at Sea
SOSs	Seaside Operating Systems
SQL	Structured Query Language
SSH	Secure Shell
SSOs	Ship Security Officers
SYN	Synchronize
TCP/IP	Transmission Control Protocol/Internet Protocol
TEU	Twenty-Foot Equivalent Unit
TFTP	Trivial File Transfer Protocol
TOSs	Terminal Operating Systems
TPMs	Trusted Platform Modules
TPUs	Tensor Processing Units
TTPs	Tactics, Techniques, and Procedures
UDP	User Datagram Protocol
UNCTAD	United Nations Conference on Trade and Development
URLs	Uniform Resource Locators
UWB	Ultra-Wideband
VIMs	Virtual Infrastructure Managers
VLANs	Virtual Local Area Networks
VNFs	Virtualized Network Functions
VTMSs	Vessel Traffic Management Systems
XDR	Extended Detection and Response
ZTA	Zero Trust Architecture

Introduction

In the contemporary maritime landscape, the rapid evolution of digital technologies has profoundly transformed port operations, enabling unprecedented efficiencies while simultaneously exposing critical systems to complex cyber threats. Ports, as vital nodes in the global supply chain, now operate within digitally interlinked environments where information systems govern logistics, coordinate stakeholder activity, and sustain operational continuity. As this digital dependence grows, so too does the imperative to manage the associated vulnerabilities. Cybersecurity and resilience are no longer peripheral technical concerns but central strategic priorities that demand integrated, forward-looking responses from port authorities, operators, and policymakers alike.

This book is situated at the intersection of port management and cybersecurity strategy. It seeks to illuminate the pathways through which ports can fortify their digital infrastructure while maintaining operational continuity in the face of increasingly sophisticated and frequent cyber incidents. It does so not only by examining the technological dimensions of cyber risks but by positioning them within broader organizational, regulatory, and strategic contexts. In doing so, it contributes to the ongoing discourse on critical infrastructure protection by offering a structured, evidence-based exploration of how cyber resilience can be embedded in port governance.

The foundational premise of this work is that cybersecurity in ports cannot be effectively addressed through technical interventions alone. Instead, it must be approached through a multidimensional strategy that encompasses people, processes, and partnerships. Chapter 1 lays the groundwork by providing a structural overview of seaports, including their core functions, operational infrastructure, and key personnel. This context is essential for understanding how digital systems are interwoven with physical port processes and how disruptions in one domain may reverberate across others.

From this foundation, Chapter 2 introduces the architecture of port information systems and the diverse technological components that support daily port functions—from terminal operations and cargo management to vessel traffic monitoring and port community coordination. It also delineates the potential attack surfaces within these systems, highlighting areas of vulnerability that are often overlooked in traditional risk assessments.

The subsequent chapters deepen this exploration by engaging directly with the technologies driving port modernization. Chapter 3 identifies major innovations—such as AI, IoT, blockchain, and cloud computing—illustrating both their transformative potential and the novel risks they introduce. The discussion is not limited to the technical; rather, it examines how these technologies reshape risk landscapes, necessitating new forms of oversight and contingency planning.

Chapters 4 and 5 offer a focused analysis of cyber threats and documented attacks on port infrastructure. Drawing from public incident reports and forensic case studies, the text dissects the anatomy of major cyber incidents, elucidating threat vectors, motivations, and systemic impacts. These chapters also identify recurring patterns and strategic lessons, enabling readers to anticipate and prepare for similar risks within their own organizational settings.

The notion of resilience, both cyber and operational, is developed more thoroughly in Chapters 6 and 7. These sections argue that building resilience involves more than reactive capabilities; it requires proactive risk management, continuity planning, and adaptive governance mechanisms. Strategies such as incident response planning, emergency recovery, and stakeholder communication are explored in depth, with emphasis on their role in maintaining service continuity and minimizing cascading disruptions.

At the regulatory level, Chapter 8 addresses the interplay between cybersecurity mandates and broader port security frameworks. It emphasizes the importance of aligning cyber defense efforts with international standards and legal obligations, a consideration increasingly relevant in the face of evolving compliance landscapes such as the IMO's cybersecurity guidelines and the European NIS2 Directive.

In technical terms, Chapter 9 evaluates the delicate balance between system integration and network segmentation, two imperatives that often present conflicting demands. This chapter explores how ports can achieve secure interoperability through architectural strategies that preserve both efficiency and isolation, supported by automation and regulatory compliance tools.

Chapter 10 returns to the theme of technology, this time focusing on the role of AI in enhancing threat detection and response. While AI presents powerful new tools for identifying and mitigating cyber risks, it also introduces challenges related to transparency, data bias, and system overreliance—issues which are critically examined in relation to port-specific applications.

Complementing these defensive strategies is the discussion in Chapter 11 of cyber insurance as a financial tool for risk transfer. As ports assess their exposure to potential liabilities, understanding the structure, limitations, and legal considerations of cyber insurance becomes a key aspect of strategic planning. The book addresses how insurers evaluate cyber risk in maritime contexts and the implications for premium determination and coverage scope.

Strategic alignment is the focus of Chapter 12, where the book introduces frameworks for integrating cybersecurity objectives with corporate goals. By mapping security measures to operational priorities and compliance requirements, ports can develop coherent strategies that support both resilience and performance.

The role of organizational culture and leadership is further explored in Chapter 13. Cybersecurity awareness, staff training, and accountability mechanisms are examined as crucial elements in sustaining long-term security. Leadership engagement, continuous monitoring, and education programs are presented as essential tools for cultivating a cyber-aware organizational ethos.

Recognizing the limits of internal capabilities, Chapter 14 explores the value of collaborative partnerships in enhancing cyber defenses. Whether through cooperation with government agencies, technology vendors, academia, or managed security service providers, ports can benefit from shared expertise, intelligence, and infrastructure. This chapter outlines practical collaboration models and the specific benefits of each arrangement.

Finally, Chapter 15 turns to governance by defining the roles and responsibilities of port cybersecurity teams. Effective cyber governance depends on clearly defined structures, cross-functional collaboration, and ongoing capacity building. The chapter details how they can serve as strategic enablers, facilitating coordination across technical and managerial domains.

Throughout the text, a deliberate effort is made to blend theoretical insight with practical application. Drawing on real-world case studies, industry benchmarks, and sector-specific challenges, the book provides a blueprint for managing cybersecurity as a dynamic and integral component of port strategy. By situating technical vulnerabilities within a broader system of organizational, regulatory, and economic dependencies, the text offers readers a holistic framework for navigating the complex cyber terrain of modern ports.

1 Overview of Seaports

1.1 Definitions and Basic Functions of Seaports

A seaport is a designated coastal facility where ships dock to load and unload cargo, transfer passengers, and access essential maritime services. Serving as a critical interface between sea and land transportation systems, seaports facilitate the movement of goods and people, playing a fundamental role in international trade, logistics, and regional economic development [1]. Functioning as logistics hubs, they enhance cargo value through integrated facilities, including docks, terminals, warehouses, and customs operations, while supporting industries such as shipbuilding and repair.

1.1.1 Key Functions of Seaports

Seaports are fundamental to the smooth operation of international trade and regional economic development. Their diverse functions encompass various critical operations that enable the efficient movement of goods and people across global transportation networks. The key functions of seaports include:

- **Cargo Handling:** Seaports are responsible for managing the transfer of cargo between vessels and other modes of transport, utilizing advanced and specialized equipment such as cranes, docks, and storage facilities. These facilities are designed to accommodate the diverse nature of cargo, ensuring its safe and efficient handling.
- **Passenger Services:** Seaports provide the necessary infrastructure for ferry and cruise operations, facilitating the efficient movement of passengers between locations, which is crucial for tourism and regional connectivity.
- **Storage and Logistics:** Seaports are equipped with warehouses, container yards, and sophisticated inventory management systems that optimize the storage, distribution, and tracking of goods. This functionality is essential for the effective management of supply chains and ensures the timely delivery of goods across borders.
- **Customs and Security Operations:** Seaports play a vital role in regulatory compliance, customs clearance, and the implementation of security

DOI: 10.4324/9781003559320-1

protocols to safeguard goods and infrastructure. The enforcement of customs regulations and security measures is critical to maintaining the integrity of international trade and preventing illegal activities.

- **Industrial Support:** The proximity of seaports to industries such as shipbuilding, repair, and processing enhances their economic significance. These industries benefit from easy access to maritime transport, facilitating the movement of raw materials and finished products and contributing to the broader economic development of the region.

1.1.2 Evolving Roles of Seaports

Seaports have traditionally served as essential interfaces between sea and land transportation, facilitating cargo transfer from vessels to other transport modes for final delivery. Over the past decades, however, they have evolved into multifaceted hubs that extend beyond their traditional roles. Today, seaports function as strategic supply chain nodes, sustainability drivers, national security assets, and centers for tourism and passenger mobility.

- **Seaports as Supply Chain Hubs:** Seaports are critical components of global supply chains, handling over 80% of global trade. They have transitioned from mere transit points to integral nodes that enhance supply chain efficiency and competitiveness [2]. Modern seaports offer value-added logistics services such as warehousing, inventory management, and distribution while optimizing multimodal connectivity by integrating rail, road, and air transport networks. Technological advancements further strengthen this role, enabling seaports to serve as strategic partners, providing competitive advantages in time and cost efficiency across interconnected industries.
- **Seaports as Drivers of Global Sustainable Development:** Seaports are critical to global trade but also major contributors to energy use and GHG emissions. Their role as multimodal logistics hubs leads to heavy reliance on fossil fuels, particularly diesel and fuel oil, which in turn generates harmful air pollutants. As international trade expands, emissions from port operations have become more visible—especially in regions where other sectors have already curbed pollution [3]. In response, the IMO has broadened its emission reduction strategies to include port activities. Still, port communities face growing pressure to mitigate health and climate risks, often without strong regulatory support for mobile emission sources like vehicles and cargo-handling equipment. Shifting toward cleaner technologies and low-emission infrastructure is essential, but progress remains constrained by high costs and policy gaps [3].
- **Seaports as Pillars of National Security:** Seaports are vital to national security, managing over 80% of international trade, including critical resources like food, fuel, and industrial components [2]. They also support energy security by facilitating the flow of oil, LNG, and coal—disruptions to which can destabilize supply chains and economies [4]. For example,

a ransomware attack by the BlackCat group disrupted 17 ports across Europe, crippling facilities such as Oiltanking and Mabanaft and forcing manual operations at gas stations in northern Germany [5]. Many ports also serve as naval hubs, supporting military logistics and rapid deployment [6]. Incidents like these highlight the strategic significance of seaports not only in the context of trade and energy but as core assets in national defense, requiring robust protection from both physical and cyber threats.

- **Seaports as Tourism and Passenger Mobility Hubs:** In addition to cargo operations, many seaports facilitate passenger movements, particularly in coastal and international tourism. These ports often serve as key nodes in the tourism supply chain, integrating with shopping centers, cultural attractions, and hospitality services. A notable example is the Phuket Deep Sea Port (PDSP) in Thailand. Originally designed for cargo operations, PDSP is undergoing upgrades so as to be able to accommodate large cruise ships, with dock extensions, channel dredging, and a new passenger terminal set for completion by 2024. Once operational, PDSP will function as a hybrid port, capable of handling cruise ships while maintaining its role in cargo logistics [7]. This transformation highlights the growing integration of tourism and trade functions at seaports, positioning them as vital hubs for economic growth and global connectivity.

1.2 Classification of Seaports by Cargo Types

Seaports can be broadly classified into two main categories based on the nature of the cargo they handle: **bulk ports** and **breakbulk ports**. This classification reflects the physical form and handling requirements of the cargo, which in turn determine the design of port infrastructure, operational procedures, and supporting equipment [6]. Within each category, ports are further specialized to manage specific cargo subtypes, with each facility tailored to meet the operational and logistical demands of the vessels and industries they serve.

1 **Bulk ports** are specialized facilities designed to handle large volumes of bulk cargo, which are goods transported in substantial quantities without individual packaging or containers. These goods are typically shipped in loose form, either directly into a ship's hold or into dedicated storage areas designed for bulk materials. Bulk cargo is categorized into dry bulk and liquid bulk, both of which are transported globally by bulk carriers, enabling economies of scale in production and distribution.

   To efficiently manage these large volumes, bulk ports are equipped with infrastructure tailored to ensure safety and operational efficiency.

   - **Dry Bulk Ports**: These ports handle solid, non-liquid commodities. The infrastructure includes conveyor belts, bucket elevators, stackers, reclaimers, and grabs for the loading and unloading of materials such as coal (for power generation), grains (wheat, corn, and rice for food production), ores (iron ore for steel manufacturing), and cement (for construction).

- **Liquid Bulk Ports**: These ports are designed for liquid commodities. Equipment such as pipelines, pumps, metering systems, loading arms, and dock manifolds is used for transferring products like crude oil (refined into fuels), chemicals, LNG, and vegetable oils (for food production).

The specialized infrastructure in both dry and liquid bulk ports ensures that cargo transfer and storage meet stringent safety and efficiency standards. Supporting critical industries such as power generation, construction, and steel production, bulk ports are essential to the global supply chain, driving economic growth and industrial development.

2 **Breakbulk ports** are structured to handle cargo that cannot be transported in bulk. These ports manage individual units of goods, typically oversized, irregularly shaped, or heavy items that must be loaded and unloaded separately. This category includes **general cargo ports**, **container ports**, and **Ro-Ro ports**, all of which serve the broader breakbulk function by accommodating non-bulk cargo types.

- **General Cargo (Breakbulk) Ports**: These facilities are traditionally associated with handling items such as machinery, industrial components, and construction equipment. Cargo is transported aboard general cargo vessels and managed through labor-intensive operations. Despite a decline in demand due to the rise of containerization, general cargo ports remain vital for specialized industries such as energy and infrastructure development, where standardized container use is not always feasible.
- **Container Ports**: Although containerized cargo is more uniform than traditional breakbulk cargo, container ports are grouped under the breakbulk category due to their handling of goods that are not transported in bulk form. These ports manage standardized 20- or 40-foot containers using gantry cranes, yard equipment, and logistics systems optimized for high throughput. Container ports support global trade in manufactured and consumer goods and are often located near economic centers to minimize inland transport costs. However, their operations contribute to environmental concerns, including emissions and urban congestion.
- **Ro-Ro Ports**: Ro-Ro facilities are specialized for cargo that can be driven directly onto and off vessels using ramps. This includes cars, trucks, trailers, agricultural machinery, and construction vehicles. Unlike bulk or container ports, Ro-Ro terminals require extensive yard space and skilled operators rather than cranes or lifts. These ports are essential in regions with strong automotive industries and play a crucial role in intermodal transport by enabling efficient transfers between ships, road, and rail networks.

1.3 Common Infrastructure Components of Seaports

Seaport infrastructure comprises the physical and structural elements essential for the operation of a seaport. These components facilitate the movement, storage, and handling of cargo and passengers while supporting vessel operations within the port's jurisdiction. Seaport infrastructure is commonly categorized into two primary types: landside infrastructure and waterside infrastructure.

1.3.1 Landside Infrastructure

Landside infrastructure encompasses the onshore physical and structural components that support cargo handling, passenger movement, and connectivity between the seaport and inland transportation networks. Key elements include:

- **Terminals** within a port serve as critical operational zones, supporting the transfer, storage, and movement of goods or passengers through specialized infrastructure [6]. While their configurations vary based on function, most terminals feature cargo-handling equipment, storage facilities, access to inland transport networks, and security and customs checkpoints. These shared elements enable efficient coordination between maritime and land-based logistics, support regulatory compliance, and ensure the safe and timely flow of goods and people. Whether handling containers, bulk materials, liquids, or passengers, terminals collectively form the operational backbone of a port, directly influencing its capacity, flexibility, and resilience.
- **Quay walls** are essential structural elements located along the shore where vessels are moored for berthing and cargo or passenger handling [6]. Constructed from reinforced concrete or steel, quay walls are designed to withstand the weight of vessels and docking impacts, ensuring operational durability. Equipped with mooring fixtures such as bollards and fenders, they secure vessels and prevent damage during docking. The capacity of quay walls is influenced by factors such as water depth and vessel size, as the depth of the water directly impacts the port's ability to accommodate larger vessels, thus affecting overall throughput.
- **Container yards** are key logistical zones within ports, used for staging and storing containers awaiting transfer to ships, trucks, or trains [6]. Their primary function is to regulate container flow and prevent congestion in terminal areas. These yards support orderly cargo movement by organizing containers based on destination, priority, or type, allowing for efficient dispatch. Equipped with handling machinery and supported by digital tracking systems, container yards enhance visibility and coordination across the supply chain. Their layout and technology directly influence a port's operational throughput and its ability to adapt to fluctuating cargo volumes.

- **Seaport gates** serve as controlled access points that manage the movement of vehicles, cargo, and personnel into and out of the port [6]. They are essential for enforcing security protocols, facilitating customs checks, and verifying cargo documentation. These checkpoints are typically equipped with surveillance, scanning systems, and digital access controls to prevent unauthorized entry and ensure regulatory compliance. Multiple gates may be designated for specific functions—such as freight, passenger, or staff traffic—to streamline flows and reduce delays, supporting both safety and operational continuity.
- **Storage facilities** are essential for managing cargo between arrival and onward transport, supporting the efficient flow of goods through the logistics chain [6]. These facilities include general-purpose warehouses, cold storage for perishables, and tank farms for liquids. Each is designed to accommodate different cargo types while meeting safety, environmental, and regulatory standards. Common features include temperature control systems, spill prevention mechanisms, and cargo-tracking technologies. Strategically located within the port, these storage zones help reduce congestion at terminals and allow for the consolidation, inspection, and temporary holding of goods prior to distribution or customs clearance.

1.3.2 Waterside Infrastructure

Waterside infrastructure encompasses the physical structures and systems located in the marine areas of a seaport, integral to accommodating ships, ensuring safe navigation, and facilitating maritime operations such as docking, loading, and unloading. Key elements of waterside infrastructure include:

- **Channels** are navigable waterways designed to facilitate the safe entry and exit of vessels to and from the port. These channels are regularly maintained to ensure clear access, with particular focus on water depth, width, and tidal variations.
- **Jetties** are structures extending from the shore into the water, typically made of stone, concrete, or steel, providing safe docking points for vessels. Jetties protect vessels from strong currents, tides, and waves during loading and unloading, while simultaneously preventing sediment buildup in channels. This reduces the need for frequent dredging and helps maintain long-term port navigability.
- **Breakwaters** are coastal structures designed to protect ports from wave impacts, ensuring safe docking and stable conditions within the harbor. Typically located offshore, breakwaters absorb and deflect wave energy, creating calm zones for vessels. This minimizes the risk of damage during docking and undocking.
- **Anchorage Areas** are designated zones within or near a port where vessels can anchor while awaiting a berth or logistical arrangements. These areas are selected based on factors such as water depth, proximity to navigational

channels, protection from adverse weather, and vessel size accommodation. Anchorage areas are ideally located at a safe distance from core port operations to avoid congestion and minimize the risk of collisions.

1.4 Ship and Cargo Operations, Process, and Equipment

Ship and cargo operations at seaports consist of a series of interdependent activities that demand effective coordination among port authorities, service providers, terminal operators, and vessel crews [8]. These activities progress through multiple stages, beginning with a vessel's approach toward the port and continuing through to its departure [9]. Figure 1.1 presents a streamlined overview of the seven key stages involved—starting with pre-arrival planning and concluding with post-departure monitoring. Further explanation of each stage is provided in the sections that follow.

1 **Pre-arrival Planning**
Prior to a vessel's arrival, preparatory steps are carried out by the vessel's operator, terminal operators, and port authorities to ensure a smooth process. The vessel's operator initiates this by submitting a pre-arrival notice, known as the Notice of Arrival or Port Call [10]. This notice includes vital details such as the vessel's type, tonnage, cargo specifications, and estimated time of arrival, enabling port authorities to ensure security and make necessary logistical arrangements.

2 **Arrival and Docking**
Upon arrival at the port, a series of coordinated procedures ensure the vessel's safe docking. A licensed marine pilot boards the vessel to navigate it through the port's waterways, leveraging expertise in local navigation to guide the ship safely through congested or shallow areas. Depending on the vessel's size and docking complexity, tugboats provide supplementary propulsion and assist in precise maneuvers, particularly in confined spaces [11].

Once positioned at the dock, mooring operations commence. Port personnel collaborate with the vessel's crew to secure the ship to the quay using mooring lines, ensuring stability during cargo handling. These mooring lines, typically composed of high-strength synthetic fibers or steel, are managed via winches to maintain the vessel's position. Supporting equipment includes pilot boats for marine pilot transport, tugboats for maneuvering assistance, and specialized mooring tools such as winches, mooring lines, and anchoring systems. These components collectively facilitate safe and efficient docking operations.

3 **Cargo-Handling Operations**
Cargo-handling operations commence once the vessel is securely docked and moored. The unloading process utilizes specialized equipment suited to the cargo type, including cranes, forklifts, and conveyor systems, ensuring efficient and secure handling. The selection of equipment varies based on

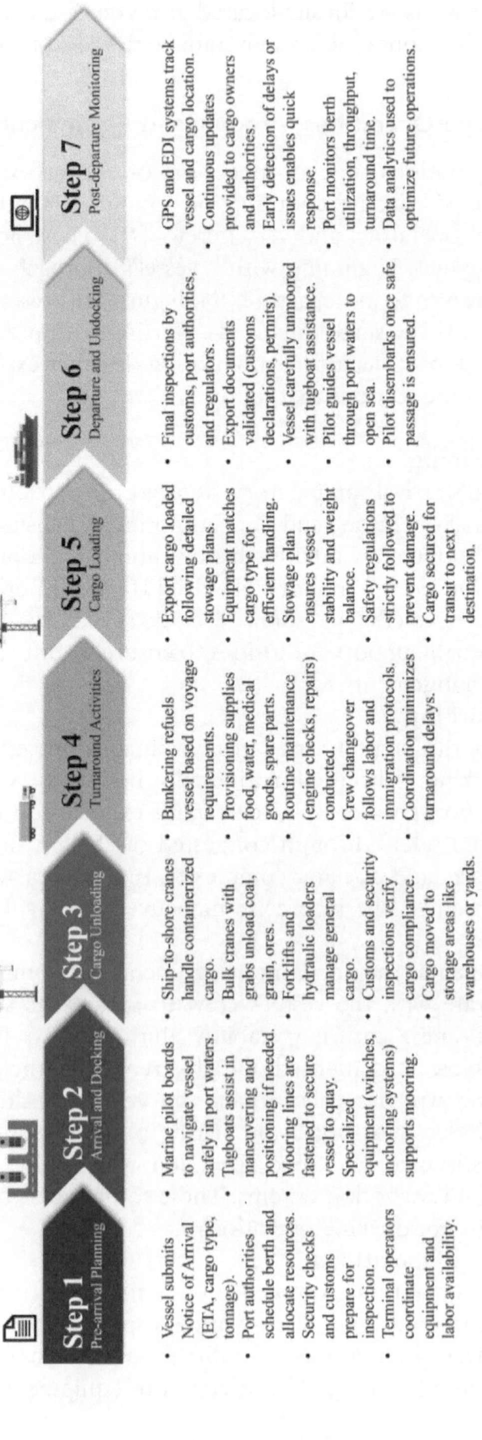

Figure 1.1 Sequential Stages of Ship and Cargo Operations at Seaports.

cargo characteristics, such as containerized, bulk, or general cargo, so as to optimize operational efficiency and safety [12].

- **Containerized Cargo:** Ship-to-shore gantry cranes lift containers from the vessel, transferring them onto the dock or directly onto trucks for transport. Within container terminals, reach stackers and forklifts manage container storage and movement, optimizing yard operations and facilitating onward distribution.
- **Bulk Cargo:** Bulk-handling cranes, equipped with grab buckets or hoppers, manage commodities such as coal, grain, and ores. Depending on operational needs, these cranes may be ship-mounted or tower-mounted. Belt conveyors transport dry bulk materials to silos or bins, ensuring continuous flow and minimizing handling time.
- **General Cargo:** Heavy machinery, vehicles, and oversized equipment require hydraulic loaders for unloading, followed by forklifts and other handling equipment for transfer to designated storage areas or staging locations.

Once unloaded, cargo undergoes inspection by customs and regulatory authorities, particularly for high-value, hazardous, or restricted goods. This process ensures compliance with import and export regulations, verifies cargo manifests, and assesses security risks. Inspections may utilize X-ray scanners for container screening, radiation detection systems for hazardous material identification, and weighing scales for cargo weight verification.

After clearance, cargo is stored in port facilities, such as warehouses or container yards, until further transport. The buyer is responsible for fulfilling customs duties, submitting required documentation—including the bill of lading, customs declarations, and clearance permits—and arranging inland transportation by truck, rail, or other means. Payments for port and shipping fees are typically processed through customs systems or port offices. Once all formalities are completed, the cargo is released for final delivery, concluding the logistics process.

4 **Turnaround Activities: Bunkering and Provisions**

During cargo operations, several critical turnaround activities take place to ensure the vessel is fully resupplied and prepared for its next voyage. These include bunkering, provisioning, maintenance, and crew changeover, all of which contribute to the vessel's operational readiness and efficiency [13].

- **Bunkering (Refueling)**

  Bunkering, or refueling, is a key process carried out while the vessel is docked. Fuel is transferred from onshore storage facilities or bunker barges directly into the vessel's fuel tanks, ensuring sufficient supply for the upcoming voyage. The required fuel quantity is determined based on the vessel's destination, projected fuel consumption, and voyage duration, with contingencies factored in for delays or route adjustments.

- **Provisioning**
  In addition to fuel, vessels require essential supplies, including food, water, medical provisions, and spare parts. Supply vessels transport these items to the ship, where they are organized using storage cages and pallets for efficient handling.
- **Routine Maintenance**
  Routine maintenance tasks are conducted during the turnaround period to uphold the vessel's operational integrity. These include inspections, minor repairs, and system adjustments, covering the engine, navigation equipment, and safety systems. Ports provide specialized facilities such as dry docks for hull inspections, cranes for lifting heavy machinery, and maintenance platforms for engine servicing.
- **Crew Changeover**
  Crew changeovers occur in accordance with labor, immigration, and health regulations. This process involves disembarking crew members who have completed their contracts and onboarding replacements. All documentation and clearances are managed to ensure a seamless transition, with timing coordinated alongside other port activities to minimize delays and maintain operational efficiency.

5 **Cargo-Loading Operations**
Once unloading is complete, the vessel transitions to the loading phase, during which export cargo is stowed according to a detailed stowage plan. Different cargo types, including containerized, bulk, and general cargo, require specific handling and loading techniques to ensure safety, stability, and efficiency [12]. The equipment used largely mirrors that of the unloading process, with gantry cranes, such as ship-to-shore cranes, handling containers while bulk-handling cranes, reach stackers, forklifts, and hydraulic loaders manage bulk and general cargo.

The stowage plan is a critical component of loading operations, ensuring proper cargo distribution across the vessel. It accounts for weight distribution, stability, and compliance with safety regulations. A well-executed plan enhances operational efficiency by optimizing space utilization, minimizing cargo damage, and maintaining vessel balance. By integrating precise handling techniques, coordinated equipment usage, and strategic planning, cargo-loading operations contribute to the vessel's safe and efficient departure for its next voyage.

6 **Departure and Undocking**
Upon the completion of cargo loading, the vessel undergoes a series of coordinated procedures to ensure a safe and efficient departure. Final inspections and clearances are conducted by port authorities, customs officials, and regulatory bodies to verify compliance with local and international requirements. This process includes the validation of export documentation such as customs declarations, bills of lading, and export permits. Additionally, safety and environmental compliance checks confirm that the vessel meets operational standards before departure [12].

Once clearances are granted, undocking operations commence. The ship is carefully unmoored from the berth, with tugboats deployed as needed to facilitate maneuvering, particularly in congested ports or when handling large vessels. Tugboat assistance ensures controlled movement, preventing collisions and optimizing the vessel's alignment as it exits the dock [13].

During the port departure phase, a harbor pilot, if engaged, provides specialized guidance through restricted waters. The pilot's expertise in local maritime conditions—such as tides, currents, and navigational hazards—enhances the vessel's safety and operational efficiency [12]. Upon reaching open waters, the pilot disembarks, and the vessel proceeds toward its next destination under the command of its bridge team.

7 **Post-departure Activities**

Following a vessel's departure, port authorities and logistics stakeholders continue to monitor shipment progress and assess operational performance. Cargo-tracking systems, integrating GPS-based positioning and electronic data interchange platforms, provide real-time updates on the vessel's location and cargo status [14]. These systems enable continuous communication among cargo owners, logistics providers, and regulatory bodies, ensuring compliance with customs procedures, import/export controls, and safety regulations.

Additionally, port performance-monitoring systems evaluate operational efficiency through automated data collection and advanced analytics [15]. These systems track key performance indicators such as berth utilization, cargo throughput, vessel turnaround time, and service efficiency. By analyzing this data, port authorities identify performance trends, optimize resource allocation, and implement strategies to reduce delays.

1.5 Key Roles and Personnel in Port Operations

As outlined in Section 1.4, Ship and Cargo Operations, Process, and Equipment, the efficiency and safety of port operations depend on specialized personnel responsible for navigation, logistics, safety, and compliance. These roles ensure seamless operations, optimize resource utilization, and uphold regulatory standards. This section categorizes these roles into three key groups.

1.5.1 Port Management and Operations Oversight

This group is responsible for the strategic and operational management of port activities, ensuring efficiency, safety, and profitability [16]. Key personnel in this category include:

- **Terminal Manager:** Oversees the operations of specific terminals (e.g., container or bulk cargo terminals), manages cargo flow, supervises terminal staff, and coordinates with the Port Operations Manager. Ensures efficient freight movement across multiple transport modes, optimizing transitions between rail, waterways, and road networks.

- **Port Operations Manager:** Handles daily port operations, including workforce scheduling, equipment availability, vessel berthing, and cargo handling, while mitigating operational bottlenecks. Coordinates multimodal transport logistics, ensuring seamless connectivity between different transportation modes to enhance supply chain efficiency.
- **Harbormaster:** Manages vessel traffic, berth assignments, and safe maneuvering within the harbor, coordinating with pilots and tugboat operators.
- **Facilities Maintenance Manager:** Oversees maintenance and repair of port infrastructure, ensuring operational continuity and safety.

1.5.2 Vessel and Cargo Handling

This group manages the physical operations of vessels and cargo, ensuring efficient loading, unloading, and storage [17]. Examples of key personnel in this group include:

1 Operators and Machinery Drivers

- **Forklift Operators:** Load, unload, and stack cargo within terminals.
- **Straddle Carrier Operators:** Transport and position containers within the terminal.
- **Reach Stacker Operators:** Handle containers in confined spaces, ensuring efficient stacking.
- **Bulldozer Operators:** Move bulk cargo and prepare terminal surfaces for operations.
- **Conveyor Belt Operators:** Oversee conveyor systems transporting bulk cargo.
- **Crane Operators:** Operate cranes to handle containers and bulk cargo safely and efficiently.

2 Signalmen

- **Signalmen:** Coordinate cargo movements, ensuring communication between crane operators and ground personnel.
- **Hatchmen:** Guide crane operators in positioning and moving cargo.
- **Hatch Tenders:** Oversee the safe transfer of cargo through ship hatches.
- **Deckhands:** Assist in securing and releasing cargo on the vessel's deck.
- **Lashers:** Secure and release cargo within the ship's hold and on the ship's deck to prevent shifting during transit.

3 Foremen

- **Gang Foremen:** Supervise cargo-handling teams, ensuring safety and efficiency.
- **Chief Tallymen:** Oversee tally clerks, ensuring accurate cargo records and compliance with documentation requirements.

- **Chief Foremen (Supervisors):** Manage multiple cargo-handling teams, enforce safety protocols, and oversee schedules.
- **Tally Clerks:** Track cargo quantity, weight, and condition, ensuring alignment with shipping records.
- **Checkers:** Inspect cargo for damage, verify shipment records, and document discrepancies.

4 **Mechanics**

- **Maintenance Technicians:** Perform preventive maintenance and repairs on port machinery.
- **Electricians:** Install, maintain, and repair electrical systems critical to port operations.

1.5.3 Safety, Compliance, and Security

This group ensures adherence to safety, environmental, and security regulations so as to protect personnel, cargo, and infrastructure [18]. This group includes professionals such as:

- **Safety and Environmental Officer:** Conducts inspections, ensures compliance with safety regulations, and manages pollution control.
- **Customs Officer:** Checks shipments for compliance with customs regulations, preventing smuggling and ensuring trade security.
- **Port Security Officer:** Monitors access points, conducts surveillance, and implements security protocols.
- **Fire Safety Officer:** Oversees fire prevention measures, emergency response planning, and firefighting equipment maintenance.
- **Health and Safety Officer:** Monitors workplace safety, provides training, and ensures compliance with occupational health regulations.

1.6 Key External Stakeholders in Port Operations

Port operations depend on the engagement of diverse external stakeholders, categorized into three primary groups: commercial, institutional, and community [6]. Each group plays a distinct role in shaping port activities, influencing policies, investments, and operational frameworks.

1.6.1 Commercial Stakeholders

From a commercial perspective, port authorities focus on attracting and retaining traffic, securing investments, and expanding infrastructure to accommodate growing trade volumes and larger vessels. This group includes businesses that engage directly with port operations, ensuring trade efficiency, infrastructure development, and economic growth.

1 **Port Users**
Port users are commercial entities that depend on port services for cargo handling and transportation. Their operations directly impact port efficiency and competitiveness. Examples of port users include:

- **Shipping Lines:** Own and operate vessels, manage cargo schedules, and ensure regulatory and safety compliance.
- **Freight Forwarders:** Act as intermediaries, coordinating cargo movement, documentation, and multimodal logistics to optimize supply chains.
- **Customs Brokers:** Facilitate customs clearance, ensuring accurate documentation and regulatory compliance so as to prevent delays and penalties.
- **Third-Party Logistics Providers:** Offer warehousing, inventory management, and distribution services, integrating port functions with broader supply chains.

2 **Service Providers**
Service providers enhance port efficiency, safety, and competitiveness by delivering essential operational support. Examples of service providers include:

- **Stevedores:** Handle cargo loading, unloading, and securing, operating specialized equipment to streamline port operations.
- **Inland Transport Providers:** Manage cargo movement between ports and inland destinations via trucking and rail, ensuring seamless multimodal connectivity.

1.6.2 Institutional Stakeholders

Port authorities function within an institutional framework that regulates infrastructure planning, decision making, and policy implementation. These institutions influence port development, funding, and governance, ensuring compliance, safety, and sustainability.

1 **Government and Regulatory Authorities**
These entities establish and enforce policies, ensuring port activities align with legal, environmental, and trade regulations. Examples of authorities include:

- **Port Authority:** Oversees port infrastructure, strategic planning, and operational management while ensuring compliance with safety and environmental standards.
- **Customs Authorities:** Regulate cross-border cargo movement, conduct inspections, enforce tariffs, and prevent illicit trade activities.
- **Port Health Authorities:** Maintain sanitary conditions, inspect vessels, and prevent the spread of infectious diseases under international health regulations.

- **Environmental Agencies:** Enforce environmental laws, regulating waste disposal, emissions, and pollution control to mitigate ecological impacts.

2 **Institutional Service Providers**
Some service providers operate under institutional oversight, ensuring compliance with navigation, safety, and environmental standards. Examples of institutional service providers include:

- **Maritime Pilots:** Guide vessels through port waters, ensuring safe navigation in congested or restricted areas.
- **Tugboat Operators:** Assist in vessel positioning, docking, and undocking, particularly in challenging conditions.

1.6.3 Community Stakeholders

Port activities have a profound impact on local communities, shaping environmental conditions, economic development, and social acceptance. Public support is essential for operational stability and future expansion, as opposition can impede trade and sustainability efforts. Active engagement with local stakeholders is necessary to address concerns such as noise pollution, traffic congestion, and environmental impact. Transparent communication regarding operations, planned projects, and environmental assessments fosters trust and strengthens community relationships.

Local communities play a pivotal role in advancing environmental sustainability by advocating for emission reductions, improved waste management, and energy-efficient technologies. They also contribute to environmental oversight by holding ports accountable for pollution control and regulatory compliance. Beyond environmental considerations, ports serve as economic drivers, generating employment and facilitating regional trade. Strengthening workforce development programs and fostering collaboration with local businesses can enhance economic benefits. Ensuring equitable distribution of port-driven opportunities enables local enterprises to participate in and benefit from port-related growth.

References

[1] A. Montwiłł, "The Role of Seaports as Logistics Centers in the Modelling of the Sustainable System for Distribution of Goods in Urban Areas," *Procedia – Social and Behavioral Sciences*, vol. 151, p. 257–265, 2014.

[2] UNCTAD, "Review of Maritime Transport 2023," 2023. [Online]. Available: https://unctad.org/system/files/official-document/rmt2023ch3_en.pdf.

[3] IMO, "Port Emissions Toolkit," 2018. [Online]. Available: https://greenvoyage2050.imo.org/wp-content/uploads/2021/01/PORT-EMISSIONS-TOOLKIT-GUIDE-NO.2-DEVELOPMENT-OF-PORT-EMISSIONS-REDUCTION-STRATEGIES.pdf.

[4] A. Rose, D. Wei and D. Paul, "Economic Consequences of and Resilience to a Disruption of Petroleum Trade: The Role of Seaports in U.S. Energy Security," *Energy Policy*, vol. 115, pp. 584–615, 2018.

[5] C. Senarak, "Port Cyberattacks from 2011 to 2023: A Literature Review and Discussion of Selected Cases," *Maritime Economics & Logistics*, vol. 26, no. 1, pp. 105–130, 2024.

[6] R. Jean-Paul and N. Theo, *Port Economics, Management and Policy*, Routledge, 2022.

[7] Marine Department, "News from the Marine Department, Issue 32/2023: The Marine Department Is Developing a Large Cruise Terminal," 2023. [Online]. Available: http://md.go.th/top-management-news/73341/.

[8] E. Demirci, "Simulation Modelling and Analysis of a Port Investment," *SIMULATION: Transactions of The Society for Modeling and Simulation International*, vol. 79, no. 2, pp. 94–105, 2003.

[9] Y. Lun, K.-H. Lai and T. Cheng, "Port Operations," in *Shipping and Logistics Management*, Springer, 2010, pp. 179–191.

[10] UNCTAD, "Monographs on Port Management," 1985. [Online]. Available: https://unctad.org/system/files/official-document/ship4944_en.pdf.

[11] Marine Department, "Pilot Officer Operating Manual," 2014. [Online]. Available: http://pilotbureau.md.go.th/2021/12/03/%E0%B8%84%E0%B8%B9%E0%B9%88%E0%B8%A1%E0%B8%B7%E0%B8%AD%E0%B8%81%E0%B8%B2%E0%B8%A3%E0%B8%9B%E0%B8%8E%E0%B8%B4%E0%B8%9A%E0%B8%B1%E0%B8%95%E0%B8%B4%E0%B9%80%E0%B8%88%E0%B9%89%E0%B8%B2%E0%B8%9E%E0%B8%99/?57.

[12] IMO, "Amendments to the Annex to the Convention on Facilitation of International Maritime Traffic, 1965," 2022. [Online]. Available: wwwcdn.imo.org/localresources/en/KnowledgeCentre/IndexofIMOResolutions/FALDocuments/FAL.14%2846%29.pdf.

[13] IMO, "Code of Practice for the Safe Loading and Unloading of Bulk Carriers," 1997. [Online]. Available: wwwcdn.imo.org/localresources/en/KnowledgeCentre/IndexofIMOResolutions/AssemblyDocuments/A.862(20).pdf.

[14] Laem Chabang Port Customs Office, "Technologies Used in Customs Operations," 2015. [Online]. Available: https://lcpcb.customs.go.th/list_strc_simple_neted.php?ini_content=technology&lang=th&left_menu=interesting_article_161221_01.

[15] T. N. Mathias, H. Inutsuka, T. Shinoda and Y. Sugimura, "Operational Performance Evaluation of a Container Terminal Using Data Mining and Simulation," *Asian Transport Studies*, vol. 10, 100127, 2024.

[16] A. Toygar, "Port Operations Manager Selection with SVNS-Critic and SVNS-Topsis Hybrid Method," in *Manager Selection Problems With Multi Criteria Decision Making Methods*, Nobel Bilimsel Eserler, 2023, pp. 161–180.

[17] ILO, "Code of Practice for Packing of Cargo Transport Units," 2014. [Online]. Available: www.ilo.org/sites/default/files/wcmsp5/groups/public/@ed_dialogue/@sector/documents/publication/wcms_492710.pdf.

[18] IMO, ISPS Code 2003, IMO, 2003. [Online]. Available: https://portalcip.org/wp-content/uploads/2017/05/ISPS-Code-2003-English.pdf.

2 Port Information Systems and Attack Surfaces

2.1 Overview of Port Information Systems

Port information systems (PISs) are digital platforms that support efficient, transparent, and compliant port operations by coordinating information exchange among various stakeholders [1]. They improve both internal workflows and external collaboration across the port ecosystem.

Internally, PISs integrate core operational systems. The terminal operating system (TOS) manages cargo handling and storage to streamline terminal activity [2]. The seaside operating systems (SOSs) focus on vessel movements and maritime safety [3], while the landside operating systems (LOSs) coordinate the flow of goods entering or exiting the port [4]. Together, these systems ensure smooth day-to-day functioning across port domains. Externally, the PCS links ports with external entities such as customs, shipping lines, freight forwarders, and regulators [5]. By enabling secure and real-time data exchange, PISs strengthen coordination, support timely decision making, and enhance the responsiveness of port operations.

PISs offer several key advantages by enhancing the management of real-time data related to critical operations such as vessel scheduling, cargo movements, and terminal activities, thereby supporting timely and accurate decision making across all levels of port management [6]. PISs also automate workflows—including berth allocation, cargo handling, and customs clearance—reducing operational bottlenecks and improving turnaround times and overall efficiency [7]. Additionally, they optimize the use of port assets such as cranes, berths, and yard space by improving resource utilization and supporting predictive maintenance strategies, which minimize equipment downtime and ensure continuous operations [8]. Furthermore, PISs strengthen operational security by ensuring regulatory compliance, automating reporting processes, and enabling real-time monitoring of port activities. Integrated security features—such as access controls, encryption, and audit trails—enhance traceability, support risk management, and facilitate prompt incident response [9].

DOI: 10.4324/9781003559320-2

2.2 Key Components of the PIS

PISs require five essential components—hardware, software, networks, human resources, and data—to function effectively and support integrated port operations. While these elements are not structural foundations of the system, they serve as critical enablers that ensure seamless operation, system reliability, and strategic value. Figure 2.1 illustrates the layered relationship between physical cargo movement, the digital systems managing port operations (PCS, LOS, TOS, and SOS), and the computing infrastructure that supports them. It highlights how logistics, data exchange, and system interdependence contribute to an integrated, technology-enabled port environment.

2.2.1 Hardware

In a PIS, hardware refers to the physical infrastructure that supports the execution of software and ensures the effective operation of port activities [10]. The key hardware elements in a PIS include:

- **Computational and Storage Infrastructure**: This includes the central processing unit, memory, storage devices, and motherboards. These components provide the computational power and data storage necessary for the execution of software applications, facilitating real-time processing, decision making, and operational efficiency within the port environment.
- **Networking Hardware**: This category encompasses routers, switches, wireless access points, and fiber-optic cables, which enable reliable communication and data exchange between systems and stakeholders within and beyond the port.
- **Communications Hardware**: This hardware is crucial for facilitating communication between different computing devices, including standard computers, embedded systems, sensors, and actuators. It ensures efficient information exchange and integration between the various subsystems that comprise the PIS.
- **Tracking and Monitoring Devices**: These devices play a critical role in enhancing operational visibility. They include tools for tracking cargo, monitoring vessel navigation, and ensuring environmental compliance. The devices facilitate data collection for decision-making processes, contributing to greater control over port operations.
- **Power Supply and Backup Systems**: These systems, including uninterruptible power supplies, generators, and power distribution units, are crucial for ensuring continuous system uptime. They safeguard against power outages and fluctuations, maintaining operational reliability under various conditions.
- **Security Hardware**: This includes surveillance cameras, biometric access systems, intrusion detection devices, and perimeter control systems. These elements protect both physical and digital assets within the port

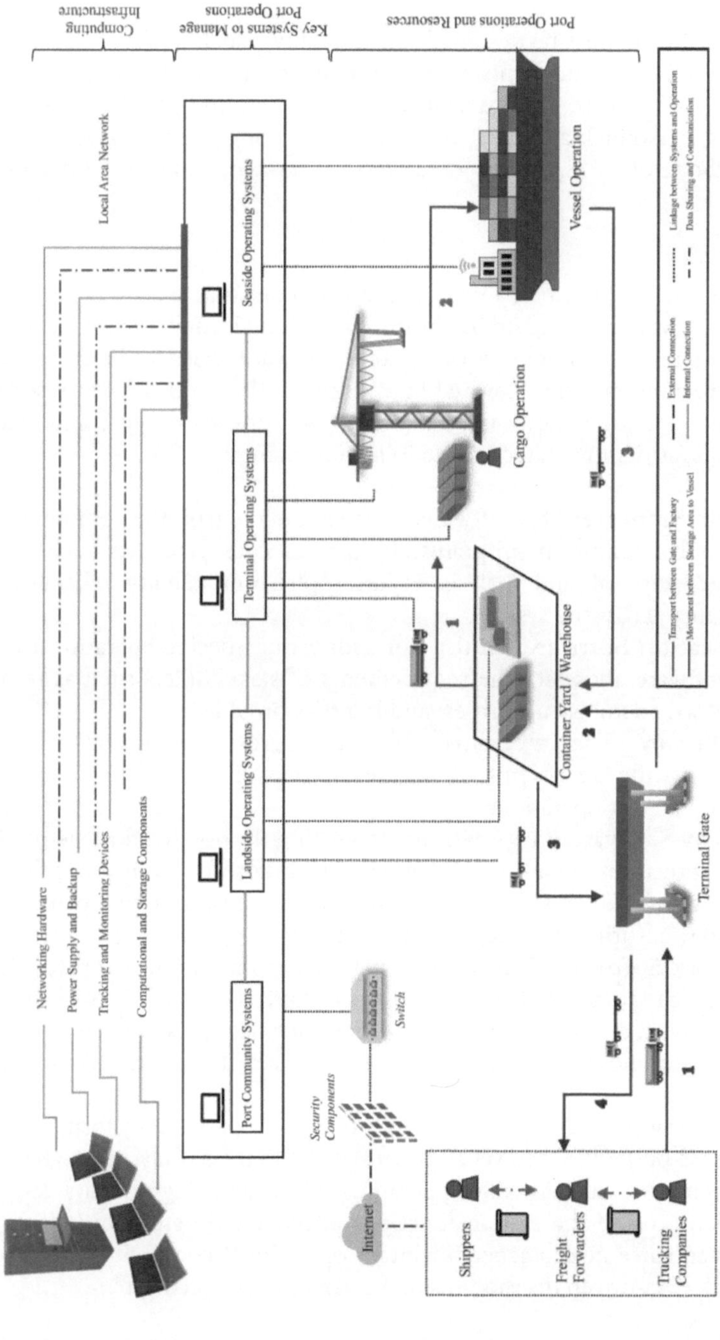

Figure 2.1 Connectivity of PIS, Components, and Operations.

and complement cybersecurity measures, forming a multi-layered defense system against potential security threats.

PIS hardware must be designed for durability, capable of withstanding the harsh conditions found in ports, including exposure to saltwater, dust, heavy machinery vibrations, and extreme weather. When integrated with software, networks, personnel, and data, these hardware components collectively form the backbone of a PIS, ensuring seamless, integrated, and secure operations.

2.2.2 Software

Software consists of instructions, data, or programs that enable digital systems to perform tasks, running on hardware and making it functional. Unlike hardware, the physical components of a system, software serves as the critical interface between users and hardware [11]. Within a PIS, various types of software are used to integrate hardware, data, and users, ensuring secure and efficient operations, as demonstrated by the following example.

- **System Software**: This software manages and controls the computer hardware and application programs. It handles core processes such as data storage, retrieval, and analysis, ensuring platform stability, reliability, and scalability across the system.
- **Application Software**: Critical for supporting specific operational needs, this software addresses the requirements of stakeholders such as terminal operators, customs authorities, and logistics providers.
- **Middleware**: This integrative software ensures interoperability between disparate software systems within the PIS, enabling a cohesive digital ecosystem for port operations.
- **Security Software**: This is vital for protecting the port's infrastructure from cyber threats and unauthorized access. Security software includes firewalls, encryption protocols, intrusion detection systems, and role-based access controls, ensuring the integrity of sensitive data.
- **Network Software:** This software manages communication protocols and data exchange across networked devices and systems. It ensures reliable connectivity, data routing, and network performance—supporting real-time information flow between internal subsystems and external stakeholders.

When software and hardware are effectively integrated, they form the operational core of the PIS. However, because the PIS is not fully automated, additional elements—such as skilled personnel and reliable, high-quality data—are essential to ensure the system functions effectively. These components collectively enhance performance, maintain operational continuity, and support informed, data-driven decision making across the port ecosystem.

2.2.3 Networks

A network consists of interconnected devices, systems, and entities that facilitate seamless data exchange, ensuring operational effectiveness and the integration of stakeholders. It serves as the foundational infrastructure for integrating hardware, software, and users within a port's operational environment [12]. As previously noted, networks combine both hardware and software components to support these functions.

- **Network Hardware:** This includes physical devices like routers, switches, servers, and modems that enable data transmission between systems and devices. These components are essential for establishing the communication infrastructure within the network.
- **Network Software:** Network software encompasses protocols, operating systems, and management tools that direct data flow within the hardware infrastructure. Examples include network operating systems, communication protocols such as TCP/IP, and management tools that ensure effective data transmission and governance.

Both network hardware and network software collaborate to ensure efficient and secure data transmission. The functions of these network components include the following:

- **Routing and Switching**: The network hardware (routers and switches) physically moves data between devices, but it relies on network software (such as TCP/IP protocols) to determine where that data should go and how it should be delivered.
- **Data Formatting and Transmission**: Network software defines the protocols that ensure data is formatted correctly for transmission over the network hardware. For example, the software uses the TCP/IP protocol to break data into packets, which are then sent through the physical network hardware (routers, switches, etc.).
- **Security and Management**: Network security software (e.g., firewalls, encryption tools) operates on the network to monitor traffic, detect unauthorized access, and ensure that data remains secure. This security software interacts with both the hardware (blocking unauthorized access points) and the software (enforcing encryption and authentication protocols).
- **Performance Optimization**: Network management software can adjust the configuration of routers, switches, and other devices to optimize performance. For example, it can reroute traffic in the event of a network failure or congestion, ensuring that data continues to flow efficiently through the network.

2.2.4 Human

The human element is essential to the efficient operation and security of a PIS [13], encompassing the expertise, decision making, and coordination required to manage, maintain, and protect the system. Personnel involved in PIS operations can be classified into three primary groups based on their roles and responsibilities: technical specialists, operational staff, and executive leadership.

- **Technical Teams** Technical personnel—comprising IT engineers and cybersecurity specialists—serve as the backbone of system maintenance and protection. IT professionals manage network infrastructure, software deployment, and systems integration, ensuring that the PIS operates reliably and scales to evolving demands. Meanwhile, cybersecurity teams focus on safeguarding system integrity, identifying vulnerabilities, and responding to potential intrusions or data breaches [14]. Together, these experts form the port's technical incident response force, providing rapid support in the event of a cyber-attack in order to limit damage and restore operations without extended delays.
- **Operational Users** Operational staff directly engage with the PIS in their daily functions, using the system to manage cargo movement, vessel scheduling, and yard logistics [14]. Their work depends on real-time system outputs to coordinate activities efficiently. When digital disruptions occur, this group is often the first to implement backup procedures, switching to manual protocols and maintaining continuity. Their familiarity with system workflows makes them central to incident recovery efforts. Enhancing their cybersecurity awareness—through training on social engineering, secure communication practices, and threat recognition—adds a critical layer of defense against internal vulnerabilities.
- **Strategic and Managerial Oversight** At the leadership level, executives and senior managers set the strategic direction for port operations and ensure that PIS security receives sustained institutional support [14]. Executives are responsible for aligning cybersecurity priorities with budget allocations, policy development, and long-term infrastructure investments. Managers operationalize these strategies by supervising system performance, enforcing compliance, and maintaining a secure working environment. This leadership tier plays a decisive role in shaping a culture of resilience and ensuring that digital risk is integrated into port governance frameworks.

  Although executive and managerial staff do not directly execute operational tasks, they rely heavily on PISs for strategic decision making and to coordinate port operations [14]. By utilizing real-time data from the PIS, they monitor operational efficiency, allocate resources, and drive continuous performance improvements. Terminal and operational managers leverage PISs to optimize terminal operations, monitor equipment utilization, and manage vessel schedules. Furthermore, leadership fosters a cybersecurity culture by ensuring that all employees—from technical staff to operational teams—understand their roles in securing the PIS. Through targeted investments in cybersecurity and a commitment to compliance, executive leadership strengthens the port's resilience, ensuring long-term operational continuity and the security of the PIS.

2.2.5 Data

Data in a PIS refers to unprocessed information collected from port operations, IoT devices, sensors, and external systems. It includes cargo manifests, vessel schedules, sensor readings, and access logs—forming the digital foundation of the system's operational capacity [15].

Within the system, data moves through structured pipelines that manage its collection, transmission, and processing. Sensors and terminal equipment generate raw data, which is securely transmitted through internal networks to centralized or distributed storage. Data management software then organizes, indexes, analyzes, and distributes the information to various applications, enabling seamless coordination between logistics modules, customs systems, and port management tools.

Supporting these processes requires an integrated data infrastructure comprising both physical and virtual components. Hardware elements—such as local servers, edge computing nodes, and cloud-based storage—provide the foundation for data retention and processing. Software components, including middleware, data platforms, and application programming interfaces, manage routing, formatting, and integration across subsystems. Managing data, therefore, depends not only on robust hardware but also on a cohesive software ecosystem.

Effective data handling also requires a well-defined architecture to ensure synchronization, integrity checks, and redundancy. Structured databases enable fast retrieval, while scalable storage accommodates variable data volumes. In this context, data serves as both the source and the output of PIS operations—driving automation, traceability, and coordination. Robust cybersecurity measures are essential throughout the data lifecycle to maintain confidentiality, integrity, and resilience [15].

2.3 Terminal Operating Systems

A TOS is an integrated software solution designed to manage and optimize key operational processes within port terminals. It enables the coordinated deployment of essential equipment—such as quay cranes and yard vehicles—that supports core terminal functions, including berth allocation and container yard management. Through centralized management, the TOS improves resource allocation and enhances overall operational efficiency [16]. As it interfaces with the majority of the terminal infrastructure, the TOS serves as an integral component of the PIS, consolidating multiple subsystems to support diverse terminal activities. The primary subsystems of the TOS are described below.

2.3.1 Berth Management Systems

The berth management system (BMS) is a specialized software platform designed to ensure the efficient, safe, and coordinated use of berths—designated docking areas for vessels—within port environments [17]. As a foundational component of port operations, the BMS facilitates the allocation, planning, and monitoring of berth usage by integrating real-time data, predictive analytics, and advanced scheduling algorithms. The BMS evaluates and processes multiple variables that influence berthing decisions, including:

- **Vessel Characteristics**: Size, draft, and cargo type.
- **Port Infrastructure**: Berth length, depth, and equipment availability.
- **Environmental Conditions**: Tidal patterns and weather forecasts.
- **Operational Schedules**: Vessel arrival and departure timetables.

By synthesizing these inputs, the BMS enables berth planners to ensure the safe and timely berthing and unberthing of vessels, optimize berth utilization, and reduce vessel turnaround times. These efficiencies contribute to reduced port congestion and mitigate the financial consequences of delays, such as demurrage charges. In addition, most modern BMSs support dynamic berth planning, enabling ports to adapt to unforeseen disruptions, including late vessel arrivals, adverse weather conditions, or temporary equipment shortages. With real-time monitoring and advanced conflict-detection capabilities, the system facilitates continuous operational adjustments to maintain uninterrupted berth activity.

2.3.2 Yard Management Systems

The yard management system (YMS) facilitates the management of yard activities associated with cargo handling after unloading from vessels or prior to loading [18]. These systems assist yard planners and controllers in optimizing container stacking, retrieval, and transportation using a range of equipment, including rubber-tyred gantry cranes, rail-mounted gantry cranes, reach stackers, straddle carriers, forklifts, top loaders, and chassis.

Advanced YMS solutions aim to minimize unnecessary container and vehicle movements, thereby reducing operational costs and minimizing delays and errors in shipment processing. To achieve these objectives, modern ports are increasingly incorporating advanced technologies into their YMS infrastructure [19]. These include:

- **Radio Frequency Identification:** Enables real-time tracking of containers and equipment, improving asset visibility and traceability.
- **Global Positioning System:** Supports accurate tracking of yard equipment such as cranes and forklifts, enhancing fleet coordination and movement efficiency.

- **Electronic Seals:** Strengthen cargo security by preventing unauthorized access.
- **Artificial Intelligence and Machine Learning:** Facilitate predictive analytics and automated decision making, improving the efficiency and responsiveness of yard operations.
- **Information Management Systems:** Aggregate and analyze data from multiple sources, increasing yard visibility and supporting data-driven decision making.

By integrating these technologies, YMSs enhance yard operations through the automation of key functions such as appointment scheduling, gate and dock management, and inventory control [19]. This automation reduces congestion and idle time, improves dock utilization, and ensures the seamless flow of goods throughout the port. In addition, YMSs contribute to lower labor costs, improved productivity, and enhanced operational security.

Moreover, as yard operations require continuous coordination among personnel and machinery, modern YMSs improve visibility into equipment, carriers, workforce activities, and inventory status. This increased visibility not only contributes to accident prevention but also enhances the flexibility and efficiency of both inbound and outbound logistics processes. As a result, YMSs play a vital role in supporting the sustainability, safety, and competitiveness of contemporary port management practices.

2.3.3 Gate Management Systems

The gate management system (GMS) is designed to enhance the efficiency, security, and traceability of vehicle movements, particularly with regard to trucks entering and exiting terminal facilities. Its core function is to regulate access by ensuring that only authorized vehicles and drivers are granted entry, in strict compliance with international port security regulations such as the ISPS Code [20]. The GMS continuously cross-references incoming vehicle and driver credentials with pre-registered data, enabling real-time verification. This process helps prevent unauthorized access, detect inconsistencies, and ensure compliance with regulatory standards.

To further optimize its capabilities, most ports have integrated advanced technologies that automate and oversee gate operations in real time. For instance, IoT and RFID technologies significantly enhance the GMS by enabling fast, accurate, and secure gate operations in smart ports [21]. The system employs RFID tags, automated license plate recognition, and fingerprint sensors to authenticate vehicles and cargo in real time. Integrated with cloud computing, the GMS cross-references data with stored records, reducing the need for manual checks, mitigating delays, and minimizing errors.

Additionally, RFID and biometric-based access control systems enhance the automation of the GMS by securely authenticating both employees and visitors [22]. These systems employ RFID tags and biometric verification (e.g., fingerprint or facial recognition) to ensure authorized access while preventing unauthorized entry. By integrating these technologies, the GMS streamlines vehicle processing, reduces manual documentation checks, decreases wait times, and improves gate throughput. These improvements, in turn, enhance terminal productivity by optimizing traffic flow and alleviating bottlenecks during peak operational periods.

2.3.4 Security and Access Control Systems

The security and access control system (SACS) plays a crucial role in managing the movement of personnel and vehicles within seaport terminals, ensuring both operational efficiency and security [23]. Unlike the GMS, which focuses primarily on regulating truck and driver access at terminal facilities, the SACS encompasses a broader spectrum of security measures. These address both physical security—focused on protecting the port's infrastructure, assets, and personnel—and cybersecurity—focused on safeguarding critical digital systems and sensitive data essential to port operations [24]. Within this framework, the GMS is considered a component of physical security, ensuring compliance with international security standards such as the ISPS Code.

- **Physical Security**
  Beyond gate access control, the SACS governs entry to critical areas within the terminal, including office buildings, operational zones, and restricted regions. These measures help prevent theft, protect cargo, and ensure the safety of personnel, while also supporting cybersecurity efforts by limiting access to sensitive digital infrastructure. The primary physical security protocols include:
  - **Access Control:** The use of biometric scanners, ID card readers, and physical barriers such as gates to restrict access to authorized personnel. Biometric technologies significantly reduce the risk of identity fraud and unauthorized access.
  - **Surveillance:** CCTV cameras are deployed throughout the port to provide real-time monitoring. Security personnel can promptly detect and address any suspicious activities.
  - **Perimeter Security:** Physical barriers, such as fencing, are employed to define and secure the boundaries of the port, preventing unauthorized entry and protecting port assets.
- **Cybersecurity**
  In parallel with physical security measures, the SACS also focuses on the protection of digital infrastructure and sensitive data vital to port operations. These cybersecurity protocols ensure the continuous functionality of port services while defending against cyber threats such as data theft, ransomware, and other forms of cyber-attacks. Key cybersecurity measures include:

- **Authentication:** Robust security protocols, including multi-factor authentication, password management, and role-based access control, ensure that only authorized personnel have access to critical systems.
- **Network Defense:** Firewalls and intrusion detection systems monitor network traffic, identify potential threats, and neutralize them before they can cause harm.
- **Data Encryption:** Encryption safeguards sensitive data both during transmission and while it is stored, ensuring confidentiality and preventing unauthorized access.
- **Continuous Monitoring and Audits:** Regular security audits and ongoing monitoring are essential for identifying vulnerabilities, addressing emerging threats, and ensuring that the system adapts to changing cyber risks.

As ports integrate more IoT technologies and other internet-based systems linked to the PIS, the convergence of physical security and cybersecurity within the SACS not only protects sensitive information and digital assets but also enhances physical security measures, ensuring operational continuity. By minimizing the risks associated with cyber-attacks and unauthorized access, the system helps mitigate potential financial losses and reputational damage, thus supporting the seamless operation of port facilities despite emerging threats [24].

2.4 Cargo Management Systems

The cargo management system (CMS) consists of land-based operational platforms that oversee cargo handling within ports and coordinate the efficient distribution of cargo to inland destinations. CMSs facilitate the integrated movement of goods, vehicles, and data across the port's landside infrastructure, ensuring a seamless transition between maritime transport and inland logistics networks, particularly those supported by storage facilities in the hinterland. These systems encompass both foundational tools that support traditional cargo handling and advanced modules tailored to logistics services, reflecting the evolving role of modern ports as integrated logistics service providers.

2.4.1 Cargo-Handling Systems

The cargo-handling system (CHS) is engineered to optimize the performance of port equipment during the loading, unloading, and internal transportation of cargo within terminal areas [25]. These systems prioritize scheduling, resource allocation, and coordination concerning equipment, with configurations varying according to the type of cargo handled [26].

- For dry bulk cargo, CHSs incorporate facilities such as power-driven conveyor belts fed by hoppers (large containers on legs) or magnetic grabs

mounted on high-capacity traveling cranes or gantries. These systems are designed to efficiently handle commodities like coal, ores, bulk sugar, and grain (using elevators or silos with pneumatic suction).
- For liquid bulk cargo—including crude oil and derivatives—CHSs are configured to transfer cargo from tankers to shore-based storage tanks via pipelines. The process involves discharging oil through a ship's manifold and transferring it via shore-based loading arms with oil-tight, flanged connections. Pumping systems on the tanker or at an onshore refinery, along with specially designated berths away from the main dock, enhance operational safety.
- For containerized cargo, CHSs manage quay cranes, container-handling equipment, and chassis to streamline the movement of containers between ships and the shore in accordance with modern logistics standards.

As cargo handling has become increasingly critical to port competitiveness, CHSs are essential for ensuring terminal efficiency and safety. Their design, tailored to the specific requirements of different cargo types, guarantees optimal performance and seamless integration within the broader supply chain. In recent years, many terminals have integrated automation, IoT sensors, and advanced data management technologies into their CHS. These innovations enhance operational efficiency by reducing vessel turnaround times, increasing cargo throughput, and minimizing equipment downtime.

2.4.2 Drayage Operation Systems

The drayage operation system (DOS) supports the transport of containerized cargo between seaports and adjacent facilities—such as warehouses, distribution centers, and intermodal rail terminals [27]. Given the increasing influence of e-commerce and integrated supply chains, drayage services have become pivotal in addressing first- and last-mile logistics challenges. DOSs facilitate door-to-door service by coordinating short-distance deliveries and long-haul intermodal container movements, thereby strengthening connectivity between ports and end-users [28]. By streamlining truck dispatching, optimizing container transfers, and minimizing delays, DOSs substantially enhance supply chain responsiveness and efficiency. Key operational functions of DOSs include:

- **Data Management and Integration**: DOSs consolidate and manage essential data—such as vehicle, driver, and container information—providing real-time visibility to support informed decision making.
- **Scheduling and Route Optimization**: Utilizing advanced algorithms, DOSs determine the most efficient transport routes based on delivery timelines, traffic conditions, and terminal availability, thereby improving operational performance.

- **Real-Time Traffic Monitoring and Adaptive Routing**: Integrated traffic data allow for real-time rerouting to avoid congestion, reduce idle time, and ensure on-time cargo delivery, even during unforeseen disruptions.
- **Dynamic Scheduling**: Drayage operation system (DOS) process continuous input from multiple variables (e.g., truck availability, container status, and infrastructure conditions), enabling dynamic rescheduling to adapt to operational delays or sudden changes.

While DOS are particularly beneficial for ports offering integrated logistics services, they may have limited relevance for ports that focus exclusively on terminal handling activities. Nevertheless, for seaports with broader supply chain responsibilities, DOS are indispensable for sustaining high levels of operational efficiency, reducing logistics costs, and enhancing competitiveness in global trade networks.

2.5 Vessel Traffic Management Systems

The vessel traffic management system (VTMS) is a comprehensive solution designed to manage maritime traffic and enhance the safety, security, and efficiency of port and coastal operations [29]. Developed in response to requirements set by the international maritime organization (IMO) for automatic identification system (AIS) on SOLAS-type vessels, the establishment of shore-based AIS infrastructure, and the mandates of the IMO ISPS Code [3], VTMSs address a range of operational challenges. These include:

- Enhancing the safety of life at sea and improving overall vessel traffic management.
- Controlling ship movements to prevent collisions and other navigational hazards.
- Protecting the environment and offshore installations.
- Preventing illicit activities such as smuggling and illegal immigration.

VTMSs integrate advanced technologies—including radar, AIS transponders, and CCTV cameras—to provide a real-time, dynamic view of maritime traffic and environmental conditions. Each sensor type underpins a dedicated subsystem within the VTMS. Central to the system is the monitoring display, which serves as the core interface [30]. It presents sensor data over electronic charts and enables remote control of external sensors and information exchange. Key functions of the monitoring display include:

- Displaying sensor information overlaid on electronic navigational charts.
- Recognizing and monitoring objects within the operational range.
- Overlaying radar images to detect and track vessels, especially under low-visibility conditions.

- Presenting AIS target information, including vessel identification, position, speed, and heading, to support tracking and collision avoidance.
- Facilitating remote sensor control and generating warnings or alarms based on user-defined criteria.
- Recording and replaying navigational scenarios and radio communications.
- Providing meteorological data, such as wind speed, wave height, and visibility, essential for safe navigation.
- Incorporating surveillance networks using CCTV and other monitoring devices to enhance situational awareness.

Workstations equipped with VTMS monitoring display software can be independently configured in terms of database connections, access rights, available functionalities, and specific information displayed. These integrated components collaborate to monitor vessel movements, assess environmental factors, and support informed decision making, ultimately reducing collision risks and enabling prompt emergency responses. Typically, VTMSs fall under the jurisdiction of governmental authorities such as port authorities or maritime departments. These entities utilize VTMS data and communication tools to manage vessel traffic, issue navigational alerts, and guide vessels through congested or sensitive areas, thereby optimizing port operations.

2.6 Port Community Systems

The port community system (PCS) is a digital platform designed to facilitate secure, standardized, and efficient information exchange among a wide array of stakeholders within the port ecosystem [31]. In the realm of international maritime transportation and global supply chains, port-related transactions are inherently complex, typically involving terminal operators, port authorities, harbor masters, shipping lines, vessel owners, freight forwarders, logistics service providers, customs administrations, and financial institutions. By promoting seamless collaboration among these entities, PCS platforms significantly enhance operational efficiency and support the advancement of international trade.

Case studies from the World Bank database demonstrate that well-implemented PCSs deliver significant advantages with regard to operational efficiency and strategic objectives [31]. PCSs facilitate the creation of Single Window environments, enabling stakeholders to submit customs declarations, regulatory forms, and trade documents through a unified digital platform, thereby reducing administrative complexity and expediting cargo clearance. The digitization of processes also shortens turnaround times and increases throughput. A notable example is Singapore's PORTNET, launched in 1984 by the Port of Singapore Authority, which evolved from a basic digital logistics portal into a comprehensive PCS supporting seamless information exchange and real-time coordination among port users. In 2022 alone, the Port of Singapore handled over 140,000 vessel calls and processed approximately 577.7 million metric tons of cargo, including 37.3 million twenty-foot equivalent units (TEUs), averaging nine vessel movements per hour across 67 berths. Beyond operational gains, PCSs contribute to broader strategic goals such as environmental sustainability, cost reduction, and regulatory compliance. For instance, Dubai's PCS eliminated more than 42 million paper exchanges, cutting carbon emissions by about 3.8 million pounds annually—equivalent to removing 347 cars from the road—while the Netherlands' PORTBASE system has achieved annual logistics cost savings nearing €245 million. Additionally, these platforms support adherence to international trade facilitation standards, including the World Trade Organization's Trade Facilitation Agreement. Together, these examples highlight how PCSs serve as both vital enablers of efficient port operations and key drivers of long-term sustainability and economic competitiveness.

The success of PCSs hinges on four critical enablers that collectively ensure efficient operation, adaptability, and sustained value within the port ecosystem [31]. First, optimizing and standardizing logistics processes is fundamental, often requiring the redesign of outdated workflows to eliminate redundancies and improve stakeholder coordination. This process streamlining is complemented by adopting international electronic data interchange (EDI) standards, which promote interoperability and scalability across diverse technology platforms. Second, the integration of advanced digital technologies plays an increasingly vital role, with Big Data analytics enabling real-time processing of complex information and artificial intelligence enhancing forecasting, planning, and scheduling in dynamic environments. These capabilities bolster operational resilience and position PCSs as core components of smart port infrastructures. Third, robust governance and institutional alignment are essential, necessitating clear role definitions and coordinated policy frameworks supported by formal governance structures. Such alignment fosters accountability, coherence, and long-term adaptability, often guided by national roadmaps that sustain institutional commitment. Finally, sound financial planning ensures economic viability, requiring strategic investment in software, hardware, cybersecurity, and ongoing IT support. As PCS platforms expand and user numbers grow, comprehensive cost estimates and cost-benefit analyses become vital for shaping funding strategies, with equitable cost-sharing models designed to reflect each stakeholder's usage and value contribution. Together, these elements form the foundation for effective PCS deployment and its ongoing success.

2.7 Attack Surfaces in the PIS

An attack surface refers to the collection of points on the boundary of a system, its components, or its operational environment where an adversary may attempt to gain unauthorized access, manipulate functionality, or extract sensitive information [32]. In the context of PISs, the attack surface encompasses all potential vulnerabilities, entry points, and vectors that malicious actors could exploit to infiltrate the system, disrupt port operations, or compromise confidential data belonging to port stakeholders. Attack surfaces are typically classified into three primary domains, each presenting distinct threats and requiring tailored mitigation measures. The subsequent sections provide a detailed analysis of these three categories of attack surfaces that are relevant to the PIS.

2.7.1 Physical Attack Surfaces

The physical attack surface (PAS) refers to all tangible access points, hardware interfaces, and infrastructure components that malicious actors may exploit to gain unauthorized access to, or manipulate, critical systems [33]. As seaports adopt increasingly advanced technologies, the scope of PASs expands accordingly. The PAS can take the following forms:

- **Unauthorized Access to Restricted Areas:** Ports contain numerous secure zones, including cargo yards, warehouses, and control centers, which must be rigorously protected [34]. Access points such as doors, gates, and terminal entrances represent potential breach locations. Insufficient security measures may allow unauthorized personnel to bypass physical barriers, facilitating activities such as equipment tampering, theft, or sabotage.
- **Exploitable Hardware Interfaces:** Physical network connections—such as USB ports, Ethernet jacks, and other exposed interfaces—present a significant attack vector [35]. Threat actors can exploit these interfaces to introduce malware, extract data, or establish unauthorized connections to critical systems.
- **Device Vulnerabilities and Theft:** Computing devices, including servers, workstations, and office phones, store and process sensitive operational data [36]. If left unprotected, these devices are susceptible to unauthorized access, tampering, or physical theft.
- **Compromised Security Infrastructure:** Surveillance cameras, alarm systems, and other security mechanisms are essential for port protection [37]. However, attackers may disable or manipulate these systems to create security blind spots, allowing undetected intrusions. A compromised surveillance network can hinder threat detection and delay incident response, increasing the risk of security breaches and operational disruptions.
- **IoT Device Exploitation:** The widespread adoption of IoT devices, including GPS trackers, RFID readers, and automated cargo handling systems, enhances operational efficiency but also introduces new risks [38]. These devices are vulnerable to physical tampering or signal interference, potentially leading to data manipulation, shipment misrouting, or supply chain disruptions.

2.7.2 Digital Attack Surfaces

The digital attack surface (DAS) is a recent concept and remains underexplored in port management literature. In the field of computer science, a DAS refers to all external or internet-facing information technology assets that are accessible from outside an organization and susceptible to exploitation by cyber attackers [39]. In the PIS context, this book defines a DAS as the totality of digital components—such as websites, cloud platforms, application programming interfaces, internet protocol addresses, and email servers—that are visible or reachable via the internet and, therefore, constitute potential targets for malicious actors.

The DAS encompasses vulnerabilities within the port's digital infrastructure, including networked devices, communication pathways, and software applications. These digital entry points present avenues for unauthorized access, operational disruption, or data compromise. As ports increasingly adopt advanced digital technologies to enhance operational efficiency and interconnectivity, the breadth and complexity of their DASs expand accordingly, introducing new cybersecurity challenges. The DAS can take the following forms:

- **Risks of Outdated Systems**: Outdated digital systems represent a critical component of the DAS [40]. These legacy technologies are frequently left unpatched, rendering them vulnerable to exploitation through known security flaws. Cybercriminals may leverage these weaknesses to deploy malicious software, extract sensitive information, or disrupt essential system functions. High-profile incidents such as the WannaCry ransomware attack highlight the urgent need for timely updates and effective vulnerability management strategies [41]. To mitigate such risks, ports should phase out outdated technologies, modernize legacy systems, and conduct proactive vulnerability assessments with corrective actions [42]. Regular maintenance and patching also enhance resilience against cyber-attacks [40].
- **Network Infrastructure Vulnerabilities:** These vulnerabilities are weaknesses in the design, implementation, or operation of an organization's network that may be exploited by cyber attackers to gain unauthorized access, disrupt operations, or steal data. These risks often stem from outdated software, misconfigured hardware, weak security protocols, human error, or exposed endpoints [43]. Such flaws can allow attackers to intercept communications, perform man-in-the-middle attacks, or compromise core systems like the TOS.
- **Exposure of Internet-Facing Assets**: Internet-facing assets, including web applications and APIs, introduce additional DASs [44]. These systems, which are exposed to external networks, are frequent targets for attackers. Improperly secured APIs can allow malicious code injections that lead to data breaches or operational disruptions in ports. With regard to mitigating these risks, implementing comprehensive security measures, such as secure coding practices, encryption, and continuous monitoring, can protect these external-facing components from exploitation [44].
- **Data Repository and Directory Management**: Shared databases and directories represent critical components within the PIS. Poorly configured or inadequately protected data repositories create opportunities for

unauthorized access, data breaches, or data manipulation [45]. To secure these assets, ports must enforce strict access controls, employ advanced encryption techniques, and conduct regular audits, ensuring that sensitive data is secure and accessible only to authorized personnel.

- **Shadow IT and Orphaned Assets**: The increasing prevalence of shadow IT—unauthorized devices or applications introduced without oversight—adds complexity to port security. These devices can act as hidden vulnerabilities, providing backdoor access for attackers [46]. Similarly, orphaned assets, or outdated systems that have not been decommissioned, represent a significant risk [39]. These unmonitored devices, still connected to the network, offer potential entry points for cybercriminals. Ports must establish clear policies for managing the lifecycle of all devices and systems, ensuring that both active and obsolete assets are properly controlled so as to prevent exploitation.

2.7.3 People Attack Surfaces

These threats—often exploited through social engineering attacks (SEA)—target human vulnerabilities such as trust, emotional manipulation, and low cybersecurity awareness to trick individuals into compromising systems or disclosing sensitive data [47]. Unlike attacks that target technical weaknesses within the PIS, SEA primarily focuses on the human element, presenting distinct and often unpredictable security challenges. As ports increasingly integrate advanced technologies that interact with or are operated by personnel, the scope of human-related vulnerabilities expands. The SEA can take the following forms:

- **Insider Threats:** Employees, contractors, and trusted third-party partners with authorized access to critical systems represent potential entry points for attackers [48]. These individuals may intentionally exploit their access for malicious purposes, such as data theft or sabotage, or unintentionally facilitate security breaches through errors or neglect [49]. Insider threats are particularly difficult to detect because they often occur under the guise of legitimate activity, which renders traditional monitoring tools less effective. To mitigate these risks, ports must implement strict access controls, conduct regular security awareness training, and monitor personnel activities to identify any suspicious behavior [14].
- **Phishing Campaigns:** In these campaigns, attackers impersonate trusted entities to trick employees into disclosing sensitive information or executing harmful actions [50]. Phishing can occur through fraudulent emails, phone calls, or websites that appear legitimate, prompting employees to disclose credentials, open malicious attachments, or grant unauthorized access to secure systems [50]. Given the interconnected nature of port operations, phishing attacks can have far-reaching consequences, including operational disruptions, data breaches, and financial losses.

- **Voice and In-Person Social Engineering:** While phishing is the most widely recognized form of SEA, attackers may use phone calls or in-person interactions to manipulate individuals [50]. By posing as company representatives, vendors, or colleagues, attackers can gather sensitive information or gain access to critical systems. These interactions can be especially deceptive as they occur in real time and may appear legitimate to unsuspecting employees. The proliferation of social media platforms has further amplified this risk. Publicly available information on platforms such as LinkedIn or Facebook allows attackers to craft highly targeted approaches, increasing the likelihood of successful manipulation and reducing the chances of detection [50].

References

[1] P. K. Bagchi and S. Paik, "The Role of Public-Private Partnership in Port Information Systems Development," *International Journal of Public Sector Management*, vol. 14, no. 6, pp. 482–499, 2001.

[2] IMO, "Guidelines for Harmonized Communication and Electronic Exchange of Operational Data for Port Calls," 2023. [Online]. Available: wwwcdn.imo.org/localresources/en/OurWork/Facilitation/FAL%20related%20nonmandatory%20documents/FAL.5-CIRC.52.pdf.

[3] IMO, "Vessel Traffic Services," 2020. [Online]. Available: www.imo.org/en/OurWork/Safety/Pages/VesselTrafficServices.aspx.

[4] D. Roy, J.-K. v. Ommeren, R. d. Koster and A. Gharehgozli, "Modeling Landside Container Terminal Queues: Exact Analysis and Approximations," *Transportation Research Part B: Methodological*, vol. 162, pp. 73–102, 2022.

[5] WPSP, "Port of Baku – Port Management Information System (PMIS)," 2020. [Online]. Available: https://sustainableworldports.org/project/port-of-baku-port-management-information-system-pmis/.

[6] L. Heilig and S. Voss, "Information Systems in Seaports: A Categorization and Overview," *Information Technology and Management*, vol. 18, no. 3, pp. 179–201, 2017.

[7] S. Nikghadam, K. F. Molkenboer, L. Tavasszy and J. Rezaei, "Information Sharing to Mitigate Delays in Port: The Case of the Port of Rotterdam," *Maritime Economics & Logistics*, vol. 25, pp. 576–601, 2023.

[8] S. Jouad and M. H. Hamri, "The Impact of Information Systems on Port Performance: The Case of Morocco's Agadir Port," *European Scientific Journal*, vol. 16, no. 1, pp. 38–49, 2020.

[9] WCO, "Guidelines on Cooperation between Customs and Port Authorities," 2023. [Online]. Available: http://wcoomd.org/-/media/wco/public/global/pdf/topics/facilitation/instruments-and-tools/tools/wco-iaph-guideline/wco-iaph-guidelines-on-cooperation-between-customs-and-port-authorities_en.pdf?la=en.

[10] B. P. Douglass, "Design Patterns for Accessing Hardware," in *Design Patterns for Embedded Systems in C*, Elsevier, 2011, pp. 79–147.

[11] M. Jazayeri, "Software Systems," in *Encyclopedia of Physical Science and Technology* (Third Edition), Elsevier, 2003, pp. 1–14.

[12] H. Rathore, "Computer Networks," in *Mapping Biological Systems to Network Systems*, Springer, 2016, pp. 11–25. https://doi.org/10.1007/978-3-319-29782-8_2
[13] C. Senarak, "Port Cybersecurity and Threat: A Structural Model for Prevention and Policy Development," *The Asian Journal of Shipping and Logistics*, vol. 37, no. 1, pp. 20–36, 2021.
[14] C. Senarak, "Cybersecurity Knowledge and Skills for Port Facility Security Officers of International Seaports: Perspectives of IT and Security Personnel," *The Asian Journal of Shipping and Logistics*, vol. 37, no. 4, pp. 345–360, 2021.
[15] G. Appell, T. Mero, T. Bethem and G. French, "The Development of a Real-Time Port Information System," *IEEE Journal of Oceanic Engineering*, vol. 19, no. 2, pp. 149–157, 1994.
[16] M. Hervás-Peralta, S. Poveda-Reyes, G. Molero, F. Santarremigia and J.-P. Pastor-Ferrando, "Improving the Performance of Dry and Maritime Ports by Increasing Knowledge about the Most Relevant Functionalities of the Terminal Operating System (TOS)," *Sustainability*, vol. 11, no. 6, p. 1648, 2019.
[17] G. Tsoukos, A. Giannopoulos and A. Bizakis, "Efficient Management of Operations in Ro-Ro/Ro-Pax Terminals Using a Cloud-Based Yard Management Platform," ," in E.G. Nathanail, N. Gavanas, G. Adamos (eds), Smart Energy for Smart Transport, CSUM 2022, Lecture Notes in Intelligent Transportation and Infrastructure, Springer, Cham, 2023. https://doi.org/10.1007/978-3-031-23721-8_97
[18] Z. Wang, An Examination of the Impact of a Yard Management System on Three Third-Party Logistics Operations Centers, Baker University, 2025.
[19] S. Kolangiammal, S. Prabha, P. Sivalakshmi, N. P, S. Kalaichelvi and S. Sujatha, "Transforming Yard Management for Optimizing Efficiency through IoT and AI Integration," in 8th International Conference on I-SMAC (IoT in Social, Mobile, Analytics and Cloud) (I-SMAC), Nepal, 2024.
[20] I. Koliousis, "A Conceptual Framework That Monitors Port Facility Access through Integrated Port Community Systems and Improves Port and Terminal Security Performance," *International Journal of Shipping and Transport Logistics*, vol. 12, no. 4, pp. 251–283, 2020.
[21] H. A. Al-Fatlawi and H. J. Motlak, "Design and Implementation of Smart Port Gate System Based on the Internet of Things," in 2023 International Conference on Information Technology, Applied Mathematics and Statistics, 2023.
[22] I. Gowtham, T. Sathishkumar, S. Lakshmiprasad, P. Arumugam and G. Rao, "Automation of Visitor Gate Pass Management System," in 2nd International Conference on Intelligent Computing, Instrumentation and Control Technologies, 2019.
[23] F. Andritsos, "Port Security & Access Control: A Systemic Approach," in The Fourth International Conference on Information, Intelligence, Systems and Applications, Greece, 2013.
[24] I. Progoulakis, N. Nikitakos, D. Dalaklis and R. Yaacob, "Cyber-Physical Security for Ports Infrastructure," in The International Maritime and Logistics Conference, Egypt, 2022.
[25] P. J. M. Meersmans, Optimization of Container Handling Systems, Thela Thesis, 2002.
[26] PFRI, "Cargo-Handling Equipment On Board And In Port," 2018. [Online]. Available: http://pfri.uniri.hr/bopri/documents/16-ME-tal.pdf.

[27] N. Huynh and C. Walton, "Improving Efficiency of Drayage Operations at Seaport Container Terminals Through the Use of an Appointment System," in *Handbook of Terminal Planning*. Operations Research/Computer Science Interfaces Series, New York, Springer, NY, 2011, pp. 323–344.

[28] R. Chen, Q. Meng and P. Jia, "Container Port Drayage Operations and Management: Past and Future," *Transportation Research Part E: Logistics and Transportation Review*, vol. 159, 102633, 2022.

[29] F. V. Javier and C. Aguado, "The Vessel Traffic Management System at the Batangas Baseport: Basis of Enhancing Vessel Traffic Services at the Batangas Bay," *International Journal of Business and Management*, vol. 1, no. 1, pp. 57–78, 2012.

[30] AMR, "Vessel Traffic Management System (VTMS)," 2560. [Online]. Available: www.marinethai.net/en/vessel-traffic-management-system-vtms/.

[31] World Bank Group, "Port Community Systems: Driving Trade in the 21st Century," 2023. [Online]. Available: www.worldbank.org/en/topic/trade/publication/port-community-systems-driving-trade-in-the-21st-century#:~:text=Port%20Community%20Systems%20(PCS)%20are,logistics%20companies%2C%20and%20freight%20forwarders..

[32] R. Ross, V. Pillitteri, K. Dempsey, M. Riddle and G. Guissanier, Protecting Controlled Unclassified Information in Nonfederal Systems and Organizations, NIST, 2024.

[33] G. Zhang, X. Dong, J. Liu and X. Zhang, "Nussbaum-Type Function Based Robust Neural Event-Triggered Control of Unmanned Surface Vehicle Subject to Cyber and Physical Attacks," *Ocean Engineering*, vol. 270, no. 15, 113664, 2023.

[34] K. Bichou, "Port Security," in *Port Operations, Planning and Logistics*, Informa Law from Routledge, 2009, p. 48.

[35] J. Clark, S. Leblanc and S. Knight, "Risks Associated with USB Hardware Trojan Devices Used by Insiders," in IEEE International Systems Conference, Montreal, 2011.

[36] J. Friedman and D. V. Hoffman, "Protecting Data on Mobile Devices: A Taxonomy of Security Threats to Mobile Computing and Review of Applicable Defenses," *Information Knowledge Systems Management*, vol. 7, no. 1-2, pp. 159–180, 2008.

[37] P. Vennam, T. C. Pramod, B. M. Thippeswamy, K. Yong-Guk and B. N. PavanKumar, "Attacks and Preventive Measures on Video Surveillance Systems: A Review," *Applied Sciences*, vol. 11, no. 12, p. 5571, 2021.

[38] U. Bhadani, "Comprehensive Survey of Threats, Cyberattacks, and Enhanced Countermeasures in RFID Technology," *International Journal of Innovative Research in Science, Engineering and Technology*, vol. 11, no. 2, pp. 1803–1809, 2022.

[39] IBM, "What Is Attack Surface Management?," 2024. [Online]. Available: www.ibm.com/think/topics/attack-surface-management.

[40] Anisetti, M., , C. Ardagna, M. Cremonini, E. Damiani, J. Sessa and L. Costa, "Security Threat Landscape," White Paper. CONCORDIA H2020 Project. 2020. www.concordia-h2020.eu/wp-content/uploads/2021/03/White_paper_SecurityThreats.pdf

[41] Q. Chen and R. A. Bridges, "Automated Behavioral Analysis of Malware: A Case Study of WannaCry Ransomware," in 16th IEEE International Conference on Machine Learning and Applications, Cancun, Mexico, 2017.

[42] C. Kuang, Q. Miao and H. Chen, "Analysis of Software Vulnerability," in The 5th WSEAS International Conference on Information Security and Privacy, Wisconsin, 2006.

[43] Ö. Aslan, S. S. Aktuğ, M. Ozkan-Okay, A. A. Yilmaz and E. Akin, "A Comprehensive Review of Cyber Security Vulnerabilities, Threats, Attacks, and Solutions," *Electronics*, vol. 12, no. 6, p. 1333, 2023.

[44] N. Albalawi, N. Alamrani, R. Aloufi, M. Albalawi, A. Aljaedi and A. R. Alharbi, "The Reality of Internet Infrastructure and Services Defacement: A Second Look at Characterizing Web-Based Vulnerabilities," *Electronics*, vol. 12, no. 12, p. 2664, 2023.

[45] A. Naguib and K. M. Fouad, "Database Security: Current Challenges and Effective Protection Strategies," in 6th International Conference on Computing and Informatics, New Cairo – Cairo, 2024.

[46] C. Senarak, "Port Cyberattacks from 2011 to 2023: A Literature Review and Discussion of Selected Cases," *Maritime Economics & Logistics*, vol. 26, no. 1, pp. 105–130, 2024.

[47] Z. Wang, H. Zhu and L. Sun, "Social Engineering in Cybersecurity: Effect Mechanisms, Human Vulnerabilities and Attack Methods," *IEEE Access*, vol. 9, pp. 11895–11910, 2021.

[48] T. Baluta, L. Ramapantulu, Y. M. Teo and E.-C. Chang, "Modeling the Effects of Insider Threats on Cybersecurity of Complex Systems," in Winter Simulation Conference, Las Vegas, 2017.

[49] N. Khan, R. J. Houghton and S. Sharples, "Understanding Factors That Influence Unintentional Insider Threat: A Framework to Counteract Unintentional Risks," *Cognition, Technology & Work*, vol. 24, p. 393–421, 2022.

[50] Z. Alkhalil, C. Hewage, L. Nawaf and I. Khan, "Phishing Attacks: A Recent Comprehensive Study and a New Anatomy," *Frontiers in Computer Science*, vol. 3, pp. 1–23, 2021.

3 New Technologies for Enhancing Port Efficiency and Associated Risks

3.1 Port Efficiency: Definition and the Role of New Technologies in Enhancement

Efficiency, in its broadest sense, refers to achieving desired outcomes with minimal use of time, effort, or resources [1]. It emphasizes optimizing outputs relative to inputs, ensuring that resources are applied in the most productive way [2]. In the seaport context, operational efficiency has become a central focus, as ports view it as a key source of competitiveness. It involves maximizing the speed and volume of cargo movement relative to the operational resources deployed—such as labor, handling equipment, and terminal space [3]. This is achieved by minimizing ship turnaround time, eliminating delays, and streamlining cargo-handling procedures. A port with high operational efficiency delivers faster and more reliable services while utilizing fewer inputs. Key processes—such as berth allocation, crane scheduling, and yard management—must convert resources like labor, capital, and time into measurable outputs, including cargo throughput, vessel service time, and customer satisfaction. Given the interdependence of these processes, operational efficiency also depends on coordination, consistency, and timely execution across the entire port system [4].

3.1.1 Dimensions of Port Efficiency

The traditional emphasis on operational output in ports has expanded in response to global trade shifts, stricter environmental policies, and rapid technological change. Port efficiency is now understood as a multidimensional concept encompassing not just speed and throughput but also environmental responsibility, economic viability, logistics performance, infrastructure utilization, and technological readiness. These dimensions are interconnected; for example, adopting automated systems can simultaneously boost cargo-handling speed, reduce energy use, and improve reliability. A holistic view of these elements is essential for evaluating and enhancing a port's overall effectiveness.

The principal dimensions of port efficiency include:

DOI: 10.4324/9781003559320-3

- **Technological Efficiency** refers to how well ports leverage digital tools, automation, and smart systems to enhance performance [5]. It involves optimizing technology to improve data processing, reduce manual tasks, and integrate with global supply chains. High technological efficiency leads to faster operations, cost savings, and improved competitiveness.
- **Infrastructure Efficiency** concerns the effective use of fixed assets—such as berths, terminals, and intermodal links—to support growing cargo volumes [6]. It measures how well these long-term capital investments support higher throughput and service reliability without requiring constant expansion. While operational efficiency emphasizes daily resource optimization, infrastructure efficiency focuses on the structural adaptability of physical systems.
- **Economic Efficiency** refers to generating economic value while minimizing the use of financial, material, and human resources [7]. It involves reducing generalized transport costs—covering time, expenses, and risk—while increasing throughput and revenue. Economically efficient ports allocate resources strategically to yield higher returns per input.
- **Logistics Efficiency** captures the smooth coordination of supply chain processes to enable timely cargo movement at lower cost and administrative burden [8]. It reflects performance across customs clearance, intermodal transfer, and documentation. Higher logistics efficiency results in fewer delays, streamlined handling, and optimal use of space and labor.
- **Environmental Efficiency** focuses on minimizing ecological impact per unit of activity [9]. It includes lowering emissions, waste, and energy consumption relative to vessel calls or cargo volumes. A port demonstrates strong environmental efficiency when it meets sustainability targets—such as carbon intensity reduction—without significantly increasing resource use.

Together, these dimensions form a robust framework for understanding and improving port performance. Evaluating input-output relationships across these areas supports informed investment decisions and guides ports toward greater sustainability, resilience, and global competitiveness.

3.1.2 The Role of New Technologies in Enhancing Port Efficiency

Technological advancement has become essential in enhancing port efficiency by enabling ports to generate greater output while using fewer inputs such as time, labor, energy, and physical infrastructure [3]. In line with the core concept of efficiency—optimizing outputs relative to resource utilization—technology enables the streamlining of operational processes, reduction of idle time, and improved reliability in service delivery. As global trade volumes increase and operational demands intensify, ports must rely on technology to maintain competitiveness, service quality, and sustainability.

A key feature shared across technological applications is their ability to support automation and data-driven decision-making [9]. These functions reduce dependence on manual labor, minimize human error, and increase the precision and speed of operations. Technologies that automate repetitive tasks, enable real-time data exchange, and improve situational awareness allow ports to handle larger cargo volumes with greater consistency and lower costs. This not only enhances throughput but also contributes to more resilient and responsive port systems.

Moreover, many technologies directly support environmental and energy efficiency by optimizing resource consumption and reducing emissions. From electrification and renewable energy integration to smart microgrids and energy-efficient equipment, technological solutions help ports meet regulatory requirements while aligning with global sustainability goals. In this regard, technology is not merely an operational tool but a strategic enabler of long-term efficiency and resilience. The following section outlines specific technological categories and explains how each contributes to enhancing port performance.

3.2 Major Groups of New Technologies in Seaports

To enhance efficiency, modern ports are adopting three major categories of technologies: digitalization, automation, and decarbonization. Each group introduces capabilities that reshape operations, logistics, and sustainability.

3.2.1 Digitalization Technologies

Digitalization in the port sector represents a fundamental reconfiguration of how ports operate and interact with their stakeholders. It goes beyond merely converting paper documents into digital files; it involves embedding digital technologies into core operational and strategic processes to enhance efficiency, coordination, and adaptability. Through tools such as mobile systems, Internet of Things (IoT) devices, robotics, artificial intelligence (AI), machine learning (ML), big data analytics, and cloud-based infrastructures, ports are evolving into more integrated and responsive systems [10].

These technologies enable real-time data exchange, predictive insights, and increased automation, laying the groundwork for smart port environments that can react swiftly to operational demands and external pressures [11]. On a practical level, digitalization improves scheduling accuracy, cargo tracking, and terminal operations, helping to reduce delays and streamline resource use. At the same time, it facilitates better coordination between key actors—such as customs, shipping firms, and inland transport providers—by simplifying information flow and accelerating administrative processes.

Beyond operational improvements, digitalization contributes to longer-term goals. Monitoring tools help manage energy use, emissions, and infrastructure wear, while analytical systems support forecasting and contingency planning. These elements strengthen both the port's environmental stewardship and its readiness for future challenges. By embedding digital capabilities into its infrastructure and governance, a port builds not only immediate efficiencies but also a foundation for resilience in the face of evolving cyber, economic, and regulatory risks [10].

3.2.2 Automation Technologies

Automation technologies are reshaping how ports function by shifting repetitive and precision-driven tasks from human labor to intelligent systems. Applied across key operational domains—such as container handling, yard logistics, gate control, and inventory tracking—these technologies enable round-the-clock operations with enhanced speed and reliability [12]. At the center of this transformation is the integration of sensing, positioning, and control systems that guide automated machinery with minimal manual input.

A fundamental component in this system is the position detection system (PDS), which uses a combination of sensors—including laser, optical, and ultrasonic devices—to determine the exact locations of equipment and containers. This spatial data ensures that automated cranes and transport vehicles move with precision and timing. Supporting technologies such as radio-frequency identification (RFID) and real-time locating systems (RTLS) further strengthen situational awareness. RFID tags automate asset identification and tracking, while RTLS—leveraging technologies like Global Positioning System (GPS), Wi-Fi, bluetooth low energy (BLE), and ultra-wideband (UWB)—provides continuous monitoring of personnel and equipment locations.

Together, these systems create a synchronized digital environment that allows port equipment to operate with greater control, efficiency, and coordination. The results are measurable: container movements are more predictable, storage systems optimize placement, and autonomous vehicles maintain consistent performance with minimal intervention. These efficiencies reduce error rates, improve throughput, and stabilize operational timelines.

Economically, automation enables ports to handle growing volumes without proportionally increasing workforce size or physical infrastructure. This leads to lower unit costs and more scalable operations. Logistical processes—such as customs coordination and modal transfers—are also accelerated through automated documentation and real-time data exchange. From an environmental perspective, the deployment of electric-powered automated equipment, as seen in ports like CTA Hamburg, contributes to emission reductions and energy conservation [12]. Over time, automation also supports smarter asset management through predictive maintenance, extending equipment life and avoiding unnecessary capital expansion.

3.2.3 Decarbonization Technologies

Decarbonization technologies are central to reducing greenhouse gas emissions and energy use in port operations, supporting broader sustainability objectives [10]. Renewable energy sources such as solar panels, wind turbines, and offshore installations play a vital role in decreasing ports' dependence on fossil fuels, cutting both emissions and operational energy expenses [13]. The integration of on-site renewable power also strengthens energy resilience, fostering more autonomous and stable energy systems within port facilities.

Electrification of equipment—like cranes and forklifts—represents another important step in minimizing environmental impact. By replacing diesel-powered machinery with electric alternatives, ports reduce air and noise pollution, improving health conditions for workers and nearby communities [14]. This transition reflects compliance with international emissions targets and demonstrates a commitment to modernizing port operations with clean technology.

Ports are also advancing the use of alternative fuels, including liquefied natural gas (LNG), hydrogen, and biofuels, to lower emissions from vessels. Given the shipping industry's significant carbon footprint, the availability of cleaner fuels at port terminals is becoming essential [15]. Supporting these fuels helps ports reduce indirect emissions and attract shipping lines with sustainability priorities, thus strengthening their competitive edge.

In addition to the environmental benefits, adopting decarbonization technologies helps ports manage regulatory risks and control compliance costs. Regulations such as the EU FuelEU Maritime Regulation—effective from January 2025—mandate reductions in greenhouse gas intensity for ships docking at EU ports, with requirements for renewable fuels and onshore power by 2030 and 2035, respectively [16]. Adhering to these rules means avoiding penalties and costly infrastructure upgrades while positioning ports advantageously in the eyes of investors focused on sustainability. Similarly, the International Maritime Organization (IMO)'s Net-Zero Framework, set to introduce emission limits and pricing mechanisms for large ships from 2027 onward, underscores the urgency of clean energy adoption [17]. By integrating these technologies and fuels, ports signal readiness for evolving regulations and demonstrate environmental responsibility that appeals to green-conscious stakeholders.

3.3 Automated Guided Vehicles

Automated guided vehicles (AGVs) are extensively employed in modern ports, revolutionizing the intra-terminal transport of containers and cargo. These unmanned, autonomous systems operate without human intervention, utilizing advanced navigation technologies to facilitate precise movement between quay cranes, stacking yards, and rail terminals [18]. While earlier AGV systems depended on buried cables for guidance, contemporary terminals now use buried beacons—embedded digital markers that emit signals enabling AGVs to determine their exact location with greater accuracy.

AGVs integrate multiple technologies for efficient and safe operation, including GPS and 5G for localization and Light Detection and Ranging (LiDAR) and radar for obstacle detection and collision avoidance [19]. Structurally, they feature a robust chassis with independently powered and steerable axles, allowing for tight maneuvering and lateral movement ("crabbing") to ensure accurate container placement. Most modern AGVs are capable of transporting either one or two twenty-foot equivalent units (TEUs) or one forty-foot equivalent unit (FEU). Importantly, AGV functionality is underpinned by sophisticated control software—typically embedded within the terminal operating system (TOS)—which manages task allocation, routing, and coordinated fleet deployment.

3.3.1 Benefits of AGVs

AGVs have markedly improved port operations by enabling consistent, around-the-clock container handling. Their continuous performance reduces vessel turnaround times and minimizes delays, enhancing overall reliability. Advanced routing algorithms further optimize transport paths, easing yard congestion and improving container placement, especially during peak periods.

By removing human operators from hazardous zones, AGVs reduce workplace injuries, supporting a safer operational environment. They also lower long-term labor costs and improve energy use. As electrically powered systems, AGVs cut emissions and align with global sustainability goals. Their scalability allows ports to handle rising demand and adjust to shifting operational loads. Integration with cranes, storage units, and other systems also strengthens process cohesion and efficiency.

3.3.2 Risks of AGVs

Despite their advantages, AGVs pose several operational and strategic risks that require proactive management [20]. Transitions to AGV systems can disrupt workflows, especially during the early stages when staff are adapting and systems require calibration. Careful planning and phased rollouts help mitigate such issues.

Cybersecurity is another major concern. AGVs depend on networked controls, making them targets for cyber-attacks that could compromise routing systems and halt movement. Their reliance on batteries also introduces challenges—recharging downtime and maintenance delays can affect availability. Disruptions in energy supply or poor battery oversight further threaten operational continuity.

Autonomous movement in shared workspaces creates safety risks. Malfunctions or routing errors, without human oversight, may lead to collisions or near misses. Insufficient monitoring, delayed maintenance, or a lack of predictive diagnostics can cause downtime and reduce equipment life, weakening long-term resilience.

AGVs also face external risks. Energy instability, whether from supply issues or geopolitical tensions, may interrupt operations. Their complex routing algorithms are sometimes slow to respond to environmental changes or disruptions, reducing planning accuracy. Moreover, while AGVs generate substantial operational data, poor integration or limited analytics can delay detection of anomalies and hinder timely intervention.

3.4 Internet of Things

IoTs have become a transformative force in the port sector, enabling real-time connectivity among physical assets through embedded sensors, software, and networked systems [10]. By facilitating continuous data exchange and autonomous decision making, IoT enhances operational visibility, optimizes cargo handling and equipment performance, and supports predictive maintenance and energy efficiency. These capabilities collectively improve throughput, reduce downtime, and advance data-driven, resilient port ecosystems.

IoT implementation depends on a convergence of advanced technologies. Central to this are sensors and actuators—devices that detect environmental and operational variables such as temperature, pressure, motion, and equipment status and execute responsive actions like activating machinery or adjusting system parameters [21]. These components are essential for automating cargo handling, monitoring equipment conditions, and managing environmental data [22]. Connectivity technologies, including Wi-Fi, Bluetooth, and cellular networks, enable seamless data transmission between distributed IoT devices and centralized systems [23]. Cloud computing provides the scalable infrastructure required to store and process the substantial data volumes generated, facilitating functions such as berth scheduling, asset tracking, and predictive analytics. In parallel, big data analytics—leveraging machine learning and predictive modeling—extracts actionable insights to improve terminal efficiency and reduce operational inefficiencies [23].

3.4.1 Benefits of IoT

IoTs bring substantial benefits to port operations, improving efficiency, safety, coordination, and decision making across the logistics chain [10, 21, 22, 23]. By embedding smart sensors in assets such as cargo, infrastructure, and machinery, IoT enables real-time tracking of movement, equipment conditions, energy usage, and environmental variables. This continuous data stream helps optimize resource use, reduce congestion, and enhance spatial planning. Greater visibility into vessel schedules and container locations improves workflow and minimizes delays.

In maintenance, IoT enables cost savings and better equipment performance through predictive analytics. Monitoring critical systems—like cranes, AGVs, and conveyors—allows early detection of faults, reducing downtime and extending asset life. IoT also enhances coordination among terminal operators, customs, logistics providers, and regulators. Shared access to real-time data on cargo status and port activities supports faster decisions, lowers errors, and streamlines compliance. This improved coordination helps mitigate disruptions and ensures smoother cargo flow.

The data generated by IoT systems supports informed, strategic planning. Ports can detect patterns, enhance operations, and develop more adaptive, sustainable models. Automated monitoring of equipment and energy use helps identify inefficiencies, reduce costs, and support environmental targets. Overall, IoT fosters more agile and resilient port ecosystems, capable of responding to shifting trade and operational conditions.

3.4.2 Risks of IoTs

While IoT improves port connectivity and operations, it also introduces critical cybersecurity vulnerabilities [22]. Weak authentication remains a major risk. Many IoT systems—used for crane controls, yard sensors, and environmental monitoring—either use default credentials or lack proper authentication altogether. These flaws open pathways for unauthorized access or allow devices to be hijacked for attacks like botnet-driven distributed denial-of-service (DDoS) [24]. Strong authentication, secure configurations, and strict password protocols are essential to securing these systems.

Another issue is limited control and visibility over connected devices. Many IoT platforms used in ports lack real-time monitoring capabilities, making it harder to detect threats or isolate compromised assets [25]. Enhanced detection systems and integrated monitoring tools are needed for timely responses and better oversight.

Unencrypted data transmission is another widespread weakness. Sensitive operational data is often sent without proper protection, making it vulnerable to interception. In complex port environments, this risk is amplified by the scale and interconnected nature of the systems. Encrypting data in transit—using protocols—is crucial for safeguarding confidentiality and integrity [26].

Shared networks also increase risk. When IoT devices run on general-purpose local area networks (LANs), attackers can move laterally across systems. For instance, a breached container sensor might be used to access vital control systems [27]. Network segmentation and the use of dedicated subnets or virtual private networks (VPNs) can help limit this exposure.

Firmware flaws and outdated software also present serious threats. Many IoT devices run on unpatched code or include vulnerable third-party components [28]. Updating is particularly difficult in port settings, where devices are spread across hard-to-reach areas. Supporting over-the-air updates and automating security patches are essential for maintaining protection without disrupting operations.

Physical tampering is another concern. Devices placed in public or semi-restricted zones are exposed to theft or manipulation [22]. SIM cards can be misused, or hardware can be altered to change configurations or extract data. Mitigation measures include tamper-resistant design, secure enclosures, and tight access control protocols to protect physical infrastructure.

3.5 Artificial Intelligence

AI encompasses a suite of advanced technologies that enable computers and machines to replicate cognitive functions traditionally associated with human intelligence, including learning, problem solving, decision making, perception, creativity, and autonomous action [10]. Contemporary AI systems can interpret complex sensory data—such as visual and linguistic inputs—generate sophisticated recommendations, and respond dynamically to evolving environments with limited human intervention. Although recent attention has focused on generative AI, which creates original text, images, and video, its foundational capabilities derive from machine learning and deep learning, which allow systems to improve performance by analyzing large volumes of data [29].

3.5.1 Benefits of AI

AI integration in port operations drives competitiveness by improving efficiency, safety, and coordination. One of its most valuable contributions lies in predictive optimization and risk reduction [30]. Drawing from historical and live data, AI sharpens vessel arrival forecasts, berth planning, and cargo volume estimates—reducing congestion and improving throughput. Computer vision and sensor analytics also enable early detection of damage, malfunctions, or intrusions, strengthening operational safety.

AI enhances productivity by automating both routine and complex functions, such as cargo allocation, container stacking, and vessel routing [31]. This improves yard space use, shortens turnaround times, and reduces equipment inefficiencies. Predictive maintenance—powered by real-time monitoring of assets like cranes and AGVs—lowers unplanned downtime. Administrative tasks, including data entry and inspections, are streamlined, allowing staff to concentrate on higher-value analytical roles.

Stakeholder communication is improved through AI-driven interfaces [32]. Chatbots and virtual assistants using natural language processing offer instant updates on vessel movements, cargo status, and customs procedures. These tools boost transparency, ease regulatory processes, and reduce administrative workload—fostering trust among port users.

From a sustainability perspective, AI promotes smarter energy and resource use [33]. By minimizing idle times, it cuts emissions and fuel consumption. It also supports waste reduction and infrastructure planning aligned with circular economy goals. Machine learning continuously refines system decisions, reducing human error and improving consistency [34]. These features are vital for maintaining safety and regulatory compliance in 24/7 operations.

3.5.2 Risks of AI

Despite its advantages, AI introduces critical risks that require structured oversight. One major concern is cybersecurity. As ports depend more on autonomous and networked AI systems, they become targets for sophisticated attacks [10]. Threat actors can exploit generative AI to mimic voices, falsify identities, or breach critical systems [35]. Such breaches jeopardize stakeholder data, disrupt traffic management, and expose ports to financial and operational threats. Strong cybersecurity protocols—including adversarial testing, encryption, and AI-specific safeguards—are needed to defend against such risks.

AI bias also presents operational risks [35]. Decisions on scheduling, cargo prioritization, or customs processing may reflect embedded biases, resulting in unfair or inefficient outcomes. These effects can impact workforce equity or trade facilitation. Mitigation involves diverse data sources, inclusive algorithm design, and oversight via ethics boards. Related to this is the issue of transparency: many AI models used in port logistics or risk scoring function as opaque "black boxes" [36]. This limits regulatory visibility, complicates dispute resolution, and reduces user trust. Explainable AI tools such as LIME and DeepLIFT can clarify decision pathways, making outcomes more interpretable and accountable.

Accountability gaps further complicate AI deployment [37]. When AI errors occur—such as container misclassification or failure to detect breaches—it's often unclear who holds responsibility. Clear governance, traceable audit logs, and alignment with frameworks like the National Institute of Standards and Technology (NIST) AI Risk Management Framework help establish accountability.

AI systems also raise privacy concerns. Applications such as biometric access, cargo tracking, and customer platforms process sensitive commercial and personal data [38]. Improper accessing or misuse of this information may breach regulations like the General Data Protection Regulation (GDPR) [39], resulting in legal and reputational consequences. Adopting strict data governance and using anonymized or synthetic data during training can help ensure compliance.

Over-dependence on AI creates systemic vulnerabilities [40]. Excessive reliance on automation for berth planning or inspections may hinder response during outages. Hybrid systems—combining human and machine oversight—can improve resilience and ensure continuity during system failures. Lastly, the environmental costs of AI infrastructure are nontrivial. Training large models consumes energy and water, raising sustainability concerns [41]. Ports should prioritize energy-efficient models, use renewable-powered data centers, and explore low-resource methods like transfer learning to align AI adoption with environmental goals.

3.6 Cloud Computing

Cloud computing refers to the on-demand delivery of computing resources—such as data storage, processing power, networking capabilities, software platforms, and AI-driven analytical tools—via the internet [42]. It eliminates the need for local infrastructure by enabling port authorities and stakeholders to remotely access and manage critical applications and data through cloud service providers. This model enhances operational scalability, flexibility, and cost-efficiency, which are essential in the dynamic and data-intensive environment of modern ports.

Key components of cloud architecture for organizations, including port environments, encompass remotely managed data centers that host the physical infrastructure; high-speed networking connections which connect users to cloud-based applications; and virtualization technologies that enable dynamic allocation and efficient utilization of computing resources [43]. Advanced networking tools, including load balancers, content delivery networks, and software-defined networking, ensure secure and efficient data transmission across systems. By leveraging cloud computing, ports can support remote work environments, enhance data-driven decision making, and integrate advanced technologies such as generative AI and predictive analytics.

3.6.1 Benefits of Cloud Computing

A major advantage of cloud computing in port environments is its scalability [44]. Cloud platforms allow dynamic resource allocation based on operational needs without requiring heavy investment in physical infrastructure. During cargo surges, ports can expand processing and storage capacity to maintain performance and efficiency.

Cloud services also improve coordination by centralizing data and enabling real-time access for stakeholders [44]. This shared environment supports faster decision making and smoother supply chain activities, such as berth scheduling and cargo handling. In terms of resilience, cloud platforms offer built-in disaster recovery features [45], including automated failover, offsite backups, and data replication across geographically dispersed centers. These capabilities minimize downtime from disruptions and support business continuity.

Financially, cloud computing shifts IT costs from capital to operational expenditure [46]. Ports can avoid large upfront costs for hardware and software, paying only for what they use. This model includes maintenance and updates, reducing the load on in-house IT teams. Cloud platforms can also support advanced tools—like AI-based analytics and predictive systems—without needing major infrastructure upgrades, enhancing adaptability and driving operational innovation.

3.6.2 Risks of Cloud Computing

Despite these advantages, cloud computing introduces risks that must be actively managed. Chief among them is cybersecurity. IBM X-Force reports show that financially motivated criminals are the most frequent threat actors in cloud environments, followed by nation-state groups [47]. Attacks often exploit misconfigured applications, unpatched systems, and unauthorized "shadow IT." Ransomware is particularly prevalent—three times more common than other malware types—alongside threats like cryptominers and botnets. Data theft, including the exfiltration of personally identifiable information (PII) and sensitive operational records, remains a persistent concern.

Cloud infrastructure itself can also be weaponized. Threat actors use it to amplify attacks such as DDoS or to run unauthorized cryptomining operations [48]. These abuses exploit the scale and anonymity of cloud platforms. In port settings, where operational and cargo data are especially sensitive, poorly secured cloud services can lead to breaches [49]. To mitigate this, ports must enforce encryption for data at rest and in transit, adopt multi-factor authentication, conduct frequent security audits, and align with global standards like GDPR and ISO/IEC 27001.

Technical dependencies also pose challenges. Cloud operations rely heavily on stable, high-speed internet access. Connectivity issues can disrupt time-sensitive services [50]. Ports should prepare for this with redundant network links, failover systems, and hybrid approaches combining edge computing with centralized cloud services.

Vendor lock-in presents another risk [51]. Relying on a single provider can lead to service disruptions if outages or failures occur. To avoid this, ports should assess providers based on – service level agreement (SLA) commitments, uptime records, and recovery capabilities. Implementing a multi-cloud strategy—using platforms like Amazon Web Services (AWS) alongside others—can improve redundancy and reduce dependency on any single vendor.

3.7 Blockchain Technology

Blockchain technology, a sophisticated form of distributed ledger technology, represents a transformative approach to recording, verifying, and securing transactions and data across decentralized digital ecosystems [52]. In this system, information is stored in sequential "blocks," each containing transaction details, timestamps, and cryptographic hashes that ensure integrity and chronological order [10]. Once recorded, these blocks form an immutable chain resistant to unauthorized alterations, thereby enhancing data security and transparency without reliance on a central authority.

Key features of blockchain include a shared ledger accessible to all authorized participants, which eliminates duplication of effort and enhances consistency in recordkeeping [52]. Its immutability ensures that once data is recorded, it cannot be altered; if an error occurs, a new transaction must be logged to reverse it, maintaining full traceability. Smart contracts—self-executing protocols embedded within the blockchain—automate processes based on predefined conditions, enabling real-time execution of agreements such as logistics coordination or insurance settlements in port operations. As each transaction is recorded, the blockchain captures comprehensive information, such as the identity of the parties involved, timestamps, asset details, and conditions. This transparency supports enhanced monitoring and accountability throughout the supply chain.

3.7.1 Benefits of Blockchain

Blockchain offers significant advantages for port operations by enhancing data integrity, transparency, and process efficiency [53]. Port ecosystems involve constant data exchange between diverse actors such as terminal operators, customs, and shipping lines, making secure, tamper-resistant systems essential. Blockchain's decentralized and encrypted infrastructure protects data from unauthorized access or alteration, while its distributed design reduces vulnerability to centralized cyber-attacks.

It also improves visibility and coordination. Traditionally, siloed systems hinder data consistency. Blockchain's shared ledger ensures all authorized parties access a unified, real-time record. Every transaction is time-stamped and immutable, reducing the risk of manipulation and reinforcing stakeholder trust. Traceability is especially valuable for compliance and verifying cargo origin—critical for goods subject to ethical or environmental regulations. Integrated with IoT or digital platforms, blockchain enables real-time, verifiable audit trails, boosting accountability and consumer confidence.

Efficiency gains are also notable. Blockchain reduces paper-based processes and manual reconciliation. Key documents—bills of lading, manifests, declarations—can be securely digitized, expediting workflows and lowering error rates. This boosts cargo throughput while cutting administrative overhead. Smart contracts further enhance automation by enforcing pre-set rules—such as releasing cargo upon payment or customs clearance—without manual oversight. These contracts streamline transactions and reduce third-party reliance, reinforcing operational agility. As ports digitize, blockchain stands out as a foundational tool for secure, transparent, and responsive logistics systems.

3.7.2 Risks of Blockchain

Despite its benefits, blockchain introduces risks requiring deliberate management [54, 55]. One major threat is a 51% attack, which occurs when one party controls over half of the network's processing power, enabling them to interfere with transaction validation and potentially alter records. This poses a critical risk in logistics, where data integrity is essential. Mitigating measures include adopting Proof of Stake and ensuring broad network decentralization.

Related threats include pool attacks and private forks, where dominant validators can alter consensus rules or fork the network. These actions can compromise data integrity and interoperability. Preventive strategies include consensus protocols that limit validator dominance and require supermajority agreement for updates.

Smart contracts are also vulnerable. Coding flaws or loopholes can be exploited to trigger unauthorized actions—disrupting customs clearance or cargo release. Tools like OYENTE, Securify, and SmartCheck, along with formal verification, are necessary to identify and correct these issues before deployment. Data injection attacks further pose risks, allowing malicious input to distort records like cargo logs or customs data. Rigorous validation and trusted oracles must verify inputs before blockchain entry.

Private key security is fundamental. If stolen, these keys can be used to initiate fraudulent transactions or alter sensitive records. Mitigations include hardware security modules, multi-signature systems, key rotation, and robust user authentication. Double-spending, though more common in cryptocurrency, is also a risk in trade documentation, where attackers may reuse digital credentials. Blockchain analytics tools help detect anomalies early and limit damage.

Public blockchains raise privacy concerns. Without proper controls, sensitive information—such as cargo contents or client data—could be exposed. Solutions include permissioned blockchains, access restrictions, and privacy-preserving methods like zero-knowledge proofs. Social engineering further threatens system security by exploiting human error. Training, strict access controls, and multi-factor authentication are necessary defenses.

Lastly, regulatory uncertainty complicates implementation. Inconsistent laws and cross-border differences can hinder adoption in maritime trade. Proactive legal engagement, transparent documentation, and alignment with compliance standards are essential for lawful and reliable blockchain use.

3.8 Renewable and Green Energy Technologies

Among the primary renewable and green energy technologies (RGETs) employed for energy generation are wind turbines, solar photovoltaic systems, and hydrogen fuel cell technologies [13]. The following provides further details.

- **Wind Energy Technologies in Ports**

  Wind energy, both onshore and offshore, is among the most widely deployed renewable solutions in ports. Coastal nations, especially in Europe, are positioning ports as strategic centers for wind energy development. Nearly 50 ports across 13 EU countries—such as Amsterdam, Galway, and Atlantique La Rochelle—are upgrading to support offshore wind projects [56, 57].

  Offshore wind relies on various core technological components [58]. Central are the offshore turbines that convert wind into electricity, designed for durability in harsh marine environments. These turbines are mounted on foundations—fixed-bottom for shallow waters and floating platforms for deep sea—chosen based on site conditions. Their installation utilizes specialized equipment like jack-up vessels, heavy-lift ships, and cable layers with dynamic positioning for precision. Once operational, systems like Supervisory Control and Data Acquisition (SCADA), remote monitoring, and autonomous inspections maintain performance. Grid integration is managed via high-voltage cables and offshore substations in order to deliver power reliably onshore. Digital technologies interconnect and optimize these stages, while cybersecurity safeguards the increasingly automated infrastructure. Together, these seven areas form an interdependent framework essential to offshore wind deployment.

- **Solar Energy Systems in Ports**
  Solar energy is being increasingly adopted by ports worldwide, with photovoltaic (PV) panels being the most common technology, often installed on port buildings and rooftops [13]. The Port of Rotterdam pioneered solar-powered mooring systems in 2014, followed by Hamburg's 2019 installation on the Elbe River. Floating solar systems have also gained attention, exemplified by Oostende's 10-kWp floating solar array as part of the EU-funded DUAL Ports initiative [59].

  Solar deployment encompasses various interconnected technological categories supporting generation, control, storage, and distribution [60]. Key components include PV panels and building-integrated photovoltaics (BIPVs) converting sunlight to electricity or heat, power conversion systems (inverters, direct current to direct current (DC/DC) converters, maximum power point tracking (MPPT) controllers) ensuring efficient energy flow, and storage/integration units like batteries and net metering for grid interaction. Environmental technologies, such as solar heat pumps and solar-integrated asphalt, extend solar use into heating and infrastructure resilience. Water and utility applications include solar desalination and irrigation.

- **Hydrogen Technologies in Ports**
  Hydrogen fuel cell technology is gaining attention for port decarbonization, aligning with the IMO's 2050 net-zero shipping goals [61]. Hydrogen offers fast refueling and a long range and suits heavy-duty cargo-handling equipment better than battery-electric options [62]. It's applicable across container, bulk, breakbulk, and inland terminals. Moreover, hydrogen supports the production of zero-carbon marine fuels like ammonia and methanol, making it a key enabler for sustainable maritime ecosystems.

  Nonetheless, hydrogen adoption faces significant challenges [62, 63, 64]. Infrastructure such as refueling and storage is costly and nascent. Hydrogen requires specialized materials and safety measures due to its flammability and storage needs under high pressure or cryogenic conditions. Supply chains remain underdeveloped, with limited green hydrogen availability and complex logistics. While fuel cell tech is progressing, commercial maturity and consistent performance under high demand are not fully achieved. Economic barriers include higher costs for green hydrogen and equipment retrofits, often without sufficient incentives. Regulatory and safety standards are stringent but still evolving, delaying implementation. These challenges mean that hydrogen's broader deployment in ports will depend on further technological progress, policy support, and coordinated investment for safe and scalable solutions.

3.8.1 Benefits of RGET

Integrating RGET into port operations significantly lowers greenhouse gas emissions, improves air and water quality, and reduces environmental impacts from port activities. As ports aim to comply with national and international climate goals, these technologies play an increasingly vital role.

Beyond environmental benefits, RGET adoption offers notable economic advantages. Although initial investments in renewable infrastructure can be substantial, the long-term savings on energy costs are significant. Prices for solar, wind, and hydropower have dropped markedly, making them more competitive. Ports that embrace these technologies reduce energy expenses and their exposure to fossil fuel price volatility. Many also leverage financial tools such as green bonds, subsidies, and public-private partnerships to offset upfront costs—critical for smaller ports or those with limited capital access.

RGET also boosts operational resilience. Hybrid energy systems combining solar, wind, ocean currents, and green hydrogen provide a steady, adaptable power supply, reducing vulnerability to grid outages or climate disruptions. These renewables lessen dependence on centralized grids, enhancing energy security. In locations with predictable tides, marine current energy offers reliable generation. Using local renewable resources further decreases reliance on imported fuels, strengthening national energy security.

Ports are also evolving as hubs for sustainable fuels like biofuels, synthetic fuels, and renewable hydrogen. These alternatives reduce maritime carbon footprints and accelerate the shift toward a fully decarbonized shipping sector. By adopting renewable technologies, ports not only advance environmental goals but also position themselves as leaders in building a sustainable and resilient global transport network.

3.8.2 Risks of RGET

Despite their promise, RGETs present several challenges in ports. Infrastructure development is costly and often nascent. For instance, solar power requires photovoltaic installations, wind energy demands port facilities capable of handling large offshore turbines, and hydrogen systems need specialized high-pressure or cryogenic storage, raising safety and complexity concerns.

Technology maturity varies widely. Solar and wind are increasingly viable but scaling in high-demand port environments remains challenging. Hydrogen fuel cells show promise but lag behind battery-electric technologies in commercial readiness, limiting widespread use in cargo equipment. Integrating these systems into existing port infrastructure can cause inefficiencies and entail retrofit expenses.

Economic risks also affect adoption. Green hydrogen and some renewables remain pricier than diesel or grid electricity, discouraging uptake without strong incentives or policies. Underdeveloped supply chains, especially for hydrogen, complicate sourcing and increase costs. Transporting hydrogen in compressed or liquid forms adds logistical complexity and expense.

Regulatory and safety issues must be managed carefully. Hydrogen's hazardous classification demands stringent safety protocols and permits. The lack of standardized guidelines for renewable tech integration further complicates implementation. Addressing these diverse challenges requires ongoing technological advances, robust policy frameworks, and coordinated investments to mitigate risks and ensure effective, sustainable integration of renewable technologies in ports.

3.9 Systemic Insights into the Benefits and Risks of Key Port Technologies

Based on the analysis in the previous sections, this part highlights key themes that cut across the six technologies examined. Rather than evaluating each technology in isolation, it presents shared areas where these tools collectively offer novel operational advantages and expose emerging categories of risk. In particular, it identifies two strategic benefits—proactive operations and integrated stakeholder coordination—and three underappreciated risks—systemic fragility, ethical and governance gaps, and growing vendor dependence. These insights are intended to support more holistic decision making as ports navigate the trade-offs of digital transformation. To assist readers in grasping these comparative insights at a glance, Figure 3.1 summarizes the specific benefits and risks associated with each technology and highlights the five cross-cutting themes on the right side of the figure.

1 **Proactive Operations as a Strategic Shift**
A shared benefit across the six technologies is their ability to shift port operations from a reactive to a proactive footing. Rather than responding to disruptions after they occur, tools like AI-based forecasting, IoT-driven asset tracking, and AGV automation allow ports to anticipate issues, minimize delays, and maintain flow. This evolution is more than just an efficiency gain—it signals a fundamental change in how ports interpret data and respond to dynamic conditions. Together, these technologies function like a digital nervous system: constantly sensing, analyzing, and enabling faster decision making across port operations.
2 **Enabling Interconnected Port Ecosystems**
Another clear advantage is the reduction of operational silos through greater interconnectivity. Technologies such as cloud platforms, blockchain networks, and IoT devices create real-time links between systems and stakeholders, allowing for smoother data sharing and coordination. The outcome is not only improved technical integration but also enhanced institutional cooperation—paving the way for ports to act less as isolated terminals and more as adaptive, interconnected ecosystems that can

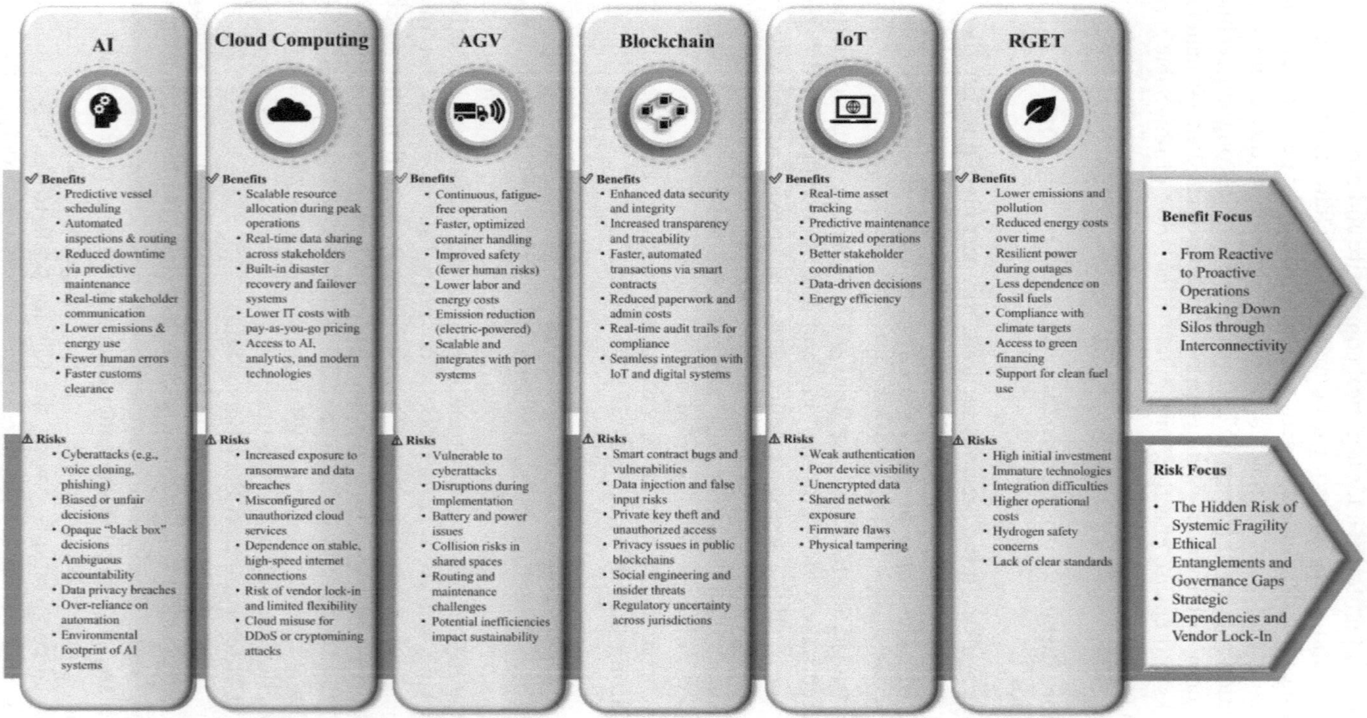

Figure 3.1 Cross-Technology Mapping of Benefits and Risks with Converging Strategic Themes.

collectively respond to market shifts, regulatory demands, and environmental pressures.

3 **Systemic Fragility from Interdependence**
While integration offers benefits, it also introduces a subtle but critical vulnerability: systemic fragility. As technologies become increasingly interconnected, a disruption in one system can propagate across others. For example, if IoT data is compromised, flawed inputs could cascade through AI systems, trigger incorrect AGV behavior, and distort blockchain records. Unlike isolated failures in legacy infrastructure, these cascading failures are harder to trace and recover from—making cross-system resilience a pressing concern in port digitalization strategies.

4 **Governance Challenges and Ethical Risks**
Emerging technologies often carry with them a false sense of neutrality. AI algorithms and blockchain mechanisms, though marketed as objective, can embed human biases or make rigid decisions with ethical implications. These risks are not merely technical—they affect fairness, accountability, and trust. Ports that view these tools as neutral infrastructure risk overlooking the ethical consequences of how decisions are automated, how data is prioritized, and how authority is encoded. Governance models must evolve accordingly, expanding beyond system performance to include transparency, oversight, and ethical safeguards.

5 **Strategic Dependence and Loss of Control**
A final, often overlooked risk involves the growing dependence on proprietary technologies and external service providers. Many AI tools, cloud infrastructures, and AGV systems are built on closed architectures, which can limit the port's ability to adapt or switch providers without incurring major costs or disruptions. This creates a form of vendor lock-in that extends beyond technical reliance—it affects long-term strategic flexibility, bargaining power, and digital sovereignty. Recognizing this risk is essential for ports aiming to maintain autonomy in an increasingly outsourced and interconnected digital environment.

Collectively, these five cross-cutting themes signal a shift in how port technologies should be understood—not merely as operational upgrades, but as catalysts for a new era of strategic thinking. They introduce a more anticipatory, interconnected, and ethically aware model of port governance that moves beyond the limits of traditional infrastructure planning. In this model, digital tools do not just support operations—they redefine the very terms of decision making, risk ownership, and institutional control. Recognizing these patterns is not just about improving efficiency; it is about preparing port leaders to navigate a future where digital complexity, stakeholder interdependence, and value-based governance are no longer optional but foundational. As such, the emerging challenge is not simply to implement smart technologies, but to govern them with the foresight and adaptability that 21st-century port resilience demands.

References

[1] S. Palmer and D. J. Torgerson, "Definitions of Efficiency," *BMJ*, vol. 318, p. 1136, 1999.

[2] J. R. Duflou, J. W. Sutherland, D. Dornfeld, C. Herrmann, J. Jeswiet, S. Kara, M. Hauschild and K. Kellens, "Towards Energy and Resource Efficient Manufacturing: A Processes and Systems Approach," *CIRP Annals*, vol. 61, no. 2, pp. 587–609, 2012.

[3] J. H. Luna, J. Mar-Ortiz, M. D. Gracia and D. Morales-Ramírez, "An Efficiency Analysis of Cargo-Handling Operations at Container Terminals," *Maritime Economics & Logistics*, vol. 20, p. 190–210, 2017.

[4] A. Pallis and J.-P. Rodrigue, "Chapter 10.2 – Port Efficiency," in *Port Economics, Management and Policy*, Routledge, 2022, n.p. https://porteconomicsmanagement.org/pemp/contents/part10/port-efficiency/

[5] K. Cullinane, T.-F. Wang, D.-W. Song and P. Ji, "The Technical Efficiency of Container Ports: Comparing Data Envelopment Analysis and Stochastic Frontier Analysis," *Transportation Research Part A: Policy and Practice*, vol. 40, no. 4, pp. 354–374, 2006.

[6] M. M. González and L. Trujillo, "Reforms and Infrastructure Efficiency in Spain's Container Ports," *Transportation Research Part A: Policy and Practice*, vol. 42, no. 1, pp. 243–257, 2008.

[7] R. O. Goss, "Economic Policies and Seaports: Strategies for Port Authorities," *Maritime Policy & Management*, vol. 17, no. 4, pp. 273–287, 2011.

[8] H. Li, L. Jiang, J. Liu and D. Su, "Research on the Evaluation of Logistics Efficiency in Chinese Coastal Ports Based on the Four-Stage DEA Model," *Journal of Marine Science and Engineering*, vol. 10, no. 8, p. 1147, 2022.

[9] J.-R. Chen, J.-W. Choi and Y.-J. Seo, "Environmental Efficiency Assessment of Coastal Ports in China: Implications for Sustainable Port Management," *Marine Pollution Bulletin*, vol. 211, 117436, 2025.

[10] C. Senarak and O. Mokkhavas, "Technology for Port Digitalization and Automation," in *Handbook of Smart Materials, Technologies, and Devices: Applications of Industry 4.0*, Springer International Publishing, 2022, pp. 1307–1320.

[11] T. Inkinen, R. Helminen and J. Saarikoski, "Port Digitalization with Open Data: Challenges, Opportunities, and Integrations," *Journal of Open Innovation: Technology, Market, and Complexity*, vol. 5, no. 2, p. 30, 2019.

[12] D. Gattuso and D. S. Pellicanò, "Perspectives for Ports Development, Based on Automated Container Handling Technologies," *Transportation Research Procedia*, vol. 69, pp. 360–367, 2023.

[13] A. G. Elkafas and I. S. Seddiek, "Application of Renewable Energy Systems in Seaports Towards Sustainability And Decarbonization: *Energy, Environmental and Economic Assessment,*" *Renewable* Energy, vol. 228, 120690, 2024.

[14] J. S. Dhupia, A. K. Adnanes, K. M. Lee and L. Kennedy, "Electrification of Port and Port Operations," in Proceedings of MTEC, Singapore, 2011.

[15] S. Alavi-Borazjani, S. Adeel, V. Chkoniya and L. Tarelho, "Sustainability-Oriented Port Management: Biomass Gasification as a Strategic Tool for Green and Circular Maritime Logistics," *Sustainability*, vol. 17, p. 2634, 2025.

[16] European Commission, "New EU Rules Aiming to Decarbonise the Maritime Sector Take Effect," 2025. [Online]. Available: https://transport.ec.europa.eu/news-events/news/new-eu-rules-aiming-decarbonise-maritime-sector-take-effect-2025-01-10_en.

[17] IMO, "IMO Approves Net-Zero Regulations for Global Shipping," 2025. [Online]. Available: www.imo.org/en/MediaCentre/PressBriefings/pages/IMO-approves-netzero-regulations.aspx.

[18] R. P. Saputra and E. Rijanto, "Automatic Guided Vehicles System and Its Coordination Control for Containers Terminal Logistics Application," in Proceedings of the Conference on International Logistic Seminar and Workshop, 2012.

[19] A. Rantala, Location- and Collision Avoidance System Technologies, Providers and Potential Applications, Finland: VTT Technical Research Centre of Finland, 2021.

[20] A. Tubis and H. Poturaj, "Risk Related to AGV Systems—Open-Access Literature Review," *Energies*, vol. 15, p. 8910, 2022.

[21] M. A. A. Mamun and M. R. Yuce, "Sensors and Systems for Wearable Environmental Monitoring Toward IoT-Enabled Applications: A Review," *IEEE Sensors Journal*, vol. 19, no. 18, pp. 7771–7788, 2019.

[22] Y. Yang, M. Zhong, H. Yao, F. Yu, X. Fu and O. Postolache, "Internet of Things for Smart Ports: Technologies and Challenges," *IEEE Instrumentation & Measurement Magazine*, vol. 21, no. 1, pp. 34–43, 2018.

[23] S. Cheruvu, A. Kumar, N. Smith and D. M. Wheeler, "Connectivity Technologies for IoT," in Connectivity Technologies for IoT. In: *Demystifying Internet of Things Security*, Apress, pp. 347–411, 2020.

[24] A. N. Alsheavi, A. Hawbani, W. Othman, X. Wang, G. Qaid, L. Zhao, A. Al-Dubai, L. Zhi, A. Ismail, R. Jhaveri, S. Alsamhi and M. A. A. Al-Qaness, "IoT Authentication Protocols: Challenges, and Comparative Analysis," *ACM Computing Surveys*, vol. 57, no. 5, pp. 1–43, 2025.

[25] G. Lyberopoulos, H. Theodoropoulou and K. Filis, "Mobile Network Threat Analysis and MNO Positioning," in *Lecture Notes in Electrical Engineering*, Springer, 2013, pp. 419–428.

[26] P. Li, J. Su and X. Wang, "iTLS: Lightweight Transport-Layer Security Protocol for IoT With Minimal Latency and Perfect Forward Secrecy," *IEEE Internet of Things Journal*, vol. 7, no. 8, pp. 6828–6841, 2020.

[27] G. Stanco, A. Navarro, F. Frattini, G. Ventre and A. Botta, "A Comprehensive Survey on the Security of Low Power Wide Area Networks for the Internet of Things," *ICT Express*, vol. 10, no. 3, pp. 519–552, 2024.

[28] X. Feng, X. Zhu, Q.-L. Han, W. Zhou, S. Wen and Y. Xiang, "Detecting Vulnerability on IoT Device Firmware: A Survey," *IEEE/CAA Journal of Automatica Sinica*, vol. 10, no. 1, pp. 25–41, 2023.

[29] G. Bansal, A. Nawal, V. Chamola and N. Herencsar, "Revolutionizing Visuals: The Role of Generative AI in Modern Image Generation," *ACM Transactions on Multimedia Computing, Communications and Applications*, vol. 20, no. 11, pp. 1–22, 2024.

[30] R. S. Khan, M. R. M. Sirazy, R. Das and S. Rahman, "An AI and ML-Enabled Framework for Proactive Risk Mitigation and Resilience Optimization in Global Supply Chains During National Emergencies," *Sage Science Review of Applied Machine Learning*, vol. 5, no. 2, pp. 127–144, 2022.

[31] N. Tsolakis, D. Zissis, S. Papaefthimiou and N. Korfiatis., "Towards AI Driven Environmental Sustainability: An Application of Automated Logistics in Container Port Terminals," *International Journal of Production Research*, vol. 60, no. 14, pp. 4508–4528, 2022.

[32] V. Ponnusamy, A. Vasuki, J. C. Clement and P. Eswaran, "AI-Driven Information and Communication Technologies, Services, and Applications

for Next-Generation Healthcare System," in *Smart Systems for Industrial Applications*, Scrivener Publishing LLC, 2022, pp. 1–32.

[33] K. Ukoba, K. O. Olatunji, E. Adeoye, T.-C. Jen and D. M. Madyira, "Optimizing Renewable Energy Systems through Artificial Intelligence: Review and Future Prospects," *Energy & Environment*, vol. 35, no. 7, pp. 3833–3879, 2024.

[34] A. H. Adepoju, B. Austin-Gabriel, A. Eweje and A. Collins, "Framework for Automating Multi-Team Workflows to Maximize Operational Efficiency and Minimize Redundant Data Handling," *IRE Journals*, vol. 5, no. 9, pp. 663–679, 2022.

[35] P. V. Falade, "Decoding the Threat Landscape: ChatGPT, FraudGPT, and WormGPT in Social Engineering Attacks," *International Journal of Scientific Research in Computer Science, Engineering and Information Technology*, vol. 9, no. 5, pp. 185–198, 2023.

[36] V. Hassija, Vinay Chamola, A. Mahapatra, A. Singal, D. Goel, K. Huang, S. Scardapane, I. Spinelli, M. Mahmud and A. Hussain, "Interpreting Black-Box Models: A Review on Explainable Artificial Intelligence," *Cognitive Computation*, vol. 16, pp. 45–74, 2023.

[37] C. Novelli, M. Taddeo and L. Floridi, "Accountability in Artificial Intelligence: What It Is and How It Works," *AI & Society*, vol. 39, pp. 1871–1882, 2023.

[38] S. Shahriar, S. Allana, S. M. Hazratifard and R. Dara, "A Survey of Privacy Risks and Mitigation Strategies in the Artificial Intelligence Life Cycle," *IEEE Access*, vol. 11, pp. 61829–61854, 2023.

[39] C. J. Hoofnagle, B. v. d. Sloot and F. Z. Borgesius, "The European Union General Data Protection Regulation: What It Is and What It Means," *Information & Communications Technology Law*, vol. 28, no. 1, pp. 65–98, 2019.

[40] I. Durlik, T. Miller, E. Kostecka and T. Tuński., "Artificial Intelligence in Maritime Transportation: A Comprehensive Review of Safety and Risk Management Applications," *Applied Sciences*, vol. 14, no. 18, p. 8420, 2024.

[41] A. Kelechi, M. Alsharif, O. Bameyi, P. Ezra, I. Joseph, A.-A. Atayero, Z. Geem and J. Hong, "Artificial Intelligence: An Energy Efficiency Tool for Enhanced High-Performance Computing," *Symmetry*, vol. 12, no. 6, p. 1029, 2020.

[42] L. Qian, Z. Luo, Y. Du and L. Guo, "Cloud Computing: An Overview," in IEEE International Conference on Cloud Computing, Beijing, China, 2009.

[43] B. Wang, Z. Qi, R. Ma, H. Guan and A. V. Vasilakos, "A Survey on Data Center Networking for Cloud Computing," *Computer Networks*, vol. 91, no. 14, pp. 528–547, 2015.

[44] R. Islam, V. Patamsetti, A. Gadhi, R. M. Gondu, C. M. Bandaru, S. C. Kesani and O. Abiona, "The Future of Cloud Computing: Benefits and Challenges," *International Journal of Communications, Network and System Sciences*, vol. 16, no. 4, 2023.

[45] A. Z. Abualkishik, A. A. Alwan and Y. Gulzar, "Disaster Recovery in Cloud Computing Systems: An Overview," *International Journal of Advanced Computer Science and Applications*, vol. 11, no. 9, 2020, pp. 702–710.

[46] S. Ibrahim, B. He and H. Jin, "Towards Pay-As-You-Consume Cloud Computing," in International Conference on Services Computing, Washington, DC, USA, 2011.

[47] A. Keskisaari, "Cybercrime in Cloud Environments: Tactics, Techniques and Procedures," Aalto University, 2021.

[48] A. Bonguet and M. Bellaiche, "A Survey of Denial-of-Service and Distributed Denial of Service Attacks and Defenses in Cloud Computing," *Future Internet*, vol. 9, no. 3, p. 43, 2017.
[49] L. Heilig and S. Voß, "A Holistic Framework for Security and Privacy Management in Cloud-Based Smart Ports," 2017. [Online]. Available: www.researchgate.net/profile/Leonard-Heilig/publication/303823550_A_holistic_framework_for_security_and_privacy_management_in_cloud-based_smart_ports/links/59a869510f7e9b2790092442/A-holistic-framework-for-security-and-privacy-management-in-cloud-.
[50] V. Mauch, M. Kunze and M. Hillenbrand, "High Performance Cloud Computing," *Future Generation Computer Systems*, vol. 29, no. 6, pp. 1408–1416, 2013.
[51] J. N. Opara-Martins, "A Decision Framework to Mitigate Vendor Lock-In Risks in Cloud (SaaS Category) Migration," Bournemouth University, 2017.
[52] A. Ramachandran and M. Kantarcioglu, "SmartProvenance: A Distributed, Blockchain Based DataProvenance System," in Proceedings of the Eighth ACM Conference on Data and Application Security and Privacy, New York, 2018.
[53] P. Guan, L. C. Wood, J. X. Wang and L. N. K. Duong., "Blockchain Adoption in the Port Industry: A Systematic Literature Review," *Cogent Business & Management*, vol. 11, no. 1, 2024, pp. 1–32.
[54] J. Liu, H. Zhang and L. Zhen, "Blockchain Technology in Maritime Supply Chains: Applications, Architecture and Challenges," *International Journal of Production Research*, vol. 61, no. 11, pp. 3547–3563, 2021.
[55] M. B. Farah, Y. Ahmed, H. Mahmoud, S. A. Shah, M. O. Al-kadri, S. Taramonli, X. Bellekens, R. Abozariba, M. Idrissi and A. Aneiba, "A Survey on Blockchain Technology in the Maritime Industry: Challenges and Future Perspectives," *Future Generation Computer Systems*, vol. 157, pp. 618–637, 2024.
[56] WindEurope asbl/vzw, "Offshore Wind Ports Platform," 2023. [Online]. Available: https://windeurope.org/policy/topics/offshore-wind-ports/.
[57] WindEurope asbl/vzw, "Ports As Key Players In The Offshore Wind Supply Chain," 2021. [Online]. Available: https://windeurope.org/wp-content/uploads/files/policy/topics/ports/Ports-Platform-Infographic.pdf.
[58] X. Su, X. Wang, W. Xu, L. Yuan, C. Xiong and J. Chen, "Offshore Wind Power: Progress of the Edge Tool, Which Can Promote Sustainable Energy Development," *Sustainability*, vol. 16, no. 17, p. 7810, 2024.
[59] Dual Ports, "Floating Solar Installed in the Port of Oostende," 2022. [Online]. Available: www.dualports.eu/floating-solar-installed-in-the-port-of-oostende/.
[60] D. Vijayan, E. Koda, A. Sivasuriyan, J. Winkler, P. Devarajan, R. Kumar, A. Jakimiuk, P. Osinski, A. Podlasek and M. Vaverková, "Advancements in Solar Panel Technology in Civil Engineering for Revolutionizing Renewable Energy Solutions—A Review," *Energies*, vol. 16, no. 18, p. 6579, 2023.
[61] UNCTAD, "Net-Zero by 2050: Achieving Shipping Decarbonization Through Industry Momentum and the New Ambition at IMO," 2023. [Online]. Available: https://unctad.org/news/transport-newsletter-article-no-108-net-zero-by-2050.
[62] V. Semchukova, K. Polemis, Z. Abdin, B. Solanki and S. Cary, "Hydrogen Infrastructure Analysis for the Port Applications," U.S. Department of Energy Office of Scientific and Technical Information, 2024.

[63] E. Vichos, N. Sifakis and T. Tsoutsos, "Challenges of Integrating Hydrogen Energy Storage Systems into Nearly Zero-Energy Ports," *Energy*, vol. 241, 122878, 2022.

[64] V. Semchukova, K. Topolski and Z. Abdin, "Hydrogen Technology for Maritime Applications: A Review of Challenges, Opportunities, and Lessons from the Port Authority of New York and New Jersey," *Renewable and Sustainable Energy Reviews*, vol. 216, 115641, 2025.

4 The Cyber Risks in Seaports

4.1 Definition and Significance of Cyber Risks in the PIS

Cyber risk involves the potential for financial loss, operational disruption, or physical harm caused by the failure or compromise of digital technologies supporting a system's informational and operational functions. These failures often stem from unauthorized electronic actions, such as access, use, disclosure, disruption, modification, or destruction of the system's technology infrastructure [1]. This risk covers a wide array of threats, vulnerabilities, and malicious acts that threaten digital ecosystem stability.

In contrast, cybersecurity risk specifically concerns the possible loss or breach of confidentiality, integrity, and availability (CIA) of data, information, or control systems. It reflects the broader impact such breaches may have on organizational operations, including mission execution, performance, reputation, assets, individuals, other entities, and national security [2]. While both concepts focus on protecting digital systems against malicious activity, cyber risk encompasses a wider scope, including operational technology threats, whereas cybersecurity risk targets core information security principles to prevent organizational harm.

Within the port information system (PIS) context, both risks underscore the growing exposure of digital infrastructure to threats that could severely impair port operations. These risks threaten the CIA of critical systems that enable coordination among port stakeholders and the larger logistics network. Cyber threats targeting data flows or automated control systems may cause operational halts, financial damage, or physical harm. A confidentiality breach could leak sensitive trade data or stakeholder communications, eroding supply chain trust. Integrity compromises can distort cargo tracking, berth scheduling, or customs data, resulting in poor decision making. Loss of availability can freeze real-time operations, undermining efficiency and competitiveness.

Ensuring CIA in the PIS is increasingly difficult due to growing digital interconnectivity. A single vulnerability can cascade through the system, causing major operational, financial, safety, and reputational damage. Cyber incidents may also ripple beyond the port, disrupting global supply chains and trade. Understanding cyber risks enables port managers to identify vulnerabilities and

DOI: 10.4324/9781003559320-4

implement targeted controls, such as comprehensive assessments, AI-driven threat detection, and collaborative information sharing among stakeholders [3]. Addressing these risks strategically helps ports build resilience, sustain operations, and maintain competitiveness in an interconnected, technology-driven world.

4.2 Key Influential Factors in Port Cyber Risks: Understanding Vulnerability, Cyber Threat, Likelihood, Impact, and Exposure in Port Information Systems

Cyber risk is assessed by combining the probability of a cyber event with the potential consequences of that event [4]. The probability, or likelihood, depends on three key factors: vulnerabilities within the system, the nature and capabilities of threats, and the degree of exposure of assets to those threats. The impact represents the scale of harm or loss that could result if a cyber incident occurs. Since these factors continuously evolve due to technological changes, shifting threat actors, and varying asset environments, cyber risk is a fluid measure that requires ongoing evaluation. Understanding this relationship provides a basis for analyzing each element of risk in greater detail.

4.2.1 Vulnerability

Vulnerability refers to inherent weaknesses or flaws within a system that can be exploited by malicious actors, thereby compromising its CIA [4]. Within the port context, vulnerabilities in PISs may originate from various sources, including outdated software, misconfigured devices, inadequate access controls, or human error. These weaknesses are critical in determining the likelihood of a cyber incident, as threat actors typically rely on exploitable vulnerabilities to initiate an attack.

In cyber risk assessments, vulnerabilities are typically evaluated using the CVSS, a standardized framework developed to assess the severity of software and system vulnerabilities [5]. CVSS assigns a numerical score ranging from 0 to 10, where a score of **0.0** indicates negligible risk, **4.0–6.9** reflects medium severity, and scores of **7.0–10.0** denote high to critical vulnerabilities. For example, a vulnerability with a score of **9.8** may allow remote code execution without authentication, posing a critical threat to system security. These scores are typically assigned by security analysts and researchers, including those from organizations such as the **National Vulnerability Database**, based on defined metrics like access complexity, exploitability, and impact [6]. By implementing CVSS, organizations, including ports, can assess the potential impact of specific vulnerabilities, prioritize mitigation efforts, and allocate resources more effectively by focusing on the most critical threats across digital and operational systems [7].

4.2.2 Cyber Threat

A cyber threat refers to any potential event or malicious action capable of exploiting vulnerabilities within PISs to compromise their CIA. Such threats may stem from a wide range of actors, including individual hackers, malicious insiders, organized cybercriminal groups, or state-sponsored entities [8]. While the overarching aim of most cyber threats is to exploit system weaknesses, the specific motivations and tactics often vary by actor type. Cybercriminal groups, for example, may deploy ransomware to encrypt port systems and demand payment, while hacktivists might launch distributed denial-of-service (DDoS) attacks to disrupt services as a form of protest. State-sponsored attackers, on the other hand, may use advanced persistent threats (APTs) or stealthy malware to conduct long-term espionage or sabotage critical maritime infrastructure. The selection of tools—whether malware, phishing, ransomware, or DDoS—typically reflects the threat actor's objectives, resources, and level of sophistication.

In cyber risk assessment, estimating the likelihood of a threat actor exploiting a system's vulnerabilities is essential. This likelihood, often expressed as a percentage, reflects the probability of an attempted cyber-attack and can be gauged using several methods. One widely used approach involves threat intelligence platforms, which compile and analyze data on global cyber incidents, particularly the tactics, techniques, and procedures (TTPs) used by malicious actors [9]. These platforms help port authorities evaluate how likely their systems are to be targeted, based on real-time trends and emerging threat patterns. In addition to threat intelligence, historical incident data offers another critical perspective. By examining the frequency and characteristics of past attacks on similar systems, organizations can infer probabilities for future threats [10]. Complementing these data-driven methods, threat actor profiling provides a more strategic layer of insight. This involves analyzing the behavior, motivations, and capabilities of known threat groups, which allows ports to align their defenses with the specific actors most likely to target maritime operations [11]. See Section 4.2.4 for likelihood details.

4.2.3 Exposure

Exposure denotes the extent to which the inoperability or inaccessibility of a technology system may contribute to end-user vulnerability [12]. Within the port environment, exposure specifically refers to the degree to which a PIS, digital network, or related infrastructure is accessible or visible to cyber threat actors. This concept encompasses not only the technical vulnerabilities inherent in the system but also the degree to which those vulnerabilities are exposed as a result of system interconnectivity, dependencies on third-party services, and integration with external platforms. For example, systems that are directly connected to the internet or dependent on external services—such as cloud-based cargo management platforms—demonstrate a higher level of exposure compared to those that are isolated or segmented from external access points.

Recognizing how exposure interplays with vulnerability and likelihood is particularly critical in the port environment. Exposure provides the conditions under which cyber risk can materialize; if a PIS is not exposed, its vulnerabilities are less likely to be exploited. Conversely, a highly exposed system—such as a public-facing interface with insufficient security controls—presents numerous attack vectors that may be leveraged by malicious actors. Vulnerabilities such as outdated terminal operating system (TOS) software, misconfigured firewalls, or unpatched AIS exacerbate this risk. Likelihood connects these factors by estimating the probability that a threat actor will exploit an exposed vulnerability. Understanding this dynamic relationship allows port authorities to make more informed risk-based decisions by reducing exposure points, addressing system vulnerabilities, and, ultimately, lowering the probability of successful cyber-attacks.

4.2.4 Likelihood

In cyber risk assessment, likelihood refers to the estimated probability that a cyber event will occur, potentially causing operational disruption or compromising the CIA of PISs. It serves as a foundational metric in cyber risk assessment, contributing to the overall risk rating when considered alongside impact [4]. The likelihood of a cyber incident is shaped by the interplay among vulnerability, threat, and exposure. This interaction is critical; for example, even when vulnerabilities are known, a low level of exposure may significantly reduce the probability of exploitation. Conversely, systems that are highly visible or easily accessible and lack adequate defenses are far more susceptible to successful cyber-attacks. Even in cases where systems exhibit both known vulnerabilities and high exposure, the likelihood of attack remains low if threat actors lack intent or capability. This dynamic underscores the necessity of comprehensive cybersecurity practices that not only address technical weaknesses but also minimize exposure and mitigate emerging threats.

In the port domain, evaluating the likelihood of cyber events involves assessing both internal conditions—such as a port's infrastructure, operational processes, and cybersecurity practices—and external conditions, including the broader threat landscape and geopolitical developments. A thorough understanding of these contextual factors enables ports to more effectively prioritize cybersecurity investments and tailor mitigation strategies accordingly [4]. In evaluating likelihood, ports may adopt either quantitative or qualitative methodologies. Quantitative approaches utilize statistical data, historical incident trends, and predictive modeling to assign numerical probabilities to specific threats [13]. In contrast, qualitative assessments rely on expert judgment, perceived system attractiveness, and the availability of exploit tools [13]. Both approaches offer distinct advantages and limitations; therefore, integrating quantitative precision with qualitative insights can enhance the reliability and contextual relevance of likelihood estimations in port cybersecurity assessments.

4.2.5 Impact

Impact refers to the potential or actual consequences that a cyber-attack can impose on a seaport's operations, assets, reputation, and overall functioning. It is typically quantified in monetary terms, such as US dollars, to enable a tangible evaluation of possible losses [4]. In the port context, the extent of impact can range from minor disruptions—such as temporary delays or localized system outages—to severe consequences that may affect the entire supply chain, cause substantial financial losses, damage the port's reputation, and trigger regulatory penalties [14]. The severity of these impacts largely depends on the nature of the cyber-attack, the criticality of the systems targeted, and the port's preparedness and response capacity. Besides, impact must be considered alongside the likelihood of an event, as the interaction between these two dimensions forms the basis for determining overall risk. For instance, a cyber-attack with a low probability of occurring but potentially catastrophic consequences—such as a targeted sabotage of critical port infrastructure—represents a high-risk scenario that demands attention. Conversely, a more frequent but less damaging event, like a minor phishing attempt, may represent a lower overall risk despite its higher likelihood. This balanced understanding helps port authorities prioritize resources effectively and tailor cybersecurity measures to address the most pressing threats.

4.2.6 Dissecting Cyber Risk Elements at the Port of Seattle (2024): A Case Study

To bridge theory and practice, this section applies a cyber risk framework—encompassing vulnerability, threat, exposure, likelihood, and impact—to a real-world event. The 2024 ransomware attack on the Port of Seattle illustrates how these interrelated elements manifest in practice, providing a grounded perspective on operational cyber risk in port environments.

On August 24, 2024, the Port of Seattle identified a ransomware intrusion linked to the cybercriminal group Rhysida [15]. Immediate containment measures were enacted, including isolating affected systems and initiating a joint investigation with cybersecurity experts and federal agencies. The attack disrupted several non-critical services—such as check-in kiosks, public display boards, Wi-Fi access, and the official website—while core airport and maritime operations remained unaffected. Systems overseen by airlines, cruise lines, and federal entities were also spared [15].

Although the attackers failed to compromise financial or passenger data, they succeeded in encrypting information stored in outdated internal systems, including sensitive personal identifiers like names, Social Security numbers, and driver's license details. Rejecting the ransom demand, the Port prioritized recovery and transparency, restoring most systems within a week, though full website functionality required additional time [15].

By April 2025, the Port began notifying affected individuals and extended credit monitoring and identity theft protection services. Simultaneously, it adopted stronger cybersecurity controls, such as improved access policies, enhanced monitoring tools, and upgraded safeguards. The Executive Director acknowledged the staff's swift response and reaffirmed the Port's commitment to digital resilience and public accountability.

The interconnected nature of these events reflects deeper systemic risk dynamics. Figure 4.1 visualizes these elements—vulnerability, threat, exposure, and impact—through a layered representation of the Port of Seattle incident, offering a practical lens for interpreting how cyber risk unfolds in operational environments. The element of likelihood is not visualized in this figure as the event under discussion has already materialized, making likelihood less relevant than in a predictive risk model. The diagram uses a layered format to show how each factor contributed to the incident, illustrating how weaknesses in systems, the presence of a capable threat actor, and system accessibility converged to cause tangible consequences.

Based on the above scenario, the attack illustrates how cyber risk arises from the interconnection of vulnerability, threat, exposure, and impact. In this case, the **vulnerability** resided in the Port's legacy internal systems, which stored sensitive personal information, including Social Security numbers and driver's license details. These systems were likely outdated and insufficiently protected, lacking modern access controls and encryption, which rendered them susceptible to exploitation.

The **threat** originated from the criminal group Rhysida, known for conducting ransomware attacks that encrypt and exfiltrate data. Their deliberate targeting of the Port reflects a growing trend in which threat actors increasingly focus on critical infrastructure to disrupt essential services and pressure victims into paying ransoms. Although the Port refused to meet the ransom demands, the attackers successfully breached and encrypted data, thereby creating substantial security and privacy risks.

Exposure, which affects the likelihood of a successful attack, was exacerbated by the Port's expansive digital surface. The disruption of public-facing systems—such as display boards, check-in kiosks, and Wi-Fi—suggests inadequate segmentation between internal and external systems. The attackers' ability to access sensitive data further points to potential weaknesses in network architecture and internal monitoring protocols.

Despite the Port's prompt incident response, the **impact** of the attack was significant. While core airport and maritime operations continued uninterrupted, several supporting services experienced temporary disruption. More critically, the breach of personal data compelled the Port to notify affected individuals and provide identity protection services. The incident triggered a reassessment of existing cybersecurity measures and led to the implementation of enhanced access controls and continuous monitoring mechanisms.

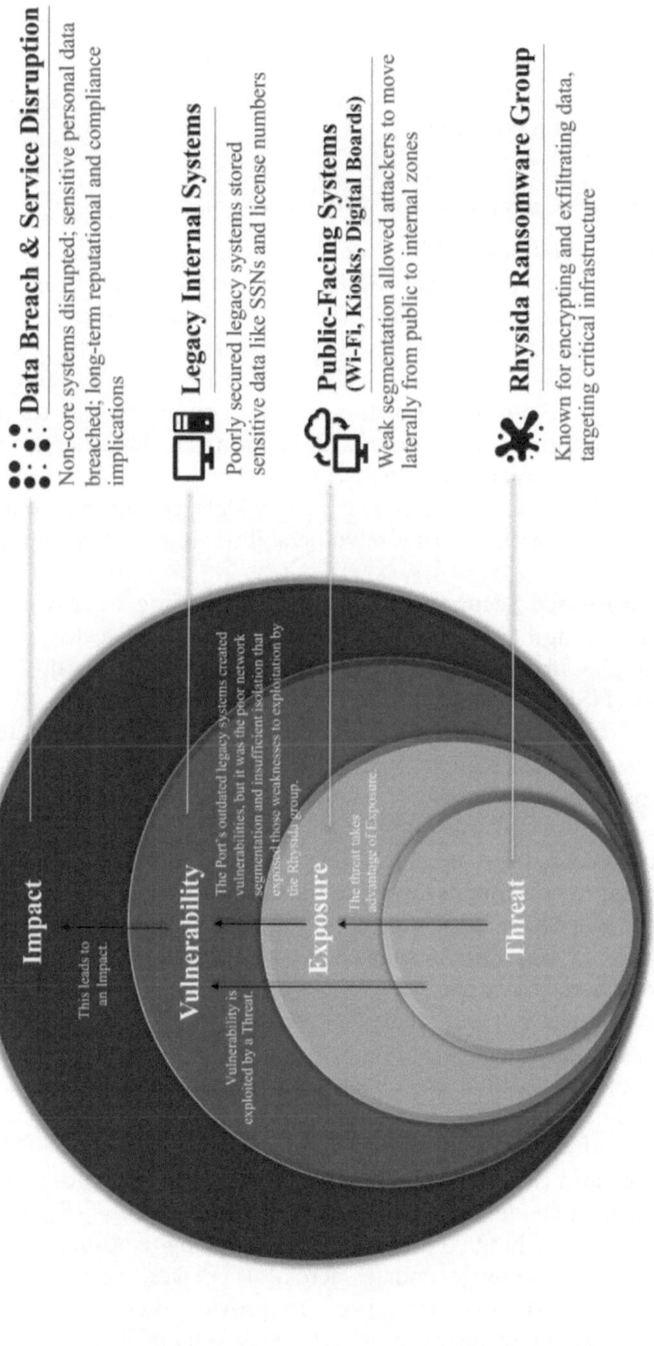

Figure 4.1 Cyber Risk Breakdown Diagram.

4.3 Cyber Vulnerabilities in the PIS and Mitigation Strategies

Cyber vulnerabilities in PISs can be broadly classified into four main categories: software, hardware, human, and configuration vulnerabilities. Each category poses unique challenges and exhibits distinct characteristics, thereby requiring targeted strategies for effective risk management and mitigation. The details are outlined below.

4.3.1 Hardware Vulnerabilities and Mitigation Strategies

Hardware vulnerabilities in PISs refer to weaknesses in the physical infrastructure and connected devices that support the port's core operational activities [8]. These may arise from outdated hardware, misconfigurations, design flaws, or insecure embedded components [16]. Given that ports rely on a variety of interconnected physical systems—including sensors, servers, cargo-handling equipment, and communication devices—any compromise at the hardware level can lead to significant operational disruption, data breaches, or unauthorized access to mission-critical systems.

The following five strategies represent widely recognized and effective approaches for mitigating hardware vulnerabilities in port environments:

1 **Hardware-Based Security Integration:** Embedding security directly into hardware strengthens critical systems by protecting device architecture. Technologies like trusted platform modules (TPMs), hardware security modules (HSMs), and secure boot provide essential defenses [17]. TPMs safeguard cryptographic keys within hardware, preventing unauthorized data access. HSMs create tamper-resistant environments for cryptographic operations, ensuring secure key handling and authentication. Secure boot verifies firmware and software integrity at startup, permitting only trusted code to execute. These measures defend against tampering, firmware alteration, and physical threats targeting port infrastructure.

2 **Routine Hardware Evaluation and Updates:** Legacy or unsupported hardware often lacks defenses against modern cyber threats. Ports must regularly assess and update hardware to preserve system security [8]. Identifying outdated devices missing secure update mechanisms or encryption is crucial. Replacing obsolete equipment with current, security-enhanced hardware aligns infrastructure with evolving standards and mitigates known vulnerabilities. Continuous evaluations support effective lifecycle management and infrastructure planning.

3 **Firmware and Software Updates:** Firmware vulnerabilities from delayed or irregular patching pose significant risks to port systems [18]. Maintaining an organized patching routine is vital to reducing exposure. Ports should ensure prompt firmware updates across all devices, especially those vital to operations. Manufacturers need to provide timely security patches, while IT and OT teams must actively track vulnerability announcements.

Coordinated patch management helps prevent exploitation of known flaws in embedded systems.

4 **Ongoing Monitoring and Threat Detection:** Vigilant surveillance of hardware behavior aids early identification of emerging threats [19]. SIEM systems work together with IDS to continuously monitor device performance, data flows, and system activities, enabling early detection of anomalies or potential security incidents. Continuous observation of servers, Programmable Logic Controllers (PLCs), and Internet of Things (IoT) sensors enables real-time detection of unauthorized access or suspicious actions indicating tampering or malware. These tools support proactive mitigation and quick incident response, reducing operational impact.
5 **Network Segmentation and Isolation:** Dividing the port network into separate zones is crucial for limiting cyber-attack spread, especially within operational technology environments [14]. Segmentation controls data flow based on device type, protocols, and source-destination criteria [20]. For example, isolating automated crane networks from administrative systems prevents lateral movement during breaches. Separating third-party or guest network connections further shields critical hardware from exposure. Effective segmentation shrinks the attack surface and enhances containment during incidents.

4.3.2 Software Vulnerabilities and Mitigation Strategies

Software vulnerabilities in PISs stem from flaws in application design, insecure configurations, unpatched systems, and inadequate encryption protocols. These weaknesses—introduced during the design, development, or maintenance stages—can expose ports to various forms of cyber threats, including malware, ransomware, and unauthorized system access. Exploiting these vulnerabilities may result in data breaches, operational disruptions, or full system compromise, ultimately threatening the security and continuity of port operations [16].

To safeguard the PIS, five approaches are widely recognized as foundational:

1 **Regular Patch Management**: Maintaining a timely and structured patch management process is one of the most effective mitigation strategies [21]. This involves maintaining an inventory of software assets, applying updates promptly, and prioritizing high-risk vulnerabilities based on impact assessments.
2 **Secure Software Development Practices**: By embedding security into the software development lifecycle, ports can prevent vulnerabilities at the design and coding stages. Best practices include secure coding standards, code reviews, and the use of static/dynamic analysis tools [22].
3 **Vulnerability Scanning and Penetration Testing**: Regular automated scans and simulated attacks help identify and address vulnerabilities before

they can be exploited in real-world scenarios, thereby reducing the system's attack surface [23].

4 **Configuration Hardening**: Ensuring that all software and systems are securely configured—by disabling unnecessary services, changing default credentials, and aligning with security benchmarks—minimizes exposure to known exploits [24].
5 **Role-Based Access Control**: Implementing role-based access control (RBAC) limits access to sensitive systems based on user roles, thereby reducing the risk of unauthorized access and privilege escalation [25].

When implemented collectively, the five core strategies—regular patch management, secure software development practices, vulnerability scanning and penetration testing, configuration hardening, and role-based access control—offer a significantly more robust defense against software vulnerabilities than they do when applied in isolation. Their integration fosters a layered security posture that not only reduces the attack surface but also enhances early threat detection, mitigates risks during development, and strengthens overall system resilience.

4.3.3 Human Vulnerabilities and Mitigation Strategies

Human vulnerabilities within PISs refer to risks arising from the actions, decisions, and behaviors of individuals responsible for operating, maintaining, and securing digital port infrastructure. These vulnerabilities typically include poor password practices, lack of cybersecurity awareness, and susceptibility to social engineering techniques such as phishing and spear-phishing [8]. Often rooted in inadequate training, insufficient threat recognition, or the absence of a security-oriented culture, such weaknesses can serve as entry points for malicious actors, potentially leading to system breaches, data manipulation, or service disruption.

To safeguard the PIS against human-induced cyber risks, five approaches are considered essential:

1 **Comprehensive Security Awareness Training**: Regular and structured cybersecurity training is a critical mitigation measure. This includes educating personnel on current threats—such as phishing, social engineering, malware, and ransomware—and equipping them with the practical skills to detect and respond to suspicious activities. Best practices emphasized in the training include secure password management, identification of malicious communications, safe mobile device usage, and proper incident reporting.
2 **Multi-factor Authentication**: Multi-factor authentication (MFA) enhances system access security by requiring two or more forms of verification, such as a password in combination with a biometric identifier or a one-time passcode. This layered authentication process mitigates the risks

posed by compromised credentials, which are often linked to human error or negligence.

3 **Role-Based Access Control**: Implementing RBAC restricts system access based on job roles and responsibilities. This principle of least privilege ensures that individuals can only access the systems and data necessary for their duties, thereby minimizing the risk of unauthorized access and accidental or intentional alterations to PIS configurations. Regular audits are necessary to ensure access rights remain aligned with organizational needs.
4 **Phishing Simulations and Social Engineering Drills**: Conducting regular simulations of phishing and other social engineering attacks provides a proactive means of evaluating personnel awareness and response capabilities. These exercises help identify gaps in training and reinforce the importance of vigilance, allowing ports to tailor educational programs and enhance readiness against manipulation-based threats.
5 **Security-First Organizational Culture**: Establishing a culture that prioritizes cybersecurity at all organizational levels is vital. This includes visible leadership commitment, consistent resource allocation to security initiatives, and open communication channels for reporting concerns. By embedding security values across the workforce, ports can cultivate shared responsibility and reduce the occurrence of human-related security incidents.

Collectively, these five measures constitute a comprehensive approach to managing human-related cybersecurity risks in port environments. By embedding these practices into daily operations and institutional policies, ports can significantly diminish the likelihood of security breaches originating from human factors and enhance their overall capacity to anticipate, withstand, and respond to evolving cyber threats.

4.3.4 Configuration Vulnerabilities and Mitigation Strategies

Configuration vulnerabilities arise from improper or insecure settings in software, network devices, or applications, including issues such as misconfigured system parameters, default configurations, mismanaged access controls, and failure to apply necessary updates or patches during system maintenance [16]. Such vulnerabilities leave systems exposed to potential cyber threats, jeopardizing their CIA. If left unaddressed, these misconfigurations can provide entry points for attackers, ultimately compromising critical systems.

To mitigate configuration vulnerabilities in PISs, five approaches are considered essential:

1 **Automated Configuration Management**: Automated tools enforce security settings across systems, ensuring alignment with organizational policies. They enable continuous monitoring, detect unauthorized changes,

and support routine audits, thereby reducing the opportunities for attackers to exploit misconfigurations. As modern networks become increasingly complex, automation in security configuration has emerged as a necessary approach to mitigate risks that stem from human error and misaligned settings [26].

2 **Security Baselines and Best Practices**: Adopting standardized baselines—such as ISO/IEC 27001—ensures systems are securely configured by default. These baselines provide structured guidance for optimal security configurations, reducing vulnerabilities and promoting uniform protection practices. As threats and technologies evolve, regularly updating these baselines enables ports to remain resilient and adaptive to emerging risks [27].
3 **System Patching and Updates**: A structured and automated patch management process is essential to mitigate risks from known vulnerabilities, as delays in applying patches can leave systems exposed for extended periods. Empirical analysis shows that attackers often exploit outdated software versions and that hosts using automated update mechanisms achieve significantly faster patching times [28].
4 **Monitoring Configuration Changes**: Real-time monitoring detects unauthorized or suspicious configuration changes, such as firewall or access control modifications. Alerts enable rapid response and reduce the risk of breaches resulting from unnoticed changes.

   Real-time monitoring of configuration changes—such as those involving firewalls or access controls—enables early detection of suspicious modifications. Tools like VisualFirewall demonstrate that multi-view monitoring and intrusion alerts significantly enhance visibility and enable faster response to unauthorized activity [29].
5 **Configuration Audits and Vulnerability Scans**: Routine configuration audits and vulnerability scans help identify weaknesses—like open ports or weak credentials—before exploitation. These practices align security measures with organizational policies, offering a clear, prioritized view of risks to support effective mitigation and resilience [30].

In addition to core strategies, several supplementary measures can further enhance the resilience of PISs against configuration-related vulnerabilities. For instance, applying secure default settings and disabling unnecessary services reduces the system's exposure by eliminating pre-configured, easily exploitable elements such as default passwords and open ports. Limiting functionality to only essential components significantly decreases the attack surface and prevents unauthorized access points. Strong access control and role-based permissions further mitigate configuration risks by ensuring that only authorized personnel can modify system settings. By enforcing the principle of least privilege and integrating audit logging, ports can prevent unauthorized configuration changes and maintain traceability of all modifications.

4.4 Common Types of Cyber Threats to the PIS and Impacts on Seaports

Academic and industry literature consistently highlight several key categories of cyber threats that have frequently affected logistics systems. While some of these threats have been directly observed in the port industry, others are emerging across critical infrastructure sectors and are increasingly relevant due to the growing digitization and interconnectedness of port operations.

The following sections present an overview of these threats, including both historically observed cases and those with plausible implications for seaport environments.

4.4.1 Social Engineering and Phishing

Social engineering manipulates human behavior to bypass security measures or extract confidential data [31]. Phishing, a leading technique, involves attackers impersonating trusted entities—such as port authorities or logistics providers—to trick individuals into revealing sensitive credentials or financial information [32]. Within ports, phishing primarily targets employees with access to critical systems [14]. These attacks often appear as legitimate emails or messages, enticing recipients to click harmful links, download malware, or enter information on fake sites. Exploiting trust, phishing grants attackers unauthorized entry into secure environments. The consequences include unauthorized access to sensitive operational data like shipping schedules and financial transactions, causing major disruptions and losses. For example, in 2011, the Port of Antwerp suffered a spear-phishing breach that enabled a drug cartel to manipulate container logistics for nearly two years, exposing significant vulnerabilities and prompting improvements in training and monitoring [14].

4.4.2 Malware

Malware, a broad category of malicious software that includes viruses, ransomware, trojans, and spyware, continues to represent one of the most pervasive and disruptive cyber threats to the PIS [8]. It often enters through phishing, compromised networks, or unauthorized devices. Once inside, malware can spread quickly, compromising key systems. Attackers may encrypt files for ransom, steal cargo or scheduling data, disable automation, or maintain hidden access. Such attacks disrupt operations, compromise safety, and inflict financial and reputational damage. Ransomware has evolved, including supply chain attacks (e.g., SolarWinds), Ransomware-as-a-Service models, use of legitimate tools to evade detection (Living-off-the-Land), and fileless malware that avoids antivirus detection [33]. Although no public reports link these advanced variants directly to ports, their growing sophistication poses a serious maritime threat, especially as ports rely more on digital and third-party services.

4.4.3 DDoS Attacks

DDoS attacks overwhelm targeted networks with massive traffic, often generated by botnets—networks of compromised devices controlled remotely [34]. Ports are vulnerable due to their interconnected infrastructure, with critical targets including public websites, cargo tracking, and communication systems. These attacks aim to disrupt service availability, delaying cargo processing, blocking customer access, and impeding logistics coordination, which undermines operational continuity and stakeholder confidence [14]. In April 2023, a coordinated DDoS attack by the Russian group NoName057(16) targeted the ports of Montreal, Quebec, and Halifax, disrupting public-facing systems and forcing manual communication despite unaffected internal operations [14]. This incident highlights how even brief digital outages can strain supply chains, damage trust, and reveal weaknesses in detection and response capabilities.

4.4.4 Insider Threats

Insider threats originate from individuals within the organization—such as employees, contractors, or other trusted personnel—who may either deliberately or inadvertently compromise the PIS. Malicious insiders may engage in activities such as data manipulation, unauthorized malware installation, or the disclosure of sensitive information [35]. Conversely, unintentional insider threats stem from negligence or lack of awareness, such as mishandling access credentials or unintentionally introducing malicious software through insecure practices [35]. Notably, current evidence from the port industry predominantly reflects the occurrence of unintentional insider threats. One common vector for these incidents is phishing, an externally initiated attack that manipulates internal personnel into executing harmful actions [14]. Although phishing attacks originate from outside actors, the resulting compromise often occurs through internal users—such as employees or contractors—who, for example, click on malicious links or provide login credentials to counterfeit platforms [14]. In these instances, internal actors become conduits for system breaches, thus classifying the event under both phishing and insider threat categories.

4.4.5 SQL Injection

SQL injection is a method of exploiting vulnerabilities within web applications to manipulate or extract data from underlying databases [36]. PISs, which often manage sensitive data, are particularly susceptible to such attacks. If an attacker exploits weaknesses within a TOS, they could potentially alter critical cargo data or execute unauthorized financial transactions. The impact of SQL injection extends beyond mere data manipulation, posing a significant risk of data theft and operational disruption. Although such attacks have not been officially reported within the port industry, the risks they present to the integrity and trustworthiness of port operations are considerable and should not be underestimated.

4.4.6 Zero-Day Exploits

Zero-day exploits target vulnerabilities in software or hardware that are unknown to the vendors, rendering these exploits especially dangerous [37]. For PISs, which rely on automated systems, the presence of unpatched vulnerabilities can create substantial risks. Attackers utilizing zero-day exploits can bypass existing security defenses to gain access to sensitive systems, often compromising operational efficiency and data integrity before mitigation strategies can be put in place. While there is no documented evidence of zero-day exploits affecting port operations to date, the potential for such attacks highlights a critical vulnerability within PISs, warranting proactive security measures.

4.4.7 Advanced Persistent Threats

APTs are long-term, targeted attacks designed to infiltrate and maintain access to systems over extended periods [38]. These sophisticated operations typically may aim at high-value data within the PIS, including shipping routes, cargo manifests, and security protocols. APTs employ a multi-phase approach involving reconnaissance, intrusion, and data exfiltration, all while evading detection [38]. The prolonged nature of APTs enables attackers to extract sensitive information while remaining undetected, presenting significant risks to both operational security and strategic decision making. Although there have been no official reports of APTs targeting ports, the potential for such threats remains a serious concern, especially as port systems continue to digitize and integrate with third-party services.

4.5 Impacts of Cyber Threats on Seaports

Cyber-attacks targeting seaport infrastructure can result in a wide range of consequences, each varying in severity and scope depending on the type and sophistication of the attack. According to cybersecurity research, these consequences are commonly classified into five major categories, reflecting their direct and cascading effects on port systems, stakeholders, and the broader maritime supply chain.

4.5.1 Data Compromise

Among the most critical consequences of cyber-attacks in port environments is the compromise of sensitive data [14]. Attacks such as phishing, malware intrusions, or SQL injection often result in unauthorized access to proprietary information, including shipping manifests, financial records, and customer data. These breaches not only violate stakeholder confidentiality but also undermine the integrity of PISs, which are central to operational decision making. The manipulation or alteration of critical datasets—such as tampered cargo descriptions or falsified vessel arrival times—can lead to substantial operational disruptions and a loss of trust among port clients. Furthermore, the exposure of confidential or classified information may compromise the port's competitive advantage, revealing logistical strategies or security protocols to malicious actors and increasing vulnerability to future targeted attacks.

4.5.2 Operational Disruption and Reputational Risks

Cyber-attacks can significantly hinder the operational continuity of seaports, which are essential nodes in the global trade ecosystem [14]. Malicious activities, particularly ransomware, have the potential to disable critical port systems such as the TOS, vessel traffic management system (VTMS), and automated equipment controls. These disruptions can result in severe delays in loading, unloading, and clearance processes, which not only affect port operations but also trigger cascading effects across regional and international supply chains.

Such interruptions diminish the efficiency of port services and can cause a ripple effect that extends well beyond the port itself. Shipping schedules are disrupted, cargo delivery commitments are compromised, and delays in one port can cause congestion at others, leading to a domino effect on global logistics networks. These delays increase operational costs, contribute to bottlenecks in the supply chain, and create dissatisfaction among stakeholders, from shipping companies to end customers.

Additionally, the long-term reputational damage caused by operational failures can undermine confidence in the affected port, resulting in a loss of business and long-term financial impact. Loss of trust may lead to the withdrawal of strategic partners, diminished customer loyalty, and a decline in investment interest. Over time, reputational damage can reduce a port's competitiveness and negatively influence its ranking within global port networks, undermining long-term business prospects. The broader implications of these disruptions are felt throughout the supply chain, as delays at seaports can lead to missed deadlines, inventory shortages, and a general decline in the reliability of shipping schedules, all of which further exacerbate the costs and reputational harm for port operators and their stakeholders.

4.5.3 Safety and Security Risks

Modern seaports rely on integrated cyber-physical systems to control cranes, access gates, surveillance networks, and other critical infrastructure. Cyber-attacks targeting these systems can endanger the physical safety of port personnel, visitors, and assets. Unauthorized access to control interfaces may result in unsafe crane operations, tampering with access control systems, or manipulation of navigational data for approaching vessels. In severe cases, such as attacks on the control systems of ports and vessels, the risk escalates to life-threatening conditions, including potential collisions, cargo accidents, or environmental hazards.

4.5.4 Financial Risks

Cyber-attacks on seaport infrastructure can result in substantial financial losses, both direct and indirect, affecting ports in multiple ways. Direct financial losses include immediate costs related to forensic investigations, system recovery, and engaging external cybersecurity services to mitigate the breach [14, 39]. These costs are essential for restoring secure operations and addressing vulnerabilities in port systems that may have been exploited during the attack.

Indirect financial losses primarily stem from operational disruptions caused by the attack. When cyber incidents cause delays in cargo handling, vessel scheduling, and other critical port functions, ports face significant revenue losses due to halted or slowed operations. For example, service interruptions can prevent ports from processing shipping orders for weeks, leading to the freezing of revenue streams and potential contractual penalties. These disruptions can ripple throughout the global supply chain, causing delays and financial strain on both port operators and their stakeholders.

In addition to these costs, ports may incur regulatory liabilities if they fail to meet data protection and cybersecurity compliance requirements. Non-compliance with frameworks and laws can result in fines, legal proceedings, and additional operational burdens as ports are required to implement corrective measures. The long-term financial impact of such penalties, along with the need for ongoing cybersecurity investments, contributes to the indirect costs of a cyber-attack.

4.5.5 Regulatory and Compliance Risks

Cyber-attacks frequently result in regulatory non-compliance due to the disruption of essential security controls and failure to meet legal obligations for data protection and operational continuity [8]. When a PIS is compromised—whether through data breaches, service outages, or unauthorized access—it may violate established requirements under national and international frameworks such as the GDPR, the ISPS Code, and regional maritime cybersecurity mandates. These frameworks often require ports to implement preventive controls, maintain secure infrastructure, and ensure timely breach reporting. A successful cyber-attack may expose deficiencies in these areas, triggering legal actions, regulatory investigations, or formal obligations to notify authorities and affected stakeholders. Beyond immediate compliance issues, such incidents can lead to intensified oversight, reputational risk, and pressure to adopt more stringent cybersecurity governance measures.

References

[1] K. Stouffer, T. Zimmerman, C. Tang, J. Lubell, J. Cichonski and J. McCarthy, "Cybersecurity Framework Manufacturing Profile," NIST, 2017. [Online]. Available: https://nvlpubs.nist.gov/nistpubs/ir/2017/NIST.IR.8183.pdf.

[2] K. Stine, S. Quinn, G. Witte and R. K. Gardner, "Integrating Cybersecurity and Enterprise Risk Management (ERM)," 2020. [Online]. Available: https://nvlpubs.nist.gov/nistpubs/ir/2020/NIST.IR.8286.pdf.

[3] IMO, "Guidelines On Maritime Cyber Risk Management," 2022. [Online]. Available: wwwcdn.imo.org/localresources/en/OurWork/Security/Documents/MSC-FAL.1-Circ.3-Rev.2%20-%20Guidelines%20On%20Maritime%20Cyber%20Risk%20Management%20(Secretariat)%20(1).pdf.

[4] S. Pandey, R. K. Singh, A. Gunasekaran and A. Kaushik, "Cyber Security Risks in Globalized Supply Chains: Conceptual Framework," *Journal of Global Operations and Strategic Sourcing*, vol. 13, no. 1, pp. 103–128, 2020.

[5] P. Mell, K. Scarfone and S. Romanosky, "Common Vulnerability Scoring System," *IEEE Security & Privacy*, vol. 4, no. 6, pp. 85–89, 2006.

[6] NIST, "NVD CVSS v4.0 Official Support," 2024. [Online]. Available: https://nvd.nist.gov/general/news/cvss-v4-0-official-support.

[7] U. K. Singh, C. Joshi and N. Gaud, "Information Security Assessment by Quantifying Risk Level of Network Vulnerabilities," *International Journal of Computer Applications*, vol. 156, no. 2, pp. 37–44, 2016.

[8] C. Senarak, "Port Cybersecurity and Threat: A Structural Model for Prevention and Policy Development," *The Asian Journal of Shipping and Logistics*, vol. 37, no. 1, pp. 20–36, 2021.

[9] S. Lee, A. A. H. Mujammami and K. Kim, "Leveraging Social Networks for Cyber Threat Intelligence: Analyzing Attack Trends and TTPs in the Arab World," *IEEE Access*, vol. 13, pp. 5679–5693, 2025.

[10] G. Wangen, "Quantifying and Analyzing Information Security Risk from Incident Data," in *Graphical Models for Security*, Springer, 2019, pp. 129–154.

[11] D. Möller, "Cyberattacker Profiles, Cyberattack Models and Scenarios, and Cybersecurity Ontology," in *Guide to Cybersecurity in Digital Transformation*, Springer, 2023, pp. 181–229.

[12] L. Robertson, A. M. Aneiros and K. Michael, "A Theory of Exposure: Measuring Technology System End User Vulnerabilities," in International Symposium on Technology and Society, Sydney, NSW, Australia, 2017.

[13] S. D. Gantz and D. R. Philpott, "Risk Management," in *FISMA and the Risk Management Framework: The New Practice of Federal Cyber Security deals with the Federal Information Security Management Act (FISMA)*, Elsevier, 2013, pp. 329–365.

[14] C. Senarak, "Port Cyberattacks from 2011 to 2023: A Literature Review and Discussion of Selected Cases," *Maritime Economics & Logistics*, vol. 26, no. 1, pp. 105–130, 2024.

[15] Port of Seattle, "Port Cyberattack Archive," 2 April 2025. [Online]. Available: www.portseattle.org/news/port-cyberattack-archive.

[16] Ö. Aslan, S. S. Aktuğ, M. Ozkan-Okay, A. A. Yilmaz and E. Akin, "A Comprehensive Review of Cyber Security Vulnerabilities, Threats, Attacks, and Solutions," *Electronics*, vol. 12, no. 6, p. 1333, 2023.

[17] A. J. Cabrera-Gutiérrez, E. Castillo, A. Escobar-Molero, J. A. Álvarez-Bermejo, D. P. Morales and L. Parrilla, "Integration of Hardware Security Modules and

Permissioned Blockchain in Industrial IoT Networks," *IEEE Access*, vol. 10, pp. 114331–114345, 2022.

[18] S. U. Haq, Y. Singh, A. Sharma, R. Gupta and D. Gupta, "A Survey on IoT & Embedded Device Firmware Security: Architecture, Extraction Techniques, And vulnerability analysis frameworks," *Discover Internet of Things*, vol. 3, no. 17, 2023, pp. 1–29.

[19] G. González-Granadillo, S. González-Zarzosa and R. Diaz, "Security Information and Event Management (SIEM): Analysis, Trends, and Usage in Critical Infrastructures," *Sensors*, vol. 21, no. 14, p. 4759, 2021.

[20] N. Mhaskar, M. Alabbad and R. Khedri, "A Formal Approach to Network Segmentation," *Computers & Security*, vol. 103, 102162, 2021.

[21] N. Dissanayake, A. Jayatilaka, M. Zahedi and M. A. Babar, "Software Security Patch Management – A Systematic Literature Review of Challenges, Approaches, Tools and Practices," *Information and Software Technology*, vol. 144, 106771, 2022.

[22] R. A. Khan, S. U. Khan, H. U. Khan and M. Ilyas, "Systematic Literature Review on Security Risks and its Practices in Secure Software Development," *IEEE Access*, vol. 10, pp. 5456–5481, 2022.

[23] S. Shah and B. M. Mehtre, "An Overview of Vulnerability Assessment and Penetration Testing Techniques," *Journal of Computer Virology and Hacking Techniques*, vol. 11, p. 27–49, 2015.

[24] A. P. H and G. Sujatha, "System Hardening Using CIS Benchmarks," in International Conference on Advances in Computing, Communication and Applied Informatics (ACCAI), Chennai, India, 2024.

[25] E. Ferrari, "Role-Based Access Control," in *Access Control in Data Management Systems*, Springer2010, pp. 61–75.

[26] D. Bringhenti, G. Marchetto, R. Sisto and F. Valenza, "Automation for Network Security Configuration: State of the Art and Research Trends," *ACM Computing Surveys*, vol. 56, no. 3, pp. 1–37, 2023.

[27] S. W. A. Hamdani, H. Abbas, A. R. Janjua, W. B. Shahid, M. F. Amjad, J. Malik, M. H. Murtaza, M. Atiquzzaman and A. W. Khan, "Cybersecurity Standards in the Context of Operating System: Practical Aspects, Analysis, and Comparisons," *ACM Computing Surveys*, vol. 54, no. 3, pp. 1–36, 2021.

[28] A. Nappa, R. Johnson, L. Bilge, J. Caballero and T. Dumitras, "The Attack of the Clones: A Study of the Impact of Shared Code on Vulnerability Patching," in Symposium on Security and Privacy, San Jose, CA, USA, 2015.

[29] C. Lee, J. Trost, N. Gibbs, R. Beyah and J. Copeland, "Visual Firewall: Real-Time Network Security Monitor," in IEEE Workshop on Visualization for Computer Security (VizSEC 05), Minneapolis, MN, USA, 2005.

[30] L. Collins, "Chapter 81 – Assessments and Audits," in *Computer and Information Security Handbook* (Fourth Edition), Elsevier, 2024, pp. 1283–1290.

[31] Z. Wang, H. Zhu and L. Sun, "Social Engineering in Cybersecurity: Effect Mechanisms, Human Vulnerabilities and Attack Methods," *IEEE Access*, vol. 9, pp. 11895–11910, 2021.

[32] Z. Alkhalil, C. Hewage, L. Nawaf and I. Khan, "Phishing Attacks: A Recent Comprehensive Study and a New Anatomy," *Frontiers in Computer Science*, vol. 3, pp. 1–23, 2021.

[33] J. Ferdous, R. Islam, A. Mahboubi and M. Z. Islam, "A Review of State-of-the-Art Malware Attack Trends and Defense Mechanisms," *IEEE Access*, vol. 11, pp. 121118–121141, 2023.

[34] N. Hoque, D. K. Bhattacharyya and J. K. Kalita, "Botnet in DDoS Attacks: Trends and Challenges," *IEEE Communications Surveys & Tutorials*, vol. 17, no. 4, pp. 2242–2270, 2015.

[35] A. Al-Harrasi, A. K. Shaikh and A. Al-Badi, "Towards Protecting Organisations' Data by Preventing Data Theft by Malicious Insiders," *International Journal of Organizational Analysis*, vol. 31, no. 3, pp. 875–888, 2023.

[36] R. Johari and P. Sharma, "A Survey on Web Application Vulnerabilities (SQLIA, XSS) Exploitation and Security Engine for SQL Injection," in International Conference on Communication Systems and Network Technologies, Rajkot, Gujarat, India, 2012.

[37] R. Zaib and K.-Q. Zhou, "Zero-Day Vulnerabilities: Unveiling the Threat Landscape in Network Security," *Mesopotamian Journal of CyberSecurity*, vol. 2022, pp. 57–64, 2022.

[38] S. Krishnapriya and S. Singh, "A Comprehensive Survey on Advanced Persistent Threat (APT) Detection Techniques," *Computers, Materials & Continua*, vol. 80, no. 2, p. 2675, 2024.

[39] F. Fotis, "Economic Impact of Cyber Attacks and Effective Cyber Risk Management Strategies: A Light Literature Review and Case Study Analysis," *Procedia Computer Science*, vol. 251, pp. 471–478, 2024.

5 Rising Port Cyber-Attacks and Discussions of Selected Publicly Reported Cases

5.1 Port Cyber-Attacks and the Current Landscape in the Global Port Industry

As ports worldwide undergo rapid digital transformation, they are increasingly exposed to sophisticated cyber threats. The integration of operational technologies, data-sharing platforms, and smart infrastructure has elevated efficiency, but it has also expanded the cyberattack surface. This section provides a regional overview of port cybersecurity incidents and responses, highlighting variations in threat exposure, digital maturity, and preparedness across major global port regions.

In the Americas, the United States has emerged as a central player in the advancement of port cybersecurity, actively implementing resilience-based frameworks and fostering interagency collaboration to protect critical maritime infrastructure. Despite these efforts, US ports have recorded the highest number of successful ransomware attacks globally, underscoring the persistent vulnerability of this region's digital port ecosystems [1]. Notable incidents include the cyber-attacks on the Port of San Diego, the Port of Vancouver, and the Port of Long Beach in 2018; the Port of Kennewick in 2020; the Port of Houston in 2021; and the Ports of Halifax, Montreal, and Quebec in 2023 [1]. Although the annual number of publicly confirmed breaches remains limited—typically two to three successful attacks per year—unsuccessful intrusion attempts are exponentially higher. For instance, the Port of Los Angeles reported over 63 million cyber-intrusion attempts in 2023 alone [2]. Cyber vulnerabilities in the US are rooted in a range of interlinked systems, including terminal headquarters, cargo-handling equipment, operational technology, and integrated communication networks. These elements are closely embedded within national logistics chains and shared data infrastructures, which complicate threat management. In response, the U.S. government has emphasized domestic development of port technologies such as cranes and automation systems to reduce reliance on foreign suppliers and minimize associated cybersecurity risks. Additionally, experts advocate for proactive risk assessments, assuming system compromise as an eventuality and focusing on network resilience and rapid recovery strategies.

DOI: 10.4324/9781003559320-5

European ports have also experienced a rise in ransomware and supply chain attacks, ranking just behind North America in terms of cyber incident prevalence. Prominent attacks include the 2017 NotPetya-related breach of APM Terminals in Ukraine—one of the most damaging maritime cyber incidents to date—the 2018 attack on the Port of Barcelona, the 2020 breach of the Port of Marseilles, and the 2022 cyber-attacks targeting the Ports of Antwerp and Lisbon [1]. A significant trend in Europe is the rise of "supply chain attacks," in which threat actors infiltrate interconnected systems across multiple logistics partners, amplifying operational disruptions. These attacks are frequently linked to state-sponsored actors, organized cybercriminal groups, and hacktivist networks. European responses have centered on enhancing port IT infrastructure, improving digital resilience, and integrating cybersecurity into broader smart port initiatives. Investments in automation, AI-enhanced logistics, smart energy systems, and digital platforms are being strategically aligned with cybersecurity enhancements. However, the growing complexity of digital ecosystems in European ports also presents a dilemma: while innovation drives efficiency and sustainability, it simultaneously increases the sector's exposure to cyber threats, necessitating continuous evaluation of security frameworks and regulatory compliance.

In Asia, home to some of the world's most advanced and high-throughput ports—including those in Singapore, China, South Korea, Japan, and Malaysia—the cybersecurity landscape is evolving alongside aggressive digitalization. While major ports in this region have demonstrated notable resilience against large-scale breaches, the number of documented attacks remains relatively low. The 2021 ransomware attack on the Port of Nagoya in Japan stands out as a key incident [1]. Nonetheless, regional reports suggest a growing number of attempted intrusions, especially in countries with less-developed cybersecurity infrastructure, such as Thailand, the Philippines, Indonesia, India, and Taiwan. According to analyses by United Nations Conference on Trade and Development (UNCTAD) [3], Asia's rapid adoption of smart port technologies, coupled with its critical role in global trade, makes it an increasingly attractive target for sophisticated cyber adversaries. Moving forward, enhanced regional cooperation, increased investment in threat detection technologies, and the adoption of internationally aligned cybersecurity standards will be pivotal to securing Asia's digital port infrastructure.

In Africa, the documented number of port cyber-attacks has remained minimal, with only one major incident reported in recent years. The most significant case occurred in 2021, when Transnet—a South African state-owned enterprise—suffered a crippling IT system failure, causing widespread cargo delays and terminal disruptions, particularly at the Port of Durban, which handles approximately 60% of the country's container volume [1]. Despite the relatively low frequency of reported incidents, African ports are particularly vulnerable due to outdated operational technologies, limited national cybersecurity capabilities, and insufficient investment in digital resilience. In response, countries such as Namibia and Ghana have begun implementing national cybersecurity strategies, awareness campaigns, and international cooperation initiatives to build more secure transport infrastructures. Some governments have also begun developing information warfare and command-control capabilities aimed at securing critical digital assets. Concurrently, major infrastructure projects at ports like Durban and Tanger Med are being supported by over USD 100 billion in combined public and private investments, with the dual aim of modernizing logistics operations and enhancing cybersecurity preparedness.

Overall, while North America and Europe confront frequent, sophisticated attacks due to their early adoption of digital systems, Asia and Africa are contending with emerging threats linked to accelerated modernization and uneven cyber readiness. These trends underscore the need for a globally coordinated, proactive, and adaptive cybersecurity strategy—one that integrates continuous risk assessment, public-private collaboration, and the development of secure-by-design port technologies to ensure the resilience of global maritime infrastructure.

5.2 Types of Cyber-Attacks and Preventive Approaches

Cyber-attacks targeting port operations can be broadly categorized into two principal types: targeted attacks and non-targeted attacks. It is estimated that targeted attacks comprise approximately 75% of all cyber incidents within the port industry, whereas non-targeted attacks account for around 25%. This disproportion underscores the greater severity and persistence of targeted threats in the port sector [1]. The primary distinction between these two categories lies in the attacker's intent, methods of execution, selection of targets, degree of customization, underlying motivations, and persistence. The specific features of each attack type are described below.

5.2.1 Targeted Attacks

Targeted cyberattacks are deliberate, highly orchestrated intrusions aimed specifically at ports, terminal operations, or critical infrastructure components. These attacks are typically preceded by an extensive period of reconnaissance, during which threat actors gather intelligence on the digital and physical attributes of the port's ecosystem. Such preparatory efforts may include the surveillance of logistics systems, cargo-handling platforms, and administrative networks. In many cases, attackers monitor these systems over extended periods—spanning weeks or months—to refine their intrusion strategies [4].

Targeted attacks are driven by diverse motivations, including financial gain, industrial espionage, operational disruption, and geopolitical objectives. These incidents are often persistent, technically advanced, and capable of causing extensive operational and financial harm. Attackers may exploit a range of tactics, including social engineering, supply chain compromise, and, in some cases, on-site reconnaissance to gather sensitive information such as credentials or access protocols [5].

These operations typically unfold in coordinated phases and are tailored to exploit specific weaknesses in the port information system (PIS). A common tactic is spear phishing, where deceptive emails—customized to target key personnel such as port administrators or shipping line operators—are used to extract credentials or deploy malware [1, 6]. Other prevalent techniques include distributed denial-of-service (DDoS) attacks and botnet-driven disruptions, which can disable communication networks and operational technology (OT) systems. In more advanced scenarios, attackers employ advanced persistent threats (APTs) for long-term infiltration, aiming to extract sensitive data such as cargo manifests, customs documentation, and vessel schedules [1, 7].

Custom-built malware is another hallmark of targeted attacks. These malicious programs are specifically engineered to exploit weaknesses in port IT or OT platforms, including systems responsible for container tracking and cargo management. Furthermore, some attackers may tamper with software or hardware during the supply chain or manufacturing process, embedding latent vulnerabilities that can be exploited at a later stage [8].

Given the impact of targeted attacks, ports must adopt a multi-layered defense strategy. This should include the implementation of maritime-specific threat intelligence systems that enable continuous monitoring for indicators of compromise. Access control protocols should follow zero-trust architecture principles and include multi-factor authentication to restrict unauthorized entry [9]. Network segmentation is equally critical, with key systems such as vessel traffic management systems (VTMSs) and terminal operating systems (TOSs) requiring isolation from general-purpose networks [10]. AI-driven endpoint detection and response (EDR) tools should be deployed to detect and respond to abnormal system behavior, particularly those associated with APT activities [11]. In addition, ports should conduct regular incident response drills, including red team exercises, to test their readiness against targeted threats [12]. Complementing these technical measures, cybersecurity awareness training and insider threat-monitoring programs should be established to strengthen the human element of port security [5].

5.2.2 Non-targeted Attacks

Non-targeted cyber-attacks, in contrast, are indiscriminate and opportunistic. Rather than focusing on a specific port asset, these attacks aim to exploit widely prevalent vulnerabilities across multiple systems and sectors. The primary motivations for such attacks often include financial gain, disruption, or experimentation with malware capabilities. Attackers rely on automated tools and generalized techniques to identify and breach weak points in cyber defenses, making ports—especially those with outdated systems—vulnerable to collateral damage [5, 13].

These attacks also exploit common human errors and system misconfigurations, using mass-scale methods that include phishing emails, drive-by downloads, and generic malware deployments. Mass phishing campaigns, for example, involve sending fraudulent emails to numerous port employees in an attempt to harvest credentials or install malware [1, 13]. Similarly, watering hole attacks compromise frequently visited websites in the maritime sector, using them as vectors to deliver malicious code to unsuspecting visitors [14]. Drive-by downloads occur when port personnel unknowingly access compromised websites, triggering automatic malware installations on their devices. Another prevalent tactic involves the deployment of ransomware, which encrypts critical data such as cargo-tracking records and demands payment for decryption [1].

To reduce non-targeted attack risks, ports should implement a robust set of baseline defenses. Regular software updates and proactive patch management are crucial to closing known security gaps in the PIS. Email- and web-filtering technologies should be employed to intercept phishing attempts and block access to malicious URLs. Firewalls and intrusion prevention systems (IPSs) are essential for detecting and halting unauthorized access attempts, such as brute-force attacks and network-scanning activities [5].

Access control measures, including strong password enforcement and the use of multi-factor authentication, are necessary to protect critical systems from unauthorized use. In addition, ports should maintain comprehensive backup and disaster recovery plans to ensure rapid restoration of operations in the event of ransomware or other data-related incidents. Cybersecurity awareness programs should also be established to educate personnel on the identification of and appropriate response to phishing threats and other common cyber risks [15].

5.3 Actors Behind Port Cyber-Attacks

Ports are increasingly exposed to cyber threats posed by a wide range of actors. The literature identifies five primary categories of cyber threat actors targeting ports: nation-state actors, hacktivists, cybercriminals, insiders, and terrorist organizations. These actors exhibit diverse motivations, methods, targets, and impacts, necessitating tailored defense strategies. An overview of each threat actor is presented below.

- **Nation-state actors** are driven by geopolitical agendas and typically pursue strategic, political, or military outcomes. Backed by state sponsorship or intelligence agencies, they conduct highly sophisticated and persistent campaigns involving APTs, custom malware, espionage, and sabotage. These actors often exploit zero-day vulnerabilities to infiltrate critical port infrastructure such as cargo-tracking systems, customs platforms, and port management networks, aiming to disrupt national security and global commerce. The repercussions of these attacks are severe, including long-term operational paralysis, data breaches, and adverse economic and diplomatic outcomes. Countermeasures require ports to adopt cutting-edge cybersecurity technologies, maintain real-time threat intelligence collaboration, and engage actively with national cybersecurity authorities [1, 16].

- **Hacktivists** are ideologically or socially motivated individuals or groups seeking to raise awareness about or protest against political, corporate, or environmental issues. They typically operate independently or as part of loosely organized activist networks, without institutional backing. Their methods include DDoS attacks, website defacement, and the unauthorized release of data. These actions often target high-visibility systems such as public terminals or online tracking portals to maximize public exposure. Although less damaging to physical infrastructure, hacktivist activity can seriously erode public trust and tarnish a port's reputation. Preventive strategies include proactive network defense, DDoS mitigation systems, and robust communication protocols to manage reputational risks [1, 15].
- **Cybercriminals** primarily pursue financial gain, targeting ports to commit fraud, steal confidential data, or extort money via ransomware. They may act independently or under the direction of organized crime groups, leveraging techniques such as phishing, ransomware deployment, and data breaches. Financial transaction platforms, cargo management software, and logistics coordination tools are common targets. Their attacks often lead to direct monetary losses, operational halts, theft of intellectual property, and reputational damage, with cascading effects on logistics partners and customs agencies. Mitigation measures include phishing awareness training, encrypted data exchange, and comprehensive response frameworks tailored to ransomware incidents [1, 5].
- **Insiders**—comprising employees, contractors, or affiliated personnel—pose distinct risks due to their direct access to sensitive systems. Motivations may range from personal dissatisfaction and financial incentive to unintentional negligence. Insiders may act alone or under the influence of external parties, engaging in data exfiltration, sabotage, or inadvertently introducing malware via unsecured devices. Their access to operational or security-critical systems makes their actions especially challenging to detect and neutralize. The consequences include data leaks, system outages, and potentially prolonged disruption of port activities. Effective mitigation involves stringent access control policies, ongoing activity monitoring, rigorous employee vetting, and fostering a cybersecurity-aware organizational culture [14, 17].
- **Terrorist organizations** view ports as strategic targets for creating fear, causing economic disruption, or advancing ideological causes. Operating independently or with state support, they often incorporate cyber-attacks into broader campaigns involving physical sabotage. Ports' security systems, vessel navigation platforms, and transportation control networks are susceptible to their attacks, which aim to inflict mass disruption and psychological

impacts. The consequences are profound, ranging from damage to infrastructure and trade disruption to heightened regional insecurity. Defense strategies demand integrated cyber-physical security protocols, interagency intelligence cooperation, and crisis response capabilities [5, 18].

5.4 Common Port Scanning Techniques

Scanning techniques are integral to the reconnaissance phase of both targeted and non-targeted cyber-attacks, allowing attackers to gather intelligence on a system, network, or application prior to launching an intrusion. In the context of port cybersecurity, these techniques are especially critical as they enable adversaries to identify and exploit vulnerabilities in PISs, digital infrastructure, and networks, which serve as virtual entry points for services such as email, file transfers, and remote access. Rather than launching indiscriminate attacks, attackers leverage scanning methods to covertly assess systems, increasing the likelihood of successful and targeted breaches. The seven most common scanning techniques are outlined below.

1 **Transmission control protocol (TCP) Connect Scan** is considered the most straightforward form of port scanning, as it relies on completing a full TCP three-way handshake to determine whether a network port is active. The attacker sends a SYN packet to the target; if a SYN-ACK is received, the connection is finalized with an ACK packet. A successful handshake indicates that the port is open and may be susceptible to unauthorized access. Because this technique uses standard system calls and establishes complete connections, it is easily detected by intrusion detection systems due to the creation of connection logs. Although effective and broadly compatible, this method lacks stealth and is typically employed when evasion is not a primary concern or when other scan types are blocked. Defensive measures include configuring firewalls to restrict unnecessary connections, enforcing rate limits, and monitoring network logs to identify suspicious activity [19].
2 **SYN Scan**, also referred to as a half-open scan, is a commonly used technique for identifying open network ports while minimizing the risk of detection. This method initiates, but does not complete, the standard TCP three-way handshake. The attacker transmits a SYN packet to a target port, and if the port is active, the system responds with a SYN-ACK packet. Rather than finalizing the connection with an ACK, the attacker immediately sends an RST (reset) packet to terminate the exchange. Because the connection is never fully established, this scan often avoids detection by the intrusion detection systems (IDS) that monitor completed TCP sessions. Although more discreet than a full connection scan, it can still be identified through network behavior. Defensive measures include configuring firewalls with SYN flood protection and implementing IDS technologies that alert administrators to a high frequency of incomplete connection attempts [19].

3 **User datagram protocol (UDP) Scan** targets connectionless services. UDP scans are used to test services that do not require a formal handshake, such as domain name system (DNS) or simple network management protocol (SNMP). The attacker sends empty messages to various ports and observes the response—or lack of one—to determine if the port is open or blocked. Attackers send empty UDP packets to various ports and infer port status from the response. An internet control message protocol (ICMP) "Port Unreachable" message typically signals a closed port, while the absence of a reply may suggest an open or filtered port. Since many IDS tools focus primarily on TCP traffic, UDP scans often go unnoticed. Services such as DNS (port 53), SNMP (port 161), and trivial file transfer protocol (TFTP) (port 69), all of which are common in port environments, are attractive targets. Defenses include disabling unnecessary UDP services, employing deep packet inspection (DPI), and implementing rate limits for ICMP responses [19].
4 **ACK Scan** is primarily used to assess firewall configurations, rather than to identify open ports. Attackers send unsolicited ACK packets to determine whether a firewall operates in a stateful or stateless manner. If a stateless firewall responds with RST (reset) packets, it suggests that the port is unfiltered, thereby revealing firewall rule behaviors. This technique enables adversaries to map how the firewall handles network traffic and potentially identify security gaps. Effective mitigation includes the use of stateful firewalls that track connection states, maintaining logs of unexpected ACK traffic, and deploying anomaly detection systems to flag irregular scanning patterns [20].
5 **FIN Scan** takes advantage of how the TCP protocol handles unexpected session terminations by sending FIN packets to target ports without initiating a connection. In accordance with RFC 793, a closed port typically responds with an RST (reset) packet, while an open port ignores the message, making this scan difficult to detect through conventional security systems focused on SYN-based traffic. This technique is also used for operating system fingerprinting. To mitigate such scans, firewalls should be configured to drop anomalous FIN packets, and continuous monitoring should be conducted to detect unusual TCP behavior that may indicate scanning activity [19, 20].
6 **XMAS Scan**, also known as the Christmas Tree scan, transmits TCP packets with multiple control flags—typically FIN, URG, and PSH—set simultaneously, creating an unusual flag combination that resembles a lit Christmas tree. This method is designed to evade standard intrusion detection systems and firewalls by exploiting variations in TCP response behavior. Closed ports generally respond with an RST packet, while open ports remain silent, making detection more difficult. Additionally, inconsistencies in how different operating systems handle such packets can aid in system fingerprinting. To counter this method, stateful firewalls should be configured to reject malformed packets and monitor for abnormal TCP flag patterns [21].

7 **Idle Scan**, or zombie scan, is a stealthy technique that allows attackers to obscure their IP address by utilizing an intermediary host, known as a "zombie." Spoofed SYN packets are sent to the target using the zombie's IP address, and the attacker observes the zombie's responses to infer the target's port status. This method is difficult to trace, making it effective at bypassing blacklist-based defenses. Mitigation strategies include implementing egress filtering to block IP spoofing, monitoring internal systems for unusual activity, and applying network segmentation to minimize the attack surface [22].

After examining individual scanning techniques, it is important to recognize that attackers may strategically combine these methods to improve the effectiveness of their reconnaissance efforts. Adversaries select scanning strategies based on their objectives and the defenses they aim to bypass. For example, a SYN scan may be used to identify open TCP services, such as secure shell (SSH) or remote desktop protocol (RDP), while avoiding detection, and a UDP scan might target services like DNS or SNMP. Attackers could also begin with an ACK scan to find unfiltered ports and then use SYN scans to confirm their status. Additionally, XMAS or FIN scans can test system responses to abnormal TCP packets, exposing potential vulnerabilities in the operating system or firewall configuration. This layered approach to scanning presents a significant concern for seaport cybersecurity, where breaches can disrupt operations, impact logistics, or compromise sensitive data. Consequently, port cybersecurity teams must be equipped not only to detect individual scanning attempts but also to identify complex multi-phase reconnaissance campaigns—an essential capability for preempting intrusions that could jeopardize cargo integrity, delay vessel scheduling, or expose customs and trade data.

5.5 Phases of Cyber-Attacks

Cyber-attacks targeting ports typically progress through a series of defined phases, each representing a step in the attacker's strategy to infiltrate systems, execute malicious activities, and achieve specific objectives. Understanding these phases is critical for enhancing the cybersecurity posture of port operations, as it enables stakeholders to implement tailored defense mechanisms, detect early-warning signals, and coordinate timely responses.

5.5.1 Reconnaissance

The reconnaissance phase marks the beginning of a cyber-attack, during which adversaries collect intelligence about the target environment [23]. This phase is primarily exploratory, involving the systematic gathering of information to identify vulnerabilities that can later be exploited. Techniques such as OSINT, footprinting, network scanning, and social engineering are commonly used [20]. For port operations, attackers may collect data from publicly accessible sources, including vessel schedules, digital interfaces for cargo handling, staff directories, and operational procedures. Such information is often gathered through analysis of the port's official websites, misconfigured databases, or unsecured network entry points. The purpose is to create a detailed map of the digital and organizational landscape, thereby identifying potential weaknesses for exploitation.

Effective mitigation at this stage involves maintaining a comprehensive and current inventory of digital assets, conducting regular risk assessments, and reducing the attack surface by limiting public access to sensitive data. The use of IDS and continuous traffic monitoring allows early detection of anomalous scanning behavior. Moreover, ports may benefit from employing decoy systems or honeypots, which mislead attackers and provide valuable insights into their tactics [24].

5.5.2 Weaponization

Following reconnaissance, attackers progress to the weaponization stage, wherein they develop or tailor malicious code or tools designed to exploit specific vulnerabilities uncovered during earlier activities [25]. This process commonly involves combining an exploit with a corresponding payload to construct an effective and deployable cyber weapon. Within the port context, weaponization may entail engineering malware intended to compromise control systems, interfere with automated crane operations, or manipulate the PIS. The success of this phase is critical in enabling the attacker to prepare a precise and potent vector capable of causing functional disruption within port infrastructure.

Preventive strategies include rigorous vulnerability management, frequent penetration testing, and software patching to close potential attack paths. Network segmentation can contain potential breaches, while endpoint protection systems equipped with behavior analysis tools can identify unusual or malicious activities before full execution. In instances where weaponization efforts are detected, rapid containment through system isolation, file removal, and forensic investigation is essential. These actions must be followed by the restoration of system integrity using verified backups and the reinforcement of relevant security protocols [10, 26].

5.5.3 Delivery

The delivery phase encompasses the transmission of the weaponized payload into the targeted port operational environment [27]. This stage is critical, as it marks the transition from preparation to active intrusion. Threat actors commonly utilize techniques such as phishing emails, malicious hyperlinks, or compromised physical media—such as infected USB drives—as delivery vectors. For port operations, attackers may craft spear-phishing messages that impersonate trusted entities. These deceptive communications often contain malware-laden attachments disguised as legitimate documents, including shipping invoices, cargo manifests, or customs declarations, thereby deceiving port personnel into initiating the malicious payload. The success of this phase relies heavily on social engineering and the exploitation of procedural trust within digital port ecosystems [1].

Mitigating delivery-based threats requires a multi-layered security strategy. Email-filtering technologies, secure web gateways, anti-malware software, and application whitelisting collectively reduce exposure to malicious content [28]. Detecting indicators of compromise through behavioral monitoring tools is also essential. In the event of an attempted or successful delivery, security personnel should immediately block further malicious communications, quarantine affected systems, and conduct a thorough investigation to ensure that no residual threats remain. Employee awareness training is also crucial, as human error remains a significant risk factor during this phase [15].

5.5.4 Exploitation

The exploitation phase represents the point at which an attacker actively takes advantage of an identified vulnerability to execute a malicious payload and obtain unauthorized access to targeted systems [27]. This process may involve the manipulation of software flaws, the use of weak or reused credentials, or the abuse of misconfigured network or system settings [29]. For port operations, such exploitation can lead to illegitimate access to critical digital platforms, including TOSs, or interfere with applications responsible for port operations [1]. The successful execution of this phase often serves as a precursor to more advanced malicious actions, such as data manipulation, surveillance, or operational disruption, thereby posing significant risks to the continuity and security of port functions.

Preventive measures include real-time vulnerability scanning, the application of security patches, and the enforcement of strong authentication mechanisms such as multi-factor authentication. The IPS deployment further helps to intercept known exploitation techniques. Once an exploitation attempt is detected, ports must isolate compromised systems, deploy containment strategies, and begin incident analysis [1]. Restoration of affected components using secure backups and review of access controls are necessary to prevent recurrence.

5.5.5 Installation

Following successful access to a target system, the installation phase marks a critical step in which attackers seek to embed malicious components that ensure continued and stealthy access to the compromised environment [30]. This is commonly accomplished through the deployment of mechanisms such as backdoors, rootkits, or remote access tools (RATs), all of which provide adversaries with persistent control while minimizing the likelihood of detection

[30]. For port operations, these malicious tools may be covertly integrated into key elements of operational technology, including programmable logic controllers (PLCs), automated gate systems, or crane control interfaces. By doing so, attackers can maintain ongoing surveillance, disrupt critical port functions, or manipulate control systems to achieve their broader objectives, all while remaining embedded within the port's digital infrastructure.

To mitigate installation risks, ports must implement advanced EDR solutions capable of identifying unauthorized software and changes to system files. Restricting administrative privileges, enforcing software whitelisting, and conducting routine audits of system activity help prevent the establishment of persistent threats [17, 31]. If installation is identified, systems must be immediately quarantined and analyzed to determine the extent of compromise. Complete removal of unauthorized software and validation through post-incident scans are necessary before restoring affected assets.

5.5.6 System Control

This phase is a critical stage, during which attackers gain the capability to remotely monitor and direct the operations of compromised systems by establishing covert communication channels [32]. These hidden pathways allow malicious actors to transmit instructions, modify or update existing malware, and extract sensitive data without detection. In the port context, this phase can have serious operational and security implications. Attackers may exploit channels to interfere with TOSs, disrupt the coordination of vessel berthing and cargo scheduling, or execute unauthorized commands within automated cargo-handling platforms. Such activities can lead to operational delays, compromise the integrity of port logistics, and expose sensitive commercial or operational information.

Detecting and preventing these activities rely on network traffic analysis and deep packet inspection to uncover irregular outbound connections, even those hidden in encrypted communications. The use of anomaly detection tools helps identify and block suspicious traffic patterns that deviate from normal port operations [33]. If activity is detected, it is essential to sever connections, isolate compromised systems, and reconfigure firewall rules. Subsequent forensic analysis provides insight into the extent of the remote control and aids in refining future preventive measures [34].

5.5.7 Actions on Objectives

During this phase, attackers actively pursue the intended outcomes of their intrusion. These objectives may vary depending on the motive of the threat actor and can include unauthorized data extraction, operational disruption, financial exploitation, or deliberate reputational damage to the targeted entity [5, 13]. Within the port environment, this phase often materializes in the form of ransomware attacks that deny access to essential port platforms, thereby paralyzing cargo coordination and delaying vessel turnaround times. Moreover, adversaries may manipulate digital cargo manifests or container-tracking data, introducing misinformation that undermines the reliability and predictability of supply chain operations. Another significant threat involves the illicit acquisition of sensitive commercial or operational data, which may be exploited for strategic or competitive advantage [1]. These malicious actions can severely compromise the operational resilience of port systems, disrupt trade flows, and erode the confidence of stakeholders across the maritime logistics ecosystem.

Defending against such activities involves implementing real-time monitoring of access attempts, logging system interactions, and restricting access to sensitive databases through encryption and access control mechanisms. Detection of abnormal system behavior—such as unexpected shutdowns, delays in cargo movements, or modifications to billing systems—must trigger immediate investigation. Once a breach is confirmed, ports must act quickly to halt unauthorized activities, restore affected systems, and assess the full impact of the breach [9, 12, 27].

5.5.8 Exfiltration

The exfiltration phase represents the final stage of a cyber-attack, during which adversaries extract compromised data from the internal systems and transmit it to external locations under their control [35]. This process is often conducted through encrypted data streams, covert communication channels, or, in some cases, physical means such as removable storage devices [35]. In the port context, exfiltration poses a significant threat to the confidentiality and integrity of critical information assets. These may include detailed shipping manifests, client and partner records, operational schedules, and sensitive financial documentation. Given the volume and strategic value of the data handled by ports, successful exfiltration can result in severe commercial, legal, and reputational consequences.

To prevent exfiltration, ports should employ data loss prevention technologies, encrypt sensitive information both at rest and in transit, and monitor data flow for anomalies [36]. Network behavior analysis can reveal unauthorized data transmissions, allowing timely intervention [37]. If exfiltration is detected, immediate action should be taken to terminate the transfer, assess the data compromised, and reinforce network security protocols. Post-incident efforts must focus on repairing vulnerabilities, restoring trust with stakeholders, and reviewing lessons learned to strengthen future resilience.

5.6 Selected Publicly Reported Cases of Port Cyber-Attacks: Penetration Techniques, Motivations, and Impacts on Port Services

5.6.1 Insights from 11 Cyber-Attacks on the Port Industry

This section presents a detailed analysis of 11 publicly reported cyber-attacks on ports, exploring the progression of each attack, the penetration methods used, the attackers' motivations, and the resulting effects on port operations and services. The analysis draws from a 2024 academic study [1], with the implications reflecting the author's perspectives. Caution is advised when interpreting this information. These case studies offer valuable insights into the vulnerabilities within port systems and highlight the broader impact of cyber threats on global trade and logistics.

5.6.1.1 Scenario1: Email-Based Malware Infiltration at the Port of Antwerp (2011)

The 2011 cyberattack on the Port of Antwerp serves as a significant example of a targeted, financially motivated intrusion that leveraged cyber means to support illicit activities. A drug cartel exploited the port's digital infrastructure to facilitate the smuggling of narcotics, primarily cocaine and heroin, through a multi-phase operation. By embedding illicit cargo within legitimate shipments and manipulating data related to container allocations and delivery schedules, the attackers circumvented traditional security checks. The Port of Antwerp was specifically targeted due to its high traffic volume and operational complexity, which provided an ideal environment for obscuring illegal activities. The attackers employed a sophisticated malware strategy initiated through spear-phishing emails aimed at port personnel and logistics firms. Once recipients opened the malicious attachments, malware was installed, granting unauthorized access to internal systems. This malware maintained persistent connectivity with external command-and-control servers, enabling the attackers to monitor and manipulate the container management system. The attack progressed in stages: reconnaissance was followed by the initial compromise, which occurred when the phishing emails were opened. The attackers then established system control through persistent malware, manipulated container data to redirect illicit cargo, and, finally, erased traces of unauthorized activity to delay detection. The breach went undetected for nearly two years until internal irregularities triggered an investigation, uncovering the cyberattack. In response, the port implemented a comprehensive cybersecurity overhaul, restoring critical defenses and enhancing monitoring protocols.

Key Lessons

This case highlights key lessons about the vulnerabilities and exposures inherent in port operations. The attackers exploited technological weaknesses within the port's digital infrastructure and human error, such as the failure to detect spear-phishing emails. While the breach was eventually identified, the delay in detection allowed the attackers to divert illicit shipments over an extended period, underscoring the insufficient capabilities of existing detection mechanisms. This breach emphasizes the importance of real-time anomaly detection, regular security audits, and personnel training to prevent similar incidents. Furthermore, the incident demonstrated the critical need for extending cybersecurity policies to cover third-party partners and supply chain collaborators. The prolonged period during which the malware remained undetected illustrates the consequences of insufficient threat monitoring, which allowed the attackers to exploit vulnerabilities for an extended period of time. This case underlines the necessity of adopting comprehensive cybersecurity frameworks that combine technical solutions, organizational resilience, and international collaboration to safeguard critical port infrastructure in an increasingly digitalized environment.

5.6.1.2 Scenario2: Ransomware from Tax Software Hits APM Terminals (2017)

In 2017, A.P. Moller–Maersk was severely impacted by a ransomware attack attributed to the state-sponsored Sandworm group, which exploited a vulnerability in Ukrainian tax preparation software, ME Doc, to deploy the NotPetya ransomware. Although Maersk was not the primary target, the attack had devastating consequences for the company's global supply chain operations. The primary objective behind the attack was political, aimed at destabilizing Ukrainian infrastructure amidst ongoing geopolitical tensions. However, Maersk, which used the ME Doc software in its Ukrainian operations, became an unwitting victim. Once the software was compromised, the NotPetya malware encrypted files and damaged the master boot record of the affected systems, rendering them inoperable. The malware spread quickly across Maersk's global network, exploiting unpatched Windows vulnerabilities and moving laterally due to weak network segmentation, shared credentials, and inadequate system hardening. The attack unfolded in several phases: reconnaissance, initial compromise via the ME Doc update, lateral movement across Maersk's systems, operational disruption, and a prolonged recovery process. As a result, terminal operations were halted or severely delayed, forcing Maersk to revert to manual procedures. The company faced direct financial losses between USD 250 and 300 million, which were related to system restoration, cargo rerouting, and business continuity measures. The attack demonstrated the vulnerability of global, digitized port operations to cascading failures, with far-reaching consequences across many countries due to Maersk's interconnected network.

Key Lessons

The Maersk ransomware attack highlights several critical lessons about the vulnerabilities and exposure of port operations to cyber threats. The attackers exploited vulnerabilities in third-party software, particularly ME Doc, which was widely used within Maersk's Ukrainian subsidiary. This incident underscores the risks of inadequate oversight of third-party software in critical supply chain functions, which can lead to significant exposure. The attack was initially detected during the operational disruption phase, when Maersk's digital systems failed and manual procedures were implemented. By the time the threat was detected, the malware had already caused widespread operational paralysis, making it too late to minimize the immediate impacts. This delay in detection illustrates the importance of timely threat monitoring and the ability to swiftly identify system anomalies. Furthermore, the attack highlighted the need for robust backup strategies and incident response planning to recover from significant disruptions. Maersk's delayed recovery, which spanned several months, exposed weaknesses in its backup systems and its preparedness for ransomware incidents. The case also emphasizes the need for comprehensive cybersecurity measures that encompass internal resilience, such as system hardening and patch management, as well as external dependencies, like third-party software and supply chain partners.

5.6.1.3 Scenario3: Ransomware Disrupts Port of San Diego (2018)

In 2018, the Port of San Diego experienced a ransomware attack that exposed critical vulnerabilities in its public-facing digital infrastructure. The incident was executed using the SamSam ransomware, which targeted systems supporting services such as parking permit applications. These systems likely harbored known but unpatched vulnerabilities, enabling the attacker to infiltrate the network. Once inside, the malware encrypted essential files and attempted to establish a command-and-control mechanism to maintain access. The primary motive appeared to be financial extortion, with the encrypted data held hostage pending ransom payment. Although there may have been a secondary intent to disrupt port operations, the prompt detection and rapid intervention by the port's cybersecurity team significantly limited the scope of the damage. The attack followed a recognizable progression, beginning with the exploitation of exposed systems, the installation of the ransomware, and the execution of its objectives through data encryption. The final stage, containment, was swiftly implemented when staff identified abnormal system behavior, isolated affected devices, and shut down certain services to prevent further propagation. As a result, while some non-critical services—such as waste reporting and permit processing—experienced temporary disruption, the port's core functions, including cargo handling and logistical coordination, remained unaffected.

Key Lessons

This incident highlights the significant cybersecurity risks posed by under-secured public access points within port systems. The attack exploited vulnerable digital entryways, demonstrating how exposure through routine public services can enable broader network compromise. The relatively early detection of the intrusion, during the containment phase, proved instrumental in minimizing damage. Had the ransomware remained undetected for longer, the outcome could have included deeper penetration into operational systems and more severe financial or logistical consequences. The rapid response of the port's staff—shutting down computers, isolating systems, and coordinating incident management—was critical in containing the threat. This case underscores the importance of continuous vulnerability assessments, especially for public-facing platforms, and the need for routine cybersecurity audits and patch management protocols. Furthermore, it highlights the necessity of having a well-defined and thoroughly rehearsed incident response plan, which enabled the port to act decisively and prevent escalation. An equally important lesson involves the role of layered defense strategies, which can reduce the likelihood of successful exploitation and facilitate quicker detection. Overall, the Port of San Diego's experience serves as a clear reminder of how even non-targeted attacks can severely challenge port systems if basic cybersecurity hygiene and monitoring are not rigorously upheld.

5.6.1.4 Scenario 4: COSCO Ransomware Incident Affects Long Beach Port (2018)

In July 2018, the Port of Long Beach encountered a ransomware incident that targeted the terminal networks of COSCO, one of its major shipping operators. While the broader port infrastructure remained largely unaffected, the attack severely disrupted COSCO's local communication and booking systems. The ransomware, likely introduced via phishing or malicious attachments, encrypted critical files, paralyzing digital operations and severely limiting COSCO's ability to manage its services. Though financial gain was the apparent motivation, the strategic significance of targeting a key terminal within one of the United States' busiest ports raises the possibility of broader geopolitical or economic aims. The attackers likely conducted preliminary reconnaissance before exploiting vulnerabilities in COSCO's internal systems to deploy the malware. As the ransomware disabled essential systems, COSCO swiftly transitioned to manual operations—such as telephone-based communication and paper documentation—to mitigate service interruptions and preserve critical workflows. Despite avoiding a total shutdown, the incident exposed substantial gaps in COSCO's cybersecurity defenses, particularly in system segmentation and contingency preparedness.

Key Lessons

This case underscores the high level of exposure ports face through third-party vulnerabilities, as the breach specifically affected COSCO's networks rather than the port's central infrastructure. The intrusion capitalized on insufficient email defenses and systemic weaknesses in local terminals, reflecting how even one operator's lapse can compromise broader operational continuity. Substantial system disruption had already occurred before the intrusion was detected, highlighting a delay in identifying and mitigating the threat during the early attack phases, particularly during delivery and exploitation. COSCO's response involved isolating the compromised systems and reverting to manual processes to sustain core operations. Although this response helped reduce the scope of the disruption, it highlighted the need for more robust detection capabilities and faster incident response mechanisms. No evidence was found of external collaboration during containment or recovery, suggesting internal coordination alone was employed. Moving forward, enhanced network segmentation, proactive threat monitoring, and interorganizational response protocols are vital for strengthening cyber resilience in port environments. The incident also points to the importance of integrating cybersecurity awareness training for personnel and developing business continuity plans capable of absorbing digital shocks without major service interruptions.

5.6.1.5 Scenario5: DDoS Attack via Infected PC at Port of Vancouver (2017–2018)

In 2017 and 2018, the Port of Vancouver, one of North America's busiest trade gateways, experienced two separate cyber incidents that revealed critical vulnerabilities in its cybersecurity infrastructure. The first incident in 2017 involved a DDoS attack launched via malware embedded in a personal device connected to the port's Wi-Fi during a live-streamed meeting. The attacker aimed to disrupt administrative operations, rather than penetrate critical port systems. This incident exploited the port's network exposure and the lack of restrictions on personal device access, resulting in temporary service interference but no direct damage to core operations. The second attack in October 2018 employed brute-force techniques to guess login credentials and encryption keys, followed by the deployment of malware within the port's internal network. Unlike the first, this intrusion appeared to pursue more severe objectives, including data theft and potential system hijacking. Despite the aggressive method, the port's timely detection and containment of the breach prevented the attacker from compromising critical systems or exfiltrating significant data. While both incidents were mitigated before they could cause widespread disruption, they exposed weak points in password management, network access control, and endpoint security, emphasizing the growing risks faced by port authorities because of both opportunistic and targeted cyber threats.

Key Lessons

These incidents demonstrate that the Port of Vancouver's exposure to cyber threats stemmed from both internal and external vectors. In the 2017 DDoS case, the use of an infected personal device on an unsecured network introduced a clear vulnerability, showcasing how poorly governed device access can create entry points for malware. The 2018 brute-force attack revealed weaknesses in credential security, suggesting a lack of sufficient access control measures such as strong password policies or multi-factor authentication. In both cases, the timing of the detection played a pivotal role in limiting the consequences. The

DDoS attack was promptly identified due to its immediate disruption of the Wi-Fi network, while the brute-force attempt was halted before the attacker could fully leverage the access gained, indicating that while monitoring systems were reactive, their efficiency minimized long-term impact. Recovery strategies primarily involved swift network isolation and system restoration, highlighting the importance of having predefined incident response protocols. Although there was no mention of collaboration with external cybersecurity agencies, the incidents underscore the value of proactive partnerships in bolstering defenses. Key strategies, moving forward, should include improved network segmentation, stricter controls over personal device connectivity, and enhanced credential security practices. Collectively, these events emphasize the need for ports to continuously assess and adapt their cybersecurity posture in response to evolving threats.

5.6.1.6 Ransomware via Local Breach at Port of Marseille (2020)

In March 2020, the Port of Marseille experienced a cyber-attack that highlights the significant risks posed by vulnerabilities within interconnected digital infrastructures. The incident was executed using Mespinoza/Pysa ransomware, which encrypted critical operational systems and temporarily disrupted port functions. Although the primary motive was financial extortion, the broader objective appeared to include operational disruption across the networked environment, exploiting the connection between the port and the AMPM network. Evidence suggests the attackers initially targeted the AMPM network and leveraged this entry point to infiltrate the port's systems, illustrating how vulnerabilities in affiliated or third-party organizations can expose critical infrastructure. The attack likely followed the typical phases of a sophisticated ransomware operation, beginning with reconnaissance to identify weaknesses, followed by the weaponization and delivery of ransomware through the shared network. Once inside, the malware exploited these weaknesses, was installed on key systems, and maintained command and control so as to facilitate the encryption of operational platforms. While no data exfiltration was confirmed, the attack remained undetected for an extended period, enabling prolonged disruption. However, the Port of Marseille activated its emergency response protocols and restored its systems in a timely manner, limiting the overall impact and duration of the incident.

Key Lessons

The Port of Marseille case underscores how exposure to external networks, particularly through poorly secured connections such as those with the AMPM organization, can significantly increase the vulnerability of port systems. In this incident, the attackers exploited the port's interconnected infrastructure, suggesting inadequate segmentation and insufficient access control protocols. The ransomware was not detected during the early stages, particularly reconnaissance and delivery, allowing the attack to progress through multiple phases without interruption. As a result, critical systems were encrypted, leading to temporary service disruptions. Although the response was ultimately effective in restoring services and minimizing long-term operational consequences, the delayed detection reduced the port's ability to prevent initial system compromise. The incident demonstrates the importance of proactive detection mechanisms and continuous monitoring to identify threats in earlier stages of the cyber-attack lifecycle. Furthermore, it illustrates the critical need for robust internal response procedures and highlights how swift action can limit damage even after a system has been compromised. While there is no evidence of external collaboration beyond the network origin point, the case draws attention to the importance of having coordinated cybersecurity strategies with external partners. Network segmentation, endpoint monitoring, and the vetting of third-party digital interfaces are necessary components of a comprehensive port cybersecurity framework. This case also reinforces the need for ports to treat connected systems as part of their extended attack surface, requiring shared governance and joint preparedness plans to protect operational integrity.

5.6.1.7 Scenario7: Software Flaw Exploited at Port of Houston (2021)

In 2021, the Port of Houston experienced a targeted cyber-attack that exploited a known vulnerability (CVE-2021-40539) in the widely used ManageEngine password management software. This breach provided unauthorized access to critical infrastructure through the port's web server, enabling the attackers to implant malicious code with the objective of extracting sensitive information, particularly login credentials. Evidence suggests that the perpetrators may have been state-sponsored, aiming to test national cybersecurity resilience or engage in espionage activities. The attack unfolded in multiple stages, including reconnaissance, exploitation, installation of malicious payloads, and attempted data exfiltration. Despite the advanced nature of the intrusion, the port's cybersecurity team detected and isolated the breach in a timely manner, containing its impact before major operational systems were compromised. Although the intrusion caused limited disruption to digital services, core port operations, such as cargo handling, remained unaffected due to the swift containment measures.

Key Lessons

This incident reveals critical cybersecurity lessons for ports and other critical infrastructure operators. The attackers gained entry through exposure in a public-facing software platform, emphasizing the need for robust security oversight of third-party systems. The exploitation of a known software flaw reflects a vulnerability that could have been mitigated through routine patch management and vulnerability scanning. Detection occurred relatively early in the attack cycle, preventing deeper infiltration and reducing potential damage. The rapid response by port authorities—particularly the isolation of the compromised server—was essential to limiting the operational impact and maintaining system integrity. This case underscores the necessity of proactive defense mechanisms, including continuous monitoring, timely software updates, and thorough risk assessments. Moreover, the potential for state-sponsored attacks highlights the increasing geopolitical dimensions of cyber threats, suggesting that ports ought to consider broader threat intelligence in their cybersecurity strategies.

5.6.1.8 Scenario8: Ransomware via Unsecured System at Port of Lisbon (2022)

In December 2022, the Port of Lisbon experienced a ransomware attack attributed to the LockBit hacker group, which exploited weaknesses within its internal network infrastructure. The attack involved unauthorized access through likely unsecured systems, followed by the encryption of critical data and the exfiltration of sensitive files, including financial records, contracts, and personal information. The attackers demanded a ransom of USD 1.5 million and threatened to publicly release the stolen data, reinforcing their financially motivated objective. Although the incident did not directly impact vessel traffic or cargo handling, internal port operations were disrupted, leading to service delays. The cyber-attack progressed through multiple phases, beginning with reconnaissance to identify vulnerabilities, followed by exploitation to penetrate the system, installation of ransomware, and subsequent data exfiltration and extortion. The response involved the activation of internal security protocols and collaboration with relevant authorities, enabling the port to restore most critical systems within one week and resume standard operations.

Key Lessons

This case underscores the critical vulnerabilities and exposure faced by port authorities when internal systems lack sufficient cybersecurity defenses. The attackers successfully infiltrated the network due to unaddressed system weaknesses, demonstrating the tangible risks posed by insufficient security controls and limited system monitoring. Although the attack did not halt core logistical functions, the encryption of internal data delayed services and revealed the broader impact of cyber threats on port operations. The incident was likely detected during or after the installation phase, indicating that the attack had already reached an advanced stage before effective containment could begin, thus limiting opportunities for early mitigation. Recovery efforts were swift, emphasizing the importance of having a well-established incident response plan and the capacity to work closely with external partners, such as cybersecurity authorities, to facilitate technical recovery and contain threats effectively. Additionally, the case illustrates the dual threat of data theft and service disruption inherent in ransomware attacks, highlighting the need for proactive threat detection, system hardening, data backup strategies, and coordinated communication protocols. This incident serves as a reminder that even non-disruptive attacks, in operational terms, can carry significant reputational and security consequences, underscoring the necessity for ports to continuously assess and upgrade their cybersecurity infrastructure.

5.6.1.9 Scenario9: DDoS Attack on Canadian Ports: Halifax, Montreal, Quebec (2023)

In April 2023, the Ports of Montreal, Quebec, and Halifax—three essential maritime gateways in Canada—were simultaneously targeted by a DDoS cyber-attack attributed to the Russian-affiliated group NoName057(16). The coordinated attack overwhelmed the ports' external communication systems, including websites and online services, rendering them temporarily inaccessible. Despite these disruptions, the internal operational infrastructure remained intact, and cargo-handling processes continued without significant delays. The attackers appeared to be motivated by ideological or political agendas, potentially in response to geopolitical tensions, rather than by financial incentives or the intent to exfiltrate data. The penetration technique involved the use of a botnet to flood the ports' digital interfaces with abnormal traffic volumes. Although malware was not deployed and no sensitive data was compromised, the volume-based nature of the attack successfully disabled public-facing systems. The incident unfolded through typical DDoS phases: initial reconnaissance to identify exposure points, weaponization through botnet deployment, execution of the traffic flood, and exploitation resulting in external service outages. The attack was eventually mitigated when the ports' cybersecurity teams intervened by shutting down affected networks and restoring communication channels. Authorities advised stakeholders to use telephones and other backup communication methods, allowing port operations to proceed largely unaffected.

Key Lessons

This case highlights several key cybersecurity insights relevant to maritime infrastructure. The attack exploited exposure in public-facing systems—specifically, websites and external communications—demonstrating that ports remain susceptible to non-invasive but disruptive cyber tactics. The threat was not detected at an early stage; abnormal traffic was identified only after external services had already failed, indicating a need for improved real-time traffic monitoring and early-warning systems. Although the operational core of each port was insulated from the attack's effects, the impact on communication systems caused confusion and delays for stakeholders. Recovery was made possible through the rapid coordination of internal IT teams, who isolated affected systems and shifted users to alternative communication channels. This underscores the importance of having contingency communication plans and predefined incident response protocols. The case also suggests the benefits of collaboration with national cybersecurity authorities, although direct mention of external agency involvement was absent. Looking ahead, ports must strengthen their cyber resilience through proactive DDoS mitigation tools, scalable network infrastructure capable of absorbing traffic surges, and continuous CTI sharing. Even attacks that do not involve data breaches or malware can cause reputational damage and operational inefficiencies, reinforcing the necessity of a holistic cybersecurity posture.

5.6.1.10 Scenario10: Ransomware Disrupts Port of Nagoya and Supply Chain (2023)

In 2023, the Port of Nagoya—Japan's largest and most vital maritime gateway for automobile exports—experienced a disruptive ransomware attack attributed to the LockBit 3.0 cybercriminal group. The attackers deployed sophisticated ransomware to encrypt key port systems, including the Nagoya-Port-Unified-Terminal System and automated check-in functions, thereby halting container-handling operations. The financial motivation of the attackers was evident in the ransom demand made in exchange for restoring access to the encrypted systems. This attack significantly affected operational continuity, particularly impacting Toyota's packaging plant, which was forced to suspend production due to delays in receiving essential auto parts. LockBit 3.0, a group known for financially driven attacks, likely infiltrated the port's network through phishing emails or exploitation of system vulnerabilities. Once inside, they weaponized and deployed ransomware to paralyze the port's critical logistics infrastructure. The attack unfolded in multiple phases—beginning with reconnaissance to identify weaknesses, followed by weaponization and delivery of the ransomware, the exploitation of control over vital systems, and, finally, the ransom demand. Although specific resolution details were not disclosed, port authorities reportedly relied on system backups and cybersecurity specialists to restore functionality and mitigate further damage.

Key Lessons

This incident reveals critical vulnerabilities and exposure points within the Port of Nagoya's digital infrastructure, particularly its susceptibility to email-based intrusions and its unpatched system weaknesses. The attackers' ability to paralyze automated operations suggests a lack of adequate segmentation between operational technology and information technology systems, as well as insufficient protective monitoring. The cyber-attack was likely detected too late—during the exploitation phase—when critical functions were already compromised. The delay in detection hindered early mitigation efforts, prolonging downtime and exacerbating operational and supply chain impacts. The port's response primarily involved deploying emergency protocols, restoring systems from backups, and enlisting external cybersecurity support, underscoring the importance of proactive incident response planning and the need for improved collaboration with security vendors and government agencies. Despite these efforts, the event exposed significant gaps in cyber readiness and resilience, particularly with regard to safeguarding ports that serve as critical logistics nodes for major manufacturers.

Furthermore, this case highlights the importance of training personnel to identify and report suspicious communications, enhancing email filtering, and implementing multi-layered defenses. Strengthening real-time threat detection and response systems would allow future threats to be intercepted earlier in the attack chain, reducing the risk of full system compromise. Strategic lessons from this event include the importance of routine system audits, updated security patches, and redundant operational protocols that ensure core port functions can continue even under cyber duress. The attack on the Port of Nagoya serves as a cautionary example of how ransomware can not only threaten port operations but also generate wider economic consequences through supply chain disruption.

5.6.1.11 Scenario11: Data Breach at DP World Terminals, Australia (2023)

In November 2023, DP World Australia, a major logistics provider responsible for handling approximately 40% of the nation's containerized freight, experienced a significant cyber incident that resulted in a targeted data breach. The breach disrupted operations across its terminals in Melbourne, Sydney, Brisbane, and Fremantle and was traced to an incident of unauthorized access through the exploitation of the CitrixBleed vulnerability—a flaw that had remained unpatched despite prior advisories. Although no ransomware was deployed and no ransom was demanded, attackers successfully infiltrated the corporate network and exfiltrated personal data belonging to current and former employees, including contact details and copies of driver's licenses. The attack unfolded across several stages of the cyber-attack lifecycle, beginning with reconnaissance and culminating in data exfiltration. The breach did not affect customer data but caused significant operational disruption following DP World's decision to disconnect its network as a containment measure. This action led to the temporary suspension of port operations and created a backlog exceeding 30,000 containers. Partial operations resumed within three days, and by November 20, the backlog had been cleared. Despite the swift recovery, the incident exposed critical weaknesses in the company's vulnerability management protocols and raised serious concerns about the protection of employee data.

Key Lessons

This incident reveals how unpatched software vulnerabilities significantly increase a port's exposure to cyber threats. The attackers exploited a known vulnerability that had been left unresolved for over a month, demonstrating the consequences of inadequate patch management and insufficient oversight of IT infrastructure. The breach reached the exploitation and exfiltration phases before being detected, indicating that the response occurred relatively late in the cyber-attack lifecycle, after damage had already been inflicted. DP World's immediate response—disconnecting its network—was effective in containing the breach but came at the cost of widespread operational delays. The swift recovery, facilitated by internal coordination and rapid technical intervention, underscores the importance of well-established incident response protocols. Although no evidence of external collaboration emerged, the case highlights the need for enhanced information sharing and threat intelligence within the broader port community. Additionally, the event emphasizes the necessity of continuous security assessments, proactive patching, and employee data protection measures. Strengthening these areas will help reduce both operational risks and the potential for personal harm resulting from identity theft or fraud following a data breach.

5.6.2 Key Lessons Learned from 11 Cyber-Attacks in the Port Industry

Building on the detailed review of 11 cyber-attacks in Section A, Figure 5.1 distills key patterns and recurring issues observed across these incidents. It highlights seven core lessons related to the progression, methods, and consequences of each case—serving as a practical reference and pointing to strategic areas where attention and improvement are most needed to strengthen cyber resilience.

1 **Vulnerabilities in Third-Party Systems, Supply Chains, and Public Interfaces**

One of the most consistent findings across major port cybersecurity incidents is the role of external systems and service providers in introducing vulnerabilities. Attacks on Maersk/APM Terminals, COSCO's operations at Long Beach, and the Port of Marseille demonstrate how malware can infiltrate port networks through compromised third-party software or logistics platforms. Similarly, incidents at Canadian ports and the Port of San Diego underscore how threats targeting public-facing digital portals—like websites or user access points—can disrupt services even when core infrastructure remains intact.

These cases reveal that ports cannot isolate their cybersecurity posture from that of their partners. In today's interconnected maritime environment, digital integration among supply chain actors has outpaced the establishment of shared security baselines. As such, ports must not only vet digital partners rigorously during onboarding but also implement continuous monitoring mechanisms. Formal contractual requirements should be established to enforce minimum cybersecurity standards, and joint responsibility frameworks must govern the security of interconnected systems.

Figure 5.1 Recurring Vulnerabilities and Strategic Lessons from Major Port Cyber Incidents.

Public-facing platforms, in particular, require robust defenses—such as web application firewalls, DDoS mitigation, and scalable cloud protections—to prevent entry points for attacks. Equally important is maintaining reliable channels of communication with stakeholders during cyber events in order to preserve trust and coordinate response efforts.

2 **Gaps in Detection and Monitoring Capabilities**

Several high-profile breaches—such as those at the ports of Antwerp, Marseille, and Lisbon and within Maersk's operations—were exacerbated by delays in identifying intrusions. In these cases, attackers remained undetected for extended periods, granting them time to move laterally within networks and escalate damage. The failure to notice anomalies early indicates a shortfall in active monitoring and threat detection protocols.

The longer a threat actor remains undetected, the more severe the operational, financial, and reputational fallout. This underscores the need for ports to invest in real-time detection systems that can continuously scan for suspicious activities across both information and operational technology environments. Artificial intelligence and machine learning tools display significant promise at sifting through log data and generating early alerts, often spotting patterns that evade traditional rule-based systems. However, technology alone is insufficient. Ports must regularly conduct threat-hunting operations and red-team exercises to identify concealed vulnerabilities and evaluate the responsiveness of their systems under simulated conditions.

3 **Deficiencies in Incident Preparedness, Organizational Culture, and Cyber Governance**

When cyber incidents struck ports like San Diego and Vancouver, the damage was mitigated by their structured internal response and clear chains of command. In contrast, other ports—where governance structures were weak or cybersecurity had not been integrated into the broader organizational culture—struggled to contain the impact. These contrasts highlight the crucial role of organizational readiness and leadership commitment in effective incident response.

Cybersecurity readiness involves more than having a plan on paper; it requires all stakeholders to know their roles, understand communication protocols, and have undergone scenario-based training. Executive leadership must play a direct role in funding, overseeing, and embedding cybersecurity within enterprise risk management frameworks. Cross-departmental collaboration is also essential, ensuring that legal, human resources, operations, and IT teams work in unison during both planning and crisis phases. Developing a cyber-aware culture within the port helps prevent errors, fosters vigilance, and enhances institutional resilience when incidents occur.

4 **Weak Network Architectures and Lack of Segmentation Between Systems**

Incidents at the ports of Nagoya, Lisbon, and Marseille revealed how quickly malware can spread when IT and operational technology systems are poorly segmented. In these cases, attackers who gained access to a single entry point were able to traverse systems freely, disrupting both administrative functions and physical operations. The absence of network segmentation significantly heightened the scale of the impact.

This reinforces the importance of adopting modern security frameworks that limit internal movement and enforce strict access controls. Zero-trust architecture, for instance, assumes that threats may already be inside the network and, therefore, restricts access based on identity, context, and continuous verification. Ports should also establish strong separation between IT and OT environments, placing monitoring points at their intersections to detect and prevent unauthorized bridging. Micro-segmentation within terminals and other complex zones can further minimize the risk of cascading failures by isolating critical systems from less secure components.

5 **Insecure Endpoints and Poor Access Control Mechanisms**

The cyber-attacks at Vancouver and Antwerp were facilitated by compromised credentials and the exploitation of poorly secured devices. In both cases, the attackers gained elevated privileges, allowing them to manipulate sensitive systems. These events expose the dangers of insufficient endpoint security and lax authentication policies.

Ports must adopt multi-factor authentication across all accounts, especially those with administrative access or remote capabilities. Equally important is the enforcement of endpoint security policies that restrict the use of unauthorized personal devices, ensure compliance with encryption and antivirus standards, and mandate regular patching. Incorporating user behavior analytics can also provide a second layer of defense by identifying suspicious activity, such as unusual login times or accessing of atypical resources, which may indicate credential compromise or insider threats.

6 **Fragile Backup Systems and Ineffective Recovery Processes**
The ransomware attacks that crippled Maersk, Nagoya, and Lisbon revealed systemic weaknesses in backup integrity and recovery readiness. In these incidents, either the backups were also compromised or the restoration processes proved to be too slow and fragmented to minimize downtime. This exposes a major operational risk, especially in high-throughput environments where every hour of disruption carries significant economic costs.

To prepare for such scenarios, ports must implement backup solutions that are both immutable and stored offline, making them resistant to encryption or deletion by ransomware. Regular drills are necessary to test the viability of these backups and identify gaps in the restoration process. Moreover, cyber recovery must be integrated into broader business continuity planning so that technical actions align with operational priorities during a crisis. The goal is to return to normalcy as swiftly and securely as possible, without reintroducing vulnerabilities.

7 **The Evolving Threat Landscape and the Need for Intelligence-Driven Defense**
The incidents at the Ports of Houston and Nagoya involved advanced threat actors, including those suspected of having state affiliations. These cases reflect an increasingly complex threat environment where traditional defenses may fall short against well-resourced adversaries capable of executing highly targeted and prolonged campaigns.

To address these evolving threats, ports must adopt an intelligence-driven approach to cybersecurity. This includes subscribing to real-time cyber threat intelligence (CTI) services that provide early warning of emerging tactics, techniques, and procedures. Participation in maritime cybersecurity coalitions and national information-sharing platforms is also critical, enabling ports to benefit from collective insights and coordinated response strategies. The integration of AI tools can further enhance situational awareness, enabling predictive modeling of potential attack vectors and faster threat triage. Staying ahead of the threat curve requires ports to move from reactive defense to anticipatory and adaptive security postures.

References

[1] C. Senarak, "Port Cyberattacks from 2011 to 2023: A Literature Review and Discussion of Selected Cases," *Maritime Economics & Logistics*, vol. 26, no. 1, pp. 105–130, 2024.

[2] S. Margaronis, "Port of Los Angeles Hit by 60 Million Monthly Cyber Attacks in 2023," *American Journal of Transportation*, 2024. [Online]. Available: www.ajot.com/insights/full/ai-port-of-los-angeles-hit-by-60-million-monthly-cyber-attacks-in-2023.

[3] UNCTAD, "Review of Maritime Transport 2024," 2024. [Online]. Available: https://unctad.org/publication/review-maritime-transport-2024.

[4] C. Hill, "What Are Untargeted and Targeted Attacks?," 2024. [Online]. Available: www.chillcybersecurity.co.uk/what-are-untargeted-and-targeted-attacks/#:~:text=The%20content%20of%20untargeted%20attacks,in%20achieving%20the%20attacker's%20goals..

[5] C. Senarak, "Port Cybersecurity and Threat: A Structural Model for Prevention and Policy Development," *The Asian Journal of Shipping and Logistics*, vol. 37, no. 1, pp. 20–36, 2021.

[6] A. J. Burns, M. E. Johnson and D. D. Caputo., "Spear Phishing in a Barrel: Insights from a Targeted Phishing Campaign," *Journal of Organizational Computing and Electronic Commerce*, vol. 29, no. 1, p. 24–39, 2019.

[7] N. Hoque, D. K. Bhattacharyya and J. K. Kalita, "Botnet in DDoS Attacks: Trends and Challenges," *IEEE Communications Surveys & Tutorials*, vol. 17, no. 4, pp. 2242–2270, 2015.

[8] J. Ferdous, R. Islam, A. Mahboubi and M. Z. Islam, "A Review of State-of-the-Art Malware Attack Trends and Defense Mechanisms," *IEEE Access*, vol. 11, pp. 121118–121141, 2023.

[9] F. Andritsos, "Port Security & Access Control: A Systemic Approach," in The Fourth International Conference on Information, Intelligence, Systems and Applications, Greece, 2013.

[10] N. Mhaskar, M. Alabbad and R. Khedri, "A Formal Approach to Network Segmentation," *Computers & Security*, vol. 103, 102162, 2021.

[11] H. Kaur, D. S. SL, T. Paul, R. K. Thakur, K. V. K. Reddy, J. Mahato and K. Naveen, "Evolution of Endpoint Detection and Response (EDR) in Cyber Security: A Comprehensive Review," in International Conference on Recent Advances in Waste Minimization & Utilization-2024 (RAWMU- 2024), 2024.

[12] Y. Diogenes and E. Ozkaya, *Cybersecurity – Attack and Defense Strategies: Infrastructure Security with Red Team and Blue Team Tactics*, Packt Publishing, 2018.

[13] M. Lehto, "Cyber-Attacks Against Critical Infrastructure," in *Cyber Security*, Springer, 2022, pp. 3–42.

[14] S. Symes, E. Blanco-Davis, T. Graham, J. Wang and E. Shaw, "Cyberattacks on the Maritime Sector: A Literature Review," *Journal of Marine Science and Application*, vol. 23, pp. 689–706, 2024.

[15] C. Senarak, "Cybersecurity Knowledge and Skills for Port Facility Security Officers of International Seaports: Perspectives of IT and Security Personnel," *The Asian Journal of Shipping and Logistics*, vol. 37, no. 4, pp. 345–360, 2021.

[16] A. Oruc, "Claims of State-Sponsored Cyberattack in the Maritime Industry," in International Naval Engineering Conference (INEC), 2020.

[17] M. Clavijo Mesa, C. Patino-Rodriguez and F. Guevara Carazas, "Cybersecurity at Sea: A Literature Review of Cyber-Attack Impacts and Defenses in Maritime Supply Chains," *Information*, vol. 15, no. 11, p. 710, 2024.

[18] T. Nazir, "Terrorist Threats to Maritime Navigation and Ports: Risk Assessment and Prevention Strategy," 2024. [Online]. Available: www.imctc.org/en/eLibrary/TerrorismIssues/Documents/Terrorism%20Issues%20-%20Is%208%20-En.pdf.

[19] M. d. Vivo, E. Carrasco, G. Isern and G. O. d. Vivo, "A Review of Port Scanning Techniques," *ACM SIGCOMM Computer Communication Review*, vol. 29, no. 2, pp. 41–48, 1999.

[20] E. Bou-Harb, M. Debbabi and C. Assi, "Cyber Scanning: A Comprehensive Survey," *IEEE Communications Surveys & Tutorials*, vol. 16, no. 3, pp. 1496–1519, 2014.

[21] R. Banu, T. Jyothi, M. Amulya, K. Anju, A. Raju and S. N. Kashyap, "MONOSEK – A Network Packet Processing System for Analysis & Detection of TCP Xmas attack using Pattern Analysis," in International Conference on Intelligent Computing and Control Systems (ICCS), Madurai, India, 2019.

[22] R. Ensafi, J. C. Park, D. Kapur and J. R. Crandall, "Idle Port Scanning and Non-interference Analysis of Network Protocol Stacks Using Model Checking," in 19th USENIX Security Symposium, Washington, DC, USA, 2010.

[23] H. P. Sanghvi and M. S. Dahiya, "Cyber Reconnaissance: An Alarm before Cyber Attack," *International Journal of Computer Applications*, vol. 63, no. 6, pp. 36–38, 2013.

[24] A. Javadpour, F. Ja'fari, T. Taleb, M. Shojafar and C. Benzaïd, "A Comprehensive Survey on Cyber Deception Techniques to Improve Honeypot Performance," *Computers & Security*, vol. 140, 103792, 2024.

[25] M. Lehto, "APT Cyber-Attack Modelling: Building a General Model," in 17th International Conference on Cyber Warfare and Security, 2022.

[26] S. Shah and B. M. Mehtre, "An Overview of Vulnerability Assessment and Penetration Testing Techniques," *Journal of Computer Virology and Hacking Techniques*, vol. 11, p. 27–49, 2015.

[27] D. Hodges and S. Creese, "Understanding Cyber-Attacks," in *Cyber Warfare*, Routledge, 2015, pp. 1–28.

[28] G. R. Galloway, "Application Whitelisting as a Malicious Code Protection Control," Capitol Technology University, Laurel, Maryland, 2020.

[29] Ö. Aslan, S. S. Aktuğ, M. Ozkan-Okay, A. A. Yilmaz and E. Akin, "A Comprehensive Review of Cyber Security Vulnerabilities, Threats, Attacks, and Solutions," *Electronics*, vol. 12, no. 6, p. 1333, 2023.

[30] P. N. Bahrami, A. Dehghantanha, T. Dargahi, R. M. Parizi, K.-K. R. Choo and H. H. S. Javadi, "Cyber Kill Chain-Based Taxonomy of Advanced Persistent Threat Actors: Analogy of Tactics, Techniques, and Procedures," *Journal of Information Processing Systems*, vol. 15, no. 4, pp. 865–889, 2019.

[31] L. Collins, "Assessments and Audits," in *Computer and Information Security Handbook* (Fourth Edition), Elsevier, 2024, pp. 1283–1290.

[32] J. Gardiner, M. Cova and S. Nagaraja, "Command & Control: Understanding, Denying and Detecting – A Review of Malware C2 Techniques, Detection and Defences," University of Birmingham, Birmingham, England, 2014.

[33] M. Bhuyan, D. Bhattacharyya and J. Kalita, "Network Traffic Anomaly Detection Techniques and Systems," in *Network Traffic Anomaly Detection and Prevention*, Springer, 2017, pp. 115–169.

[34] K. Kent, S. Chevalier, T. Grance and H. Dang, "Guide to Integrating Forensic Techniques into Incident Response," 2006. [Online]. Available: https://nvlpubs.nist.gov/nistpubs/Legacy/SP/nistspecialpublication800-86.pdf.

[35] F. Ullah, M. Edwards, R. Ramdhany, R. Chitchyan, M. A. Babar and A. Rashid, "Data Exfiltration: A Review of External Attack Vectors and Countermeasures," *Journal of Network and Computer Applications*, vol. 101, pp. 18–54, 2018.

[36] H. AlKilani, M. Nasereddin, A. Hadi and S. Tedmori, "Data Exfiltration Techniques and Data Loss Prevention System," in International Arab Conference on Information Technology (ACIT), Al Ain, United Arab Emirates, 2019.

[37] S. Fayssal, S. Hariri and Y. Al-Nashif, "Anomaly-Based Behavior Analysis of Wireless Network Security," in Fourth Annual International Conference on Mobile and Ubiquitous Systems: Networking & Services, Philadelphia, PA, USA, 2007.

6 Port Cybersecurity and Cyber Resilience

6.1 Definitions and Roles of Cybersecurity in PIS Protection

In port environments, cybersecurity refers to safeguarding digital assets—particularly the port information system (PIS)—from threats that may disrupt safety, operations, or service continuity [1]. Its core function is to protect the CIA of port data and systems. This involves blocking unauthorized access (confidentiality), ensuring data reliability (integrity), and maintaining system uptime (availability). Equally crucial is ensuring that port systems remain operational during and after cyber incidents. This resilience requires capabilities to detect threats early, respond quickly to limit damage, and restore systems without major delays [2].

Achieving both CIA protection and resilience calls for integrated security measures. For instance, encryption secures data at rest and in transit, while multi-factor authentication restricts access. Network segmentation limits lateral movement in the event of a breach, and intrusion prevention systems help block attacks like malware or DDoS [1]. Resilience is further supported by intrusion detection tools and event monitoring platforms that identify anomalies and trigger timely responses [2]. These strategies are aligned with international standards, such as the IMO's MSC-FAL.1/Circ.3, ISO/IEC 27001, and the NIST Cybersecurity Framework.

As ports increasingly depend on the PIS and adopt advanced technologies like IoT and AI, the role of cybersecurity—especially through legal and regulatory frameworks—has become critical [3]. While digital innovation enhances efficiency, it also increases system complexity and expands the attack surface [4]. Regulations not only enforce minimum cybersecurity standards but also promote broader risk management. Their implementation varies globally. European ports must meet NIS2 Directive requirements, which include strict reporting and governance measures [5]. In North America, CISA guidelines and public–private collaboration shape port cybersecurity [6]. Asian ports, such as those in Singapore and Japan, embed security within national digitalization agendas. In contrast, many African ports remain in the early stages, relying on international support to build cybersecurity capacity. These

DOI: 10.4324/9781003559320-6

regional approaches reflect a shared understanding of cybersecurity as central to modern port governance.

6.2 Concepts of the CIA Model in Port Cybersecurity

The CIA model serves as a foundational framework for securing digital environments in modern ports. As port operations increasingly rely on interconnected information systems, the need to safeguard against unauthorized access, data tampering, and system downtime becomes critical. By applying the CIA model, ports can adopt a structured approach to minimizing cyber risks and enhancing the resilience of maritime logistics networks.

Figure 6.1 illustrates the CIA model in a triangular format tailored to port cybersecurity. Each section of the triangle—red for confidentiality, blue for integrity, and green for availability—presents the core objective of the component, key challenges faced in port contexts, and targeted mitigation strategies.

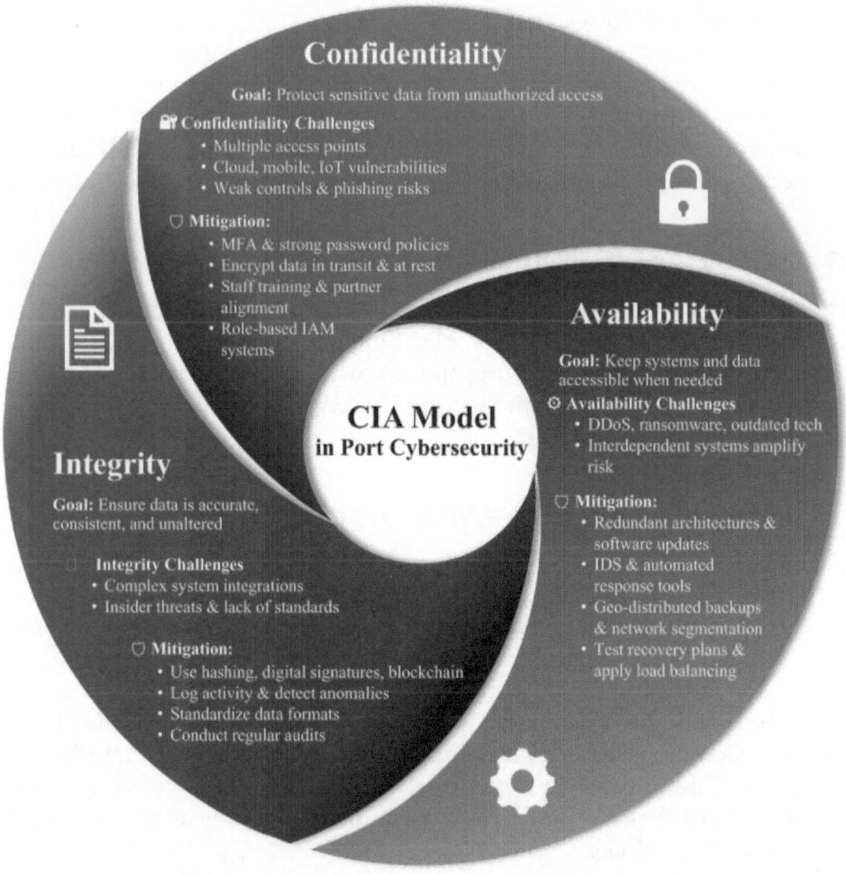

Figure 6.1 The CIA Triad in Port Cybersecurity.

This visual aid reinforces the model's practical relevance and provides a reference point for port cybersecurity teams and decision-makers. Further details on each component of the CIA model, including their specific application and relevance to port operations, are provided in the sections that follow.

- **C – Confidentiality** focuses on protecting sensitive data from unauthorized access, ensuring only approved individuals can view, alter, or transmit critical port information [7]. Ports handle large volumes of confidential records, including cargo manifests, customs data, and financial details. A breach of this data can lead to fraud, operational interference, or trade manipulation.
- **I – Integrity** ensures that digital data remains accurate and unchanged from its original state [7]. In port settings, reliable data—such as shipping schedules and customs declarations—is crucial for logistics coordination and regulatory compliance. Cyber-attacks targeting integrity, including ransomware and data tampering, can corrupt these datasets, causing delays, errors, or financial losses.
- **A – Availability** ensures access to systems and data when needed [7], supporting continuous port operations. As ports become more dependent on digital platforms for automation and tracking, attacks like DDoS and ransomware can disrupt systems, stall cargo, and interrupt supply chains, directly undermining availability.

6.3 Challenges and Methods for Maintaining the CIA of the PIS

Maintaining the CIA of the PIS becomes increasingly challenging as digital port ecosystems grow more complex and interconnected. Figure 6.1 summarizes key mitigation measures applied to each element of the CIA triad. The following sections detail the specific challenges ports face in preserving these elements and the strategies used to address them.

6.3.1 Confidentiality Challenges and Mitigation Strategies

Safeguarding confidentiality in port cybersecurity is complex due to the number of stakeholders interacting with the PIS. Each entity introduces potential access points, often operating under inconsistent cybersecurity standards, which weakens protection for cargo data, financial records, and operational reports. The growing use of cloud systems, mobile tools, and IoT devices further broadens the attack surface, exposing communication channels to new risks. Common vulnerabilities include poor access controls, insufficient encryption, and mismanaged credentials. Human factors—such as credential mishandling or falling for phishing—remain difficult to fully address through technical solutions alone.

To mitigate these risks, ports must adopt standardized, layered security measures. Encrypting sensitive data in transit and at rest ensures that intercepted content remains unreadable. Role-based access controls, multi-factor authentication (MFA), and secure communication protocols restrict unauthorized access and reduce data misuse. Strong password policies and consistent enforcement of MFA help prevent breaches from weak or reused credentials. Identity and access management (IAM) tools should enforce least-privilege principles. Training programs are essential to reduce human errors, particularly in handling data and detecting phishing attempts. Finally, aligning cybersecurity standards across external partners is critical to ensure secure and consistent data exchange throughout the port system.

6.3.2 Data Integrity Challenges and Mitigation Strategies

Maintaining data integrity in PIS environments is increasingly difficult due to the integration of diverse systems and external platforms. These connections raise the risk of unauthorized modifications to critical information, such as customs documents, vessel schedules, and cargo records. Threats include malware attacks that corrupt data, as well as insider actions—whether malicious or accidental—that alter or delete essential files. The absence of unified data standards among port actors further complicates reliable information exchange across the supply chain.

To mitigate these risks, ports apply verification tools to detect unauthorized changes within internal and external systems. Techniques like hashing, digital signatures, and checksums help confirm data authenticity during transfer and storage. Some ports implement blockchain solutions to create tamper-proof records, enhancing traceability and auditability. Addressing insider risks requires role-based access, change-logging, and anomaly detection to track unauthorized activities. Standardized data protocols across stakeholders improve consistency in handling. Regular audits and real-time monitoring enable early detection of integrity breaches, preserving confidence in digital port operations.

6.3.3 System Availability Challenges and Mitigation Strategies

Ensuring system availability in port operations is increasingly difficult due to the rising frequency and complexity of cyber-attacks. Threats like DDoS and ransomware can disable essential platforms by targeting outdated software, weak network configurations, or slow incident responses. Given the interconnected structure of port systems, a disruption in one area—such as the terminal operating system (TOS)—can rapidly affect broader operations. This risk is compounded by limited redundancy, insufficient backups, and delayed threat detection.

To mitigate these vulnerabilities, ports must adopt layered strategies aligned with system interdependencies. Redundant infrastructure, frequent data backups, and disaster recovery protocols help restore services after incidents. Firewalls, intrusion prevention systems, and regular drills support early threat containment. Updated software, segmented networks, and geographically distributed backups reduce exposure and limit the spread of failures. Real-time IDS and automated threat response tools allow faster mitigation. Load balancing and traffic management tools help avoid single points of failure. These coordinated defenses strengthen availability by addressing the structural weaknesses targeted by modern cyber threats.

6.4 Definitions and Roles of Port Cyber Resilience in Enhancing Ports' Operational and Supply Chain Resilience

Port cyber resilience refers to the capacity of a port to anticipate, withstand, and recover from cyber incidents while preserving essential functions [8, 9]. As ports increasingly integrate digital systems into core operations, the ability to recover from cyber disruptions is critical. Unlike traditional cybersecurity, which primarily emphasizes threat prevention, cyber resilience encompasses broader objectives—ensuring continuity, adapting to unforeseen events, and restoring normalcy without compromising port performance or supply chain integrity [1].

The concept of cyber resilience is central to operational resilience in ports, where core systems such as the TOS, IoT networks, and port community system (PCS) are interdependent. These systems, while improving operational efficiency, also increase the attack surface. A cyber-attack on cargo-tracking or customs clearance modules could paralyze scheduling operations, disrupt inter-agency coordination, and trigger cascading failures across connected systems [10]. The complexity of digital interconnectivity necessitates resilience-focused strategies that allow ports to absorb shocks, isolate faults, and resume service with minimal delay.

Cyber resilience also plays a crucial role in preserving supply chain continuity [9]. As pivotal nodes within global logistics networks, ports facilitate the movement of goods among manufacturers, customs agencies, logistics providers, and consumers. A breach in logistics systems may lead to cargo misrouting, delayed manifests, and system-wide port congestion, with downstream effects on inventory levels and trade reliability. Strengthening cyber resilience in ports mitigates these risks by ensuring secure data exchange, timely recovery from disruptions, and preservation of service reliability. Moreover, it fosters stakeholder trust and reinforces collaboration through data integrity and system availability.

6.5 Importance of Port Cybersecurity in Ensuring the Cyber Resilience

Cybersecurity and resilience are closely interconnected. In port operations, cybersecurity serves as a fundamental enabler of resilience by providing the tools and processes necessary to prevent, detect, respond to, and recover from cyber threats. Without robust cybersecurity, the mechanisms that support resilience—such as rapid recovery, secure communication, and effective incident containment—cannot function properly. To illustrate this relationship, the NIST CSF offers a widely recognized reference point.

The NIST Cybersecurity Framework outlines five core functions—Identify, Protect, Detect, Respond, and Recover—that collectively contribute to cyber resilience [11]. These functions offer a structured and integrated approach to managing cybersecurity risks, particularly relevant in complex, digitalized port environments. In practice, each function aligns with specific resilience objectives: the Identify function supports early risk awareness by mapping critical assets, such as TOSs or communication networks; the Protect function implements controls like access restrictions and system hardening to prevent disruptions to cargo handling or customs procedures. The Detect function ensures timely identification of anomalies, which is vital for recognizing breaches that could delay operations or compromise vessel coordination. Meanwhile, the Respond and Recover functions are central to resilience—enabling ports to contain damage, maintain communication channels, and restore operations swiftly after an incident. By applying these functions, the relationship between cybersecurity and cyber resilience becomes more tangible. Resilience, in this context, is not merely the ability to bounce back but also to maintain continuity of essential services during a cyber incident. Port cybersecurity serves as the foundation for this capability, as it ensures the operational integrity of interconnected digital systems critical to logistics, customs, and vessel traffic management.

In addition to the NIST core functions, specific cybersecurity techniques—such as network segmentation, firewalls, MFA, and data encryption—play a crucial role in strengthening port cyber resilience. These measures not only protect digital infrastructure from unauthorized access but also help isolate and contain incidents when breaches occur. For instance, network segmentation can prevent malware from spreading across systems that manage cargo tracking, billing, or terminal access. Similarly, encryption safeguards sensitive customs and trade data, even if systems are compromised. By limiting the reach and severity of cyber-attacks, these strategies preserve situational awareness and operational command during crises—both of which are essential for resilient performance and swift recovery in port environments.

Cybersecurity plays a critical role in enhancing cyber resilience by enabling swift recovery following a cyber incident. Real-time monitoring and threat detection facilitate the early identification of intrusions, while well-defined response plans and backup systems ensure that damage is minimized and operations are restored promptly. By reducing downtime and preventing escalation, cybersecurity strengthens operational continuity, which is vital for resilient port performance. Given ports' essential function in global trade, any disruption can have ripple effects on international supply chains. Resilient cybersecurity frameworks ensure that ports can maintain their role in global commerce, swiftly resuming operations to preserve the stability of trade flows. Moreover, robust cybersecurity practices foster stakeholder trust and facilitate compliance with international regulations, reinforcing the overall resilience of port operations in an increasingly interconnected world.

6.6 Business Continuity Planning and Its Role in Port Cyber Resilience

Business continuity planning (BCP) encompasses the strategic design and execution of policies, procedures, and resources that enable an organization to sustain critical operations during emergencies and restore full functionality following disruptions [12]. In port environments, BCP holds particular importance due to the significant economic and operational consequences of extended service outages. These disruptions, whether caused by cyber-attacks or technical failures, can lead to delays, financial losses, and compromised safety and security [1]. As part of a proactive risk management strategy, BCP aims to mitigate such adverse effects by ensuring operational continuity and facilitating timely recovery.

With the growing reliance on digital technologies to support various port operations and supply chain functions, BCP frameworks must explicitly incorporate cybersecurity considerations. Cyber-attacks—including ransomware and DDoS incidents—pose considerable threats to port infrastructure and digital assets. Consequently, an effective BCP must integrate robust cybersecurity controls [13], such as firewalls, intrusion detection systems, data encryption, and MFA. Additionally, a structured incident response plan is essential to enable the timely detection, containment, and resolution of cyber threats, thereby minimizing service interruptions and reinforcing port cyber resilience.

A comprehensive BCP framework typically comprises several key components: risk assessment, BIA, and the establishment of recovery time Objectives (RTOs) and recovery point objectives (RPOs) [14]. The initial stage, risk assessment, involves identifying potential disruptions, including both digital threats and physical hazards. Following this, the BIA evaluates the potential impact of these disruptions on critical port functions, thereby aiding in the prioritization of recovery efforts. RTOs and RPOs are subsequently defined to establish acceptable thresholds for service interruptions and data loss, which serve to guide the formulation of appropriate mitigation and recovery strategies. Once these core elements are in place, ports must develop, implement, and regularly test contingency procedures to ensure stakeholder readiness and the ability to maintain or restore operations within the defined parameters—especially in response to cyber incidents.

To operationalize BCP effectively, ports can rely on several internationally recognized standards that offer structured methodologies for continuity planning and implementation. Among these, ISO 22301 plays a pivotal role in reinforcing port cyber resilience by providing a comprehensive framework for establishing a Business Continuity Management System [15]. This standard emphasizes risk assessment, impact analysis, and continual improvement, ensuring systematic preparedness for a range of disruptions, including cyber threats. Achieving ISO 22301 certification not only enhances a port's demonstrable resilience but also strengthens stakeholder trust and facilitates compliance with regulatory requirements. Beyond ISO 22301, additional frameworks such as NIST SP 800-34 and NFPA 1600 provide valuable guidance. NIST SP 800-34 outlines a methodical approach to developing information systems and contingency plans and identifying preventive measures, while NFPA 1600 offers a comprehensive model encompassing prevention, mitigation, response, and recovery strategies—each contributing to a more resilient port infrastructure.

References

[1] C. Senarak, "Port Cybersecurity and Threat: A Structural Model for Prevention and Policy Development," *The Asian Journal of Shipping and Logistics*, vol. 37, no. 1, pp. 20–36, 2021.

[2] A. Staves, T. Anderson, H. Balderstone, B. Green, A. Gouglidis and D. Hutchison, "A Cyber Incident Response and Recovery Framework to Support Operators of Industrial Control Systems," *International Journal of Critical Infrastructure Protection*, vol. 37, 100505, 2022.

[3] WPSP, "Port of Baku – Port Management Information System (PMIS)," 2020. [Online]. Available: https://sustainableworldports.org/project/port-of-baku-port-management-information-system-pmis/.

[4] IBM, "What Is Attack Surface Management?," 2024. [Online]. Available: www.ibm.com/think/topics/attack-surface-management.

[5] European Commission, "NIS2 Directive: New Rules on Cybersecurity of Network and Information Systems," 2025. [Online]. Available: https://digital-strategy.ec.europa.eu/en/policies/nis2-directive#:~:text=The%20NIS2%20Directive%20establishes%20a,cross-border%20reaction%20and%20enforcement..

[6] CISA, "Cybersecurity Framework Implementation Guidance," 2020. [Online]. Available: www.cisa.gov/sites/default/files/publications/Commercial_Facilities_Sector_Cybersecurity_Framework_Implementation_Guidance_FINAL_508.pdf.

[7] Y. Cherdantseva and J. Hilton, "A Reference Model of Information Assurance & Security," in International Conference on Availability, Reliability and Security, Regensburg, Germany, 2013.

[8] I. Linkov and A. Kott, "Fundamental Concepts of Cyber Resilience: Introduction and Overview," in *Cyber Resilience of Systems and Networks*, Springer, 2018, pp. 1–25.

[9] E. Punt, J. Monstadt, S. Frank and P. Witte, "Navigating Cyber Resilience in Seaports: Challenges of Preparing for Cyberattacks at the Port of Rotterdam," *Digital Policy, Regulation and Governance*, vol. 25, no. 4, pp. 420–438, 2023.

[10] C. Senarak, "Port Cyberattacks from 2011 to 2023: A Literature Review and Discussion of Selected Cases," *Maritime Economics & Logistics*, vol. 26, no. 1, pp. 105–130, 2024.

[11] NIST, "The CSF 1.1 Five Functions," 2024. [Online]. Available: www.nist.gov/cyberframework/getting-started/online-learning/five-functions#:~:text=detection%20%2F%20response%20activities-,Recover,impact%20from%20a%20cybersecurity%20incident..

[12] V. Cerullo and M. J. Cerullo, "Business Continuity Planning: A Comprehensive Approach," *Information Systems Management*, vol. 21, no. 3, pp. 70–78, 2004.

[13] K. Kosmowski, E. Piesik, J. Piesik and M. Śliwiński, "Integrated Functional Safety and Cybersecurity Evaluation in a Framework for Business Continuity Management," *Energies*, vol. 15, no. 10, p. 3610, 2022.

[14] N. Bajgorić, L. Turulja and A. Alagić, "Business Continuity Management, Disaster Recovery Planning: Compliance in Practice," in *Always-On Business*, Springer, 2022, pp. 51–78.

[15] I. Tikanmäki, J. Savolainen and H. Ruoslahti, "The Role of Standards in Enhancing Cybersecurity and Business Continuity Management for Organizations," *Information & Security: An International Journal*, vol. 55, no. 1, pp. 63–78, 2024.

7 Proactive Risk Management for Port Cyber Resilience and Business Continuity

7.1 Concepts of Proactive Risk Management and Importance to Port Cyber Resilience and Business Continuity

Proactive risk management (PRM) is a systematic, forward-looking approach aimed at identifying potential risks, assessing their likelihood and impact, and implementing preventive measures before disruptions occur. In contrast to reactive strategies, which address incidents after they materialize, proactive management emphasizes early detection, continuous monitoring, and preemptive planning. This approach fosters a culture of preparedness by integrating risk assessments into routine operations and encouraging risk awareness across all organizational levels. By developing contingency plans, establishing redundancy measures, and implementing recovery protocols in advance, proactive risk management enhances operational continuity and resilience in increasingly complex and digitalized environments [1, 2].

The necessity of PRM in ports has become increasingly critical due to the rapid digitalization of port operations and the widespread adoption of advanced technologies. As ports integrate complex digital platforms, automated systems, and cloud-based networks, they face a significantly expanded attack surface. These innovations, while enhancing operational efficiency, introduce a range of cybersecurity vulnerabilities—such as outdated software, misconfigured systems, and weak access controls—that can be exploited by malicious actors. Additionally, the high degree of interconnectivity and dependency on external systems increases exposure, making ports more susceptible to external threats. Cyber threat actors increasingly target ports using tactics like ransomware, which can disrupt core systems, paralyze supply chain flows, and result in substantial financial losses. In this evolving threat landscape, PRM is essential for identifying and addressing these vulnerabilities, reducing exposure, and preparing for sophisticated cyber-attacks before they occur. By integrating continuous risk assessment, early detection, and preemptive planning into their operational frameworks, ports can strengthen the resilience of their digital infrastructure, protect sensitive information, and maintain continuity of service in the face of growing cyber risks.

DOI: 10.4324/9781003559320-7

While PRM is vital for preventing cyber risks, effective incident response and recovery (IRR) strategies are equally essential for minimizing the impact of a cyber-attack when it occurs. IRR encompasses a set of coordinated procedures designed to detect, contain, respond to, and recover from cybersecurity incidents in a timely and efficient manner [3]. These strategies ensure that ports can resume critical operations, minimize downtime, and reduce financial and reputational damage following an attack. Key components of IRR include predefined incident response protocols and data backup and restoration procedures, all of which contribute to rapid containment and recovery. Integrating IRR with PRM ensures a comprehensive approach to cyber resilience, covering both the prevention and the resolution of cyber disruptions.

Contemporary cybersecurity standards, such as the NIST Cybersecurity Framework and ISO 31000, provide comprehensive guidance for implementing effective risk management practices. These frameworks support ports in systematically identifying, assessing, mitigating, and continuously monitoring cyber risks. By embedding these practices into daily operations, port authorities can protect critical infrastructure, secure sensitive information, and ensure the uninterrupted flow of trade—thereby reinforcing their strategic role within the global logistics network.

To clarify how the concepts of PRM and IRR translate into actionable measures, Figure 7.1 presents seven foundational steps that collectively support a comprehensive port cybersecurity strategy. The first five steps emphasize proactive risk management, beginning with identifying port-specific cyber threats and progressing through assessment, prioritization, monitoring, and mitigation. These measures are designed to reduce vulnerabilities before incidents occur. The final two steps reflect incident response and recovery priorities, focusing on structured response protocols and robust backup and restoration procedures to ensure rapid recovery when disruptions do happen. Together, these seven steps offer a practical framework for anticipating cyber threats, minimizing risk exposure, and maintaining operational continuity. The sections that follow examine each step in detail, offering guidance on how ports can implement and sustain this integrated approach in the face of an evolving threat landscape.

7.2 Identifying Cyber Risks in Seaports

Cyber risk identification in ports involves a structured process that begins with the recognition and prioritization of critical assets across both IT and OT infrastructures [4]. These assets may include cargo-handling systems, the port information system (PIS), and communication networks vital to port operations. This initial phase emphasizes understanding the types of data managed, identifying ownership, and evaluating the potential impact if confidentiality, integrity, and availability (CIA) is compromised. Such analysis enables port authorities to determine which assets require the highest level of protection.

Figure 7.1 Seven Core Steps of Port Cybersecurity Strategy.

Once critical assets are defined, the next step focuses on identifying threats that could compromise them. These threats range from external adversaries—such as hackers, ransomware operators, and state-sponsored attackers—to internal risks, including insider threats and supply chain compromises [4]. Effective threat identification draws on multiple sources, including historical incident reports, threat intelligence feeds, cybersecurity advisories, and consultations with experts. Identified threats must be mapped to the relevant systems and services like the PIS, the port community system (PCS), and automation networks [5, 6]. This mapping clarifies which components are most at risk, helps identify threat-specific vulnerabilities, and enables ports to develop targeted defense strategies. It ensures that resources are allocated efficiently to protect the most operationally significant systems.

Following threat identification, evaluating vulnerabilities is essential. These include weak access controls, outdated or unsupported legacy systems, and limited cybersecurity training among personnel [7]. Understanding how these vulnerabilities align with specific threats and critical assets supports the development of focused mitigation strategies. Vulnerability assessments—such as penetration testing—simulate cyber-attacks to uncover exploitable weaknesses. This phase also aligns with international standards, such as those from the IMO and NIST, reinforcing resilience and guiding investment in cybersecurity.

Complementing vulnerability assessments is exposure analysis, which evaluates how easily digital assets can be accessed by potential attackers [8]. This includes identifying externally facing systems, auditing network connections, locating unmanaged or unknown devices, and analyzing publicly available data that could aid attackers. However, exposure analysis is often challenged by limited system visibility, the presence of shadow IT, and dynamic attack surfaces. To overcome these obstacles, ports are increasingly adopting threat intelligence platforms and continuous monitoring tools. These tools scan across digital spaces—including the surface web, dark web, and online forums—for early warning indicators like leaked credentials, spoofed domains, or planned attacks. Timely detection of such indicators enables swift countermeasures such as domain takedown requests or implementation of stricter access controls.

Finally, effective cyber risk identification relies on robust communication and awareness strategies [9, 10]. Given the evolving nature of cyber threats, it is vital that all stakeholders—port authorities, terminal operators, shipping agents, third-party vendors, and cybersecurity teams—maintain a shared understanding of asset priorities and risks. Communicating threat intelligence and vulnerability information strengthens collaboration and improves accuracy in risk identification. Additionally, raising awareness about the operational implications of CIA breaches helps personnel recognize the importance of the data they manage. Training programs should emphasize data ownership, system interdependencies, and the consequences of compromise. By fostering ongoing communication and education, ports can adapt more effectively to emerging threats, detect weaknesses early, and support a dynamic, collaborative risk identification process tailored to complex maritime environments.

7.3 Assessing and Analyzing Cyber Risks in Seaports

Assessing and analyzing cyber risks is a structured process designed to evaluate the potential impacts and likelihood of cyber incidents that could disrupt port operations, damage infrastructure, or compromise sensitive information. Following the identification of cyber threats, this phase centers on understanding the probability of such events occurring and the magnitude of their impact.

In the port environment, impact assessments are essential for evaluating how security incidents may disrupt operations, damage reputations, and erode stakeholder trust [11]. This process combines both quantitative and qualitative measures to examine potential consequences, such as increased operational costs from cargo delays or terminal shutdowns, reduced revenues due to halted services, and competitive disadvantages if clients shift to ports perceived as more secure. Reputational harm is particularly critical in globally interconnected logistics systems, where breaches can undermine trust among shipping lines, customs authorities, and supply chain partners. To forecast these ripple effects, ports often employ business impact analysis (BIA), which helps illustrate how cyber incidents may affect not only port operations but also broader logistics chains and port-dependent industries [12].

Another crucial component in cyber risk assessment is analyzing the likelihood of cyber incidents [13]. Likelihood is primarily influenced by potential threats, level of exposure to those threats, and system vulnerabilities—analyzed in earlier phases. By integrating findings from exposure analysis with insights from threat and vulnerability assessments, ports can develop a more accurate understanding of the likelihood of cyber incidents. This comprehensive view enables a proactive rather than reactive cybersecurity posture, ultimately improving decision making and resource allocation in subsequent steps of the risk management process. With both the impact and likelihood of cyber risks now assessed, the next logical step is risk prioritization, where these evaluated risks are ranked to ensure that mitigation efforts focus first on the most critical threats to port operations.

7.4 Prioritizing Cyber Risks in Seaports

Following the assessment and analysis phase, the next critical step in cyber risk management is the prioritization of risks in ports. This stage involves systematically evaluating identified threats based on their likelihood, potential impact, and the port's capacity to mitigate or manage them [7]. In contemporary port environments, the primary goal is to strengthen cybersecurity posture by focusing on risks that pose the greatest threat to operational continuity, financial stability, and reputational integrity. This approach allows ports to address high-impact threats proactively—threats that could otherwise result in cargo delays, service disruptions, or diminished stakeholder trust [14].

In addition to enhancing operational resilience, effective ranking of risks supports compliance with international cybersecurity standards. Frameworks established by organizations such as the IMO and the NIST emphasize the importance of structured risk assessments and the implementation of appropriate mitigation measures. Aligning with these frameworks not only facilitates regulatory adherence but also bolsters the security of both digital and physical port infrastructure [15].

This process typically follows a structured methodology that integrates both qualitative and quantitative assessments. A widely used tool is the risk matrix, which categorizes risks into high, medium, or low priority levels based on predefined criteria [16]. These criteria generally include the probability of a risk occurring and the severity of its consequences for port operations. For this method to be effective, it is essential to establish consensus on how these criteria are defined and measured, as this influences both the precision of the assessment and subsequent decisions regarding risk treatment.

Once the criteria are set, each risk is evaluated using a consistent scale. Many organizations use a three-tier scale (high, medium, low), while others prefer a more granular 5×5 matrix to capture varying degrees of likelihood and impact. These tools help decision-makers identify which risks require immediate action and which can be managed through routine security measures. Some ports may also use cumulative risk scores, calculated by combining or weighting likelihood and impact values, to better align prioritization with operational needs. Regardless of the scoring method, it is essential that the process be formally documented to promote consistency, transparency, and adaptability across the organization.

The final stage involves comparing risk rankings against the established criteria and developing a response plan that targets the most significant threats [17]. Since cyber risks are dynamic, this process must remain flexible. The matrix and its underlying assumptions should be reviewed and updated regularly—at least once per year, or more often in response to emerging threats—to ensure alignment with the port's evolving threat landscape and strategic goals. By systematically ranking cyber risks, ports can make informed decisions that enhance resilience, protect critical systems, and ensure continuity in an increasingly digital maritime environment. This step also lays a foundation for the subsequent phase in the cybersecurity framework: implementing targeted risk treatment strategies.

7.5 Monitoring and Detection of Cyber Risks in Seaports

Effective monitoring and detection of cyber risks in ports are essential for translating risk prioritization into proactive security action. As discussed in the previous section, prioritizing cyber risks enables port authorities to focus on the most critical assets and threats. This prioritization informs where monitoring efforts should be concentrated, ensuring that surveillance resources are aligned with the most significant operational risks. Monitoring and detection thus serve as the operational backbone of a risk-based cybersecurity strategy, enabling real-time visibility into threat activity across both IT and OT systems.

Monitoring activities involves the continuous observation of digital environments to identify suspicious behavior, system anomalies, or indicators of compromise (IOCs) [18]. Ports and other organizations increasingly rely on advanced tools such as security information and event management (SIEM) systems, IDS, and EDR technologies to collect and analyze log data across diverse network segments [19, 20]. These tools allow security teams to correlate events across platforms and detect patterns that may suggest unauthorized access, malware presence, or potential insider threats. In OT environments, where deterministic behavior is expected, monitoring may also extend to SCADA systems and industrial protocol traffic to detect deviations from normal control logic [21]. In parallel, threat intelligence gathering enhances the effectiveness of monitoring by supplying contextual information about known vulnerabilities, adversary tactics, and ongoing attack campaigns. By integrating threat intelligence feeds from governmental sources, industry groups, and commercial providers, ports can recognize evolving risks and tailor their monitoring rules to detect specific threat signatures. This intelligence-led approach ensures that port security teams remain vigilant and responsive to emerging threats.

A core component of these monitoring efforts is anomaly detection, which focuses on identifying deviations from established system baselines that may signal a cyber threat. Positioned as a proactive layer within the broader monitoring strategy, anomaly detection leverages machine learning and data analytics to define normal activity profiles across IT and OT systems and flag unusual behaviors—such as unauthorized login attempts, irregular data flows, or unexpected configuration changes. These early-warning indicators enable timely investigation before an incident escalates. The anomaly detection process also includes classification and triage, where alerts are evaluated to distinguish genuine cyber threats from false positives, which may arise from operational errors or benign anomalies [22]. This filtering process is essential to conserve investigative resources and maintain operational efficiency. Effective classification relies on close collaboration between cybersecurity teams and operational units to validate detected anomalies and assess potential business or system impacts.

7.6 Incident Response and Control Procedures

Following the monitoring and detection phase, implementing incident response and control procedures is critical when threats are identified and pose potential risks to port systems. These procedures provide a systematic approach to managing cybersecurity incidents that could disrupt operations [23]. Given the increasing reliance on digital systems, a well-defined incident response framework—which includes preparation, containment, and recovery actions—is vital. The core objectives of this framework are to maintain operational continuity, protect sensitive data, swiftly contain threats, minimize financial and regulatory risks, and ensure compliance with international standards such as those set by the IMO (e.g., the ISPS Code) and NIST. Additionally, a proactive strategy allows ports to continuously improve their cybersecurity posture and enhance readiness for evolving threats.

The incident response process is organized into distinct phases to ensure a rapid and coordinated response to cybersecurity incidents:

- **Preparation Phase**: This phase focuses on proactive measures to ensure the port is prepared for potential incidents. Key actions include the development and regular maintenance of an incident response plan (IRP), which defines roles, responsibilities, and clear communication protocols. Regular training and scenario-based exercises familiarize staff with the plan and enhance response capabilities. Testing backup systems, ensuring up-to-date threat intelligence, and maintaining coordination with external partners, such as regulatory bodies, are also essential for strengthening readiness [3].

- **Response Phase (During the Incident)**: Once an incident is detected, the focus shifts to containment. Immediate actions are taken to isolate compromised systems, cut off access to infected networks, and prevent the lateral spread of the attack within the port's digital infrastructure. This minimizes operational disruption and helps maintain continuity. Effective communication and coordination during the incident are crucial. Internal teams, including IT staff and cybersecurity specialists, work closely with external stakeholders such as regulatory bodies and external experts. This collaboration ensures a unified response, maintains transparency, reduces misinformation, and fosters trust among stakeholders, including logistics providers, governmental agencies, and international partners [3, 24].

The successful application of these procedures ensures that the core objectives of the incident response framework are met, including maintaining operational continuity, protecting sensitive data, swiftly containing threats, minimizing financial and regulatory risks, and ensuring compliance with international standards. These objectives lead to multiple operational and strategic benefits, including faster recovery times, enhanced threat detection through artificial intelligence (AI) and predictive analytics, and greater cyber resilience through continuous refinement of response strategies. Compliance with regulatory requirements further reduces legal and financial liabilities, while efficient incident handling minimizes operational downtime and mitigates economic disruptions, particularly in global supply chains. A robust and timely response builds confidence among port stakeholders and strengthens the overall security ecosystem.

7.7 Cyber Emergency Backup and Recovery

Following a cyber incident, the eradication and recovery phases are critical to restoring the security and functionality of port operations. During eradication, ports must ensure that all residual malicious code, unauthorized access mechanisms, or compromised components are entirely removed from affected systems. This is a prerequisite to avoid re-infection or further exploitation. Recovery then focuses on returning digital infrastructure to fully operational conditions under secure parameters. This involves reestablishing functionality without reintroducing previous vulnerabilities. Robust backup and recovery mechanisms serve as the foundation for this phase, enabling ports to restore essential data and services promptly while minimizing operational disruptions and financial impact [23, 25].

A central component of the recovery phase is the implementation of robust backup and restoration systems, which allow ports to reestablish operations securely and efficiently. Developing a reliable backup and recovery framework begins with defining the scope of critical data, setting backup intervals, and selecting appropriate storage solutions—whether cloud-based, off-site, or hybrid models. Data is replicated using incremental, differential, or full backup methods and protected through encryption, access controls, and multi-factor authentication to maintain confidentiality and integrity. Given the interconnected nature of port operations and PISs, a dependable recovery system is vital for ensuring operational continuity. Upon detection of a cyber emergency, the recovery process is triggered: systems are evaluated, compromised elements isolated, and restoration protocols deployed. This involves reinstalling software, reconfiguring infrastructure, validating systems, and resuming essential functions such as cargo management and vessel scheduling. The benefits of such mechanisms include improved data availability, reduced downtime, enhanced cyber resilience, and compliance with international cybersecurity standards [24].

Once port operations have been restored and systems are stabilized, attention shifts to the lessons learned phase, which plays an indispensable role in advancing a port's long-term cybersecurity posture [26]. This phase involves a thorough assessment of the incident response process, including an evaluation of backup and recovery effectiveness, identification of root causes, and incorporation of corrective actions into future protocols. By continuously refining strategies based on practical insights, ports can strengthen their preparedness and adaptability to evolving cyber threats. The integration of lessons learned not only ensures that vulnerabilities are addressed but also reinforces a culture of resilience, contributing to more secure and sustainable maritime operations.

7.8 Cyber Risk Mitigation Strategies

In addition to conventional cybersecurity practices, cyber risk mitigation strategies offer structured approaches to manage, minimize, or neutralize threats targeting seaport systems. These strategies are vital for protecting the CIA of PISs and associated data. By effectively implementing mitigation strategies, seaport authorities can reduce the likelihood and impact of cyber incidents, thereby preventing operational disruptions, financial losses, and reputational harm.

This section classifies cyber risk mitigation into four primary categories: risk avoidance, risk transfer, risk reduction, and risk acceptance. Each category offers distinct advantages and is supported by specific methods tailored to the unique operational and technological context of seaports. When selected appropriately, these strategies contribute to enhanced cyber resilience, operational continuity, and compliance with regulatory standards.

7.8.1 Risk Avoidance

Risk avoidance involves proactively eliminating exposure to cybersecurity threats by discontinuing, replacing, or significantly altering high-risk technologies, processes, or operational practices [27]. In the port context, this may include retiring unsupported software, isolating critical infrastructure from external networks, or preventing third-party devices from connecting to sensitive systems. These deliberate actions aim to reduce potential entry points for cyber-attacks. As one of the core cyber risk mitigation strategies, risk avoidance is particularly relevant when the likelihood or impact of a threat is deemed unacceptable, making the complete removal of the risk more effective than attempting to manage it [28].

This strategy is most applicable when identified cyber risks pose serious threats to the port's essential services, and other mitigation methods are either ineffective or too costly. For example, if a system's architecture is inherently flawed or incompatible with current security standards, continued use may create more harm than good. In such cases, eliminating the associated risks—rather than controlling them—becomes the more responsible and sustainable course of action. Risk avoidance is particularly useful when external dependencies, such as outdated vendors or untrusted third-party applications, introduce uncontrollable variables into the cybersecurity environment.

Several key factors guide the decision to implement risk avoidance. These include the severity of potential impact, especially if a successful cyber-attack could result in operational paralysis or major financial losses; the limited effectiveness of available mitigation measures; and the feasibility of eliminating or replacing vulnerable assets. Furthermore, when the cost of continuing with a high-risk process exceeds the investment required for replacement or redesign, risk avoidance becomes the economically rational choice. Strategic alignment with security compliance requirements and industry standards also plays a critical role in shaping this decision.

As a long-term, proactive measure, risk avoidance contributes to the development of a resilient cybersecurity infrastructure. By focusing on eliminating root causes—such as outdated systems or insecure communication channels—this strategy enhances overall system integrity and reduces the likelihood of future incidents. It supports uninterrupted port operations by preventing disruptions that could arise from unaddressed vulnerabilities. Additionally, it limits financial exposure by reducing the chances of cyber-attacks that might otherwise lead to costly service downtime, data breaches, or reputational damage. Beyond immediate protection, risk avoidance helps ports maintain regulatory compliance and fosters a culture of preemptive security planning.

In the broader context of cyber resilience, risk avoidance offers ports the opportunity to secure critical systems without relying solely on reactive defense mechanisms. By removing threats at their origin, this strategy enables ports to focus their cybersecurity resources on strengthening sustainable and compliant digital operations. Ultimately, risk avoidance not only fortifies ports against existing vulnerabilities but also prepares them to adapt to future cyber challenges with greater agility and assurance.

7.8.2 Risk Transfer

Risk transfer refers to the strategic allocation of cyber risk responsibilities to external entities through mechanisms such as contractual arrangements, cyber insurance policies, or outsourced cybersecurity services [29]. Within port operations, this strategy allows ports to shift the burden of managing certain cyber threats—such as data breaches, ransomware attacks, or operational disruptions—to third-party cybersecurity providers or insurance firms [30]. For example, a port may engage specialized external vendors for continuous network monitoring, incident response, or compliance management, or it may purchase cyber insurance to offset the potential costs of recovery and liability. The fundamental objective of risk transfer is to reduce the internal strain associated with complex or high-cost cyber threats by leveraging the capabilities and financial safeguards provided by external actors.

Risk transfer is most effectively employed when a port faces cyber risks that exceed its internal capacity to manage, whether because it lacks the necessary technical expertise, does not have sufficient financial resources to invest in cybersecurity infrastructure, or lacks the necessary tools and systems to adequately address certain threats. This strategy is particularly suitable when the external party—such as a specialized cybersecurity firm or insurance provider—has superior capabilities for handling specific threats, such as advanced persistent threats (APTs) or large-scale ransomware attacks. In these cases, third-party experts offer continuous monitoring, rapid incident response, and specialized knowledge that the port might lack internally. Additionally, risk transfer becomes a practical choice when the cost of transferring the risk, through mechanisms like cyber insurance or outsourcing, is less than the potential financial and operational damage from a cyber incident. In the future, or in specific regions with strict national regulations, regulatory requirements or contractual obligations may make risk transfer necessary, particularly when sensitive data is handled by third-party partners. In such cases, national laws or industry-specific regulations might require ports to delegate certain cybersecurity responsibilities to external entities, such as specialized service providers or insurers, to ensure compliance with data protection standards.

The implementation of a risk transfer strategy yields several tangible benefits. By shifting responsibility to entities better equipped to handle specific threats, ports can alleviate the financial burden associated with cyber incidents. Cyber insurance, for example, can cover expenses related to data restoration, legal liabilities, and system recovery, thereby reducing the economic impact of breaches. The use of third-party cybersecurity firms enhances the port's overall resilience by introducing continuous threat monitoring, improved compliance oversight, and access to specialized response teams. These measures not only enhance preparedness but also allow the port to concentrate its internal resources on maintaining operational continuity. Moreover, the strategic distribution of cyber risk contributes to a more stable and secure environment, particularly when dealing with risks that are difficult to manage directly. Ultimately, risk transfer reinforces a port's cybersecurity posture while ensuring that critical services remain protected against the financial and operational consequences of cyber threats.

7.8.3 Risk Reduction

Risk reduction is a proactive cybersecurity strategy aimed at minimizing both the likelihood and impact of cyber incidents by implementing technical safeguards, infrastructure enhancements, and operational improvements [31]. In the port environment, this involves deploying multi-layered cybersecurity controls such as network segmentation, firewalls, intrusion detection systems, and multi-factor authentication. Regular employee training, vulnerability assessments, and incident response simulations further improve the port's capacity to identify and neutralize threats before they escalate. Rather than avoiding risk entirely, the goal of risk reduction is to manage it to acceptable levels while allowing ports to maintain regular operations.

This strategy is particularly appropriate when identified cyber risks are significant but manageable through feasible and cost-effective interventions. Ports may choose risk reduction when practical measures—such as enhanced security protocols or system updates—can meaningfully reduce exposure without requiring the cessation of operations or technologies. Key decision factors include the availability of internal resources (such as budget and skilled personnel), the feasibility of implementing risk mitigation actions, and the need to maintain operational continuity. It is especially suitable for risks with moderate to high likelihood and considerable, but not catastrophic, impacts.

When implemented effectively, risk reduction strategies lead to early detection and mitigation of cyber threats. Regular software updates, employee awareness programs, and continuous vulnerability assessments help ports identify weaknesses before they are exploited [24]. Security infrastructure improvements such as encrypted communications, strict access control policies, and real-time threat monitoring reinforce the port's cybersecurity posture, reducing both the frequency and severity of incidents. Furthermore, risk reduction supports long-term business continuity by ensuring ports are prepared to recover quickly from attacks. Recovery plans, backup systems, and routine incident response exercises enable a swift return to normal operations with minimal disruption [23]. Importantly, this strategy fosters a culture of continuous improvement—cybersecurity measures are regularly reviewed and adapted to address new vulnerabilities and evolving attack methods. This dynamic approach ensures ports remain resilient in an increasingly complex threat landscape.

7.8.4 Risk Acceptance

Risk acceptance occurs when mitigation efforts are considered impractical, cost-prohibitive, or unnecessary due to the low probability or limited impact of a potential cyber incident [32]. For example, a port may choose to tolerate the risk of minor phishing attempts, provided that basic safeguards—such as staff awareness training—are in place. This approach acknowledges that certain risks may be unavoidable or too inconsequential to warrant substantial investment. Rather than eliminating or transferring these risks, ports formally recognize their presence and determine that the best course of action is to tolerate them while ensuring mechanisms are in place to monitor changes in the risk landscape. The goal of this strategy is to preserve operational efficiency and allocate resources more effectively without compromising the port's overall cybersecurity posture.

Risk acceptance is appropriate when the likelihood of an incident is low and the potential consequences are minimal or when the costs of mitigation would exceed the anticipated benefits [32]. It is also used when certain risks are inherent to the port's operations—such as occasional low-impact cyber threats—and cannot be fully eliminated but are unlikely to cause major disruption. This strategy is most viable when the port has the capability to continuously monitor accepted risks and respond promptly if circumstances evolve. Decision-makers must consider factors such as the magnitude and likelihood of the risk, the cost-effectiveness of mitigation options, and the practicality of alternative solutions. Additionally, contingency planning and risk-tracking mechanisms must be in place to ensure a rapid shift in strategy should the threat escalate.

By adopting a risk acceptance approach, ports can focus their resources on addressing higher-priority cyber threats while avoiding unnecessary expenditures on low-impact vulnerabilities. This results in a more cost-effective and balanced cybersecurity strategy, allowing for efficient resource allocation and sustained operational performance [32]. While accepted risks are not actively mitigated, they are closely monitored to ensure early detection of any changes that may require reevaluation. This strategy helps avoid overburdening cybersecurity teams with disproportionate protective measures and ensures that investments are directed toward threats with the highest potential for disruption. Ultimately, risk acceptance supports long-term resilience by preserving flexibility and responsiveness in the face of a dynamic cyber threat environment.

7.9 Communicating Cyber Risks to Port Stakeholders

Effective communication of cyber risks is essential to strengthening port cybersecurity, guiding stakeholders through the phases of risk awareness, mitigation, and recovery. Communication plays a central role in each phase of incident management: during the preparation phase, it establishes frameworks for identifying and addressing potential threats; during the incident phase, it supports real-time coordination and response; and in the post-incident phase, it facilitates recovery efforts and the sharing of lessons learned [24]. Across all stages, strategic communication ensures that stakeholders understand their responsibilities, enabling timely responses and promoting overall resilience. Furthermore, clear and consistent communication supports regulatory compliance and enhances transparency in risk management processes. This transparency not only reinforces internal accountability but also provides external stakeholders—such as shipping lines and port customers—with critical information needed to assess disruptions, identify alternatives, and adjust operational plans accordingly.

A foundational element of effective cyber risk communication is recognizing the diverse range of stakeholders involved and tailoring messages to their specific roles and responsibilities. Each group—whether internal stakeholders such as port management, IT personnel, and security teams, or external entities like vendors, regulatory bodies, and supply chain partners—has distinct information needs. For example, senior port management requires strategic overviews of risk exposure and mitigation priorities, while IT and security teams need detailed technical data on vulnerabilities, threat vectors, and response protocols. External partners demand transparency and assurances that the port's cybersecurity posture aligns with industry norms. Designing communication strategies that reflect these differences ensures that all parties are informed, engaged, and capable of taking appropriate action.

The following scenarios illustrate how tailored communication supports cybersecurity across key activities:

- **Identification of Cyber Risks:** Port executives require summarized assessments to guide long-term strategic planning, whereas IT personnel need granular insights into system vulnerabilities and detection metrics. External vendors must be alerted to risks affecting service continuity or supply chain stability so they can adapt accordingly.
- **Incident Response and Recovery:** During a cyber incident, real-time updates and coordination are essential for security teams tasked with containment and restoration. Senior management relies on high-level briefings to evaluate operational impacts and prioritize recovery resources. Meanwhile, regulatory bodies require formal reporting to verify compliance and facilitate transparent post-incident reviews.
- **Cyber Risk Mitigation Strategies:** IT and security professionals need specific instructions for implementing technical controls such as patch management, firewall updates, and access restrictions. In contrast, management requires strategic insights into risk transfer, acceptance, or avoidance, helping guide decisions with operational and financial implications. Supply chain partners must be kept informed of mitigation efforts that may affect logistics, schedules, or collaborative workflows.

The effectiveness of these efforts depends not only on content but also on the communication tools and formats selected. These should be adaptable to stakeholder needs and the urgency of each situation. Formal documentation—such as reports, briefings, and incident response plans—ensures the accuracy and traceability of communications. In contrast, real-time tools like alerts, dashboards, and secure messaging systems enable rapid coordination and situational awareness during incidents. Public communication platforms, such as X (formerly Twitter) and Instagram, can also serve as valuable tools during high-impact events by delivering time-sensitive updates to port users, shipping lines, and the broader community [24]. These platforms foster transparency and engagement when public awareness is essential. Additionally, interactive formats—such as simulation exercises and digital training modules—help staff practice communicating under pressure, refining how messages are delivered, coordinated, and escalated during cyber incidents and, thereby, strengthening overall institutional communication readiness.

Nevertheless, even the most well-designed communication plans may fall short if stakeholder engagement is limited or siloed. A common challenge in port environments is the development of communication protocols and cyber drills that are conducted in isolation, involving only internal departments. Given the highly interconnected nature of port operations—spanning terminal operators, IT service providers, logistics firms, shipping lines, and government agencies—such fragmentation can impede information flow and hinder coordinated incident response. As a result, communication strategies should be embedded within broader joint preparedness initiatives, including multi-stakeholder training and exercises [33]. These collaborative activities clarify expectations, foster trust, and improve interoperability, thereby enhancing collective situational awareness and response efficiency. In addition, ongoing stakeholder engagement through forums, feedback loops, and regular knowledge-sharing sessions contributes to a culture of proactive cybersecurity. These efforts help disseminate lessons learned and support the continuous improvement of communication protocols in response to evolving threats and operational complexity.

References

[1] B. Fernández-Muñiz, J. M. Montes-Peón and C. J. Vázquez-Ordás, "Safety Leadership, Risk Management and Safety Performance in Spanish Firms," *Safety Science*, vol. 70, pp. 295–307, 2014.

[2] C. Fang and F. Marle, "A Simulation-Based Risk Network Model For Decision Support in Project Risk Management," *Decision Support Systems*, vol. 52, no. 3, pp. 635–644, 2012.

[3] E. C. Thompson, *Cybersecurity Incident Response: How to Contain, Eradicate, and Recover from Incidents*, Apress, 2018.

[4] H. I. Kure, S. Islam, M. Ghazanfar and A. R. &. M. Pasha, "Asset Criticality and Risk Prediction for an Effective Cybersecurity Risk Management of Cyber-Physical System," *Neural Computing and Applications*, vol. 34, pp. 493–514, 2022.

[5] I. Zografopoulos, J. Ospina, X. Liu and C. Konstantinou, "Cyber-Physical Energy Systems Security: Threat Modeling, Risk Assessment, Resources, Metrics, and Case Studies," *IEEE Access*, vol. 9, pp. 29775–29818, 2021.

[6] I. Koliousis, "A Conceptual Framework That Monitors Port Facility Access Through Integrated Port Community Systems and Improves Port and Terminal Security Performance," *International Journal of Shipping and Transport Logistics*, vol. 12, no. 4, pp. 251–283, 2020.

[7] C. Kapalidis, S. Karamperidis, T. Watson and G. Koligiannis, "A Vulnerability Centric System of Systems Analysis on the Maritime Transportation Sector Most Valuable Assets: Recommendations for Port Facilities and Ships," *Journal of Marine Science and Engineering*, vol. 10, no. 10, p. 1486, 2022.

[8] L. Robertson, A. M. Aneiros and K. Michael, "A Theory of Exposure: Measuring Technology System End User Vulnerabilities," in International Symposium on Technology and Society, Sydney, NSW, Australia, 2017.

[9] A. V. Jha, A. N. Ghazali, B. Appasani and D. K. Mohanta, "Risk Identification and Risk Assessment of Communication Networks in Smart Grid Cyber-Physical Systems," in *Security in Cyber-Physical Systems*, Springer, 2021, pp. 217–253.

[10] M. Zwilling, G. Klien, D. Lesjak, Ł. Wiechetek, F. Cetin and H. N. Basim, "Cyber Security Awareness, Knowledge and Behavior: A Comparative Study," *Journal of Computer Information Systems*, vol. 62, no. 1, pp. 82–97, 2020.

[11] H. Bahşi, C. J. Udokwu, U. Tatar and A. Norta, "Impact Assessment of Cyber Actions on Missions or Business Processes: A Systematic Literature Review," in 13th International Conference on Cyber Warfare and Security, Washington DC, 2018.

[12] E. H. Budiyanto, R. O. S. Gurning and T. Pitana, "The Application of Business Impact Analysis Due to Electricity Disruption in a Container Terminal," *Sustainability*, vol. 13, no. 21, 12038, 2021.

[13] S. Pandey, R. K. Singh, A. Gunasekaran and A. Kaushik, "Cyber Security Risks in Globalized Supply Chains: Conceptual Framework," *Journal of Global Operations and Strategic Sourcing*, vol. 13, no. 1, pp. 103–128, 2020.

[14] M. Dhahri, M. Elmsalmi, A. Aljuaid and W. Hachicha, "Seaport Terminals Risks Prioritization Using a Structural Modeling-Based Approach: A Real Case Study," *Journal of Marine Science and Engineering*, vol. 10, no. 2, p. 217, 2022.

[15] N. Adams, R. Chisnall, C. Pickering and S. Schauer, "How Port Security Has to Evolve to Address the Cyber-Physical Security Threat: Lessons from the SAURON Project," *International Journal of Transport Development and Integration*, vol. 4, no. 1, pp. 29–41, 2020.

[16] L. Anthony (Tony) Cox Jr, "What's Wrong with Risk Matrices?," *Risk Analysis: An International Journal*, vol. 28, no. 2, pp. 497–512, 2008.

[17] N. Shinde and P. Kulkarni, "Cyber Incident Response and Planning: A Flexible Approach," *Computer Fraud & Security*, vol. 2021, no. 1, pp. 14–19, 2021.

[18] H. Balisane, E. I. Egho-Promise, E. Lyada and F. Aina, "Towards Improved Threat Mitigation In Digital Environments: A Comprehensive Framework For Cybersecurity Enhancement," *International Journal of Research – GRANTHAALAYAH*, vol. 125, pp. 108–123, 2024.

[19] Z. B. Yusof, "Effectiveness of Endpoint Detection and Response Solutions in Combating Modern Cyber Threats," *Journal of Advances in Cybersecurity Science, Threat Intelligence, and Countermeasures*, vol. 8, no. 12, pp. 1–9, 2024.

[20] M. Li, J. Zhou, S. Chattopadhyay and M. Goh, "Maritime Cybersecurity: A Comprehensive Review," arXiv preprint arXiv, vol. 2409, no. 11417, pp. 1–23, 2024.

[21] K. Raghunandan, "Supervisory Control and Data Acquisition (SCADA)," in *Introduction to Wireless Communications and Networks*, Springer, 2022, pp. 321–337.

[22] J. Meira, R. Andrade, J. C. Isabel Praça, V. Bolón-Canedo, A. Alonso-Betanzos and G. Marreiros, "Performance Evaluation of Unsupervised Techniques

in Cyber-Attack Anomaly Detection," *Journal of Ambient Intelligence and Humanized Computing*, vol. 11, pp. 4477–4489, 2019.

[23] A. Staves, T. Anderson, H. Balderstone, B. Green, A. Gouglidis and D. Hutchison, "A Cyber Incident Response and Recovery Framework to Support Operators of Industrial Control Systems," *International Journal of Critical Infrastructure Protection*, vol. 37, 100505, 2022.

[24] C. Senarak, "Port Cyberattacks from 2011 to 2023: A Literature Review and Discussion of Selected Cases," *Maritime Economics & Logistics*, vol. 26, no. 1, pp. 105–130, 2024.

[25] E. Punt, J. Monstadt, S. Frank and P. Witte, "Navigating Cyber Resilience in Seaports: Challenges of Preparing for Cyberattacks at the Port of Rotterdam," *Digital Policy, Regulation and Governance*, vol. 25, no. 4, pp. 420–438, 2023.

[26] F. Quader and V. Janeja, "Insights into Organizational Security Readiness: Lessons Learned from Cyber-Attack Case Studies," *Journal of Cybersecurity and Privacy*, vol. 1, no. 14, pp. 638–659, 2021.

[27] J. Mendes, M. Marques and C. Guedes Soares, "Risk Avoidance in Strategic Technology Adoption," *Journal of Modelling in Management*, vol. 19, no. 5, pp. 1485–1509, 2024.

[28] S. S. Oren, "Risk Management vs. Risk Avoidance in Power Systems Planning and Operation," in IEEE Power Engineering Society General Meeting, Tampa, FL, USA, 2007.

[29] M. Benaroch, "Cybersecurity Risk in IT Outsourcing—Challenges and Emerging Realities," *in Information Systems Outsourcing*, Springer, 2020, pp. 313–334.

[30] F. Wang, "The Role of Insurance in Regulating Cyber Risks in the Shipping Industry," in *Research Handbook on Marine Insurance Law*, Edward Elgar Publishing, 2024, pp. 306–332.

[31] F. Dine, "Cyber Threat Analysis and the Development of Proactive Security Strategies for Risk Mitigation," 2024. [Online]. Available: www.researchgate.net/profile/Faizal-Dine/publication/384365805_Cyber_Threat_Analysis_and_the_Development_of_Proactive_Security_Strategies_for_Risk_Mitigation/links/66f64413f599e0392fa7054b/Cyber-Threat-Analysis-and-the-Development-of-Proactive-Sec.

[32] F. Kitsios, E. Chatzidimitriou and M. Kamariotou, "The ISO/IEC 27001 Information Security Management Standard: How to Extract Value from Data in the IT Sector," *Sustainability*, vol. 15, no. 7, p. 5828, 2023.

[33] National Cyber Security Centre, "Guidance on Effective Communications in a Cyber Incident," 2024. [Online]. Available: www.ncsc.gov.uk/guidance/effective-communications-in-a-cyber-incident.

8 Strengthening Port Cybersecurity Regulations

8.1 Importance of and Relationships between Port Security Regulations and Cybersecurity

As ports adopt increasingly advanced digital systems—such as automated cranes, cargo-tracking platforms, and smart access controls—the line between physical and cyber threats continues to erode. Cyber-attacks are no longer confined to data breaches; they can halt cargo operations, disrupt navigation, and compromise safety-critical infrastructure. This convergence demands a unified security approach, where cybersecurity is treated as an integral part of physical security. The ISPS Code, developed under the SOLAS Convention, remains the foundational framework for safeguarding port facilities from unlawful interference. While originally focused on physical threats like terrorism, its flexible, risk-based design makes it adaptable to the digital threat landscape. Recognizing this, the IMO now requires the integration of cyber risk into port security management through measures such as MSC-FAL.1/Circ.3 and Resolution MSC.428(98), which embed cyber risk within the ISM Code. Ports are also encouraged to align with global standards—including the IAPH Cybersecurity Guidelines, ISO/IEC 27001, and the NIST Framework—to ensure system resilience and incident readiness. Meanwhile, regional and national regulations reinforce these expectations. For instance, the EU's GDPR imposes strict data security rules, while US agencies like CISA and the TSA set sector-specific cybersecurity obligations. Together, these frameworks promote the convergence of physical and cyber safeguards, allowing ports to embed digital risk into existing assessments, plans, and drills—enhancing both regulatory compliance and operational resilience.

When cybersecurity regulations are integrated seamlessly into port security protocols, the result is a more agile and robust operational environment. Such alignment allows ports to respond swiftly to emerging threats, minimizing service disruptions in core activities like cargo movement, vessel coordination, and customs processing. Consolidating physical and digital risk management also streamlines oversight, reducing regulatory friction and simplifying audits. Importantly, adherence to recognized standards fosters confidence among trading partners, logistics firms, and border control authorities—encouraging

DOI: 10.4324/9781003559320-8

smoother digital exchanges and operational transparency. Conversely, overlooking cybersecurity as a key element of overall port security exposes critical vulnerabilities. Cyber incidents can quickly ripple through interconnected systems, stalling port activity and triggering cascading financial losses. Non-compliance may also invite regulatory penalties or compromise a port's standing in public–private investment negotiations. In a globally connected sector, reputational harm from security failures can be difficult to recover from, particularly when trust underpins long-term commercial relationships. These risks underscore the urgency of embedding cybersecurity within the same strategic and operational frameworks used to manage physical threats, ensuring a unified approach that anticipates and neutralizes disruption before it spreads.

8.2 Linking Port Cybersecurity to Key Security Regulations

8.2.1 International Convention for the Safety of Life at Sea

Since its establishment in 1914, the SOLAS Convention has been the principal international framework for maritime safety, designed to protect human life through regulations that cover various aspects such as ship stability, lifesaving equipment, fire protection, and navigational safety [1]. As maritime technology continues to advance, SOLAS has adapted to incorporate new safety standards, reflecting changes in both the maritime industry and the types of threats encountered at sea. The primary focus of SOLAS is on preventing accidents and mitigating the effects of unforeseen events that could endanger human life, such as structural failures or operational mistakes [2]. SOLAS sets standards for ship design, equipment, and operational procedures to ensure ships remain safe for passengers, crew, and cargo.

In today's increasingly digital maritime environment, cybersecurity has become a growing concern that threatens not only the confidentiality of data but also the physical safety and operational stability of vessels. With critical systems such as navigation, propulsion, and communication increasingly relying on digital infrastructure, the maritime sector faces new vulnerabilities that traditional safety frameworks were not originally designed to address. The SOLAS Convention's continued relevance now depends on how well it accommodates the risks introduced by digital transformation. Although SOLAS does not directly mandate technical cybersecurity controls, it reflects a shift toward acknowledging cyber threats as part of maritime safety. In response, ship and port operators are expected to implement cybersecurity measures—such as protecting communication channels, securing operational technologies, and managing data transmission—to uphold the safety objectives set by the Convention. Likewise, operators must ensure their personnel are trained to handle cyber risks alongside traditional safety responsibilities. Incorporating cybersecurity into operational procedures and crew training is increasingly seen as essential to maintaining the safety and continuity of maritime operations in a digital era [1, 2].

8.2.2 Integrating Cybersecurity into ISPS Code

The ISPS Code, established under Chapter XI-2 of the SOLAS Convention in response to the September 11, 2001, terrorist attacks [2], is the key international security regulation that ports should consider when seeking to integrate cybersecurity measures into existing frameworks, as it provides a globally recognized standard for port security practices.

Several key components of the ISPS Code provide clear opportunities for incorporating cybersecurity into existing port security practices [2]. First, port facility security assessments—required under Regulation XI-2/6—could be expanded to include evaluations of critical digital infrastructure, such as automated terminal systems and equipment, control servers, port information systems (PISs), and connected devices used in cargo operations. Second, measures to prevent unauthorized access should not only cover physical entry points but also address digital access control. This includes enforcing role-based access to operational systems, implementing multi-factor authentication for management platforms, and securing remote access pathways. Third, emergency response procedures—which traditionally focus on physical incidents like unauthorized boarding or sabotage—should also account for cyber incidents, such as ransomware attacks that disrupt port operations or data breaches that compromise sensitive cargo information. By aligning cybersecurity practices with the ISPS Code's existing structure, ports can strengthen their overall security posture, reflecting the growing interdependence between digital and physical operations.

Integrating cybersecurity into the ISPS Code's framework offers several significant advantages for ports, particularly from the perspectives of safety, security, and operational resilience. From a safety standpoint, securing digital infrastructure can prevent catastrophic incidents, such as cyber-attacks that target automated systems or interfere with safety-critical operations [3]. For example, a cyber-attack on an automated crane system could result in physical damage to cargo or, worse, pose a direct safety risk to port personnel. By securing these systems, ports ensure the safe and efficient movement of goods without the risk of cyber-induced disruptions.

From both security and operational resilience standpoints, integrating cybersecurity into the ISPS Code framework enables ports to build a more robust defense against evolving and multidimensional threats. As digital systems become integral to port functions, the risk of cyber incidents intensifies, especially when these digital threats converge with physical vulnerabilities. Embedding practices such as real-time network monitoring, threat detection, and structured incident response into port security procedures would allow ports to detect and respond to cyber risks swiftly, limiting potential disruptions. A breach targeting both digital controls and physical systems—such as automated cranes or access points—could severely impact operations and safety. By aligning cybersecurity with the ISPS Code, ports can reduce their exposure to such hybrid attacks. Furthermore, clearly defined cyber risk management strategies and emergency protocols can accelerate recovery efforts, enabling ports to restore essential functions efficiently. By sustaining operational continuity and reassuring stakeholders in the wake of cyber disruptions, these measures help minimize financial losses, service delays, and reputational harm.

8.2.3 Port Facility Security Plans and Cybersecurity Integration

Port facility security plans (PFSPs) form the operational core of the ISPS Code, serving as the primary tool for managing security risks at port facilities. These plans outline the procedures for safeguarding personnel, cargo, and infrastructure from threats such as unauthorized access, cargo tampering, and perimeter breaches. PFSPs are developed based on comprehensive port facility security assessment (PFSAs), which identify potential vulnerabilities and define the preventive measures needed to address them. Once established, the PFSP must be implemented and periodically reviewed to ensure its effectiveness in responding to evolving security threats. Oversight of these plans is the responsibility of designated port facility security officers (PFSOs), who are tasked with ensuring compliance with ISPS Code requirements and keeping the plans up to date [3]. PFSPs outline critical procedures such as access control, surveillance, personnel identification, and coordinated responses to changing threat levels. These tasks are carried out in collaboration with ship security officers (SSOs) and company security officers (CSOs), who together form a structured security chain. Their coordination ensures that security protocols are consistently enforced across both port and vessel operations and that relevant authorities are engaged in threat detection and information exchange when necessary.

As digital technologies become embedded in nearly all aspects of port operations, the need to incorporate cybersecurity into PFSPs has become both urgent and practical. PFSPs—already structured around identifying threats, defining protective measures, and assigning security responsibilities—offer a suitable platform for integrating cyber-specific safeguards. By expanding existing provisions to account for risks such as system intrusion, data manipulation, and unauthorized access to control platforms, PFSPs can evolve into comprehensive, dual-domain security tools. This integration does not require building a parallel structure but, rather, adapting current PFSP elements to include cybersecurity dimensions. The following areas illustrate where and how cybersecurity considerations can be systematically incorporated into PFSPs:

- **Access Control, Surveillance, and Personnel Identification**: These existing PFSP elements can be enhanced with cybersecurity protocols to prevent unauthorized digital access. Measures such as encrypted credentials, biometric authentication, and multi-factor login systems can strengthen access control for sensitive IT assets. Surveillance systems should be upgraded with real-time network monitoring tools capable of detecting anomalies in both physical and digital environments. Integrating these technologies ensures that access points—whether physical gates or remote terminal servers—are secured in tandem.

- **Response Protocols for Security Threat Levels**: Current procedures for escalating physical threat responses should be mirrored with cyber-specific escalation plans. PFSPs can include predefined responses to incidents such as malware infections, ransomware attacks, or denial-of-service disruptions. These should be aligned with physical security measures to allow a synchronized reaction when cyber-attacks coincide with physical threats. Including cyber risk indicators in threat level assessments improves preparedness and facilitates faster containment and recovery.
- **Designation of Security Roles**: PFSPs can be expanded so as to assign clear responsibilities for cyber risk management alongside physical security duties. While PFSOs, SSOs, and CSOs oversee traditional security, designated cyber officers (COs) should be incorporated to manage digital infrastructure protection. This role may include monitoring network activity, assessing system vulnerabilities, and coordinating incident response. Embedding cyber roles within the existing command structure improves communication, ensures accountability, and supports integrated decision making across both domains.
- **Coordination with National, Regional, and International Authorities**: PFSPs should promote formal collaboration with cybersecurity agencies, maritime computer emergency response teams (CERTs), law enforcement, and intelligence networks. This can involve shared incident-reporting protocols, joint threat assessments, and participation in cybersecurity drills. By institutionalizing these connections within the PFSP, ports improve their situational awareness and resilience to rapidly evolving threats that may originate beyond their operational boundaries.

By effectively integrating cybersecurity measures into the core components of PFSPs, ports can ensure that their security frameworks remain resilient in the face of evolving threats. This integration is no longer optional but essential, as ports increasingly rely on digital systems for daily operations.

8.3 Using International Frameworks to Strengthen Port Cybersecurity

International frameworks offer essential guidance to help ports integrate cybersecurity into their overall security strategies. Key frameworks include the IMO's cybersecurity guidelines, the IAPH Cybersecurity Guidelines, ISO/IEC 27001, and the NIST Cybersecurity Framework. The following section outlines how each of these frameworks can support ports in enhancing their digital resilience and operational continuity.

8.3.1 IMO Guidelines on Cyber Risk Management

To support the maritime sector in mitigating these risks, the IMO has issued two key cybersecurity frameworks: MSC-FAL.1/Circ.3 and Resolution

MSC.428(98) [4]. These guidelines provide structured approaches for ports, shipping companies, and other maritime operators to integrate cyber risk management into their existing safety and security management systems. Although adoption of these guidelines is not legally binding, many countries have incorporated them into national regulations, effectively making compliance mandatory for port authorities and maritime operators. The following section presents a detailed examination of each guideline and its specific implications for port operations.

1 **MSC-FAL.1-Circ.3: Guidelines on Maritime Cyber Risk Management**
MSC-FAL.1-Circ.3 provides high-level recommendations on maritime cyber risk management [4]. This guideline emphasizes a risk-based approach, integrating cyber risk management into existing safety and security practices established by the IMO. It focuses on identifying, protecting against, detecting, responding to, and recovering from cyber threats in maritime operations, particularly those affecting IT and OT systems, such as navigation and cargo-handling systems. Operators are expected to recognize the dual nature of cybersecurity risks across both IT and OT domains, with critical systems encompassing not only administrative networks and databases but also cargo-handling equipment, industrial control systems, navigational aids, and vessel traffic services. The guideline underscores the significant role of the human element, highlighting personnel actions, errors, and awareness levels as pivotal factors influencing the overall cybersecurity posture [5].

To implement MSC-FAL.1/Circ.3 effectively, ports should begin by identifying and mapping their critical assets. They must assess potential cyber threats and evaluate system vulnerabilities, considering the operational, financial, and reputational risks. It is essential for ports to adopt a comprehensive view of risk, understanding both direct and cascading impacts that could affect interconnected systems. By embedding cybersecurity risk management within existing safety and security management systems, ports can avoid inefficiencies or oversight from introducing parallel frameworks. Additionally, ports must establish formal cybersecurity policies, assign clear roles and responsibilities within the organization, and implement technical safeguards like access controls, data encryption, secure network architecture, and intrusion detection systems to protect their critical infrastructure [5].

Training and raising awareness among personnel are also a vital aspect of MSC-FAL.1/Circ.3 implementation. Ports should establish continuous education programs to keep staff informed on good cybersecurity practices and emerging threats. Furthermore, it is crucial for operators to develop comprehensive incident response and recovery plans. These plans should outline procedures for identifying, reporting, containing, mitigating, and recovering from cyber incidents. Effective communication protocols should be incorporated to facilitate rapid coordination within the organization and with external partners. Ongoing monitoring of cyber threats, regular vulnerability assessments, and the periodic revision of risk management measures will ensure the system remains resilient to the evolving threat landscape [5].

2 **Resolution MSC.428(98): Maritime Cyber Risk Management in Safety Management Systems**
Resolution MSC.428(98) presents a formal approach to incorporating cyber risk management into the safety management systems (SMS) under the ISM Code [6]. While the resolution primarily addresses the management of cyber risks on ships, it is equally relevant to ports, which play a crucial role in the safety and security of maritime operations. The resolution mandates that cyber risks be considered an integral part of safety management, and while the compliance deadline is set for the first annual verification of the DoC after January 1, 2021, the importance of cybersecurity at ports is also emphasized. Ports, alongside shipowners and operators, must incorporate cyber risk management into their SMS. By doing so, they not only comply with the ISM Code but also help ensure the broader safety of the maritime industry, linking this requirement to regulatory enforcement and audits that span both ships and the port infrastructure that supports them [6].

To comply with MSC.428(98), the first step in incorporating cyber risk management into SMS is for ports to identify and assess the cyber risks associated with their systems and operations. This includes evaluating critical infrastructure, such as communication systems, navigation equipment, cargo-handling systems, and control systems, which are susceptible to cyber threats. By considering both IT and OT, ports can identify vulnerabilities that may affect the safety of human life at sea, the protection of vessels, cargo, and port infrastructure. This comprehensive risk assessment will highlight existing gaps in safety protocols and indicate where additional cybersecurity measures are needed [6].

Once cyber risks are assessed, ports must integrate cyber risk management into their existing SMS frameworks. This involves establishing clear policies and assigning roles for the identification, assessment, mitigation, and monitoring of cyber risks. These policies must be aligned with the ISM Code to avoid redundancy and confusion, ensuring that cybersecurity efforts are seamlessly integrated with the broader safety and security strategies already in place. Given the dynamic nature of cyber threats, ports must also ensure that cyber risk management procedures are regularly evaluated and updated. Ongoing monitoring, audits, and risk assessments are necessary to keep pace with emerging threats and evolving regulatory requirements. A dynamic risk assessment process ensures that new technologies, tactics, and vulnerabilities are consistently addressed and that mitigation strategies remain relevant [6].

A critical aspect of implementing MSC.428(98) is ensuring compliance verification. Ports are required to incorporate cyber risk management into their DoC, which is subject to annual audits. The DoC must confirm that cybersecurity protocols are robust and embedded within the overall safety management system. This compliance verification process ensures that cybersecurity practices are rigorously audited and meet the necessary standards. In addition to these operational measures, training and capacity-building efforts are essential for the effective application of MSC.428(98). Ports and operators must ensure that staff members are trained in both cybersecurity and safety management. Training programs should address the intersection of traditional safety management practices with emerging cybersecurity threats, ensuring that all personnel, from senior management to operational staff, understand their roles in maintaining cybersecurity and mitigating cyber risks [6].

While both guidelines focus on cybersecurity, they differ significantly in their approach and level of enforcement. MSC-FAL.1-Circ.3 is a voluntary guideline, offering general, high-level recommendations to raise awareness and guide the integration of cyber risk management into existing frameworks. It provides a flexible approach for stakeholders with regard to following best practices across the maritime industry. On the other hand, Resolution MSC.428(98) mandates the formal integration of cyber risk management into existing SMS, with a clear deadline and regulatory enforcement through audits. This makes it a compliance-driven guideline that focuses on ensuring cyber risks are managed systematically within established safety frameworks.

8.3.2 IAPH Cybersecurity Guidelines for Ports

The IAPH Cyber Guidelines are globally recognized for their practical approach to enhancing port cybersecurity. Developed by IAPH, a leading non-governmental organization, these guidelines align with the IMO's MSC-FAL.1/Circ.3, which offers non-prescriptive recommendations for maritime cybersecurity resilience [7]. The guidelines provide a structured, port-specific framework for integrating cybersecurity into daily operations, addressing a wide range of areas which are broadly classified into four key categories, as follows.

1 **Executive Leadership and Strategic Commitment**
The IAPH emphasizes the critical role of port executives in advancing cybersecurity at a strategic level. To ensure cybersecurity is prioritized throughout the organization, executives must lead by example, fostering a culture of commitment and actively participating in developing and implementing a comprehensive cybersecurity risk management strategy aligned with global standards and best practices. This involves establishing a defense-in-depth posture to address emerging cyber risks and vulnerabilities,

ensuring cybersecurity is embedded in the port's long-term vision and operational goals. Central to this commitment is the appointment of the chief information security officer CISO or the chief information officer (CIO) to oversee and centralize cybersecurity efforts. These leadership roles are pivotal in ensuring accountability, signaling to the organization that cybersecurity is not just a technical issue, but a core element of the port's strategic direction. Through these roles, port executives can align cybersecurity objectives with broader organizational goals, integrating it into decision-making processes and long-term planning [8].

2 **Risk Management and Holistic Cybersecurity Management**

The IAPH Cybersecurity Guidelines emphasize the need for ports to adopt a proactive approach to managing cybersecurity risks. The process begins with the identification of cyber risks specific to the port environment, ensuring that threats unique to port operations, infrastructure, and digital systems are clearly recognized. This is followed by a comprehensive risk assessment and analysis to evaluate vulnerabilities across critical assets and operational systems. After completing the assessment, ports must prioritize identified risks based on their likelihood of occurrence and potential impact on operations. This prioritization allows for the effective allocation of resources and ensures that protection efforts focus on the most critical areas [8].

Continuous monitoring, detection, and control of emerging threats are essential to maintaining situational awareness and responding promptly to changes in the cyber threat landscape. Subsequently, ports should implement targeted mitigation strategies to reduce exposure to cyber threats and enhance the overall resilience of their systems. In parallel, establishing a well-defined incident response and recovery plan is crucial to ensure that, in the event of a cybersecurity breach, swift and coordinated actions are taken to contain damage, restore normal operations, and minimize disruption [8].

Throughout these processes, the IAPH guidelines stress the importance of continuous information sharing, communication, and coordination—both internally and with external stakeholders—to reinforce collective cyber resilience. Furthermore, cybersecurity maturity must be systematically assessed, with iterative improvements integrated to adapt to the evolving threat environment. By adhering to this comprehensive and dynamic approach, ports can significantly strengthen their digital resilience, operational continuity, and long-term security posture against emerging cyber threats [8].

3 **Organizational Structures and Governance**

A critical element contributing to the success of effective port cybersecurity is the establishment of clear organizational structures and robust governance frameworks. Ports must start by identifying all stakeholders within their digital ecosystems, including administrative staff, operational personnel, external vendors, and government partners who interact with digital assets. Given the dynamic nature of port ecosystems, regular reviews and updates of the stakeholder list are essential to ensure its comprehensiveness. Following stakeholder identification, ports must delineate specific roles and responsibilities for individuals involved in cybersecurity activities. Authority should be assigned based on expertise, ensuring that only qualified personnel manage and oversee digitally connected assets and infrastructures. These organizational structures ensure that cybersecurity is adequately managed and protected across all operational facets of the port [8].

In addition to identifying stakeholders, it is crucial to appoint key figures responsible for leading and overseeing cybersecurity efforts within the port. The IAPH stresses the need for a designated CISO to centralize cybersecurity management and accountability. The Board of Directors should also play an active role in overseeing cyber risk management, ensuring that cybersecurity remains a key discussion at the strategic level. Regular updates on cyber risks, incidents, and mitigation strategies must be provided to the Board, enabling informed decisions about resource allocation and risk management. Furthermore, the IAPH calls for the creation of a cybersecurity steering committee, which will coordinate cross-functional cybersecurity initiatives, ensuring that cybersecurity objectives align with the port's broader operational and strategic goals. These structures and roles collectively enhance the port's governance, ensuring that cybersecurity remains a priority and is integrated effectively into the port's overall strategy [8].

4 **Awareness, Training, and Workforce Development**

Ports should prioritize building a strong cybersecurity culture within their workforce to enhance port security. Ensuring that employees at all levels are well-trained and aware of cybersecurity risks is essential for strengthening the overall resilience of port operations. Ports should foster a cybersecurity-conscious culture throughout the organization to create a proactive workforce that can effectively mitigate potential threats [8]. Regular training sessions, coupled with continuous awareness programs, should be implemented to keep personnel informed about current risks, vulnerabilities, and emerging cyber threats. Furthermore, ports should provide ongoing learning opportunities to ensure staff stay up-to-date with evolving best practices and regulatory requirements. In addition to awareness efforts, ports should equip cybersecurity leads with the necessary tools, resources, and knowledge to develop and execute effective cybersecurity strategies. Regular cybersecurity drills and simulations are also recommended to prepare the workforce to respond quickly and effectively to real-world cyber-attack scenarios. These drills should provide hands-on experience, allowing staff to familiarize themselves with incident response procedures, and post-drill assessments should be conducted to measure improvements in response times and incident handling.

8.3.3 ISO/IEC 27001

ISO/IEC 27001 is a globally recognized standard for ISMS, providing a comprehensive framework to manage sensitive information security risks. Endorsed by the IMO as a recommended guideline for ports, ISO/IEC 27001 offers a structured, risk-based approach to safeguard critical data and ensure operational continuity [4]. For port facilities, adopting this standard is a strategic move to enhance cybersecurity resilience, offering a systematic method for managing risks from increasingly sophisticated cyber-attacks. Its implementation safeguards vital systems against a wide range of cyber threats [9]. By embedding ISO/IEC 27001 principles into organizational culture and day-to-day operations, ports can clearly define cybersecurity roles and responsibilities, align security initiatives with business objectives, and institutionalize ongoing risk assessment, asset identification, and proactive system monitoring at all management levels.

A key strength of ISO/IEC 27001 is its focus on five essential domains that help safeguard the complex digital infrastructure of modern ports: access control, incident management, data protection, business continuity, and dynamic risk management [10]. First, the standard promotes strict access control measures to restrict system access to authorized personnel, reducing risks from insider threats and external breaches. Second, it mandates the creation of comprehensive incident management protocols, ensuring timely detection of, response to, and recovery from cybersecurity incidents, thus minimizing disruptions to port operations. Third, to protect sensitive data, ISO/IEC 27001 advocates using encryption technologies for both data in transit and at rest, preserving the CIA of operational and customer data. Fourth, the standard encourages developing robust business continuity and disaster recovery plans, ensuring that ports can continue operations or quickly resume services during disruptive events. Finally, ISO/IEC 27001 emphasizes a dynamic risk management framework that continually evaluates emerging and existing cyber threats, allowing ports to adjust their security measures to an evolving threat landscape, ensuring ongoing resilience.

Moreover, ISO/IEC 27001 goes beyond compliance by fostering a culture of continuous improvement. Regular audits and assessments enable ports to evaluate their security practices, identify areas for enhancement, and create a feedback loop that strengthens overall resilience. This process is essential for ports increasingly dependent on interconnected systems and digital technologies, where vulnerabilities can emerge rapidly in response to evolving cyber threats. By institutionalizing continuous improvement, ports ensure not only adherence to global security standards but also position themselves as leaders in safeguarding critical infrastructure. This proactive approach builds trust with partners, stakeholders, and customers, ensuring both immediate protection and long-term strategic security benefits.

8.3.4 NIST CSF

The NIST CSF is organized around five core functions—Identify, Protect, Detect, Respond, and Recover [11]. These functions work together to create a comprehensive, cyclical process that helps organizations continuously improve their cybersecurity posture. This cycle allows for adaptability in addressing both current threats and emerging risks, making it a vital approach for ports and other critical infrastructure [12]. The five functions offer an integrated structure that provides guidance in all aspects of cybersecurity, from initial risk assessments to post-incident recovery. For ports, with their complex, interconnected digital operations, this structured approach is essential for building resilience against an ever-evolving threat landscape.

1. **Identify:** The first step involves understanding and managing cybersecurity risks related to systems, assets, data, and capabilities essential to port operations. Ports need to conduct thorough assessments of their infrastructure, including automated cargo-handling systems and port community systems, identifying potential vulnerabilities. This phase also includes understanding the port's risk environment, such as possible cyber-attack vectors, and establishing a cybersecurity governance framework. A clear understanding of risk helps ports prioritize where to allocate resources and efforts to mitigate potential threats.
2. **Protect:** Building on the insights gained from the Identify function, the Protect function focuses on implementing safeguards to ensure the CIA of critical systems. Ports must establish strong access controls, encryption, and data protection measures for the digital systems that manage operations like cargo tracking, vessel management, and communications. Additionally, physical security measures should complement these digital efforts, ensuring security protocols are enforced across both virtual and physical infrastructures. Employee training programs to increase cybersecurity awareness are also crucial in protecting against human error, a common vulnerability.
3. **Detect:** Even with robust protective measures in place, threats can still emerge—making the Detect function essential. This function emphasizes the timely identification of cybersecurity events to minimize damage. Ports must implement systems that monitor digital assets and operations for unusual activities that could signal a cyber-attack. Tools such as intrusion detection systems (IDSs), security information and event management (SIEM) solutions, and regular audits help detect and analyze suspicious activity. Early detection allows ports to quickly identify malicious actions like malware, ransomware, or unauthorized access, enabling a swift response that limits operational disruptions.
4. **Respond:** When a threat is detected, ports must be prepared to act—this is the role of the Respond function. It focuses on taking immediate and appropriate actions to contain and mitigate the impact of a cybersecurity

incident. Ports should have a detailed incident response plan that includes clear protocols for communication, coordination, and technical actions. For example, if an attack compromises the port's cargo management system, the response could involve isolating affected systems, notifying relevant stakeholders, and initiating recovery processes. A well-executed response minimizes downtime and prevents significant disruptions to port operations, which are critical for global supply chain continuity.

5 **Recover:** Following response efforts, the Recover function ensures that impaired systems and services are restored efficiently and securely. This phase involves implementing robust business continuity and disaster recovery plans so that backup systems can resume operations with minimal delay. Just as importantly, it includes reviewing the incident to identify lessons learned and improve future resilience. These insights feed back into the Identify function, supporting continuous improvement and reinforcing the cyclical nature of the NIST CSF in strengthening port cybersecurity.

By implementing the NIST CSF's core functions, ports can build a robust security posture that protects critical infrastructure, ensures operational continuity during cyber incidents, and supports ongoing improvement. To enhance the effectiveness of this approach, NIST regularly updates its guidelines, offering practical tools and recommendations for each function. These include resources for asset inventory and mapping, risk assessment, data protection, and identity management—key areas for addressing vulnerabilities and adapting to an evolving cybersecurity landscape [13]. The structured and regularly updated nature of these guidelines ensures that organizations have access to best practices and actionable strategies that are adaptable, scalable, and capable of addressing both existing and emerging cybersecurity challenges—capabilities that are especially critical for ports as they manage complex, interconnected digital operations.

Apart from its core guidelines, NIST also addresses the unique cybersecurity challenges presented by evolving technologies by issuing updated frameworks that help organizations align their practices with the latest standards. For example, the AI Risk Management Framework, developed with input from over 240 organizations, offers voluntary guidance for integrating trustworthiness into artificial intelligence (AI) systems by identifying, assessing, and managing AI risks [14]. Ports can apply this framework to enhance the security and transparency of AI applications in cargo tracking, vessel management, and security operations. Similarly, NIST's Special Publication 800-228 provides guidelines for securing application programming interfaces (APIs)—critical to cloud-native architectures—by addressing vulnerabilities across the API lifecycle [15], helping ports strengthen the security of services such as automated cargo handling and port community systems. In addition, the National Cybersecurity Center of Excellence has developed solutions for securing emerging 5G networks, outlined in Special Publication 1800-33 [16], which support ports in protecting real-time data exchanges and automation systems. Collectively, these evolving guidelines enable ports to better manage the cybersecurity risks of new technologies, ensuring operational efficiency, infrastructure resilience, and public trust in an increasingly digital environment.

8.3.5 Comparative Analysis of Major Cybersecurity Frameworks for Ports

This section aims to provide a concise comparison of the commonalities and differences among these frameworks, helping readers connect the detailed framework descriptions from earlier sections with a clear, visual synthesis.

Figure 8.1 offers a visual summary that complements the detailed textual analysis provided earlier. It presents an integrated overview of both shared principles and the distinct emphases of each framework. The figure highlights key areas of alignment and divergence—such as governance models, risk focus, adaptability to port-specific needs, integration of emerging technologies, and regulatory compliance orientation—enabling readers to grasp each framework's relative strengths and unique contributions at a glance.

- **Common Foundations Across Major Cybersecurity Frameworks**
  Despite being developed by different organizations and for varied purposes, the **IMO Cybersecurity Guidelines**, **IAPH Cybersecurity Guidelines**, **ISO/IEC 27001**, and the **NIST CSF** share a number of foundational principles relevant to the port industry. Their convergence on several critical cybersecurity areas reflects a consensus on what is considered essential for effective cyber risk governance within the maritime and port sectors.

  A key commonality is the use of a **risk-based approach**. All four frameworks emphasize the need to assess, prioritize, and address cyber risks according to their likelihood and potential impact. IMO and IAPH guidelines make this a stated requirement, directly tying it to maritime safety and leadership responsibilities. ISO/IEC 27001 incorporates it through its structured ISMS methodology, while NIST constructs its entire framework on the principle of risk-informed decision making.

  Another shared theme is the importance of **continuous monitoring and improvement**. These frameworks all encourage regular review cycles to ensure that cybersecurity strategies remain relevant and effective. This includes audits and reviews under ISO/IEC 27001, lifecycle-based feedback loops in the NIST model, and reevaluation mechanisms found in the IMO and IAPH guidelines. Each framework also insists that **cybersecurity be fully embedded into operational and strategic contexts**, rather than treated as a standalone technical function. IMO mandates its integration into the SMS, IAPH aligns it with executive strategies, ISO/IEC

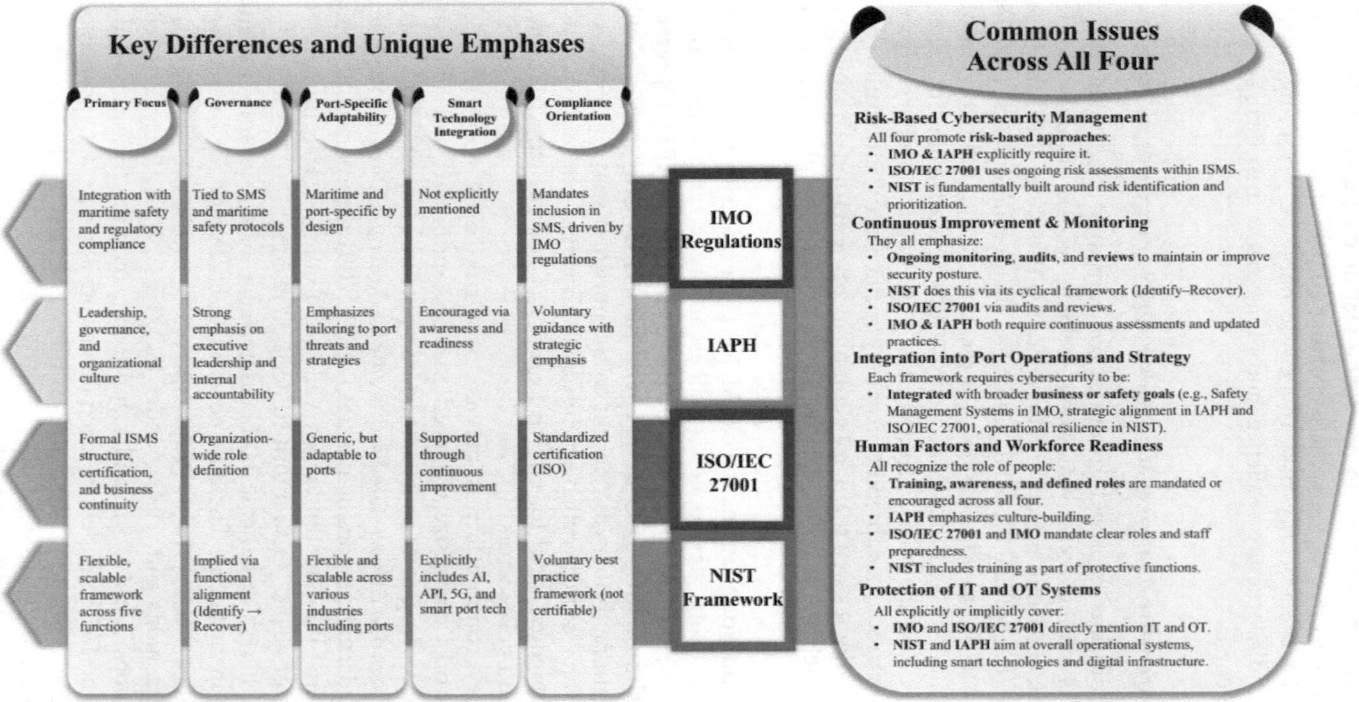

Figure 8.1 Commonalities and Differences in Major Port Cybersecurity Frameworks.

27001 promotes linkages with business continuity, and NIST positions cybersecurity as a pillar of operational resilience.

Furthermore, the **human element** is consistently addressed. All four frameworks stress the importance of staff awareness, defined responsibilities, and regular training. IAPH puts particular weight on cultivating a cybersecurity-conscious organizational culture, while ISO/IEC 27001 and IMO focus on role designation and preparedness. NIST includes human readiness within its "Protect" function. Lastly, attention to **both IT and OT systems** is another point of alignment. Although the degree of specificity varies, all frameworks acknowledge the increasing convergence of these systems in ports. IMO and ISO/IEC 27001 directly reference both domains, while IAPH and NIST take a broader view that includes smart infrastructure and digitally integrated operations.

- **Key Differences and Unique Contributions**
While the four frameworks align on many principles, their differences are equally important—particularly when it comes to their origins, use cases, and the level of formality they demand.

The **IMO Guidelines** are tightly coupled with maritime regulatory structures, focused on integrating cybersecurity within existing SMSs. Their strength lies in ensuring compliance, particularly for facilities and vessels governed by international conventions. Their prescriptive nature makes them indispensable for ports with mandatory obligations under IMO jurisdiction. In contrast, the **IAPH Guidelines** are voluntary and strategic, designed to support internal governance improvements rather than meet regulatory benchmarks. They prioritize leadership accountability and cultural transformation. Their unique contribution lies in encouraging executive-level commitment and risk ownership across all levels of port operations.

ISO/IEC 27001 stands out for its structure and certifiability. It offers a rigorous, globally recognized standard for establishing and managing an ISMS. While not designed specifically for ports, its flexibility allows for adaptation, especially for operators seeking formal recognition or alignment with international supply chain security standards. **NIST**, meanwhile, provides a highly modular and scalable model, making it ideal for organizations that value flexibility or are in the earlier stages of cybersecurity development. Its five-function structure—Identify, Protect, Detect, Respond, and Recover—presents a clear and logical path for managing cyber risks. Notably, it addresses modern digitalization trends more directly than the other frameworks, explicitly referencing AI, APIs, 5G, and other emerging technologies.

The frameworks also diverge in **adaptability to port environments**. IMO and IAPH are purpose-built for maritime and port settings. ISO/IEC 27001 is industry-agnostic but adaptable, while NIST is intentionally broad, encouraging ports to tailor its functions to their own operational and technical contexts. Finally, differences in **compliance orientation** are pronounced. IMO Guidelines are mandatory under international maritime law. ISO/IEC 27001 offers third-party certification, valuable for ports needing formal external validation. IAPH and NIST, by contrast, provide best-practice models without regulatory force.

References

[1] P. K. Mukherjee, "The ISM Code and the ISPS Code: A Critical Legal Analysis of Two SOLAS Regimes," *WMU Journal of Maritime Affairs*, vol. 6, p. 147–166, 2007.

[2] IMO, "International Convention for the Safety of Life at Sea (SOLAS), 1974," 2024. [Online]. Available: www.imo.org/en/About/Conventions/Pages/International-Convention-for-the-Safety-of-Life-at-Sea-(SOLAS),-1974.aspx.

[3] C. Senarak, "Cybersecurity Knowledge and Skills for Port Facility Security Officers of International Seaports: Perspectives of IT and Security Personnel," *The Asian Journal of Shipping and Logistics*, vol. 37, no. 4, pp. 345–360, 2021.

[4] IMO, "Maritime Cyber Risk," 2024. [Online]. Available: www.imo.org/en/OurWork/Security/Pages/Cyber-security.aspx.

[5] IMO, "Guidelines On Maritime Cyber Risk Management," 2022. [Online]. Available: wwwcdn.imo.org/localresources/en/OurWork/Security/Documents/MSC-FAL.1-Circ.3-Rev.2%20-%20Guidelines%20On%20Maritime%20Cyber%20Risk%20Management%20(Secretariat)%20(1).pdf.

[6] IMO, "Maritime Cyber Risk Management in Safety Management Systems," 2017. [Online]. Available: wwwcdn.imo.org/localresources/en/OurWork/Security/Documents/Resolution%20MSC.428(98).pdf.

[7] IMO, "Measures to Enhance Maritime Security," 2021. [Online]. Available: https://events.iala.int/content/uploads/2021/09/MSC-104-7-1-IAPH-Cybersecurity-Guidelines-for-Ports-and-Port-Facilities-IAPH.pdfMeasurestoEnhanceMaritimeSecurity.

[8] IAPH, "IAPH Cybersecurity Guidelines for Ports and Port Facilities," 2021. [Online]. Available: https://sustainableworldports.org/wp-content/uploads/IAPH-Cybersecurity-Guidelines-version-1_0.pdf.

[9] IMO, "Guidelines on Port Community Systems (FAL.5/Circ.54)," 2024. [Online]. Available: wwwcdn.imo.org/localresources/en/OurWork/Facilitation/FAL%20related%20nonmandatory%20documents/FAL.5-Circ.54.pdf.

[10] ISO/IEC, "Information Technology — Security Techniques — Information Security Management Systems — Requirements," ISO/IEC, Switzerland, 2013.

[11] NIST, "The CSF 1.1 Five Functions," 2024. [Online]. Available: www.nist.gov/cyberframework/getting-started/online-learning/five-functions#:~:text=detection%20%2F%20response%20activities-,Recover,impact%20from%20a%20cybersecurity%20incident..

[12] D. Trimble, J. Monken and A. F. L. Sand, "A Framework for Cybersecurity Assessments of Critical Port Infrastructure," in 2017 International Conference on Cyber Conflict (CyCon U.S.), Washington, DC, USA, 2017.

[13] NIST, "Guidelines and Tools," 2020. [Online]. Available: www.nist.gov/privacy-framework/resource-repository/browse/guidelines-and-tools.

[14] Trustworthy & Responsible AI Resource Center, "AI Risk Management Framework," 2025. [Online]. Available: https://airc.nist.gov/airmf-resources/airmf/.
[15] NIST, "Guidelines for API Protection for Cloud-Native Systems," 2025. [Online]. Available: https://csrc.nist.gov/pubs/sp/800/228/ipd.
[16] NIST, "5G Cybersecurity," 2025. [Online]. Available: https://csrc.nist.gov/pubs/sp/1800/33/ipd.

9 Balancing the Port Network Integration and Segmentation

9.1 Definitions and Purposes of Port Network Integration

Port network integration (PNI) involves aligning and connecting the various digital systems, infrastructure elements, and operational processes that support port activities. Rather than functioning in isolation, these components are structured to operate as an interconnected framework that supports synchronized, real-time decision making. The goal is to ensure seamless interaction among key systems—such as terminal operating systems (TOSs), seaside operating systems (SOSs), landside operating systems (LOSs), and any logistics coordination tools—thereby enabling efficient cargo movement, regulatory compliance, and coordinated stakeholder engagement. Through standardized data formats and interoperable workflows, this integration reduces operational silos, enhances visibility across the supply chain, and supports the strategic demands of modern, digitally connected ports.

This concept of integrated PNI is illustrated in Figure 9.1. In the left box, four subsystems—BMS, YMS, GMS, SACS—are integrated into a unified TOS, while CHS and DOS are typically consolidated under a cargo management system (CMS). In contrast, vessel traffic management systems (VTMSs) remain separate, reflecting their distinct operational role and real-time control requirements. This architecture exemplifies how integration enables seamless data exchange, centralized oversight, and reduced duplication of effort across traditionally siloed functions. However, it also underscores a critical vulnerability: when multiple systems are tightly linked, a cyber-attack on one component can cascade across the entire TOS or CMS, potentially halting several operational processes at once. Thus, while integration improves efficiency and coordination, it simultaneously expands the potential impact of cyber incidents—making cybersecurity considerations central to integration planning.

Translating the concept of PNI into practice requires more than connecting software systems—it demands a deliberate and coordinated effort to align physical infrastructure, operational workflows, and human expertise [1, 2]. Technologies such as sensors, programmable controllers, and communication networks must be integrated not only with digital tools like middleware and

DOI: 10.4324/9781003559320-9

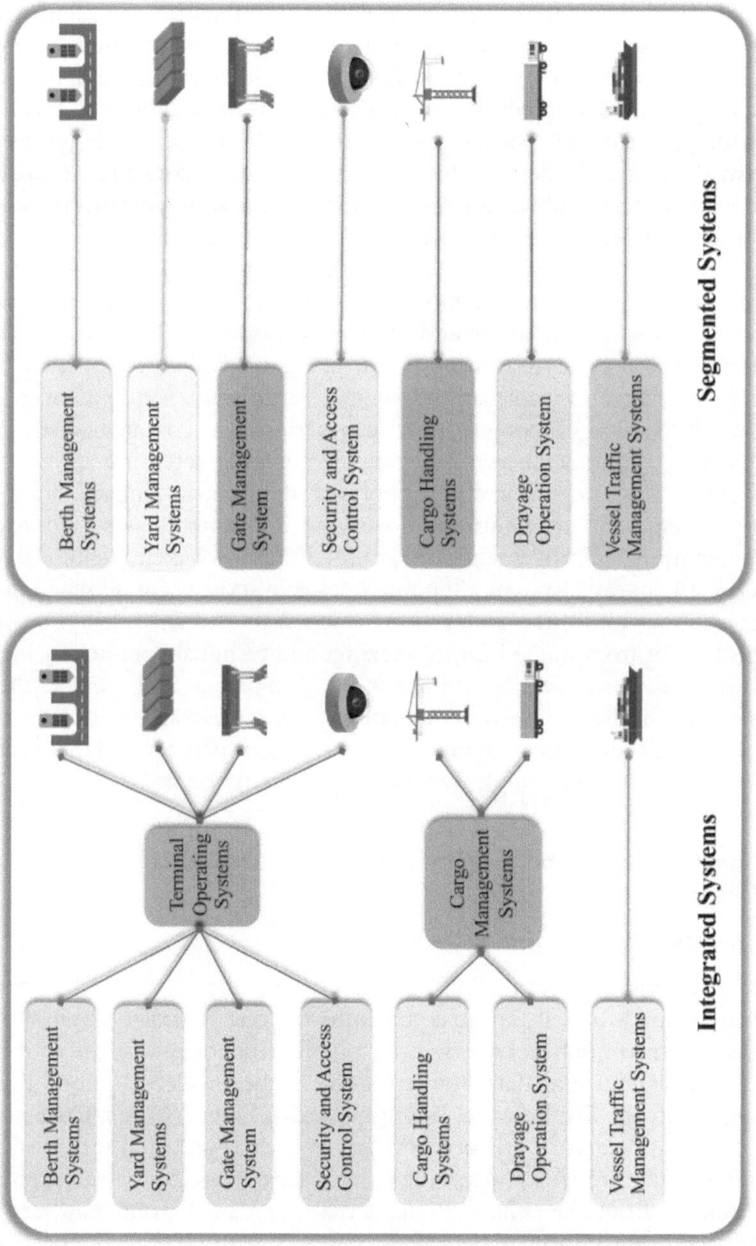

Figure 9.1 Comparison of Integrated and Segmented Port System Architectures.

APIs but also with the day-to-day activities of port personnel. This level of coordination cannot happen passively; it must be supported by a clear strategic vision, dedicated budgets, and governance mechanisms that anticipate both technical dependencies and operational constraints [3]. Without such foresight, integration efforts may fall short—leading to fragmented systems, inefficiencies, or critical vulnerabilities. Ports must therefore approach integration as a long-term investment that requires careful resource allocation, skilled implementation teams, and ongoing oversight. In this context, the success of port network integration depends less on individual technologies and more on the port's ability to mobilize and align its technical and organizational assets toward a shared operational objective.

When effectively implemented, the PNI significantly enhances operational efficiency. Real-time synchronization across terminals, berths, and hinterland links enables ports to reduce vessel waiting times, optimize berth usage, and prevent congestion at key transition points like gates and customs. By automating the exchange of information—such as cargo status, equipment availability, and inspection outcomes—ports can better align container discharge schedules with yard operations, reducing demurrage, detention costs, and idle resources. This integration also supports predictive maintenance, drawing from equipment data to minimize downtime and extend asset lifecycles. Beyond operational improvements, integration improves stakeholder collaboration across the port ecosystem. Shipping lines gain more accurate scheduling insights; customs authorities receive timely access to clearance data; logistics providers benefit from unified cargo tracking; and terminal operators achieve better resource allocation. Inland transport companies and port authorities alike benefit from improved situational awareness and coordination. Ultimately, a well-integrated port network fosters transparency, reliability, and responsiveness in an increasingly complex logistics environment.

9.2 Definitions and Cybersecurity Benefits of Port Network Segmentation

9.2.1 Segmenting Port IT Infrastructure

Port network segmentation (PNS) refers to the intentional architectural division of a port's digital infrastructure into discrete logically or physically isolated segments or sub-networks. Each segment operates with its own set of access permissions and data flow controls, aligned with its unique functional requirements. To illustrate, the right box of Figure 9.1 depicts a conceptual layout in which seven core port systems are segmented into distinct zones. This figure presents an extreme case of separation, where each system is fully isolated from the others. While actual implementations may vary in granularity, the illustration underscores how segmenting systems based on operational roles can reduce interdependencies and prevent lateral movement of threats. By confining each system within its own zone, ports can tailor security controls to the risk level and criticality of each function, enhancing both containment and resilience. This segmentation approach reinforces zero-trust principles and allows for more precise monitoring, aligned with industry-specific guidance such as the IAPH Cybersecurity Guidelines for Ports and Port Facilities [4].

Implementing effective PNS offers a range of cybersecurity advantages that bolster both technical control and operational resilience. A primary benefit is the reduction of the attack surface. By isolating mission-critical systems from administrative networks, ports can significantly limit the pathways available for cyber intrusions. This architectural separation ensures that vulnerabilities in one zone are less likely to propagate laterally, confining potential breaches and minimizing the risk of systemic compromise. Segmentation also plays a key role in threat containment. If malware or unauthorized activity occurs within a particular domain, the threat can be swiftly contained before it spreads to critical infrastructure governing logistics, navigation, or safety operations. This localized containment allows security teams to respond quickly and decisively, preserving the continuity of broader port activities. Additionally, clearly defined segmentation boundaries enhance anomaly detection, making irregular traffic patterns easier to isolate and investigate within each zone.

Furthermore, segmentation supports the enforcement of fine-grained access controls based on functional roles and responsibilities. For instance, only authorized personnel with specific clearance may interact with the VTMS, which manages maritime traffic and ensures safety by preventing collisions. In contrast, general administrative staff are confined to less sensitive segments. Similarly, access to the cargo-handling system (CHS), responsible for scheduling and coordinating port equipment, is restricted to operators and technicians who manage the equipment. This alignment of access with operational roles enforces the principle of least privilege and supports zero-trust security models, minimizing the risk of insider threats and unauthorized lateral movement [5]. Security measures can be customized according to the sensitivity of each segment—allowing ports to deploy stronger encryption, authentication, and monitoring tools where necessary, without burdening lower-risk systems with excessive restrictions. Finally, segmentation supports compliance with global cybersecurity frameworks. By clearly delineating zones within the network, ports streamline monitoring, auditing, and forensic investigations [4]. This clarity not only aids in meeting regulatory requirements but also enhances the port's reputation among stakeholders, insurers, and international partners as a secure and reliable participant in the global maritime supply chain.

9.2.2 Key Approaches to Network Segmentation

While segmenting all systems can improve cybersecurity, it may hinder operational and managerial efficiency due to reduced integration. Therefore, ports should apply segmentation selectively, based on functional requirements and risk profiles. This section outlines five widely used approaches to network segmentation, highlighting their respective benefits and challenges when it comes to balancing security and operational effectiveness.

1 **Virtual local area networks (VLANs)** are a network configuration technique that groups devices into separate, logical sub-networks within the same physical infrastructure [6]. Rather than relying on physical separation, VLANs use software-defined boundaries to isolate traffic. This approach allows for the logical division of a physical network into multiple isolated segments. These VLANs enable ports to group devices based on operational functions regardless of their physical location within the infrastructure. For instance, cargo management systems, security systems, or administrative networks can be segmented into different VLANs to enhance both operational efficiency and security. VLANs work by separating traffic between different groups, ensuring that systems in one group do not interact with others unless specifically permitted. This controlled isolation helps enforce internal boundaries within the port's digital infrastructure.

   The main advantage of VLANs is ensuring improved security by isolating sensitive systems [7] such as cargo management or port authority operations, thereby reducing the risk of unauthorized access. VLANs also enhance network performance by limiting unnecessary broadcast traffic and allowing more efficient use of network resources. However, managing numerous VLANs can be complex and prone to misconfiguration without careful planning. Furthermore, enabling communication between separate VLANs requires specific settings, which can add operational complexity and potential risks if not carefully managed.

2 **Firewalls and access control lists (ACLs)** are essential network security tools that work together to control traffic flow between network segments [8]. A firewall acts as a barrier between trusted internal networks and untrusted external networks, filtering incoming and outgoing traffic based on predefined security rules [9]. On the other hand, ACLs, typically configured on routers or switches, allow administrators to define which types of traffic are permitted or denied based on specific criteria like IP addresses, protocols, or ports [10]. For example, ACLs can allow communication between security systems but block unnecessary traffic to less sensitive areas. This combination of firewalls and ACLs creates a multi-layered defense, reducing the risk of unauthorized access and limiting the spread of potential threats if one part of the network is compromised.

   One of the key benefits of using firewalls alongside ACLs is the creation of robust, fine-grained access control, enhancing overall security. This layered defense helps to reduce the risk of unauthorized access, making it more difficult for attackers to move freely between network segments. However, while offering strong security, the use of firewalls and ACLs can introduce performance overhead, especially when managing large volumes of traffic or implementing complex security rules. Additionally, setting up and maintaining firewalls and ACLs requires a deep understanding of network configurations. Misconfigurations or overly complex rule sets may lead to unintended access, which could disrupt the flow of traffic or reduce security effectiveness.

3 **Demilitarized zones (DMZs)** are specialized subnetworks designed to separate public-facing services from internal systems, thereby limiting the exposure of critical infrastructure to external threats [11]. The concept of a DMZ emerged as a response to the limitations of traditional security mechanisms—such as encryption, intrusion detection and prevention, patch management, and system monitoring—which, while essential, are not always sufficient to prevent cyber breaches. By isolating services that must be accessible from the internet, DMZs ensure that even if a public-facing system is compromised, attackers cannot directly access sensitive internal networks [11].

   In the context of port environments, DMZs serve to protect vital operational systems—such as TOSs and VTMSs—by placing public-facing services like port authority websites or external APIs in a separate network zone. This configuration allows users to interact with publicly available services without exposing the internal port infrastructure to direct access. Typically, DMZs are implemented using a dual-firewall architecture: one firewall regulates traffic between the internet and the DMZ, while another controls communication between the DMZ and the trusted internal port network. This layered approach ensures that any potential compromise of external services is contained within the DMZ, thereby safeguarding critical port operations from cyber intrusions.

   The primary advantage of a DMZ in port networks is enhanced security ensured by isolating public-facing services, reducing the risk of external cyber-attacks affecting core port operations. However, establishing and maintaining a DMZ for port systems requires careful planning to determine which services should be exposed to the outside world. Additionally, the setup can be resource-intensive and increase operational complexity, particularly in large-scale port networks where multiple services must be carefully managed.

4 **Air gaps** are the physical or logical isolation of critical systems from unsecured networks, particularly the internet, to prevent unauthorized access and reduce the risk of cyber-attacks [12]. The core principle is the deliberate absence of any wired or wireless communication between the isolated network and external systems. This is typically enforced by removing network cables, using electromagnetic shielding, or housing systems in physically secure locations. The result is a system that is extremely difficult to compromise remotely, as data cannot enter or leave through conventional digital channels. Air gaps are widely adopted in environments where the protection of sensitive information, high-value assets, and critical infrastructure is paramount. These include military and government systems, financial computing systems, backup environments, and similar domains requiring uninterrupted and secure operations [12].

In port environments, air gaps are particularly effective in protecting core systems—such as control servers or backup databases—from exposure to broader IT networks or the internet. For example, a TOS may be hosted in an air-gapped environment to ensure continuous operation even if other parts of the network are compromised. By limiting data exchange to manual transfers or tightly controlled interfaces, air-gapped systems offer a high-assurance defense against cyber threats. The key advantage in port operations is near-total immunity to remote attacks, as the absence of external connectivity eliminates most threat vectors. However, maintaining an air gap poses challenges: manual data handling is time-consuming and vulnerable to human error. As ports grow more interconnected, sustaining fully isolated systems becomes increasingly impractical.

5 **Software defined networking (SDN)** is a modern approach to designing and managing networks that improves flexibility, efficiency, and control. Unlike traditional networks—where each device (like a switch or router) makes its own decisions—SDN separates the decision-making part of the network (called the control plane) from the part that moves the data (called the data plane) [13]. This separation allows the entire network to be managed by a central software-based controller, which acts like the brain of the system. This central controller has a complete view of the network and can automatically adjust how data flows through it, based on current conditions and needs. Because it is software-driven, network settings can be changed quickly without having to physically reconfigure hardware. This makes SDN especially helpful for handling growing network traffic and for managing complex or large-scale environments [13]. In the port context, the SDN manages the diverse and interconnected systems that support port operations and surveillance networks. By providing a centralized control mechanism, SDN enables ports to better coordinate networked systems, prioritize critical data flows, and respond to operational demands in real time.

The primary benefit of SDN is its dynamic flexibility, enabling administrators to quickly reconfigure network segments in response to real-time security or performance requirements [13]. Its centralized management streamlines oversight and policy enforcement across complex port systems. However, SDN introduces operational complexity and requires specialized expertise for effective deployment and maintenance. Moreover, because the network relies on a centralized controller, it may introduce a potential single point of failure. Without appropriate redundancy and security measures, this could pose risks to the network's stability and resilience [13]. Therefore, while SDN offers substantial advantages, its implementation in port environments must be carefully planned and supported by skilled personnel.

9.2.3 Challenges and Strategies for the PNS

While PNS offers substantial cybersecurity benefits, its successful implementation within port environments presents several challenges. The following section outlines key challenges and proposes strategies to mitigate such challenges.

- **Complexity of Port Network Architecture:** Port network architectures are inherently complex, often encompassing a wide range of interconnected IT and OT systems. This complexity makes segmentation difficult, as isolating systems without disrupting workflow requires a deep understanding of the network's interdependencies. To manage this complexity, ports must begin with comprehensive network mapping and risk-based segmentation planning. Identifying critical systems and mapping data flows allows ports to design segmentation that reflects operational priorities while minimizing risk. Threat modeling further helps by simulating attack scenarios to identify how breaches might propagate across interconnected systems. Implementing segmentation in phases, testing each segment before deployment, can reduce operational disruptions. This gradual rollout, supported by clear architectural planning, ensures that segmentation enhances security without compromising the continuity of essential port functions.
- **Cost and Resource Constraints:** Financial and personnel constraints often hinder the implementation and maintenance of effective segmentation. The need for additional hardware, security software, and skilled personnel can quickly escalate costs. To manage these constraints, ports can adopt a risk-prioritized approach that focuses resources on high-value or high-risk segments first. Automation tools can help enforce policies and monitor traffic with minimal manual intervention, reducing labor demands and response time. Outsourcing specialized tasks or engaging in public-private partnerships can provide access to cybersecurity expertise when in-house capabilities are limited. Concurrently, investing in targeted training programs for existing staff can gradually build internal capacity, supporting sustainable management over time of segmented environments.
- **Impact on Operational Efficiency:** The introduction of PNS can inadvertently slow down data flow between segments, affecting real-time operations. Overly rigid segmentation may also hinder staff productivity if access to necessary systems becomes burdensome. To avoid these pitfalls, segmentation designs must consider performance and latency, aligning with operational needs. Adaptive access controls and real-time monitoring can maintain security without sacrificing efficiency. Collaboration between IT and OT teams is essential to balance technical safeguards with functional demands, ensuring that segmentation protocols are aligned with the requirements of both business systems and physical operations.
- **Legacy Systems Integration:** Legacy operational technology systems present another major obstacle, as many were never designed with modern cybersecurity in mind. These systems often lack support for modern segmentation and authentication practices, increasing exposure to potential attacks. To mitigate this, ports can deploy intermediary devices or network gateways that shield legacy systems without requiring direct modification. Where upgrades are not immediately feasible, compensating controls such

as strict access rules and network isolation can reduce exposure. Ports should maintain dedicated zones for legacy assets, monitor them closely, and document all access and configuration changes to ensure traceability. Over the long term, phased modernization plans supported by regular audits will help to transition away from vulnerable systems while preserving operational continuity.

9.3 Types of Network Segmentation Strategies

Network segmentation encompasses a variety of methods, each offering unique advantages and serving specific purposes within a network. The following sections provide an in-depth explanation of each segmentation approach, highlighting their key features and practical applications in port operations.

9.3.1 Micro-Segmentation

Micro-segmentation is a network security approach that focuses on isolating individual workloads, applications, or devices rather than broader network zones [14]. This granularity significantly limits lateral movement within the network, making it harder for attackers to propagate if they breach a single-entry point. In port environments, where both OT and IT systems coexist, micro-segmentation helps isolate sensitive components such as TOSs, IoT devices, and cargo-tracking systems. It is especially effective in situations where critical systems must be shielded from less secure parts of the network, such as regulatory zones, legacy infrastructure, or third-party interfaces. Ports dealing with hybrid environments or high-value assets can use micro-segmentation to maintain strict control over internal communications and minimize attack exposure. By ensuring that each of these systems only communicates with authorized counterparts, micro-segmentation provides a robust barrier against internal and external threats.

Micro-segmentation offers several advantages, including minimizing lateral movement, reducing the attack surface, and increasing visibility and control over network traffic. However, it also presents challenges. Its implementation can be complex, requiring specialized knowledge and tools, especially in environments with diverse legacy and modern systems. Additionally, the increased volume of security policies and inspections can introduce performance overhead, which may affect real-time operations in high-traffic areas. Despite these challenges, micro-segmentation is a valuable strategy in port cybersecurity, particularly where operational continuity and data protection are essential.

9.3.2 Physical Segmentation

Physical segmentation is a network security strategy that isolates network segments through hardware-based solutions like firewalls, routers, and switches, creating clear security boundaries between different parts of the network [15]. In port environments, physical segmentation protects sensitive systems, particularly OT systems, which control critical port operations such as machinery and automated systems. Ports often have a mix of IT and OT environments, and physical segmentation helps ensure that these distinct systems are securely separated to prevent unauthorized access and potential compromise.

Physical segmentation offers several significant benefits in port environments. First, it provides strong isolation between different network segments, preventing unauthorized access to critical systems. This is essential for protecting sensitive networks from threats that may arise from IT systems. Another advantage is that it reduces the risk of cross-network attacks, as a breach in one segment does not easily spread to others. However, there are notable disadvantages. One of the most significant is the high cost of implementing and maintaining the required hardware infrastructure. Ports must invest in additional routers, switches, firewalls, and cabling, which can be expensive, especially in large-scale environments. Furthermore, managing multiple physically separated network segments can be complex and resource-intensive, requiring dedicated personnel and tools for monitoring and maintenance.

9.3.3 Perimeter Segmentation

The term *perimeter* generally refers to the boundary that separates an organization's internal network from external environments, where mechanisms such as traffic filtering and access control are applied to manage potential risks [16]. In OT settings, this boundary plays a crucial role in separating enterprise IT networks from critical control environments like ICS or SCADA, reducing their exposure to external threats [17]. According to NIST SP 800-18 Rev. 1, the *security perimeter* encompasses all system components within a defined accreditation boundary, explicitly excluding any external systems connected to it [18]. Within this context, *Perimeter Segmentation* refers to the deliberate structuring of this boundary into smaller, enforceable zones that constrain external access, isolate threats, and minimize the attack surface. This is achieved by deploying targeted controls—such as firewalls, intrusion detection or prevention systems, secure gateways, and demilitarized zones—that inspect traffic and enforce communication policies at key entry points [16]. These controls ensure that only authorized, policy-compliant exchanges occur between external entities and internal systems, thereby strengthening the overall security posture.

Perimeter segmentation offers notable defensive value. One of its key advantages lies in its ability to filter external traffic, thereby reducing the system's exposure to threats. By enforcing inspection at the network boundary, it can stop many intrusion attempts before they penetrate critical systems. This boundary-focused approach also supports traffic monitoring, which helps security teams identify irregular patterns and respond to potential threats at an early stage. Moreover, the establishment of well-defined zones and trust boundaries aligns with regulatory expectations—such as those outlined in IEC 62443—by facilitating structured control over conduits and inter-zone communication [17].

However, perimeter segmentation is not without limitations. Once an attacker gains entry, this approach does little to prevent movement within the internal network, leaving systems vulnerable to lateral attacks. The model also becomes increasingly difficult to maintain in environments that rely on interconnected legacy systems, fluctuating access needs, or third-party integrations. Misconfigurations or overly rigid rules can block legitimate operations, causing inefficiencies or unintended disruptions. Sustaining accurate and up-to-date segmentation policies across diverse port operations often requires significant coordination and administrative oversight, especially when managing multiple systems under varying operational demands.

9.3.4 Application Segmentation

Application segmentation refers to the deliberate isolation of individual applications or services within a network to prevent security threats in one from propagating to others. Unlike broader network segmentation, which often divides large network zones [14], Application segmentation focuses on protecting specific applications by controlling their communication paths, user access, and exposure to threats. It frequently integrates micro-segmentation techniques to enforce fine-grained, application-specific traffic rules. This bridge between the two approaches means that while micro-segmentation controls data flows between workloads [14], application segmentation directly targets the services themselves, especially those exposed to users or third-party integrations.

The main advantage of application segmentation is its ability to significantly reduce the attack surface within a port's digital infrastructure. By ensuring that applications operate in isolation, it minimizes the risk of lateral movement, especially in multi-application environments where a single compromised service could otherwise jeopardize multiple operational layers. Tailored access control policies allow each application to enforce its own security posture—critical when sensitive systems like payment processing or vessel tracking are at stake. It also improves visibility, making it easier to detect suspicious behavior within isolated application segments.

However, these benefits come with operational costs. Configuring segmentation for dozens of applications can become complex, particularly when dealing with legacy OT systems that require custom security handling. The use of application-layer firewalls and containers can introduce performance overhead, especially in time-sensitive environments like ports, which demand low-latency processing for cargo movement and real-time communication. Furthermore, as applications evolve, their segmentation policies must be continuously updated and monitored, adding administrative burden and increasing the potential for misconfigurations if not properly managed.

9.3.5 User Segmentation

User segmentation is the classification of users into distinct groups based on their behavior, roles, or security-related characteristics in order to apply tailored security controls and training strategies [19]. The core idea is that users represent a significant vulnerability in any information system, particularly in operational environments like ports where both administrative staff and field operators interact with critical digital infrastructure. Unlike technical segmentation that focuses on traffic or applications, user segmentation targets the human factor, aiming to reduce insider threats, phishing susceptibility, and misconfiguration risks through differentiated access and education strategies [19]. In port environments, personnel can be logically segmented according to their operational roles, risk exposure, and required access to sensitive systems. For instance, crane operators, controllers, and planners who routinely interact with OT assets face different security challenges compared to administrative personnel working on billing platforms. Segmenting these groups accordingly allows for targeted enforcement of access controls and the implementation of role-specific cybersecurity training, reducing unnecessary exposure and strengthening overall risk management.

User segmentation contributes significantly to a port's cybersecurity by enabling security teams to tailor controls to the behavioral patterns, access needs, and risk levels of different user groups. This approach not only reduces technical vulnerabilities but also mitigates risks arising from human error. For instance, restricting the system access of seasonal staff or external vendors—while ensuring they receive focused cybersecurity training—can minimize the chances of accidental or unauthorized disruption. It also helps align operational practices with regulatory expectations concerning role-based access and accountability. Still, implementing segmentation is not without obstacles. Privacy considerations may arise when monitoring user behavior, and the effort to maintain current user profiles—particularly in dynamic operational settings—can stretch administrative capacity. Even so, when applied with foresight, user segmentation becomes a practical tool for linking human-centered risks with broader technical safeguards, reinforcing the port's defensive posture.

9.4 Using Automation and Orchestration Tools in Simplifying Network Integration and Segmentation

Automation and orchestration tools play a pivotal role in managing the increasing complexity of modern port networks, especially when grounded in SDN and network function virtualization (NFV). SDN enables centralized control of network operations through software, replacing distributed, hardware-dependent management, while NFV substitutes physical appliances with flexible, software-based services. Together, these technologies enable greater agility, scalability, and consistency in configuring and managing port infrastructure. They support dynamic provisioning, reduce manual tasks, and optimize resource allocation across diverse systems.

Orchestration, in this context, refers to the intelligent coordination of multiple systems to automatically distribute and assign resources based on service needs [20]. Within a port environment, this means integrating control across various zones—such as operational technology areas, enterprise IT, and guest networks—into a single, policy-driven framework. This becomes especially critical where containerized applications, automated cranes, or sensor networks are involved, as they require uninterrupted, high-performance connectivity that bridges disparate systems. Hierarchical orchestration models simplify this task by abstracting the complexities of individual segments while still allowing centralized oversight and policy enforcement.

Central orchestration tools typically interface with SDN controllers, hypervisors, and virtual infrastructure managers (VIMs) to deploy virtualized network functions (VNFs), including firewalls, intrusion detection systems, and traffic shapers. In ports, such tools are invaluable for quickly creating secure, temporary network environments to support seasonal operations or short-term deployments. These orchestrators ensure that VNFs are provisioned correctly and in the right sequence, facilitating efficient traffic management and policy compliance. As noted in [20], orchestration is essential for enabling logic that spans beyond hardware, creating virtual links between distributed containers and virtual machines across remote terminal locations.

A more specialized form—service orchestration—focuses on chaining together multiple network functions with defined connectivity rules and performance targets [21]. This allows ports to guarantee quality-of-service parameters for mission-critical platforms such as berth scheduling, customs systems, or gate automation. The orchestrator handles real-time adjustments to compute and network configurations, ensuring these services continue to meet bandwidth, latency, and security requirements regardless of the underlying infrastructure.

While orchestration handles the high-level coordination, automation ensures routine tasks—like deploying configurations or applying segmentation policies—occur without manual intervention. This is particularly valuable in port settings that feature equipment from multiple vendors and legacy systems. Using SDN APIs, automation frameworks can enforce uniform traffic rules across devices, allowing, for instance, micro-segmentation of networks in container terminals. Different VLANs or virtual overlays can be automatically applied for control systems, safety sensors, or third-party service access.

The NFV MANO framework provides the architecture for orchestrating and managing these virtual services. It consists of the NFV Orchestrator for resource coordination, VNF Managers for function-specific oversight, and VIMs for controlling the underlying virtual infrastructure [20, 21]. For ports, this allows the dynamic management of edge compute nodes deployed near quay cranes or inland hubs. These edge systems can process local data streams or facilitate real-time communications without overloading core networks and can be spun up or decommissioned based on shifting operational demands.

Nonetheless, orchestrating large-scale, distributed networks introduces complexity. As noted in [21], orchestration systems in port environments must account for scalability challenges, ensuring high availability and fault tolerance while maintaining data consistency across geographically dispersed zones. The CAP theorem illustrates this tradeoff: systems cannot fully optimize availability, consistency, and fault tolerance simultaneously. Therefore, orchestration platforms must be carefully designed with synchronization mechanisms and failover strategies to uphold critical service operations, even during partial system disruptions.

9.5 Port Network Segmentation in Compliance with GDPR

The GDPR, introduced by the European Union, is widely regarded as one of the most far-reaching and rigorous frameworks for personal data protection [22]. In force since May 25, 2018, its scope extends beyond the borders of the EU. Any organization, regardless of location, that handles the personal data of EU citizens or residents—whether through logistics operations, passenger records, or crew information—is subject to its provisions. This extraterritorial application has significant implications for ports worldwide. Even those outside the EU must adhere to GDPR requirements if their operations involve European stakeholders, with non-compliance carrying the risk of substantial financial penalties [22].

In the port context, GDPR compliance becomes especially critical due to the volume and sensitivity of the personal data handled—such as crew identification records, cargo manifests linked to individual identities, surveillance footage, and digital access logs. Given that this data often traverses multiple systems—from access control terminals to cloud-based logistics platforms—ensuring compliance requires more than just policy alignment. PNS emerges as a central strategy in managing these data flows securely and lawfully. The following sections detail how the PNS directly supports compliance with key GDPR obligations in port environments.

- **Translating GDPR Principles into Segmentation Strategies**
  GDPR Article 5 outlines seven core data protection principles: lawfulness, fairness and transparency; purpose limitation; data minimization; accuracy; storage limitation; integrity and confidentiality; and accountability [23]. Network segmentation serves as a technical foundation for embedding these principles within port systems.

  For instance, data minimization can be implemented by isolating personal data systems—such as entry logs or customs documents—from general IT infrastructure, ensuring only essential and authorized access. The principle of purpose limitation is similarly reinforced when systems collecting data for specific regulatory or security functions are separated from systems used for analytics or administration, preventing unauthorized cross-use. Segmentation also enhances the enforcement of confidentiality and integrity by restricting internal data movement, applying encryption protocols, and monitoring access within discrete zones.

- **Defining Data Control Roles and Applying Segmentation**
  GDPR distinguishes between data controllers, who determine the purpose and means of processing, and processors, who act on their behalf [22]. In ports, the authority typically serves as the controller, while external IT firms, cloud hosts, or surveillance contractors often act as processors.
  This distinction is not only legal but also architectural. Proper segmentation ensures that processors only access the data necessary for their function. For example, surveillance systems may be confined to a secure VLAN accessible solely to designated security staff, while customs-related data is restricted to a trusted segment managed under explicit processing agreements. Segmenting networks by role and function aligns with GDPR's requirement to define responsibilities clearly and restrict access accordingly.
- **Security Measures, Breach Containment, and Design Compliance**
  Articles 32 and 25 of the GDPR mandate "appropriate technical and organizational measures" to secure personal data [22]. Network segmentation addresses this by reducing lateral movement—limiting the potential scope of any breach. For example, biometric data collected at quay gates can be confined to a micro-segment separate from general operational systems, protecting it from broader intrusion attempts.

  Segmentation also supports GDPR's "data protection by design and by default" requirement by embedding access controls and isolation into the network architecture from the outset. In a breach scenario, segmented networks help contain the impact, preventing unauthorized spread and enabling ports to meet the 72-hour breach notification window. If encryption and segmentation render the data unintelligible, breach reporting obligations may be reduced or waived under GDPR.

  The combination of proactive segmentation and reactive containment forms a cornerstone of resilient and compliant port cybersecurity strategies.
- **Embedding GDPR into Port Network Architectures**
  To make GDPR compliance actionable, ports must integrate data protection across the entire IT lifecycle—from system design to ongoing operations. This starts with mapping where personal data is stored and how it flows across segmented zones. Each segment must correspond to specific legal roles, security needs, and processing boundaries. Advanced architectural models like SDN and zero-trust networking enable this dynamic segmentation. These approaches allow real-time control over data paths, role-based access enforcement, and adaptive responses to new regulatory interpretations—without requiring structural overhauls.
  Ultimately, GDPR compliance in port environments is not about checking regulatory boxes; it's about building systems that are transparent, accountable, and resilient. Network segmentation, when used intentionally,

transforms legal requirements into enforceable practices that protect data, ensure compliance, and strengthen operational trust in maritime digital ecosystems [22].

References

[1] C. S. Chapman and L.-A. Kihn, "Information System Integration, Enabling Control and Performance," *Accounting, Organizations and Society*, vol. 34, no. 2, pp. 151–169, 2009.

[2] S. Vercauteren and B. Lin, "Hardware/Software Communication and System Integration for Embedded Architectures," *Design Automation for Embedded Systems*, vol. 2, pp. 359–382, 1997.

[3] R. Holdsworth, "Practical Applications Approach to Design, Development and Implementation of an Integrated Management System," *Journal of Hazardous Materials*, vol. 104, no. 1-3, pp. 193–205, 2003.

[4] IAPH, "IAPH Cybersecurity Guidelines for Ports and Port Facilities," 2021. [Online]. Available: https://sustainableworldports.org/wp-content/uploads/IAPH-Cybersecurity-Guidelines-version-1_0.pdf.

[5] F. Andritsos, "Port Security & Access Control: A Systemic Approach," in The Fourth International Conference on Information, Intelligence, Systems and Applications, Greece, 2013.

[6] N. S. Tarkaa, P. I. Iannah and I. T. Iber, "Design and Simulation of Local Area Network Using Cisco Packet Tracer," *The International Journal of Engineering and Science*, vol. 6, no. 10, pp. 63–77, 2017.

[7] G. Leischner and C. Tews, "Security Through VLAN Segmentation: Isolating and Securing Critical Assets Without Loss of Usability," in 9th Annual Western Power Delivery Automation Conference, Spokane, Washington, 2007.

[8] R. Deal, *Cisco Router Firewall Security*, Cisco Press, 2004.

[9] U. Murthy, O. Bukhres, W. Winn and E. Vanderdez, "Firewalls for Security in Wireless Networks," in Proceedings of the Thirty-First Hawaii International Conference on System Sciences, Kohala Coast, HI, USA, 1998.

[10] R. Parthasarathy, M. Krishnan, I. Perumal, P. Ayyappan, L. Rajamanickam and S. B. Alias, "Configuration of Access Control List Applications: Route Filtering and Traffic Control for Enterprise Network Design Using Cisco Packet Tracer Simulation Tool," *Science International*, vol. 33, no. 3, pp. 265–271, 2021.

[11] S. Shrimali, "DeMilitarized Zone: Network Architecture for Information Security," *International Journal of Computer Applications* (0975 – 8887), vol. 174, no. 5, pp. 16–19, 2017.

[12] M. Rajkumar Na and K. B. Sundharakumar, "A Study on Air-Gap Networks," in 2024 5th International Conference on Innovative Trends in Information Technology (ICITIIT), Kottayam, India, 2024.

[13] J. Xie, F. R. Yu, T. Huang, R. Xie, J. Liu and C. Wang, "A Survey of Machine Learning Techniques Applied to Software Defined Networking (SDN): Research Issues and Challenges," *IEEE Communications Surveys & Tutorials*, vol. 21, no. 1, pp. 393–430, 2019.

[14] A. George, "The Critical Role of Micro-Segmentation in Modern Cybersecurity Architectures: A Comprehensive Review," *Partners UniversalMultidisciplinary Research Journal*, vol. 2, no. 2, pp. 24–34, 2025.

[15] S. Bellamkonda, "Network Segmentation and Micro Segmentation: Reducing Attack Surfaces in Modern Enterprise Security," *International Journal of Innovative Research in Computer and Communication Engineering*, vol. 8, no. 6, pp. 2499–2507, 2020.

[16] G. UÇTU, M. ALKAN, İ. A. Doğru and M. Dörterler, "Perimeter Network Security Solutions: A Survey," in 2019 3rd International Symposium on Multidisciplinary Studies and Innovative Technologies (ISMSIT), Ankara, Turkey, 2019.

[17] A. Ribeiro, "Addressing Role of Network Segmentation, Perimeter Strategies in OT Cybersecurity to Reinforce Industrial Defenses," 2025. [Online]. Available: https://industrialcyber.co/features/addressing-role-of-network-segmentation-perimeter-strategies-in-ot-cybersecurity-to-reinforce-industrial-defenses/.

[18] NIST, "Security Perimeter," 2025. [Online]. Available: https://csrc.nist.gov/glossary/term/security_perimeter.

[19] D. Fujs, S. Vrhovec, and D. Vavpotič,, "Know Your Enemy: User Segmentation," *IEEE Access*, vol. 9, pp. 157306–157315, 2021.

[20] R. Casellas, R. Martínez, R. Vilalta and R. Muñoz, "Control, Management, and Orchestration of Optical Networks: Evolution, Trends, and Challenges," *Journal of Lightwave Technology*, vol. 36, no. 7, pp. 1390–1402, 2018.

[21] C. Rotsos, D. King, A. Farshad, J. Bird, L. Fawcett, N. Georgalas, M. Gunkel, K. Shiomoto, A. Wang, A. Mauthe, N. Race and D. Hutchison, "Network Service Orchestration Standardization: A Technology Survey," *Computer Standards & Interfaces*, vol. 54, no. 4, pp. 203–215, 2017.

[22] B. Wolford, "What Is GDPR, the EU's New Data Protection Law?," 2020. [Online]. Available: https://gdpr.eu/what-is-gdpr/.

[23] GDPR.EU, "Art. 5 GDPR Principles Relating to Processing of Personal Data," 2020. [Online]. Available: https://gdpr.eu/article-5-how-to-process-personal-data/.

10 Advancing Port Cybersecurity by Artificial Intelligence

10.1 Concepts and Key Abilities of AI in Port Cybersecurity

10.1.1 Definition, Key Abilities, and Architecture of AI

Artificial intelligence (AI) refers to the simulation of human cognitive capabilities in machines, enabling them to process information, learn from data, adapt to new situations, and make decisions independently. It encompasses a spectrum of technologies including machine learning, computer vision, and natural language processing, all of which allow systems to perform tasks traditionally requiring human intelligence [1]. These technologies do not operate in isolation but function within a layered and dynamic system capable of continual learning and adaptation, reinforcing their potential to manage increasingly complex environments.

The structure of AI systems is typically organized into four interconnected layers, each responsible for a distinct function that contributes to the system's overall intelligence and responsiveness [2]. As illustrated in Figure 10.1, this layered architecture begins with the infrastructure layer, which supplies the essential computing power, network connectivity, and data storage needed to support AI operations. Above this, the perception layer captures incoming data through sources such as sensors and cameras, allowing the system to observe and register real-time environmental conditions. The cognitive layer follows, transforming raw inputs into meaningful insights by detecting patterns, interpreting anomalies, and applying contextual understanding. At the top, the decision-making layer uses these insights to trigger actions, execute responses, and adapt system behavior to meet shifting demands. Together, the four layers form a cohesive framework that enables AI to move beyond basic automation and toward more predictive, adaptive, and intelligent performance [2].

Once all four layers are working in unison, AI systems become capable of exhibiting five core abilities: **perception**, **reasoning**, **learning**, **decision making**, and **interaction**. These abilities define the functional intelligence of AI in real-world applications. *Perception* enables machines to sense and monitor their surroundings by collecting data from external sources. *Reasoning* allows systems to interpret that data, establish connections, and draw conclusions

DOI: 10.4324/9781003559320-10

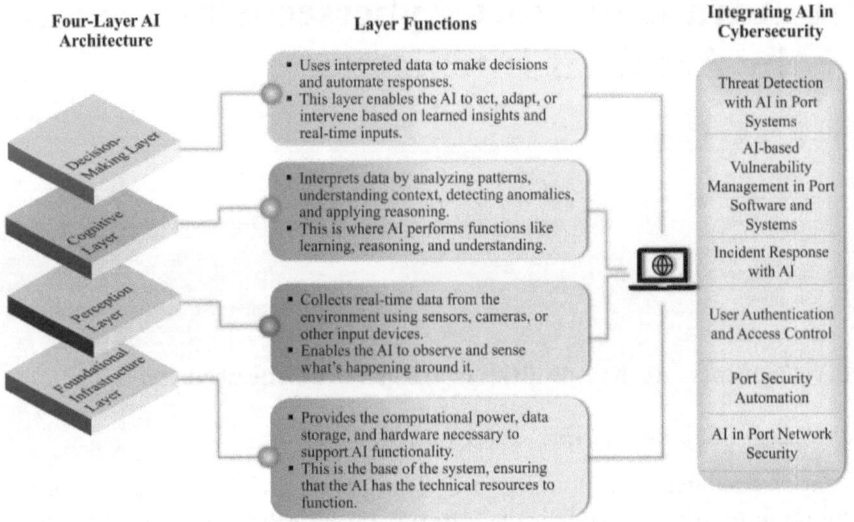

Figure 10.1 Layered Architecture and Functional Applications of AI in Port Cybersecurity.

even when information is partial or uncertain. Through *learning*, AI improves performance over time by recognizing patterns and refining its internal models. *Decision making* builds on the insights from perception and reasoning to select suitable actions within dynamic environments. Last, *interaction* supports communication between AI systems and humans or other machines, typically via natural language interfaces or predefined protocols. When implemented together, these abilities shape how effectively AI can replicate and support complex human problem-solving processes [3, 4].

10.1.2 AI's Role in Enhancing Port Cybersecurity Systems

AI plays a strategic and operational role in strengthening port cybersecurity systems. Its integration enhances threat detection, accelerates incident response, and supports risk mitigation in increasingly complex digital environments. At the technical level, AI operates through a layered architecture—perception, cognition, and decision making—which altogether enables ports to move from reactive security approaches to proactive, adaptive defense.

The **perception layer** receives continuous data streams from IoT devices and sensors deployed across port zones. These include access points, cargo-handling systems, and surveillance equipment. By capturing real-time data on environmental changes, equipment usage, and system activity, AI significantly improves situational awareness. This early-warning capability is essential for identifying anomalies that may signal security breaches or cyber-physical threats.

Building on this, the **cognitive layer** processes contextual data to determine the relevance and urgency of threats. In the port context, this means navigating a hybrid environment where operational technology OT and information technology (IT) coexist. AI can identify interdependencies across these domains—for example, recognizing that a malware infection in terminal software could compromise ship-to-shore communications. This level of insight enables prioritized, risk-based decision making that accounts for cascading effects within the system.

The **decision-making layer** adds the capacity for automated responses. When an incident occurs, AI can isolate affected systems, redirect traffic, and alert security teams in real time—critical actions when ports are operating at full capacity and delays could disrupt global supply chains. These capabilities do not replace human decision-makers but complement them, freeing personnel to focus on strategic oversight rather than routine diagnostics. Over time, AI improves its responses by learning from previous incidents, enhancing the resilience of port infrastructure.

To maximize AI's contribution, port cybersecurity systems must be designed for human-machine collaboration. Staff must not only operate AI tools but also interpret their outputs, understand their thresholds, and adjust actions when needed [4]. This shift requires investment in training and culture as much as in technology. As ports increasingly adopt AI across their cybersecurity architecture, its role expands from technical enhancement to a cornerstone of strategic risk management.

10.2 Applications and Benefits of AI-Based Cybersecurity in the Port Industry

This section outlines the primary ways AI contributes to enhancing cybersecurity within the port sector. As shown in Figure 10.1, six core application areas are identified, and each of these areas reflects how AI technologies are being leveraged to address the unique cybersecurity demands of modern port environments, offering both practical safeguards and strategic advantages.

10.2.1 Threat Detection with AI in Port Systems

An IDS is composed of critical cybersecurity tools designed to monitor network traffic and flag suspicious activities or policy violations. In complex maritime environments—where port networks, shipboard systems, and smart terminal infrastructures form interconnected digital ecosystems—IDSs provide frontline defense against cyber threats. These systems analyze data flows to detect anomalies or known malicious signatures before operational continuity is compromised [5]. Broadly, IDSs fall into two categories: signature-based and anomaly-based. Signature-based systems compare traffic patterns against databases of known threats, offering high accuracy for previously identified attacks. Yet, they are ineffective against novel or evolving threats.

Anomaly-based IDSs, on the other hand, learn normal system behavior and detect deviations. While this method helps identify zero-day exploits, it often generates excessive false positives and struggles with integration into the maritime domain's diverse and dynamic systems [5].

To address these specific shortcomings, AI-enhanced IDS architectures offer more nuanced threat detection capabilities. For example, to overcome the rigidity of signature-based systems, machine learning algorithms can continuously update threat recognition models using both historical and live maritime data, allowing them to identify unfamiliar threats that would evade static databases [5]. Similarly, to mitigate the false positives common in anomaly-based IDSs, AI systems apply context-aware analysis—filtering out harmless anomalies such as routine schedule deviations and focusing on those with malicious indicators. In the port environment, where numerous devices communicate across interlinked subsystems, this intelligence allows IDSs to distinguish between operational irregularities and true cyber intrusions. Techniques like neural networks, supervised learning, and behavior-based classification can be tuned to maritime-specific traffic, making detection more accurate across various network layers. However, realizing the full benefit of AI-driven IDSs also hinges on human readiness; port personnel must be equipped to interpret automated alerts and adjust system parameters when needed [5].

Despite their benefits, IDS deployment continues to face technical and logistical barriers. Retrofitting legacy ships and port systems with IDS capabilities often involves complex hardware and software integration. Analyzing encrypted traffic without violating privacy, operating within limited bandwidth, and maintaining functionality under harsh environmental conditions further complicate the performance of IDSs, since privacy requirements limit the depth of inspection while bandwidth constraints restrict real-time analysis. To address these constraints, a virtual testing framework called MaCySTe has been introduced to simulate port-relevant scenarios and assess IDS performance under realistic maritime conditions. This testbed supports iterative design and evaluation, ensuring that IDS solutions are optimized for actual deployment environments [5].

10.2.2 AI-Based Vulnerability Management in Port Software and Systems

Vulnerability management in software and systems refers to the process of identifying, evaluating, and addressing weaknesses in software that could be exploited by cybercriminals. It involves scanning software for security vulnerabilities, assessing their potential impact, and taking appropriate steps to mitigate or remediate them. Traditional vulnerability management relies heavily on manual procedures, including the use of scheduled vulnerability scans, manual log reviews, and referencing external vulnerability databases such as CVE lists. Security teams interpret scan results, assess contextual risk, and manually prioritize remediation actions based on system criticality. Patching, configuration changes, and follow-up testing are also performed manually, often requiring coordination across different teams. This approach is time-consuming, prone to oversight, and difficult to scale in complex environments [6].

AI-based vulnerability management enhances cybersecurity by enabling systems to proactively identify, assess, and address software weaknesses. Unlike traditional methods that depend on manual reviews and periodic scans, AI-powered tools automate the detection of outdated software versions, misconfigurations, and exploitable flaws, while also prioritizing threats based on their potential impact [7]. In the port context, this capability is especially valuable. AI systems can assess vulnerabilities across critical platforms, flagging abnormal access behavior or third-party integration risks. For example, if a flaw is detected in a terminal operating system (TOS) module that manages scheduling or cargo data exchange, AI can evaluate its severity, isolate the affected component, and propose a targeted response—often without interrupting core port functions. This approach minimizes reliance on manual audits, reduces remediation time, and helps maintain operational continuity in high-throughput environments.

Despite its advantages, implementing AI-based vulnerability management in ports presents significant operational and technical hurdles. Port environments are inherently heterogeneous, often combining legacy systems with modern digital infrastructure. This diversity—further complicated by differences across terminals and governing authorities—makes standardization difficult. Additionally, many AI models are developed using datasets that fail to capture the distinct network architecture and risk landscape of maritime systems, limiting their initial effectiveness. Regulatory frameworks like the GDPR also constrain how vulnerability data can be gathered and processed, especially when multiple international stakeholders are involved. To be effective, AI tools must be both modular and interoperable, integrating seamlessly with existing systems such as SIEM platforms and endpoint security tools. Moreover, they need to learn and adapt to local operational patterns—such as fluctuations in cargo volume or shifts in vessel activity—to maintain accuracy. By focusing on adaptability, contextual awareness, and ease of integration, ports can better leverage AI to secure their digital infrastructure.

10.2.3 Incident Response with AI

Incident response refers to the combination of processes and technologies used to detect, manage, and mitigate cyber threats or breaches. It encompasses identifying, containing, and resolving incidents to prevent further impact. Traditionally, these efforts have relied on manual workflows such as evidence collection, threat identification, and forensic analysis. In large-scale environments like ports—where complex systems and high data volumes intersect—manual responses can delay action and increase the risk of errors when handling electronic evidence [8]. Moreover, conventional systems are often inadequate for real-time decision making in maritime environments characterized by continuous operations and dynamic cyber risks.

AI technologies are increasingly deployed to enhance incident response by automating threat detection and containment. Machine learning algorithms can process large datasets to identify anomalies, anticipate risks, and correlate incidents with historical attack patterns—significantly improving response speed and precision [8]. These capabilities are often integrated into platforms such as SIEM and SOAR, helping to streamline triage processes and reduce reliance on human judgment [7].

In the port environment, AI provides additional advantages by enabling situational awareness across interconnected domains, including vessel tracking, cargo operations, and customs management. AI-driven tools monitor traffic patterns, system behaviors, and endpoint activity to detect unauthorized access or manipulation of operational technologies. For instance, SOAR solutions can automatically quarantine compromised systems—such as infected terminal servers—without halting port-wide operations. Likewise, AI models trained on past port-specific threats can recommend tailored responses to ransomware or denial-of-service attacks. These enhancements reduce both resolution time and business disruption—critical for high-throughput facilities where delays can trigger global ripple effects. By transitioning from reactive routines to proactive, adaptive measures, ports can leverage AI to manage cyber incidents more effectively.

Despite these advantages, deploying AI-based incident response in ports presents significant technical, organizational, and regulatory challenges. Many ports still rely on legacy systems that lack compatibility with modern AI platforms, making integration costly and time-consuming. Data quality and availability are another issue: AI systems require high volumes of accurate, labeled data, which may not exist in legacy maritime networks. There are also concerns about AI model transparency and explainability, especially when decisions involve regulatory reporting or legal evidence. Inaccurate alerts, model bias, or poor generalization across different port environments may further erode operator trust. In addition, compliance with data protection laws—such as the GDPR—can restrict how security data is collected, processed, or shared among stakeholders. Addressing these issues requires not just modular and interoperable tools like EDR or extended detection and response (XDR) but also investment in skilled personnel, robust governance frameworks, and continuous validation of AI performance. Without these foundations, AI-based incident response risks becoming a brittle overlay on an already complex maritime cyber landscape.

10.2.4 User Authentication and Access Control

User authentication and access control are central to IAM, ensuring that only verified and authorized individuals can interact with sensitive systems, applications, or datasets under defined access policies [9]. Traditional IAM systems, which often depend on static credentials and fixed rule sets, struggle to adapt to modern digital ecosystems shaped by cloud computing, mobile access, and fluid operational roles. These static mechanisms lack the agility to detect contextual anomalies—such as unauthorized access from remote endpoints or unexpected privilege escalations—leaving critical systems open to exploitation through compromised credentials or insider manipulation.

AI introduces a more responsive, behavior-aware layer to IAM by moving beyond identity verification based solely on credentials [9]. Machine learning models monitor a range of contextual indicators—such as device type, geolocation, access timing, and prior user behavior—to determine access legitimacy in real time. These systems can continuously reassess user sessions and adjust access rights dynamically, enabling capabilities like adaptive multi-factor authentication, real-time biometric verification, and anomaly-triggered lockdowns. For example, an AI-enabled IAM platform might restrict access when a user logs in from a suspicious location or exhibits usage patterns inconsistent with their normal operational profile. This allows for granular, context-sensitive access decisions that better reflect the complexity and variability of today's digital environments.

In port operations—where thousands of users, contractors, and automated systems interact across a patchwork of logistics, customs, and operations platforms—AI-enhanced IAM is especially valuable. These systems can model typical access behavior across distinct port roles and detect irregularities that signal potential threats. Supervised learning helps classify expected user actions based on role and time, while unsupervised methods flag behaviors that deviate from baseline norms, such as anomalous access to terminal servers or login attempts during off-rotation hours. These models can enforce real-time decisions without relying on static permissions, offering more precise control over access to systems like the TOS, port community systems (PCS), and databases. The result is tighter control over human and machine identities interacting with vital infrastructure.

However, integrating AI into IAM frameworks at ports presents structural and operational barriers. Many port systems remain siloed and rely on legacy platforms that lack the flexibility to accommodate intelligent authentication protocols. Interfacing these environments with AI-driven controls demands customized integration so as to avoid workflow disruptions, particularly in cargo-handling or customs clearance operations. Moreover, AI-based IAM depends on robust data flows for effective modeling, yet data is frequently fragmented across disconnected systems operated by shipping lines, customs, and third-party logistics providers. Addressing these limitations may require hybrid IAM architectures, combining rule-based access with AI-driven anomaly detection tailored to maritime workflows. For ports with constrained or unreliable network connectivity, edge-based AI modules can maintain access governance locally, enabling responsive and resilient authentication processes even in bandwidth-limited conditions.

10.2.5 AI-Enhanced Security Automation in Cyber-Physical Port Environments

The growing integration of digital infrastructure into port operations has blurred the line between physical security and cybersecurity. While frameworks such as the ISM Code and the ISPS Code provide structured guidance on safety and security management [10], their practical implementation increasingly relies on interconnected digital systems that require cyber-resilient enforcement. Modern port security no longer functions in isolation—it depends on digital surveillance platforms, biometric access systems, smart cargo monitoring, and networked sensors, all of which present new cyber-physical vulnerabilities.

AI offers transformative potential in automating and securing these hybrid environments. For instance, AI-powered video analytics can detect unauthorized access attempts not only by identifying human intrusions but by correlating physical events with digital anomalies—such as concurrent unauthorized network access or the disabling of surveillance feeds. Similarly, machine learning algorithms can enhance cyber-physical threat detection by linking irregular access badge usage with unusual activity in IT systems, allowing for earlier and more targeted incident responses.

AI-driven systems also enable continuous compliance monitoring for port safety and security frameworks by automating audit trails, flagging inconsistencies in access logs, and ensuring that digital logs of physical activities are complete and tamper-resistant. Moreover, adaptive AI models can assess combined data from physical and digital systems—such as smart gates, container-tracking software, and access management tools—to build real-time risk profiles and prioritize responses accordingly.

To be effective, these solutions must be deeply integrated into existing port infrastructure and supported by clean, interoperable data. Collaborative implementation between cybersecurity teams and physical security personnel is essential to ensure that AI tools function as an intelligent bridge—strengthening protection against cyber threats that manifest through physical channels or target operational technologies.

10.2.6 AI in Port Network Security

Port network security encompasses a layered defense strategy designed to protect the CIA of data as it flows through increasingly digitized maritime infrastructure [11]. This includes technologies such as intrusion prevention systems, identity verification mechanisms, encryption protocols, and network segmentation, all of which are tasked with safeguarding critical assets. However, in modern port environments—where IT and OT converge across customs, cargo management, and navigation systems—traditional defenses alone are insufficient. Threats like ransomware and zero-day exploits can traverse these systems rapidly, overwhelming manual incident response efforts and causing significant disruption.

AI introduces a critical advancement by transforming network security into a more proactive and scalable function. In port contexts, AI-powered systems can identify subtle indicators of compromise—such as anomalous traffic patterns or lateral movement between isolated zones—faster than human operators. This capability is essential for containing threats that could affect cargo operations, port logistics, or customs clearance in real time. For example, AI-driven analytics may detect an unauthorized data exfiltration attempt from a SCADA-linked subsystem, triggering automated containment protocols before the breach can spread.

Nonetheless, effective implementation of AI within network security demands compatibility with existing systems. Many ports continue to operate legacy infrastructure that lacks the interoperability required for full AI integration. Moreover, the diversity of platforms—from IoT-enabled sensors and container management systems to enterprise customs applications—necessitates AI solutions that are modular and adaptive. To address this complexity, ports can adopt hybrid AI architectures through solutions such as SOAR, EDR, and XDR. These tools enable incremental enhancements across network layers without necessitating complete infrastructure overhauls.

10.3 Be Aware of the Risks of AI-Based Cybersecurity and the Corresponding Mitigation Measures

As AI-driven tools take on a greater role in securing port environments—particularly in threat monitoring and response—new categories of risk also emerge. These risks, if left unaddressed, may expose vulnerabilities within both digital and physical port systems. This section presents eight critical risk areas and discusses practical measures that port managers and cybersecurity teams can adopt to limit their impact and maintain operational trust in AI-based defenses.

10.3.1 Data Availability and Training Constraints

Effective anomaly detection in AI-driven cybersecurity depends on access to extensive, high-quality datasets [12]. These data are central to training models to distinguish between normal and suspicious behavior. In ports, the challenge is compounded by the diversity of operational systems—cargo management, vessel tracking, and surveillance—each producing unstandardized data. Additionally, external sources like global shipping data or meteorological inputs add complexity. Acquiring, integrating, and updating such datasets are resource-intensive. To address this, ports should invest in streamlined data collection and harmonization processes, enforce data quality standards, and ensure compliance with privacy regulations. Periodic updates and expert feedback loops can further enhance dataset relevance and model precision.

10.3.2 Computational Resource Requirements

Training and deploying AI models, especially deep learning systems, demand substantial computational power, often requiring graphicspProcessing units GPUs or tensor processing units (TPUs) [12]. These resources can drive up energy consumption and infrastructure costs, which may be prohibitive in port settings characterized by continuous, real-time operations. For example, security systems processing large video and sensor feeds must detect anomalies without latency. To mitigate this, ports can employ edge computing solutions to reduce the load on central servers. Edge processing enables faster detection by analyzing data near its source. Investing in scalable, energy-efficient infrastructure ensures that cybersecurity systems can evolve alongside growing operational demands.

10.3.3 Opacity and Interpretability of AI Decisions

Many advanced AI systems operate as opaque 'black boxes', providing minimal insight into how conclusions are drawn [12, 13]. This lack of interpretability can hinder operational decision making in ports, particularly during security incidents requiring fast, informed responses. For instance, if a system flags unusual cargo activity without explaining its rationale, security teams may face delays. One response to this challenge is the adoption of explainable AI models, which aim to provide transparency with regard to system outputs. Incorporating human oversight—such as expert validation of high-risk alerts—further ensures that decision making remains accountable and understandable.

10.3.4 Detection Errors: False Positives and False Negatives

AI systems face a persistent challenge in balancing detection sensitivity. High false positive rates can burden personnel with unnecessary alerts, while false negatives may allow threats to slip through unnoticed [12]. In dynamic port settings, where daily operations vary widely, this issue becomes critical. Training models with diverse, port-specific datasets can reduce error rates. Additionally, hybrid systems that combine AI predictions with human verification help to filter and prioritize alerts, mitigating the risks of both alert fatigue and oversight.

10.3.5 Susceptibility to Adversarial Manipulation

AI models are vulnerable to adversarial attacks—deliberate manipulations of input data designed to mislead or disrupt system performance [12, 13]. In port environments, attackers might feed false data to achieve misclassification of threats or bypass surveillance. For example, vessel-tracking systems could be deceived into identifying suspicious routes as routine. To counteract this, ports should adopt adversarial training methods that expose models to potential manipulation during development. Using ensemble detection frameworks—where multiple models corroborate findings—also strengthens resistance to deceptive inputs. Routine testing against adversarial scenarios is essential for maintaining system integrity.

10.3.6 Human Oversight and Decision-Making Erosion

While AI enhances speed and scale in cybersecurity tasks, excessive dependence on it can erode human judgment [13]. Ports operating in high-stakes, multicultural environments cannot afford to rely solely on automated decisions. Contextual nuances—such as diplomatic sensitivities or complex cargo anomalies—may be missed by algorithms. To prevent this, ports should adopt human-in-the-loop protocols, where critical alerts are escalated for human review. Training programs that develop both AI literacy and traditional analytic skills will help ensure a balanced, resilient decision-making process.

10.3.7 Technical Integration and Maintenance Burdens

Integrating AI systems into existing port cybersecurity frameworks presents logistical and technical challenges [12]. AI tools must interact with legacy systems, physical security measures, and real-time logistics platforms. Beyond deployment, ongoing model training, updates, and performance monitoring are required to maintain effectiveness. A phased implementation strategy—beginning with pilot projects—can ease this transition. Cross-functional teams combining cybersecurity, IT, and domain-specific expertise will facilitate smoother integration. Long-term support and training programs are also necessary to manage the evolving system landscape.

10.3.8 Privacy, Bias, and Ethical Governance

Deploying AI in ports raises ethical questions, especially regarding surveillance, data protection, and potential algorithmic bias [14]. Large-scale monitoring generates sensitive operational and personal data that must comply with privacy laws such as the GDPR [15]. Moreover, biased training data can lead to discriminatory outcomes in personnel screening or access control decisions. To mitigate these risks, ports should adopt strong privacy safeguards—encryption, anonymization, and access controls—and perform routine audits to assess algorithmic fairness. Embedding ethical principles into AI system design and governance will foster trust and reduce the risk of misuse.

References

[1] M. H. Jarrahi, "Artificial Intelligence and the Future of Work: Human-AI Symbiosis in Organizational Decision Making," *Business Horizons*, vol. 61, no. 4, pp. 577–586, 2018.

[2] Y. Xu, X. Liu, X. Cao, C. Huang, E. Liu, S. Qian, X. Liu, Y. Wu, F. Dong, C.-W. Qiu, J. Qiu, K. Hua, W. Su, J. Wu, H. Xu, Y. Han, C. Fu, Z. Yin, M. Liu, R. Roepman and S. Dietman, "Artificial Intelligence: A Powerful Paradigm for Scientific Research," *The Innovation*, vol. 2, no. 4, 100179, 2021.

[3] S. J. Russell and P. Norvig, *Artificial Intelligence A Modern Approach*, Pearson Education, 2010.

[4] L. Markauskaite, R. Marrone, O. Poquet, S. Knight, R. Martinez-Maldonado, S. Howard, J. Tondeur, M. D. Laat, S. B. Shum, D. Gašević and G. Siemens, "Rethinking the Entwinement between Artificial Intelligence and Human Learning: What Capabilities Do Learners Need for a World with AI?," *Computers and Education: Artificial Intelligence*, vol. 3, 100056, 2022.

[5] M. J. C. Samonte, E. N. B. Laurenio and J. R. M. Lazaro, "Enhancing Port and Maritime Cybersecurity Through AI – Enabled Threat Detection and Response," in 2024 8th International Conference on Smart Grid and Smart Cities (ICSGSC), Shanghai, China, 2024.

[6] V. B. Komaragiri and A. Edward, "AI-Driven Vulnerability Management and Automated Threat Mitigation," *International Journal of Scientific Research and Management*, vol. 10, no. 10, pp. 980–998, 2022.

[7] S. Wan, J. Saxe, C. Gomes, S. Chennabasappa, A. Rath and K. Sun, "Bridging the Gap: A Study of AI-based Vulnerability Management between Industry and Academia," in 54th Annual IEEE/IFIP International Conference on Dependable Systems and Networks – Supplemental Volume (DSN-S), Brisbane, Australia, 2024.

[8] R. Hasan, A. Raghav, S. Mahmood and M. A. Hasan, "Artificial Intelligence Based Model for Incident Response," in 2011 International Conference on Information Management, Innovation Management and Industrial Engineering, Shenzhen, China, 2011.

[9] G. Nzeako and R. A. Shittu, "Leveraging AI for Enhanced Identity and Access Management in Cloud-Based Systems to Advance User Authentication and Access Control," *World Journal of Advanced Research and Reviews*, vol. 24, no. 3, pp. 1661–1674, 2024.

[10] P. K. Mukherjee, "The ISM Code and the ISPS Code: A Critical Legal Analysis of Two SOLAS Regimes," *WMU Journal of Maritime Affairs*, vol. 6, pp. 147–166, 2007.

[11] M. Kaeo, *Designing Network Security*, Cisco Press, 2004.

[12] M. J. Goswami, "AI-Based Anomaly Detection for Real-Time Cybersecurity," *International Journal of Research and Review Techniques*, vol. 3, no. 1, pp. 45–53, 2024.

[13] M. Stoltz, "Artificial Intelligence in Cybersecurity: Building Resilient Cyber Diplomacy Frameworks," *Cryptography and Security*, 2024, pp. 1–13. https://arxiv.org/abs/2411.13585

[14] D. Elliott and E. Soifer, "AI Technologies, Privacy, and Security," *Frontiers in Artificial Intelligence*, vol. 5, pp. 1–8, 2022.

[15] B. Wolford, "What Is GDPR, the EU's New Data Protection Law?," 2020. [Online]. Available: https://gdpr.eu/what-is-gdpr/.

11 Purchasing Insurance for Cyber Risks

11.1 Overview of Cyber Insurance for Port Managers

11.1.1 Principle of Insurance and Cyber Insurance

Insurance operates as a mechanism for sharing risk, where entities contribute premiums into a collective pool overseen by an insurer. In exchange, these contributors are entitled to compensation when specific adverse events occur. The insurer takes on a dual role: as a custodian responsible for settling valid claims and as an owner with an interest in maintaining the fund's viability and profitability. Premiums are calculated based on each participant's individual risk profile rather than applied uniformly. This structure enables risk to be redistributed across a wider base, stabilizing financial exposure and converting uncertain future losses into foreseeable, manageable costs [1].

Expanding on this risk-sharing foundation, cyber insurance has developed as a specialized response to the mounting challenges posed by cyber threats. These risks—encompassing data breaches, system failures, and cyber-attacks—have become increasingly significant as digital dependency grows across sectors. With expanded use of technologies such as mobile platforms, cloud services, and networked infrastructures, the potential damage from cyber incidents has also grown. Despite ongoing efforts to fortify digital defenses, many organizations still experience serious operational disruptions and financial setbacks. Because complete prevention is often out of reach, businesses are increasingly turning to cyber insurance to offset residual risks and ensure financial continuity following an attack [2].

Cyber insurance provides both monetary protection and post-incident support. While its foundations mirror those of conventional insurance, its structure reflects the complex nature of digital threats. Coverage is usually split into two core areas: **first-party coverage**, which includes compensation for losses like data recovery, operational downtime, or ransomware response; and **third-party coverage**, which applies to external liabilities such as legal defense costs, regulatory penalties, or breach notifications. Importantly, cyber insurance can also drive improvements in organizational security. Insurers often offer premium discounts to companies with robust cybersecurity controls,

DOI: 10.4324/9781003559320-11

thereby promoting a culture of proactive risk management. As adoption of cyber insurance grows, it also yields broader systemic benefits: encouraging higher cybersecurity standards, fostering accountability, and enhancing visibility around cyber incidents. While there are still challenges—such as limited data on cyber losses, unpredictable attack patterns, and difficulty in modeling risk—cyber insurance is increasingly regarded as a critical layer of protection, supplementing traditional security measures in today's uncertain digital environment [2].

11.1.2 Framing Cyber Risk and the Role of Cyber Insurance in Ports

The shift toward digitalized port infrastructure—encompassing Internet of Things (IoT) sensors, automated cargo systems, digital surveillance, and integrated logistics platforms—has created new exposures to cyber risk [3]. Unlike generic enterprise systems, ports operate at the intersection of physical movement and digital control. A cyber-attack can not only disrupt IT services but stall crane operations, sever vessel tracking, or compromise customs data—delays with cascading economic and geopolitical consequences. Cyber risk in this context includes targeted ransomware campaigns, phishing schemes exploiting supplier networks, and advanced persistent threats embedded in industrial systems. The complexity and interdependence of port systems mean that recovery can be slow and costly without prior planning.

In this environment, cyber insurance is more than a financial buffer—it becomes a mechanism to support operational resilience. Effective policies are designed around specific port vulnerabilities, covering scenarios such as cargo diversions, third-party service outages, and regulatory penalties for data loss. However, value is maximized only when policies are aligned with broader cybersecurity governance. Embedding insurance into risk management practices—through maturity assessments, standardized frameworks like ISO/IEC 27001, and active engagement with underwriters—helps shape both affordable coverage and more disciplined internal safeguards.

As insurers increasingly assess digital maturity, incident history, and control environments during underwriting, insurance becomes not just a response tool but a catalyst for improving cybersecurity posture. For port managers, this shift demands proactive integration of insurance into cyber risk strategy—not as an afterthought, but as an essential pillar of resilience planning.

11.2 Various Types of Cyber Risk Coverage

Cyber insurance policies tailored to the needs of port operations generally fall into two primary categories: **First-Party Coverage** and **Third-Party Coverage**. Both play essential roles in cushioning the financial and operational consequences of cyber-attacks. In addition, there are five specialized areas of coverage that are increasingly relevant as ports advance their digital capabilities.

11.2.1 First-Party Coverage

First-party cyber insurance focuses on covering internal losses directly experienced by the insured organization as a result of cyber incidents. This type of policy primarily supports the organization itself, aiming to restore operations and limit disruptions without relying on third-party claims. Typical areas covered include business interruption, cyber extortion, data loss or corruption, and theft involving digital or financial assets [2].

Within port environments, this coverage is especially important. For example, if ransomware disables a terminal operating system (TOS), the result could be halted container movements, delayed ship schedules, and demurrage charges. Ports may also incur emergency IT response costs, expenses for data recovery, or the need to implement temporary manual processes. Business interruption insurance helps recover lost income during such outages, while coverage for digital asset loss ensures the restoration of essential information like cargo manifests or vessel berthing data. In highly automated ports, where uptime is closely linked to performance and revenue, first-party insurance is critical for limiting vulnerabilities and avoiding wider disruption across maritime logistics chains.

A real-world example comes from a Thai cyber insurance product tailored to enterprises. This policy offers tiered first-party protection with annual coverage limits ranging from about USD 145,000 to USD 870,000 and premiums between USD 435 and USD 6,400. The package includes support for breach investigations, business downtime, cyber extortion events, forensic services, and legal obligations such as customer notifications [4]. Higher tiers also cover income loss due to network failures and ransomware payments. Eligibility is conditional: applicants must maintain basic cybersecurity controls, such as firewalls, antivirus tools, access management protocols, and regular backups. The policy also excludes high-risk sectors—such as online gambling or digital asset trading—and applicants with unresolved claims. This risk-based, tiered structure enables insurers to manage exposure while motivating policyholders to enhance their cyber defenses.

Port authorities can draw several key takeaways from this example. First, it is important to select a policy tier that aligns with the scale and complexity of port operations. Tailored coverage for incidents like ransomware attacks, system outages, or investigative needs is essential for digitally reliant functions such as gate automation, cargo tracking, and vessel scheduling. Second, demonstrating cybersecurity readiness significantly improves insurability. Implementing foundational protections such as firewalls, antivirus systems, and robust backup routines not only reduces risk but also improves eligibility and potentially lowers premiums. Ports lacking such controls may face higher premiums or be denied coverage altogether. Given their critical economic and logistical role, ports may also be subject to increased scrutiny by insurers. Ensuring compliance with security expectations is therefore essential for minimizing exclusions and maintaining access to favorable insurance terms.

11.2.2 Third-Party Coverage

Third-party cyber insurance protects the insured organization from financial liabilities that arise when external parties—such as clients, vendors, or stakeholders—are harmed due to the insured's cyber incident. While first-party coverage handles internal recovery, third-party coverage addresses claims related to legal or financial responsibilities involving outside entities [2].

This category often includes liability for privacy breaches, regulatory fines, customer notification costs, and legal representation. Policies may also cover reputational damage stemming from online content and losses involving third-party data [2]. Some advanced policies extend further, offering contractual indemnification for obligations to compensate business partners or clients. Coverage limits typically range from USD 10 million to USD 100 million, depending on the selected tier. In some cases, insurers such as QBE also provide access to cyber response professionals and crisis management teams so that they can investigate incidents and guide recovery—services that can be instrumental in mitigating further harm [2].

In a port setting, third-party insurance is critical due to the interconnected nature of operations. Port systems interface with shipping lines, freight forwarders, customs agencies, and cargo owners. A cyber event that compromises a system—such as one used for cargo release, customs clearance, or berth management—can trigger contractual and legal claims from partners. For example, delays in container handling caused by a cyber-attack might result in penalties for breaching service-level agreements. Third-party insurance helps cover legal expenses, compensation for affected stakeholders, and fines resulting from privacy violations. In addition, indemnity clauses in these policies can absorb financial risk related to failure in operational obligations. Given the potential for high-value claims and reputational fallout, this coverage is indispensable for protecting a port's standing and continuity in the aftermath of cyber-related disruptions.

Figure 11.1 illustrates the distinct but complementary roles of first-party and third-party cyber insurance in managing cyber risk within digitally enabled port environments. First-party coverage concentrates on internal vulnerabilities, providing financial protection for losses directly suffered by the port due to incidents such as ransomware attacks, business interruptions, or data loss. This type of coverage is critical in ensuring operational continuity and supports faster recovery when core digital systems are compromised. Conversely, third-party coverage focuses on the port's responsibilities to external stakeholders, including shipping lines, freight forwarders, and regulatory agencies. It addresses legal and financial liabilities resulting from service disruptions, data breaches, or delays that negatively impact partners. This includes compensation for privacy violations, breach notification costs, reputational repair, and contractual penalties.

By comparing these two categories, Figure 11.1 highlights how each serves a different layer of cyber risk exposure: first-party policies shield the port's

Aspect	First-Party Cyber Insurance	Third-Party Cyber Insurance
Primary Focus	Covers internal losses suffered directly by the insured port organization due to cyber incidents.	Covers liabilities and damages the port may owe to external parties affected by its cyber incidents.
Typical Coverage Areas	▪ Business interruption ▪ Cyber extortion ▪ Data corruption ▪ Theft of digital/financial assets ▪ Data breach investigations ▪ Reputational repair ▪ Forensic analysis ▪ Legal breach notification obligations	▪ Security and privacy breach liability ▪ Forensic investigations ▪ Customer notification and PR expenses ▪ Multi-media liability ▪ Loss of third-party data ▪ Contractual indemnification
Operational Relevance	Critical for ports relying on TOS and digital infrastructure. Helps mitigate disruptions from ransomware or system outages by restoring logistics functions such as container movements and vessel scheduling.	Protects ports when cyber disruptions affect stakeholders (e.g., delays in vessel scheduling or data breaches). Helps avoid legal penalties or reputational loss due to failing to meet service obligations or protect sensitive third-party data.
Financial Terms	▪ Tiered coverage: ~$145,000–$870,000 (USD) per year ▪ Premiums: ~$435–$6,400 ▪ Covers ransom, data recovery, business interruption, breach costs ▪ Requires minimum security standards (firewalls, antivirus, backup) ▪ Excludes high-risk sectors (e.g., gambling, digital asset trading) ▪ Requires clean claims history	▪ Indemnity coverage typically ranges from $10M–$100M USD, depending on policy tier ▪ May include access to external cyber experts and crisis response teams (e.g., QBE) ▪ Includes coverage for legal liabilities, penalties, and PR/crisis communication costs
Cybersecurity Requirements	Applicants must demonstrate basic controls such as firewalls, antivirus software, data backups, and access controls to qualify. High cybersecurity readiness can reduce premiums; poor security may lead to rejection or higher costs.	Ports must show due diligence in safeguarding stakeholder data. Policies may require terms for contractual liability, and external services help ensure appropriate breach response and third-party communication.
Strategic Benefits	▪ Enables rapid internal recovery and system restoration ▪ Reduces downtime and cascading supply chain disruptions ▪ Encourages continuous cybersecurity improvement to qualify for better coverage terms	▪ Protects legal and commercial relationships with partners, vendors, and clients ▪ Minimizes reputational and contractual damage after a cyber incident ▪ Supports trust and continuity in the port's stakeholder ecosystem

Figure 11.1 Comparison of First-Party and Third-Party Cyber Insurance in Port Operations.

internal functions, while third-party policies protect its legal and reputational obligations to others. For ports that operate as digital hubs in the maritime supply chain, both coverages are essential. Together, they form a holistic risk management strategy—one that ensures recovery from internal failures and maintains trust and compliance in the face of external obligations.

11.3 Limitations and Exclusions within Cyber Insurance Policies

11.3.1 Key Limitations of Cyber Insurance Policies

Cyber insurance policies often include structural constraints—commonly known as limitations—that affect when, how, and to what extent a claim can be made. These limitations may involve financial caps on payouts, time restrictions for incident reporting, or exclusions based on specific types of attacks or affected data. For instance, some policies might only reimburse losses up to a fixed amount or apply coverage solely to breaches involving regulated personal information. Although these limits do not eliminate coverage outright, they can substantially affect its practical value in different operational scenarios [4].

Importantly, cyber insurance is not standardized. Policy terms differ widely based on the insurer, industry context, and organizational needs. A port authority, for example, encounters cybersecurity risks that are fundamentally different from those faced by a retail chain or financial institution. Many standard policies fail to adequately address third-party risks—such as breaches originating from vendors or supply chain partners. For ports, where complex digital infrastructures rely on interconnected stakeholders, such blind spots can leave critical vulnerabilities unaddressed. Tailoring coverage to include contractor and supplier risks is essential to avoid exposure during cross-network incidents.

Another significant limitation involves insurer-imposed restrictions on incident response. Some policies require the insured to work only with pre-approved service providers or vendors during a cyber event. While this control helps insurers contain costs and ensure expertise, it can hinder a port's ability to act swiftly. In high-stakes environments like seaports, where disruptions can cascade rapidly—halting container movements or delaying vessel schedules—any delay in response can amplify the financial and operational fallout.

Equally problematic is the false confidence that cyber insurance may foster. Organizations sometimes treat coverage as a substitute for internal safeguards, assuming that any damage will be reimbursed. However, insurance policies are designed to absorb the financial aftermath—not to prevent incidents from occurring in the first place. Critical losses such as reputational harm or penalties for regulatory non-compliance often fall outside a policy's scope. For ports, the costs of prolonged downtime, stakeholder distrust, or reputational damage could far exceed insured losses. Therefore, insurance must be seen as a fallback—not a frontline defense.

11.3.2 Common Exclusions in Cyber Insurance Policies

Unlike policy limitations, which restrict the *extent* or *conditions* of coverage, exclusions eliminate specific risks from coverage altogether. They define circumstances where no payout will be made, regardless of the financial damage involved. These clauses are explicitly stated in the policy and often relate to high-impact but hard-to-quantify threats, such as acts of cyberwarfare or intentional wrongdoing by employees [5].

For port operators, understanding exclusions is just as critical as knowing what is covered. The global, interconnected nature of port infrastructure means that even a narrowly defined exclusion can lead to major gaps in protection. Misjudging or overlooking these clauses during policy negotiation can result in significant out-of-pocket losses when a breach occurs.

One notable example is the **Prior Knowledge Exclusion**, which denies coverage for incidents that the insured knew—or should reasonably have known—could occur before the policy took effect. For instance, if a known vulnerability in a port's cargo-tracking system is left unresolved and later exploited, any resulting claims could be rejected. Ports should keep detailed records of known risks and remediation efforts to ensure transparency and protect future claims.

Another critical clause is the **War and Terrorism Exclusion**, which typically excludes coverage for cyber incidents connected to acts of war or state-sponsored attacks. Given the strategic importance of ports, they may be prime targets in geopolitical conflicts. Without additional endorsements that specifically cover cyber warfare, losses from such attacks may fall outside the policy's scope. Ports with heightened geopolitical exposure should explore options for supplementary or standalone cyber terrorism coverage.

Another important exclusion involves **regulatory fines and penalties**. Many cyber insurance policies specifically exclude coverage for penalties imposed by regulatory bodies, such as those under the GDPR or maritime safety regulations. For ports, which operate in heavily regulated environments, this can create a significant coverage gap. If, for example, a data breach exposes sensitive shipping or personal information, any resulting fines from regulators may not be reimbursed. To address this, ports should review policy language carefully and consider add-on endorsements that extend coverage to certain regulatory actions—particularly those tied to unintentional compliance failures rather than deliberate negligence.

Contractual Liability and Vicarious Liability exclusions are also particularly relevant. Ports often engage with multiple vendors and digital service providers and may assume legal responsibility through contracts. Yet, if an incident arises from a third party's failure and the port has contractually accepted liability, standard policies may not cover these costs. A careful review of all third-party agreements—aligned with the insurance terms—is essential to ensure risks are not inadvertently assumed.

Additionally, exclusions tied to **portable device loss** or **employee misconduct** can be problematic. A lost laptop lacking sufficient encryption or remote access controls may not be reimbursed under some policies. Similarly, if a breach results from deliberate employee actions, such as credential sharing or unauthorized access, insurers may deny claims. To minimize these risks, ports should enforce strong endpoint security, data encryption standards, and employee awareness programs targeting insider threats.

Finally, **Unapproved System Modifications** represent a frequent but often overlooked exclusion. If internal IT teams bypass formal cybersecurity protocols—such as by applying unauthorized patches or installing unofficial software—insurers may argue that the breach was avoidable and deny compensation. Strict change management policies, regular internal audits, and documented configuration practices are essential to maintaining insurability under such clauses.

11.4 Influential Factors in Insurers' Assessment of Cyber Risks

As discussed in Chapter 4, cyber risk arises from five interconnected factors: vulnerability, threat, exposure, likelihood, and impact. These components shape how insurers evaluate whether a digital environment—like a port's IT infrastructure—is insurable. Rather than looking at each in isolation, insurers assess how they intersect to determine appropriate coverage terms, exclusions, and pricing. This section explains how each factor influences underwriting decisions in practice.

11.4.1 Underwriting System Weaknesses

Insurers evaluate a port's approach to managing system vulnerabilities by focusing on key areas such as patch management, endpoint protection, and internal security audits. They review evidence like patch deployment logs, vulnerability scan results, and security process documentation to understand how effectively weaknesses are identified and addressed. Ports that maintain consistent and proactive controls in these areas demonstrate a lower risk of compromise, which often translates into more favorable insurance terms. Conversely, signs of outdated software, irregular testing, or insufficient security governance increase perceived risk, leading insurers to impose higher premiums or more restrictive coverage conditions.

11.4.2 Probability of Attack

The likelihood of a cyber-attack on a port is shaped by several factors, including its strategic value, history of incidents, and the broader cyber threat environment. Insurers assess this risk using a mix of threat intelligence, past attack data, and evaluations of vulnerabilities specific to the port sector. Ports are particularly vulnerable to attacks by state-sponsored actors, organized crime groups, and malicious insiders. A port's attractiveness as a target—driven by factors such as geopolitical importance, cargo volume, or known security gaps—plays a central role in how insurers judge risk. When the likelihood of attack is deemed high, especially in politically sensitive regions or where recent breaches have occurred, insurers may respond by increasing premiums or imposing stricter coverage limitations. To mitigate these outcomes, ports must stay current on emerging threats and demonstrate strong cyber defense measures to secure more favorable insurance terms.

11.4.3 Visibility and Attack Surface

Exposure measures how accessible a port's systems are to cyber attackers. A larger attack surface means more opportunities for exploitation. Insurers look closely at how interconnected a port's digital environment is—this includes internet-facing applications, cloud services, and reliance on third-party software. Ports that don't properly separate their IT and OT networks risk greater vulnerabilities, especially through third-party vendors and supply chain links.

To evaluate exposure, insurers often rely on questionnaires and technical assessments to uncover weaknesses such as open network ports or unsecured access points. When exposure is high, ports may face demands for stronger security measures or tighter insurance conditions. Demonstrating effective controls to limit exposure—particularly around third-party connections and network segmentation—is crucial for securing favorable coverage.

11.4.4 Composite Risk Probability

The likelihood of a cyber incident is a combined measure that reflects how probable such an event is within a certain timeframe. This assessment draws from an analysis of vulnerabilities, threat intelligence, and exposure levels. Insurers use actuarial models, historical data, and risk scoring tools to calculate this probability. For instance, a port with numerous security gaps, high exposure, and frequent targeting would receive a high likelihood rating, indicating greater risk.

This score plays a key role in underwriting decisions, influencing coverage limits, premium costs, and security requirements. Ports with elevated likelihood scores may face higher premiums, limited coverage options, or conditions that require them to strengthen their cybersecurity posture before coverage is granted. Evaluators pay particular attention to how well a port can detect and respond to incidents, as strong defense capabilities can reduce the perceived risk.

11.4.5 Loss Magnitude and Claims Scenarios

Impact refers to the potential severity of a cyber-attack's consequences, including operational disruptions, financial losses, and damage to reputation.

Insurers apply scenario modeling to estimate the financial fallout from various incidents, such as ransomware outbreaks, port closures, or breaches involving sensitive cargo data. These projections help determine policy details like coverage limits, deductibles, and sublimits.

For ports, the expected impact plays a significant role in shaping insurance terms and premium costs. Facilities that oversee critical infrastructure or handle valuable shipments typically face higher premiums or stricter coverage conditions. Additionally, insurers often use catastrophe modeling to evaluate the risk of widespread disruptions, which can lead to liability caps or exclusions for certain high-risk scenarios.

11.5 Factors Influencing Cyber Insurance Premiums

Building on the technical risk factors outlined in Section 11.4, insurers consider several additional elements when determining cyber insurance premiums for ports. These factors reflect not only the port's exposure to cyber threats but also its operational scale, historical claims experience, and choices regarding coverage.

- **Port Size and Revenue:** Larger ports with extensive and complex operations tend to face higher premiums. Their broad attack surface— including critical systems like automated cargo handling and vessel traffic management— increases the potential impact of a cyber incident. Ports acting as major hubs in international shipping networks may be especially vulnerable to large-scale disruptions, which insurers factor into pricing.
- **Claims History:** A port's track record of previous cyber incidents plays a significant role in premium calculations. Frequent or severe past claims, such as repeated ransomware attacks or breaches, signal higher future risk. Insurers also weigh how effectively the port responded to prior events; unresolved or poorly managed claims can lead to increased premiums or more restrictive policy terms.
- **Security Posture:** Robust cybersecurity measures, such as implementing zero-trust models, conducting regular penetration tests, and deploying advanced threat detection, can help ports secure lower premiums. Active risk management demonstrates to insurers a reduced likelihood of breaches and a stronger capacity to mitigate incidents, which positively influences pricing.
- **Industry Risk Context:** The maritime logistics sector faces elevated cyber risks given its critical role and reliance on complex IT and OT infrastructure. This industry-wide risk profile contributes to generally higher premiums for ports compared to less exposed sectors. Insurers factor in common threats such as ransomware, denial-of-service attacks, and automation disruptions when setting rates.
- **Coverage Levels and Deductibles:** Premiums are also shaped by the chosen insurance terms. Ports opting for higher coverage limits or lower

deductibles generally pay more, reflecting the insurer's increased potential liability. Conversely, selecting reduced coverage or higher deductibles may lower premiums but increases financial exposure in the event of a serious cyber incident. Striking the right balance between cost and protection is key.

11.6 Legal Considerations Related to Cyber Insurance

Cyber insurance coverage for ports is deeply intertwined with various legal obligations. Gaining a clear understanding of these legal factors enables port managers to select policies that are enforceable, minimize gaps in coverage, and reduce the chances of disputes. The primary legal considerations can be grouped into three categories: insurance law, data protection requirements, and contractual and regulatory risks.

11.6.1 Insurance Law: The Foundation for Policy Enforcement

Insurance law regulates how policies are created, interpreted, and enforced, outlining the legal duties of both insurers and insured parties [6]. From the perspective of port operators, this framework governs the application of exclusions, the process of claim evaluation, and what constitutes proper disclosure during underwriting [7]. It is critical that ports confirm their policies and comply with the jurisdiction in which they operate, as vague wording or policy limitations—such as exclusions for negligent cybersecurity measures or pre-existing vulnerabilities—can lead to conflicts.

Additionally, cyber incidents at ports frequently affect third parties like cargo owners, shipping lines, or terminal operators. Insurance law is pivotal in defining whether such third-party liabilities fall within the scope of coverage, especially if the policy includes liability protections. Given the global nature of maritime operations, port authorities must also be mindful of potential conflicts of law that arise if the insurer operates under a different legal jurisdiction. Knowing which legal system governs the policy can be decisive in dispute resolution or claiming denial scenarios. Therefore, obtaining legal counsel during policy negotiations is not merely beneficial but a strategic imperative to ensure the port's cyber insurance coverage is comprehensive and legally sound.

11.6.2 Data Protection and Security Laws: Legal Triggers for Claims

Data protection and security regulations represent another significant legal factor influencing port cyber insurance. Laws such as the PDPA and the GDPR do not regulate insurance directly but often underpin the liabilities cyber insurance is designed to mitigate. As ports increasingly rely on digital platforms to manage cargo, personnel data, and vessel operations, they become subject to legal requirements regarding the collection, usage, and protection of personal and sensitive information.

Failure to comply with these laws—through insufficient safeguards, delayed breach notifications, or improper data handling—can result in regulatory fines, investigations, or lawsuits [8]. These legal consequences often activate cyber insurance claims. However, insurers may restrict or refuse coverage if a port's non-compliance is judged reckless, intentional, or grossly negligent according to applicable laws or policy terms.

For port managers, adhering to data protection laws is therefore more than a legal obligation; it directly influences the port's ability to receive insurance benefits. Legal violations that could have been avoided may not only result in penalties but also disqualify the port from compensation under its insurance policy. To mitigate such risks, port authorities should adopt robust data governance frameworks, regularly review compliance status, and consult legal experts as needed. Aligning legal compliance with cybersecurity practices is vital to upholding regulatory standing and maintaining effective insurance protection.

11.6.3 Contractual and Regulatory Risks: Less Visible but Insurable

A third area of legal concern affecting cyber insurance for ports relates to risks emerging from contractual duties and regulatory mandates. Port operators are typically bound by service contracts with shipping lines, logistics providers, terminal operators, and technology vendors. These agreements often include commitments regarding service availability, system uptime, data confidentiality, and timely cargo processing. Cyber incidents disrupting port IT systems can hinder the fulfillment of these contracts, leading to legal and financial liability.

In addition to contractual risks, ports—especially those classified as critical infrastructure—are subject to national cybersecurity regulations and sector-specific standards issued by maritime authorities or cybersecurity agencies. These rules often set minimum requirements for cyber hygiene, threat reporting, and incident response readiness. Non-compliance can result in regulatory penalties and may be considered gross negligence by insurers, potentially limiting or voiding coverage. Managing these contractual and regulatory risks is critical for port managers. Legal oversight during contract negotiations, regular assessments of regulatory compliance, and thorough reviews of insurance policy language can help ensure the port remains protected from cyber threats and the legal and financial repercussions of failing to meet obligations. Addressing these challenges proactively strengthens both the port's legal defenses and insurability.

For example, a cyber-attack causing extended downtime that delays shipment processing could constitute a breach of contract. Likewise, exposing customer or operational data due to weak cybersecurity controls might breach confidentiality agreements, leading to contractual claims or liquidated damages. While some cyber insurance policies cover such liabilities, coverage is not automatic unless explicitly stated. Furthermore, if a port is found to have neglected basic cybersecurity responsibilities, insurers may invoke exclusions based on negligence or poor risk management.

An illustrative case is Thailand's Cybersecurity Act, B.E. 2562, which mandates that operators of critical information infrastructure—including ports—implement preventive and responsive cyber measures. Failure to comply not only invites regulatory sanctions but also weakens the port's insurance standing.

References

[1] P. M. Liedtke, "What's Insurance to a Modern Economy?," *The Geneva Papers on Risk and Insurance – Issues and Practice*, vol. 32, pp. 211–221, 2007.

[2] A. Marotta, F. Martinelli, S. Nanni, A. Orlando and A. Yautsiukhin, "Cyber-Insurance Survey," *Computer Science Review*, vol. 24, pp. 35–61, 2017.

[3] G. Tonn, J. P. Kesan, L. Zhang and J. Czajkowski, "Cyber Risk and Insurance for Transportation Infrastructure," *Transport Policy*, vol. 79, pp. 103–114, 2019.

[4] OECD, "Encouraging Clarity in Cyber Insurance Coverage," 2020. [Online]. Available: www.oecd.org/content/dam/oecd/en/publications/reports/2020/02/encouraging-clarity-in-cyber-insurance-coverage_c2dea16f/40beab07-en.pdf.

[5] National Cybersecurity Society, "Cyber Insurance FAQs," 2018. [Online]. Available: https://nationalcybersecuritysociety.org/wp-content/uploads/2019/02/TIP-Cyber-Insurance-FAQs.pdf.

[6] WTO, "Insurance Law," 1994. [Online]. Available: www.wto.org/english/thewto_e/acc_e/hrv_e/wtacchrv29_leg_2.pdf.

[7] The University of Law, "Insurance Law," 2024. [Online]. Available: www.law.ac.uk/employability/legal-practice-areas/insurance-law/.

[8] W. B. Chik, "The Singapore Personal Data Protection Act and an Assessment of Future Trends in Data Privacy Reform," *Computer Law & Security Review*, vol. 29, no. 5, pp. 554–575, 2013.

12 Strategic Alignment of Port Cybersecurity Policy and Corporate Strategy

12.1 Defining Strategic Alignment, Corporate Strategy, Goals, and Objectives

An effective strategic management process begins with a clear understanding of corporate SGOs, which together guide decision making across all levels of the organization. **Corporate strategy** defines the organization's overarching direction by outlining its scope of operations, resource allocation, and long-term market positioning in relation to financial performance and growth opportunities [1]. This high-level strategy sets the foundation for the development of **goals**—broad, qualitative outcomes the organization intends to achieve—and **objectives**, which are the specific, measurable actions required to fulfill those goals. These elements exist within a structured hierarchy, where corporate strategy is shaped by the organization's societal role and ethical responsibilities—known as **enterprise strategy**—and is further translated into business and functional strategies that guide operational and departmental execution [1].

To be effective, these strategic components must be internally aligned. Internal alignment refers to the coherence between strategies, structures, goals, and activities within the organization. It ensures that corporate objectives, business-level strategies, and operational initiatives reinforce one another, creating a unified direction and purpose [2]. This alignment operates on two levels: vertical alignment, which connects strategic priorities across organizational tiers, and horizontal alignment, which promotes consistency across functions and departments. When SGOs are logically connected in this way, it strengthens coordination, improves performance, and ensures that actions taken at all levels are consistent with the organization's strategic intent [2]. However, rigid enforcement of alignment across all units may limit flexibility, especially in diverse organizations with decentralized operations [2].

For instance, in a retail company, **vertical alignment** can be observed when corporate leadership sets a goal to improve customer satisfaction, which then informs business-level objectives such as reducing delivery times. This is further translated into departmental objectives like improving warehouse

DOI: 10.4324/9781003559320-12

efficiency or upgrading inventory tracking systems. At the same time, **horizontal alignment** is achieved when marketing, logistics, and customer service departments coordinate efforts to ensure consistent messaging, faster responses, and seamless service. Together, these alignments ensure that strategic intentions are supported at all levels and across all units.

Beyond internal coordination, strategic alignment also involves adjusting to the external environment. This broader dimension, known as **external alignment**, refers to the degree to which an organization's strategy fits with its external conditions—such as market demands, technological changes, and regulatory expectations [2]. For example, a firm operating in a highly dynamic industry may need to realign its strategic direction frequently in response to emerging threats or opportunities. External alignment ensures that the organization remains relevant and competitive, even as internal goals evolve. Unlike internal alignment, which focuses on internal consistency, external alignment emphasizes **responsiveness and adaptability** to forces outside the organization.

While alignment—both internal and external—is often associated with improved strategic execution and performance, overemphasizing alignment can create rigidity. Especially in diversified firms, business units may require autonomy to adapt their strategies to local market conditions. Therefore, alignment should not be pursued at the expense of **organizational agility**. A balanced approach that allows for both consistency and responsiveness is essential for sustainable strategic management [2].

12.2 The SGO Commonly Used by Leading Seaports

Like other complex organizations, ports depend on structured strategic planning to guide operations and align their activities with broader institutional aims. A well-articulated **SGO** framework is especially important in the port sector, where digital transformation, environmental obligations, and operational resilience converge. Leading ports distinguish among strategic directions, long-term goals, and actionable objectives to ensure coherence across policy, investment, and daily execution. This section presents how the SGO framework is typically implemented by examining three common strategic directions: **smart port transformation**, **environmental sustainability**, and **resilience and connectivity**. In each case, the alignment of strategy with objectives illustrates how ports translate vision into measurable outcomes.

The **smart port strategy** focuses on transforming port operations through advanced technologies to increase efficiency, transparency, and real-time responsiveness. This overarching strategy is typically supported by several high-level **goals**, such as enhancing digital infrastructure, improving decision making through data analytics, and reducing operational bottlenecks. Under each goal, ports define **objectives** that are concrete and measurable. For example:

- To support the goal of enhancing digital infrastructure, objectives might include deploying 5G connectivity or integrating Internet of Things (IoT) devices across terminal equipment.
- To improve data-driven decision making, ports may aim to install artificial intelligence (AI)-enabled control towers or predictive maintenance systems using digital twins.
- To reduce inefficiencies, they may target the full automation of gate access or cargo inspection points.

In this structure, objectives serve as stepping stones to achieve goals, which collectively reinforce the strategic commitment to smart transformation. The alignment ensures that each technical implementation contributes to a larger digitalization vision.

The **environmental sustainability strategy** positions ecological responsibility as a fundamental component of port development and compliance. This strategy is typically expressed through **goals** such as minimizing carbon emissions, increasing energy efficiency, and meeting regulatory requirements. These goals are pursued through **objectives** that are quantifiable and time-bound:

- To reduce emissions, a port may set the objective of cutting Scope 1 and Scope 2 emissions by 30% over five years.
- To improve energy efficiency, ports might aim to install LED lighting and electrify yard cranes within three years.
- To align with regulations, they may target certification under ISO 14001 or establish shore power connections at 70% of berths.

Each objective is tied to a corresponding goal, and each goal is rooted in the broader strategy of environmental stewardship. This hierarchy ensures accountability and provides measurable benchmarks for progress toward sustainability targets.

The **resilience and connectivity strategy** reflects a growing emphasis on ensuring operational continuity amid digital threats, climate-related disruptions, and geopolitical risks. The **goals** associated with this strategy often include securing digital infrastructure, enhancing logistics flexibility, and preparing for emergencies. These goals translate into **objectives** such as:

- Conducting semi-annual cybersecurity audits to protect digital assets.
- Diversifying inland transport options to reduce dependency on single corridors.
- Organizing annual multi-agency disaster drills and updating continuity plans accordingly.

By ensuring that each objective maps directly to a resilience-related goal, ports can systematically reduce vulnerabilities and improve responsiveness.

This SGO structure supports a holistic resilience approach that bridges both physical and digital systems.

12.3 The Benefits of Aligning Port Cybersecurity Policy with the SGO

In leading seaports, cybersecurity policies are no longer developed in isolation or delegated solely to technical departments. Instead, they are increasingly crafted in alignment with the port's SGO, such as smart transformation, environmental sustainability, and resilience and connectivity, as discussed in Section 12.2. This alignment enhances both the strategic coherence of the organization and the practical impact of cybersecurity initiatives by ensuring that risk management is embedded within the broader trajectory of port development.

The following discussion presents eight key benefits of aligning cybersecurity policy with the port's SGO, covering strategic, operational, and financial dimensions.

1. **Strategic Coherence and Resource Allocation:** When cybersecurity policy is aligned with the SGO, it becomes part of the organization's strategic narrative rather than a standalone initiative. This ensures that cybersecurity receives executive attention, dedicated funding, and is factored into long-term planning decisions. For instance, a port pursuing a smart logistics hub strategy is more likely to allocate resources toward securing data infrastructure, integrating real-time monitoring tools, and developing secure APIs for third-party integration. Strategic coherence also promotes continuity across leadership transitions, reducing the likelihood that cybersecurity investments are deprioritized or inconsistently maintained over time.
2. **Innovation and Future-Readiness:** Smart ports embracing digital transformation—through IoT networks, AI-driven analytics, or blockchain-enabled trade facilitation—require a cybersecurity policy that not only defends existing systems but anticipates emerging risks. Aligning policy with innovation-focused SGOs allows cybersecurity teams to work proactively with developers and technology partners. For example, if AI is used to optimize cargo flow, cybersecurity must ensure model integrity and protect sensitive training data. Ports that embed security within their innovation strategies are more capable of scaling new technologies without compromising safety, reliability, or trust.
3. **Culture of Cyber Awareness and Shared Responsibility:** SGO alignment strengthens the cultural integration of cybersecurity by making it relevant to all departments and roles. When cybersecurity goals are tied to broader strategic objectives, employees view them not as technical mandates but as shared responsibilities that support the port's overall mission. In a port working toward environmental sustainability, staff may be more invested in securing automated power-switching systems if they recognize that cyber intrusions could cause energy waste or emissions surges. This shared

understanding fosters a sense of accountability and reduces reliance on isolated technical enforcement.

4 **Cross-Sector Coordination and Operational Resilience:** Cybersecurity cannot be implemented effectively in isolation from operational or commercial functions. Alignment with the SGO enhances both vertical and horizontal integration across the organization. Vertically, strategic intent is translated from board-level decisions into everyday protocols for frontline workers. Horizontally, it encourages departments—such as IT, operations, engineering, and environment—to collaborate on securing interdependent systems. A port adopting shore power to reduce vessel emissions, for example, must ensure that the system is safeguarded from cyber-physical attacks, which requires coordination across technical, environmental, and infrastructure teams. This integrated approach reinforces both cyber and operational resilience.
5 **Stakeholder Trust and Ecosystem Reliability:** As ports become increasingly reliant on complex supply chain ecosystems, alignment between cybersecurity and strategic objectives becomes essential for maintaining stakeholder trust. Business partners, regulators, shipping lines, and local communities are more confident in ports that can demonstrate secure, future-focused operations. For instance, demonstrating that cybersecurity protections extend across digital customs platforms and trade documentation systems reassures clients and governments of data integrity and transaction reliability. In competitive maritime environments, such credibility can influence port selection decisions and long-term business relationships.
6 **Compliance Integration and Audit Efficiency:** Ports face multiple overlapping regulatory requirements, from IMO cybersecurity guidance and the ISPS Code to ISO/IEC 27001 and national data protection laws. When cybersecurity policy is aligned with strategic objectives, it provides a unifying framework for meeting these varied obligations. This reduces redundancy in audit preparation and improves overall governance. For example, ports with sustainability-linked objectives may already implement environmental monitoring systems; integrating cybersecurity into these systems ensures compliance with both environmental and cyber regulations simultaneously. This dual-purpose approach supports audit readiness and reduces bureaucratic friction.
7 **Crisis Preparedness and Adaptive Capacity:** Strategically aligned cybersecurity planning improves a port's ability to detect, respond to, and recover from disruptive cyber incidents. Instead of treating cybersecurity incidents as isolated crises, ports can embed them into wider business continuity and resilience planning. This alignment ensures that recovery plans prioritize mission-critical operations that support strategic goals. For example, in the event of a ransomware attack, a port with resilience-centered SGOs will prioritize restoring operational systems that support real-time cargo tracking or emergency communication,

thereby minimizing the impact on service continuity and stakeholder coordination.

8 **Financial Risk Reduction and Insurance Benefits:** Cyber risk insurers increasingly assess not only a port's technical controls but also the extent to which cybersecurity is embedded into strategic and governance structures. Ports with cybersecurity policies aligned to their SGO can demonstrate long-term risk awareness and institutional maturity, which may result in more favorable terms during insurance underwriting. This could include lower premiums, fewer exclusions, or increased coverage limits. Additionally, clear cybersecurity governance improves transparency during claims processes and strengthens a port's financial resilience in the face of cyber-related disruptions or liabilities.

12.4 The Common Goals, Measures, and Indicators of Port Cybersecurity

12.4.1 Translating Strategy into Measurable Outcomes

Indicators are quantifiable metrics used to evaluate how well an organization is progressing toward its SGOs. In corporate settings, these are often referred to as key performance indicators (KPIs) [3]. While strategic goals articulate the long-term direction and high-level ambitions of an organization—such as becoming a digitally resilient or environmentally sustainable port—these goals are typically broad and not directly measurable. Their abstract nature makes it difficult for decision-makers to assess progress without the aid of supporting metrics. KPIs serve this purpose by translating high-level goals into measurable terms, enabling consistent monitoring and performance management across all levels of the organization. Crucially, these indicators should not be selected based solely on available operational data; instead, they must be derived from a deliberate review of the overarching strategy to ensure they are meaningfully linked to the SGO. This alignment guarantees that each KPI reflects the organization's core intent and contributes to the realization of its long-term vision [3].

Indicators are applicable and necessary across all levels of the SGO framework. They form the foundation for cascading strategic objectives from the top level (corporate strategy) down to individual initiatives, enabling coherent performance tracking throughout the organization. Within any frameworks, indicators are distributed across financial, customer, internal process, and learning and growth perspectives, with clearly mapped cause-and-effect relationships that support strategic goal achievement [3]. Effective implementation requires consensus among management to define indicators that are both strategically meaningful and operationally measurable. These indicators evolve over time and must be regularly reviewed to remain relevant, ensuring that they continue to provide actionable insights and foster continuous improvement [3].

12.4.2 Indicators and Strategic Goal Hierarchies in Port Cybersecurity

In the port cybersecurity context, indicators provide the means to operationalize and track security-related goals that stem from strategic, regulatory, and risk management priorities. Many ports are increasingly aligning their cybersecurity strategies with international frameworks such as the IMO guidelines, ISO/IEC 27001, and the NIST Cybersecurity Framework. These strategies are often structured as a hierarchy, linking long-term strategic aspirations to specific objectives and concrete operational practices. Within this structure, indicators play a critical role in evaluating performance and guiding adjustments across all levels of implementation.

At the strategic level, cybersecurity goals express a port's broader vision, such as achieving digital resilience or ensuring continuity of operations during cyber disruptions. These long-term aims often emerge from senior leadership's assessment of cyber risk in relation to core business functions. Indicators at this level serve to evaluate whether the overarching strategy is producing the intended outcomes. For example, a port might use the annual percentage reduction in downtime due to cyber incidents as an indicator of improved resilience. Likewise, strategic indicators can include the number of successful system-wide recovery drills or improved ratings in cybersecurity audits. These metrics help leadership assess whether strategic investments in cybersecurity are translating into meaningful resilience gains over time.

At the middle level, this level focuses on defining clear objectives and coordinating the allocation of resources across departments. This level acts as the bridge between strategic direction and day-to-day execution. Indicators here assess progress on intermediate goals that are critical for strategic fulfillment. For instance, if a port's strategic aim is to reduce cyber-related operational disruptions, a middle-level objective might be to improve threat visibility across all critical systems. Relevant indicators could include the percentage of critical assets covered by continuous monitoring systems or the frequency of cross-departmental cybersecurity coordination meetings. This level also ensures that cybersecurity policies and processes are adapted to evolving threats and are appropriately integrated into business operations.

At the operational level, attention turns to the practical implementation of cybersecurity measures and the execution of tasks by technical teams. This is where the strategy becomes tangible, through technologies and procedures that mitigate risk on the ground. Indicators at this level focus on specific activities such as detection, response, training, and system hardening. For example, a port may track the average time to detect and respond to security incidents, the success rate of phishing simulation tests among employees, or the completion rates of patching cycles for IT and OT assets. These indicators offer granular feedback on how well frontline practices are supporting broader cybersecurity objectives. Operational indicators are especially valuable for identifying bottlenecks and ensuring that corrective actions are timely and effective.

To illustrate how ports effectively manage cybersecurity strategies, consider a hypothetical port focused on enhancing resilience against ransomware attacks on container terminal operations, as shown in Figure 12.1. The port's cybersecurity approach cascades through three levels—strategic, managerial, and operational—demonstrating essential horizontal and vertical alignment.

Horizontally, each organizational level translates broader intentions into measurable components to ensure clarity and accountability:

- **Strategic Level:** The port sets a high-level strategy to enhance digital resilience and guarantee business continuity during major cyber incidents. This is broken down into strategic goals, such as minimizing operational disruptions from ransomware by improving preparedness and recovery capabilities. Progress is tracked using key indicators, including a targeted 30% reduction in system downtime within 12 months, at least two full-system recovery drills annually, and achieving an external cybersecurity audit rating of "Very Good" or higher.
- **Managerial Level:** These strategic goals become actionable objectives. For example, establishing a port-wide ransomware response and recovery protocol aligned with ISO/IEC 27001 and NIST Incident Response frameworks. Measures at this level include developing an integrated incident response and recovery plan (IRRP) and conducting cross-departmental ransomware training sessions. Indicators assess engagement and effectiveness, such as 100% department participation in IRRP workshops, three ransomware simulation exercises per year, and rapid incident escalation within 15 minutes.
- **Operational Level:** Objectives guide concrete actions, such as deploying EDR tools across IT and operational technology environments and running phishing simulations. Tactical tasks include weekly updates to endpoint protections and quarterly patching of industrial control systems. Operational performance is monitored with indicators like detection and isolation of ransomware activity within 10 minutes, over 85% staff success in phishing tests, and 95% patch completion on OT systems within scheduled windows.

Vertically, this framework creates a clear linkage from strategic vision through managerial planning to operational execution. The strategic goals set the direction, which informs managerial objectives and resource allocation, guiding the frontline actions that implement cybersecurity measures daily. This cascading alignment ensures that all efforts, from boardroom decisions to staff tasks, are synchronized toward strengthening the port's cyber resilience.

Together, this horizontal and vertical alignment supports consistent, measurable cybersecurity management, enabling ports to identify weaknesses—such as delayed incident response—and adjust strategies or resources accordingly. Ultimately, this integrated approach fortifies the port's defenses against

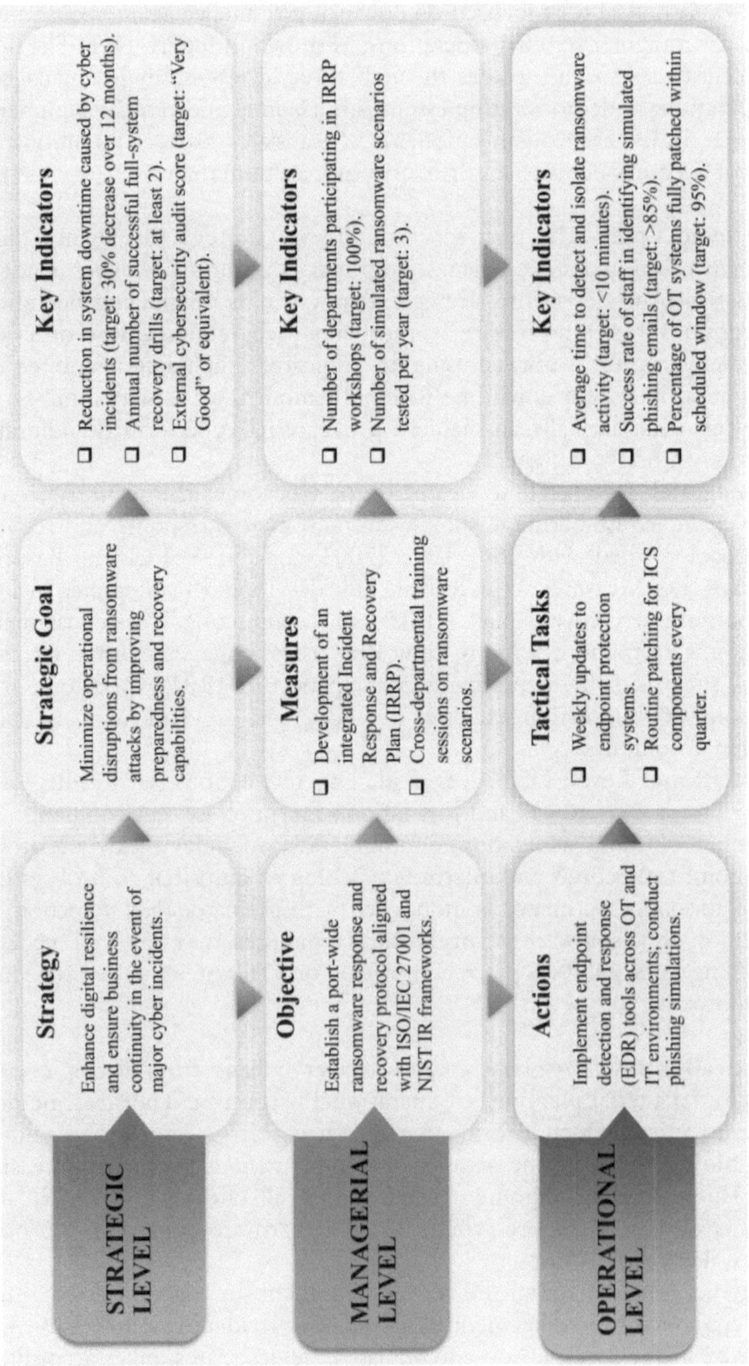

Figure 12.1 Alignment of Port Cybersecurity Strategy Across Organizational Levels.

ransomware and other cyber threats by turning high-level ambitions into practical, accountable actions.

12.5 Mapping Port Cybersecurity Goals to the SGO

12.5.1 Strategy Maps: Defining the Framework for Cybersecurity Strategy

Integrating cybersecurity into a port's strategic framework requires managing the often complex relationships between high-level ambitions, managerial objectives, and operational activities. This complexity can make it difficult to maintain consistency in execution or clearly communicate cybersecurity's value to stakeholders. Strategy maps address this issue by visually articulating how strategic objectives relate to one another, revealing the causal connections that link actions to outcomes.

Evolving from the Balanced Scorecard methodology, strategy maps offer a structured, visual approach for translating broad strategic intent into measurable, actionable goals [4]. They highlight the interdependence among key perspectives—such as financial outcomes, customer service, internal processes, and learning and growth—and help align them in a coherent sequence that supports execution. This approach bridges the gap between corporate vision and operational realities, reducing misalignment and ensuring each department understands its role in achieving enterprise-wide goals [4].

In the port cybersecurity context, strategy maps offer a valuable tool for illustrating how specific initiatives—like implementing intrusion detection systems, improving incident response capabilities, or enhancing data governance—contribute to broader organizational aims. For example, a cybersecurity initiative that secures real-time tracking systems can enhance service continuity, build customer trust, and reduce reputational risk, which ultimately supports the port's financial and operational targets.

These maps typically adopt a top-down format. Strategic outcomes such as reduced financial loss or improved customer confidence sit at the top, while enabling activities—like staff training or infrastructure upgrades—form the base. The idea is that lower-level tasks and capabilities are the drivers of higher-level success. For instance, investments in employee cybersecurity awareness programs (learning and growth) can improve breach detection (internal processes), which then reduces customer disruptions and safeguards revenue. This layered mapping helps organizations visualize how cybersecurity is not an isolated concern, but a driver of long-term performance.

12.5.2 Six-Step Process for Mapping Port Cybersecurity Goals

While strategy maps provide a clear visualization of the desired outcomes and the steps required to achieve them, the real challenge lies in executing the strategy effectively. Scholey (2005) outlines a six-step process for creating strategy maps that ensure a well-understood, actionable strategy is in place.

Each step builds on the previous one, progressively refining the organization's goals and aligning them with the necessary internal actions.

1 **Choose the Overriding Objective**
The first step in the strategy-mapping process is defining the overriding objective, which serves as the organization's primary goal. For a port cybersecurity strategy, the overriding objective could be to reduce the risk of cyber-attacks by 30% over the next 12 months through the implementation of advanced threat detection systems and continuous employee training. Additionally, the goal could be to decrease downtime from cyber incidents by 25% within the same period. This objective should be specific and measurable, reflecting the organization's most critical aspirations.

To ensure alignment and clarity across the organization, this objective should be clearly communicated to all stakeholders, grouped into three categories:

- Internal Operational Stakeholders: This includes port management and executives, cybersecurity teams, IT department, operations teams, and port staff, all of whom are directly involved in day-to-day cybersecurity functions and response efforts.
- External Support and Compliance Stakeholders: These include third-party service providers, legal and compliance teams, and insurance providers who play a role in supporting and enforcing cybersecurity policies and procedures.
- Regulatory and Policy Stakeholders: This group encompasses local authorities, government bodies, and industry regulatory bodies responsible for overseeing compliance with cybersecurity standards and regulations.

Clear communication of the overriding objective to these groups ensures that everyone, from internal teams to external partners, understands the strategic direction and their role in achieving the port's cybersecurity goals.

2 **Select the Appropriate Value Proposition**
The second step involves selecting the value proposition, which defines how the port will create value in the cybersecurity space. Depending on the port's priorities, the value proposition could focus on operational excellence (e.g., implementing cost-effective cybersecurity solutions), product leadership (e.g., adopting cutting-edge technologies for threat detection), or customer intimacy (e.g., ensuring robust data privacy for port users). By aligning the value proposition with the port's strategic focus, the organization can ensure that its cybersecurity efforts are directly tied to the broader value it offers to stakeholders.

3 **Determine the General Financial Strategies**
Once the value proposition is selected, the next step is to define the financial strategies that will support it. For port cybersecurity, this could involve balancing revenue growth (e.g., through increased efficiency and reduced

operational costs due to better cybersecurity measures), productivity (e.g., reducing costs associated with cyber incidents), and asset utilization (e.g., optimizing existing cybersecurity infrastructure). The goal is to find a financial approach that supports the port's cybersecurity initiatives while maintaining fiscal responsibility.

For example, the port may decide to invest USD 1.5 million in advanced threat detection systems, with the goal of reducing the likelihood of a cyber-attack that could result in significant downtime. By improving threat detection, the port could potentially save USD 3 million annually by preventing or mitigating cyberattacks that would otherwise cause prolonged operational disruptions. Additionally, the port could aim to reduce its operational costs by 15% over the next year, by automating certain cybersecurity functions and streamlining the response processes, thus minimizing labor costs during incidents. The financial strategy, in this case, would ensure that the port not only mitigates cyber risks but also achieves cost savings and productivity gains over time.

4 **Determine Customer-Focused Strategies**
The next step is to decide on strategies aimed at customers—whether that be port clients, operators, or partners. This step involves defining how the cybersecurity strategy will improve customer experience and security. For example, providing secure access portals and real-time shipment tracking for shipping lines and freight forwarders can enhance transparency and operational confidence. Additionally, offering assurance of compliance with international data protection standards can strengthen trust among importers, exporters, and customs authorities who rely on the port's digital infrastructure for secure documentation and transaction handling. Furthermore, transparent cybersecurity policies and incident notification procedures can reassure external stakeholders such as shipping lines, freight forwarders, and customs authorities that their data and operational dependencies are well-protected. These customer-focused strategies should complement the port's value proposition and align with overall financial and operational goals.

5 **Decide How Internal Processes Will Support Execution**
With the overarching strategies in place, the next step is to map out the internal processes necessary for executing the cybersecurity strategy. These processes could include staff training, incident response protocols, or the integration of automated cybersecurity tools. These internal processes ensure that the strategy is executable and that the necessary infrastructure is in place to support cybersecurity goals. Proper execution of these processes is crucial to ensuring that the strategic intent translates into tangible results.

6 **Implement Skills, Capabilities, and Employee Programs**
The final step focuses on ensuring that the organization has the right mix of skills and capabilities to support its cybersecurity goals. This includes providing role-specific training—basic cyber hygiene for all employees, operational response training for frontline port staff, and technical workshops

for IT and OT teams. Recruitment efforts should target professionals with expertise in areas such as maritime cybersecurity, industrial control systems, and digital forensics. These specialists can help address key cybersecurity challenges unique to port operations, such as securing PISs, protecting critical infrastructure like cranes and container-handling equipment, and ensuring the integrity of digital transaction records and logistics systems. By filling these gaps, they ensure that the port is equipped with the necessary skills to manage and mitigate cyber risks effectively. Additionally, investments in supportive technologies—like real-time monitoring systems or automated threat detection—can reinforce these human-centered efforts. Together, these initiatives help build a workforce and infrastructure capable of withstanding cyber disruptions.

By following these six steps, ports can create a comprehensive strategy map that clearly outlines their cybersecurity goals and provides a roadmap for achieving them. This process ensures that cybersecurity is not just a technical issue but a strategic priority that supports the broader organizational objectives.

12.6 Integrating Cybersecurity Measures into Port Operational Processes

Effectively integrating cybersecurity into port operations requires more than high-level strategies—it demands a clear understanding of internal workflows and how they can be fortified against digital threats. Process mapping plays a pivotal role in this effort. It is a technique used to visually document, analyze, and improve operational workflows by identifying each step in a process, the people involved, the technologies used, and the expected outcomes. This approach not only clarifies how a task is performed but also helps expose hidden vulnerabilities, inefficiencies, and interdependencies between systems [5]. Mapping port processes offers a foundation for embedding cybersecurity controls where they are most needed. By documenting real-world procedures and engaging frontline personnel in the process, ports gain visibility into both routine and exceptional operations. This visibility is essential for aligning cybersecurity strategies with actual workflows, ensuring that protections are not generic but tailored to the operational realities of the port environment.

In the context of port logistics, several core operational processes require careful mapping before cybersecurity measures can be effectively integrated. These include:

- **Pre-Arrival Planning**: Involves port call notifications and scheduling, supported by secure digital communications between vessels, shipping agents, and port authorities. Infrastructure components such as navigation channels and vessel traffic management systems (VTMSs) play a critical role here.

- **Vessel Arrival and Docking**: Includes pilotage, tug assistance, and berth assignment. These operations rely on real-time data from automatic identification systems (AIS) systems, mooring equipment, quay walls, and jetty infrastructure.
- **Cargo-Handling Operations**: Covers container, bulk, and general cargo movement, supported by terminal operating systems (TOSs), automated gantry cranes, conveyor belts, and container yards.
- **Customs Inspections and Cargo Clearance**: Requires secure data exchange between customs systems, port databases, and scanning equipment such as X-ray and RFID readers at entry gates and inspection zones.
- **Turnaround Services**: Encompasses bunkering, provisioning, maintenance, and waste disposal, involving coordinated scheduling and digital monitoring systems that track service completion and compliance.

Each of these processes represents a critical node where operational continuity and cybersecurity intersect. Effective integration of cybersecurity into these workflows means embedding protective mechanisms directly into the systems and infrastructure that support each stage.

For pre-arrival planning, ports should secure submission portals with authentication and encryption, ensuring that vessel scheduling data is not intercepted or manipulated. In vessel arrival and docking, network segmentation and AIS spoofing detection systems help maintain control over navigation and berthing information. During cargo handling, cybersecurity must extend to both the software controlling cranes and the IoT devices used for cargo tracking. This includes real-time anomaly detection, device integrity checks, and access control mechanisms. In the customs clearance phase, the use of secure APIs, blockchain-based documentation, and audit trails can help maintain transparency and integrity of shipment data. Turnaround services benefit from cybersecurity integration by protecting service coordination platforms and maintenance records from tampering, which could otherwise lead to safety incidents or environmental violations.

To illustrate, consider a cyber-attack on the TOS during container handling. If cybersecurity protocols—such as endpoint protection, encrypted communications, and live failover systems—are integrated into this process, the system can detect and isolate the threat early. This allows for a swift switch to backup systems, preserving cargo flow and minimizing terminal disruption. Similarly, in customs clearance, secure, blockchain-based platforms allow verification of cargo records even during a system outage or cyber-attack, reducing clearance delays and maintaining regulatory compliance. These examples underscore that cybersecurity integration must be embedded within critical operational workflows—not layered on top—so ports can ensure both continuity and resilience in the face of escalating digital threats.

12.7 Utilizing Regulatory and Compliance Requirements to Reinforce Strategic Alignment

Regulatory and compliance requirements are no longer just instruments for legal adherence; they have emerged as powerful tools for reinforcing strategic alignment. Frameworks such as the ISPS Code, MSC-FAL.1/Circ.3, ISO/IEC 27001, and the NIST Cybersecurity Framework provide structured pathways that port authorities can *utilize proactively* to integrate cybersecurity into strategic governance, enhance operational resilience, and cultivate a culture of accountability.

Rather than treating these frameworks as isolated mandates, forward-leaning ports interpret them as enablers of governance coherence—embedding cybersecurity principles across planning, operations, technology adoption, and stakeholder engagement. Each regulatory instrument contributes uniquely to this alignment:

- **ISPS Code: Embedding Cybersecurity into Established Security Governance**
  The ISPS Code, although developed to counter physical threats, offers a foundational structure that port authorities can strategically extend to digital risks. Strategic alignment begins by integrating cyber risk into mandatory PFSAs. By evaluating OT, port information system (PIS), and digital access points within the existing ISPS framework, port managers can ensure that cybersecurity assessments inform broader safety and risk strategies.

  Moreover, aligning digital access control with physical access requirements strengthens holistic threat management and reinforces role-based accountability across departments. Incorporating cyber scenarios—like ransomware or data breaches—into emergency preparedness plans transforms crisis response from reactive to strategically aligned business continuity. Through this adaptation, the ISPS Code supports a unification of physical and cyber domains, enabling ports to align compliance activities with broader strategic objectives such as resilience, risk integration, and incident preparedness.
- **MSC-FAL.1/Circ.3: Integrating Cyber Risk into Organizational Strategy**
  The IMO's MSC-FAL.1/Circ.3 circular advances the concept of embedding cyber risk into the operational fabric of port safety management systems. It promotes a risk-based approach that supports strategic decision making by encouraging ports to map digital dependencies across IT and OT environments. Utilizing this guidance, port leaders can tie cybersecurity to enterprise risk management frameworks, aligning protective actions with strategic outcomes like service reliability and supply chain continuity. Defining roles and responsibilities as mandated by the circular reinforces internal governance and strategic clarity—ensuring cybersecurity efforts are championed at the leadership level.

  Additionally, the focus on continuous personnel awareness, incident response, and technical safeguards ensures that cyber practices are not siloed, but integrated into a shared operational vision. By internalizing this framework, ports transform compliance into a mechanism for building strategic cohesion and resilience.

- **ISO/IEC 27001: Institutionalizing Strategic Cyber Governance**
  ISO/IEC 27001 enables ports to institutionalize cybersecurity as a governance priority. Rather than a technical checklist, the standard serves as a strategic framework that supports long-term alignment through continuous improvement and leadership accountability. Utilization of ISO/IEC 27001 allows ports to formalize cybersecurity goals that directly support strategic imperatives such as operational continuity, stakeholder trust, and regulatory reputation. The standard's emphasis on risk assessment, documented policies, and executive involvement ensures that cybersecurity is embedded in strategic planning cycles and not managed in isolation.

  By conducting regular audits, engaging stakeholders, and assigning clear responsibility for information security, port authorities reinforce strategic coherence across departments. This proactive posture aligns cybersecurity investments with performance metrics and competitive positioning, turning compliance into a tool for enterprise-wide alignment.
- **NIST CSF: A Strategic Compass for Adaptive Cybersecurity**
  The NIST CSF offers ports a flexible, outcome-oriented approach to align cybersecurity with strategic imperatives. Its five core functions—Identify, Protect, Detect, Respond, and Recover—map directly onto critical areas of port strategy such as infrastructure resilience, digital transformation, and customer assurance.

  - **Identify**: Supports strategic asset prioritization by enabling ports to catalogue critical digital systems and align cybersecurity investments with operational risk profiles.
  - **Protect**: Facilitates integration of protective measures into workforce culture and operational protocols, reinforcing reliability and service integrity.
  - **Detect**: Enhances strategic visibility by embedding monitoring capabilities into operational oversight functions.
  - **Respond**: Aligns with crisis management and stakeholder communication strategies, reinforcing reputation management.
  - **Recover**: Embeds learning and adaptation into strategic planning, ensuring cybersecurity contributes to long-term agility.

Beyond the core CSF, supplemental resources such as the AI Risk Management Framework, SP 800-228 (API Security), and SP 1800-33 (5G Security) provide ports with guidance to secure digital innovation. By adopting these extensions, ports ensure that advanced technologies like AI, IoT, and 5G are governed with strategic intent, aligning emerging capabilities with trust, resilience, and scalability goals.

References

[1] B. Steyn, "From Strategy to Corporate Communication Strategy: A Conceptualisation," *Journal of Communication Management*, vol. 8, no. 2, p. 168–183, 2003.

[2] P. Wadström, "Aligning Corporate and Business Strategy: Managing the Balance," *Journal of Business Strategy*, vol. 40, no. 4, pp. 44–52, 2019.

[3] A. Janeš and A. Faganel, "Instruments and Methods for the Integration of Company's Strategic Goals and Key Performance Indicators," *Kybernetes*, vol. 42, no. 6, pp. 928–942, 2013.

[4] C. Scholey, "Strategy Maps: A Step-by-Step Guide to Measuring, Managing and Communicating the Plan," *Journal of Business Strategy*, vol. 26, no. 3, pp. 12–19, 2005.

[5] J. Rowell, "Do Organisations Have a Mission for Mapping Processes?," *Business Process Management Journal*, vol. 24, no. 1, pp. 2–22, 2018.

13 Enhancing Cyber-Aware Culture in Port Organizations

13.1 Role of Human Factors in Cybersecurity Incidents and Cybersecurity

Human factors are a central element in the cybersecurity landscape of port environments. As ports become more reliant on interconnected digital systems, the behavior, awareness, and decisions of individuals—both internal staff and external partners—significantly influence cybersecurity outcomes. These individuals are embedded in core operational processes and can either serve as points of vulnerability or act as a critical line of defense against cyber threats [1].

A large proportion of cybersecurity breaches in port operations are rooted in human-related weaknesses rather than advanced technical attacks. Common errors include clicking on phishing links, poor password hygiene, or misconfigured system settings by operational staff [2]. Employees working with cargo, vessel logistics, or safety systems regularly interact with digital platforms—such as cargo-tracking software, automated gates, and control dashboards. Even brief lapses in attention or gaps in training can compromise the integrity of these systems. Research highlights that such incidents often arise from low cybersecurity awareness, inadequate or uneven training, and the inconsistent enforcement of security policies across departments [1].

At the same time, the very individuals who may pose these risks are also essential to a strong cybersecurity posture. When trained properly and supported by clear procedures, employees can play a decisive role in identifying suspicious activity, reporting anomalies, and initiating quick responses [1]. A port supervisor may detect unexpected behavior in scheduling software, while crane operators or gate personnel might recognize interface malfunctions that signal a compromise. Security teams contribute by monitoring surveillance systems and verifying access, ensuring rapid containment of potential threats [3]. Personnel at every level can become active participants in defense if roles are clearly defined and communication lines are open.

Cyber risks also extend beyond internal personnel. Contractors, shipping agents, information technology (IT) vendors, and maintenance technicians often have system access or infrastructure clearance. Their behavior—whether

DOI: 10.4324/9781003559320-13

careless or deliberate—can introduce vulnerabilities that bypass internal safeguards [2]. Managing these third-party interactions requires clear access policies, contractual obligations for cybersecurity compliance, and regular auditing to reduce external risk exposure.

Ultimately, human factors should be seen not only as a source of incidents but also as a cornerstone of resilience. The ability of individuals to prevent, respond to, and recover from cyber threats is shaped by the surrounding culture, training systems, and operational clarity. Treating human elements as an integrated part of cybersecurity strategy—rather than an afterthought—ensures that both incident reduction and long-term protection are achievable goals. The next section examines how ports can operationalize these insights by strengthening responsibility, awareness, and collaboration across all stakeholder groups.

13.2 Phishing Awareness and Social Engineering

Phishing and social engineering attacks continue to pose significant risks to port cybersecurity, serving as common initial vectors for deeper system compromises. These methods exploit human behavior—rather than technical vulnerabilities—to bypass security controls, often targeting staff across various departments, including operations, administration, and logistics. In the port context, where multiple stakeholders interact daily and where cybersecurity awareness levels may vary, this threat becomes amplified. Ports are particularly vulnerable due to their reliance on email-based communications, third-party logistics coordination, and legacy systems that may lack robust identity verification measures [2].

To address phishing, ports need traditional defenses such as basic awareness training and email filtering, as discussed in Chapter 4. However, the following section presents advanced, proactive strategies that ports may incorporate to enhance resilience against phishing and social engineering.

- **Behavioral Anomaly Detection**: Behavioral anomaly detection (BAD) is a cybersecurity technique used to detect actions that deviate from established behavioral patterns of users or systems, signaling potential compromises [4]. Unlike traditional rule-based approaches, BAD builds high-resolution models that reflect both the distinctiveness and consistency of individual behavior [4]. In port environments, BAD enables the identification of irregular activities—such as unusual login times or unauthorized file access—offering real-time monitoring that helps contain threats before they escalate. The increasing availability of behavioral data, driven by 5G, Internet of Things (IoT), and mobile Internet technologies, has improved BAD's effectiveness by supporting machine learning algorithms that analyze both event-level behavior and underlying user properties. Recent advances, including graph neural networks and composite event-property models, enhance detection accuracy by combining fine-grained and coarse-grained behavioral insights.

- **AI-Driven Threat Simulations**: To effectively train personnel, ports can use customized, artificial intelligence (AI)-powered simulations that mimic real-world attack scenarios. These simulations, tailored to the specific workflows and operations of the port, enhance staff readiness and help them react effectively to social engineering attempts.
- **Zero Trust Architecture**: ZTA is a modern cybersecurity approach that assumes no person or device should automatically be trusted, even if they are inside the network [5]. Instead of relying on traditional methods that only check someone at the point of entry, ZTA continuously verifies the identity and behavior of users and devices throughout their interaction with a system. It gives access only to the information or systems needed for specific tasks and blocks everything else. This approach is especially important for protecting critical systems—like those in ports—where many devices and people connect from different locations [5]. By using tools like secure logins, restricted access to port control systems, and real-time monitoring of network activity, ZTA helps prevent cyberattacks and protect critical port operations such as cargo handling, vessel traffic management, and customs processing. It also incorporates technologies like AI to detect unusual behavior—such as unauthorized access attempts or abnormal data flows—allowing port cybersecurity teams to respond swiftly before disruptions or safety risks occur.
- **Human Digital Twins**: This emerging strategy involves creating digital simulations of employee behavior patterns under attack. These models can help forecast potential vulnerabilities and guide the development of targeted security interventions to bolster defense mechanisms.

While basic cybersecurity training remains a cornerstone of defense, these advanced techniques are crucial for adapting to increasingly sophisticated adversaries. Ports that adopt these innovative strategies will better position themselves to prevent and mitigate the risks posed by phishing and social engineering attacks.

13.3 The Role of Organizational Leaders in Championing Cybersecurity Initiatives and Cyber-Aware Culture

13.3.1 Executive Leadership in Cybersecurity

Championing means actively leading efforts to build a stronger, more security-aware organization [6]. It is not just about approving policies or assigning tasks; it involves taking ownership, setting the tone from the top, and driving change through action and influence. A cybersecurity champion—especially at the executive level—acts as a role model who inspires others, communicates the importance of cybersecurity clearly, and makes it a visible priority throughout the organization.

In port settings, such leadership ensures cybersecurity is treated as a critical part of business continuity and operational safety [7]. Drawing on concepts from innovation theory, champions are seen as individuals who push for change, overcome resistance, and help people adopt new ways of thinking [6]. Effective champions combine influence, communication skills, and persistence to shift organizational culture. Leaders at ports, therefore, must act as both promoters of innovation and protectors of digital resilience, using their authority and networks to remove barriers, embed cybersecurity into everyday practice, and foster a culture where security awareness becomes part of daily behavior [6, 7].

Leadership in ports goes beyond setting policies—it requires direct accountability for cybersecurity risks. This includes clearly assigning who makes decisions, who reports to whom, and how information flows between departments—for instance, defining whether the chief information security officer (CISO) reports directly to the port's executive board or through the chief information officer (CIO) and clarifying how cybersecurity updates are communicated between the IT department, operational control rooms, and terminal managers. By establishing defined roles and reporting structures, leaders ensure that cyber risk management is not fragmented or left to chance. Regular engagement with cybersecurity teams or trusted external advisors helps executives stay informed about emerging threats. When leadership shows visible commitment—by asking questions, attending briefings, and incorporating cybersecurity into board-level discussions—it signals that security is a shared priority. This kind of involvement creates a ripple effect, encouraging employees at every level to pay closer attention to cybersecurity in their own work.

One of the most practical ways for port leaders to champion cybersecurity is to guide the development of a capability maturity model—a structured framework that helps assess the current level of performance in specific areas, such as cybersecurity, and outlines steps for improvement over time—tailored to the port's operational context. Once implemented, the model supports targeted improvements across departments—such as IT, legal, operations, compliance, and staff training—by identifying priority gaps and aligning initiatives. Senior leaders must drive this effort by fostering cross-department collaboration, allocating necessary resources, and setting long-term improvement goals [7]. The model is more than a diagnostic tool; it promotes shared accountability and provides a roadmap for embedding cybersecurity into daily operations. By involving department heads in regular assessments and strategic planning, leadership cultivates a culture where progress is tracked, vulnerabilities are addressed, and every individual understands their role in maintaining cyber resilience. Over time, this structured approach helps shape a cyber-aware culture by reinforcing the idea that security is a shared, continuous responsibility across all functions.

13.3.2 Mid-Level and Frontline Leadership in Cybersecurity

Mid-level leaders—such as IT directors, cybersecurity managers, port managers, and operations supervisors—play a tactical role in translating strategic cybersecurity priorities into enforceable, day-to-day practices. Positioned between executive decision-making and frontline operations, they serve as critical enablers who align technical capabilities with organizational goals. Their leadership ensures that cybersecurity policies are integrated into key operational systems, such as terminal operating systems (TOSs) and other cargo management platforms, without hindering performance. Through the formation of incident response teams, implementation of vendor risk assessments, and execution of regular vulnerability scans, they embed cybersecurity into core business functions. Mid-level leaders also drive workforce awareness by tailoring training programs to specific roles and leading simulation exercises that test readiness. In doing so, they champion a culture of accountability and preparedness, reinforcing the idea that cybersecurity is not confined to policy documents but is part of every department's responsibility.

Frontline leaders—including shift managers, dockside supervisors, and physical security coordinators—are instrumental in maintaining the behavioral integrity of cybersecurity policies at the operational level. Their proximity to daily workflows allows them to influence the habits, vigilance, and compliance of the workforce. By enforcing secure work practices, such as access restrictions and multi-factor authentication, and ensuring prompt reporting of anomalies or suspected breaches, they act as custodians of cyber hygiene. Their role in real-time monitoring and incident escalation is critical in minimizing human-factor vulnerabilities, which remain a leading cause of cyber incidents. Moreover, by fostering a culture of trust where employees feel comfortable reporting suspicious activities without fear of blame, these leaders promote early detection and collective responsibility. Their everyday commitment to protocol adherence and responsive action transforms abstract cybersecurity goals into tangible, consistent practices, anchoring a culture of awareness at the ground level.

Figure 13.1 provides a visual representation of how leadership roles are structured within port organizations to support cybersecurity and build a culture of awareness. The pyramid shape reflects the organizational hierarchy, beginning with executive leadership at the top, followed by mid-level managers, and ending with frontline supervisors at the base. Each tier carries distinct responsibilities, yet all are connected in maintaining cyber resilience. Executives focus on setting strategic goals and driving change; mid-level leaders turn these goals into coordinated actions; and frontline leaders integrate security protocols into daily routines and oversee workforce behavior. The layered format underscores how leadership at all levels contributes collectively to embedding cybersecurity across operational, managerial, and strategic domains. Together, these roles form the foundation of a resilient and security-conscious organizational culture—reinforcing the principle that cybersecurity is not the responsibility of one individual or team, but a shared commitment across all levels of leadership.

13.4 Education and Training Programs

In the context of port cybersecurity, effective leadership requires tailored education and training programs that align with each leadership tier's specific roles and responsibilities. Strategic, middle, and operational leaders must develop

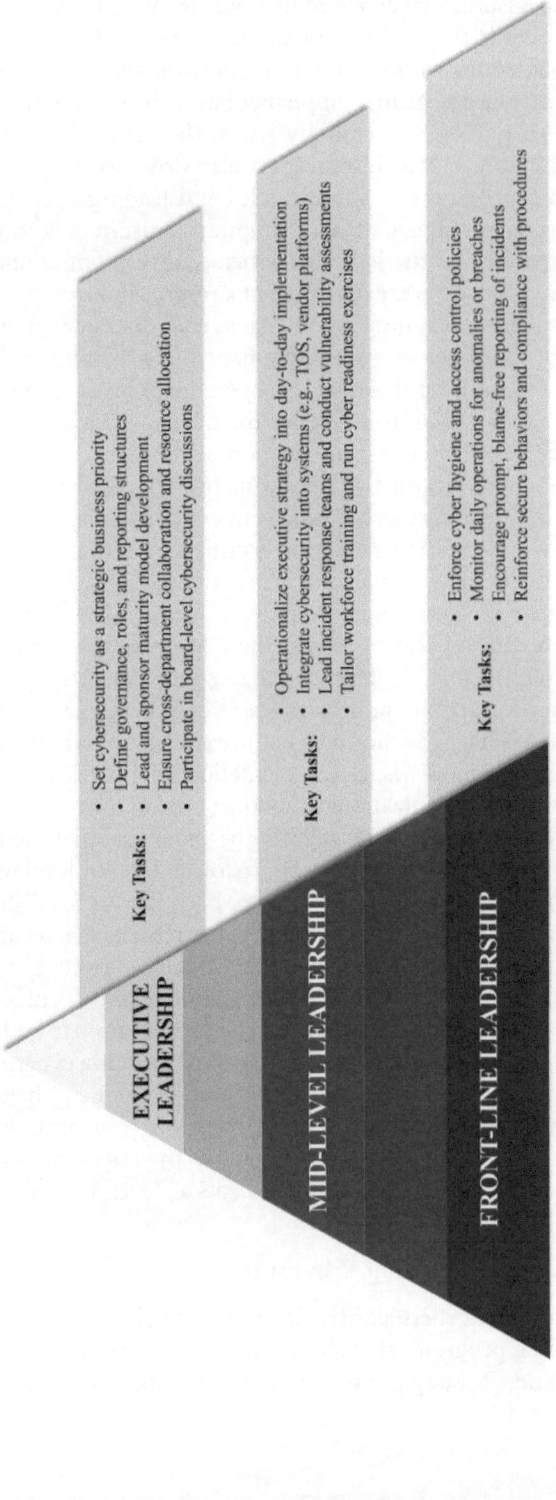

Figure 13.1 Leadership Pyramid for Championing Cybersecurity in Ports.

the necessary skills, abilities, and knowledge to not only uphold cybersecurity policies but also to drive continuous improvement in cybersecurity resilience across the organization. A targeted approach ensures that leadership at every level can effectively contribute to mitigating cyber risks and responding to incidents, from governance to day-to-day operations.

For **strategic leadership**, the focus of training is on integrating cybersecurity into the broader governance, risk management, and investment planning frameworks. Senior leaders must understand how to align cybersecurity initiatives with corporate objectives, ensuring that these efforts are supported by adequate resources and prioritized at the highest organizational levels. Training should cover international cybersecurity frameworks such as the International Maritime Organization (IMO)'s Cyber Risk Management Guidelines, the International Ship and Port Facility Security (ISPS) Code, and ISO/IEC 27001 standards. Additionally, strategic leaders need to develop expertise in evaluating the financial implications of cyber risks, including the impact of ransomware attacks and data breaches. Crisis management training, including the formulation of executive-level incident response plans and coordination with external stakeholders, ensures that senior leaders can make informed decisions in times of crisis. Training methods should include scenario-based simulations, executive briefings, and strategic workshops to foster informed decision making and proactive risk management. To support this level of preparedness, senior leaders may consider enrolling in specialized courses such as:

- Cybersecurity for Executives (Harvard Kennedy School or equivalent) [8].
- Cyber Risk Management for Senior Leaders (SANS Institute) [9].
- Cybersecurity for Leaders: Managing Risk in a Digital World (MIT Sloan Executive Education) [10].

For **middle leadership**, the training is designed to translate strategic cybersecurity goals into operational actions. Mid-level leaders must be equipped with the technical skills necessary to implement cybersecurity measures and oversee their enforcement within the port's daily operations. Key areas of training should include the secure integration of technology, such as TOSs and IoT platforms, and the development of compliance checklists for third-party vendors. Additionally, middle leaders must be proficient in managing cyber incident response teams (CIRT) and conducting vulnerability assessments to identify and mitigate potential threats. Training should also emphasize effective communication and coordination with both operational and strategic leadership. Practical training methods, such as hands-on cybersecurity labs, real-world attack simulations, and cross-departmental drills, will ensure that middle leadership is prepared to address both routine and critical cyber challenges. Relevant training programs for mid-level managers may include:

- National Institute of Standards and Technology (NIST) Cybersecurity Framework Implementation Workshop [11].

- Cybersecurity for Managers: A Playbook (MIT Sloan School of Management) [12].
- Certified Incident Handler (EC-Council) [13].
- Industrial Control Systems/Supervisory Control and Data Acquisition (ICS/SCADA) Cybersecurity for Industrial Control Systems (SANS ICS410) [14].

Operational leadership focuses on the frontline detection, reporting, and prevention of cybersecurity threats within the daily tasks of port operations. Training for operational leaders should emphasize best practices for securing devices, identifying social engineering tactics, and responding to suspicious activities such as phishing or unauthorized system access attempts. Leaders at this level must be well-versed in basic network monitoring and incident reporting procedures. Ensuring the rapid escalation of threats and coordinating with middle leadership to mitigate potential disruptions is a core responsibility. Operational leadership training must include real-time cybersecurity simulations and role-based exercises that enable leaders to recognize and respond to emerging threats in real time. By fostering a culture of vigilance and rapid response, operational leaders play a critical role in safeguarding port operations from cyber risks on a daily basis. Practical training opportunities for operational leaders may include:

- Cybersecurity Foundation Course (Thailand National Cyber Academy) [15].
- Cybersecurity Awareness for Operational Personnel (IMO- or port authority-endorsed).
- Network Monitoring Basics and Threat Detection (Cisco CyberOps Associate) [16].
- Maritime Cyber Security Awareness (Lloyd's Register) [17].
- Cyber Security in the Maritime Industry (Det Norske Veritas) [18].

Education and training across these three leadership tiers creates a robust, multi-layered defense against cyber threats. By addressing the specific competencies required at each level, ports can build a culture of cybersecurity awareness and resilience that permeates every part of the organization. Tailored programs ensure that each leader, whether at the strategic, middle, or operational level, has the tools to make informed decisions, enforce security measures, and respond effectively to threats, ultimately contributing to the port's overall cybersecurity strength.

13.5 Emphasizing Accountability and Responsibility in Protecting Data and Systems

13.5.1 Embedding Accountability in Port Cybersecurity

Accountability plays a central role in cybersecurity, extending beyond the fulfillment of policy checklists or regulatory compliance. It entails the ability to demonstrate that appropriate safeguards are in place, that risks are known and addressed, and that responsible parties can be clearly identified and held answerable for outcomes [19]. Regulatory frameworks such as the General Data Protection Regulation (GDPR) and ISO/IEC 29100 emphasize this expectation by requiring organizations to assume full responsibility—that is, the duty assigned to individuals or teams to execute specific cybersecurity tasks or manage particular systems and data—for the personal and operational data they handle, regardless of whether the infrastructure is managed internally or through cloud service providers. In port environments, this responsibility becomes especially significant due to the sensitive and high-value nature of the data processed daily. Information related to vessel movements, cargo details, customs documentation, employee identification, and video surveillance is often distributed across cloud-based and hybrid platforms. Despite the complexity, ports remain ultimately accountable for any breach, data leakage, or misuse that occurs under their purview.

To translate accountability into practice, ports must embed it across all operational and strategic layers of cybersecurity. This involves assigning ownership of risk at the executive level, conducting regular assessments to identify new vulnerabilities, and ensuring that personnel—from crane operators to IT administrators—understand their roles in protecting data. Beyond assigning roles, effective accountability demands visibility. Mechanisms such as activity logs, access monitoring, and change-tracking systems provide a factual record of who did what, when, and why—forming a crucial component of incident response, internal audits, and external reporting. Ports that work with multiple contractors and external vendors need particularly robust systems for managing access rights and ensuring that third-party behavior aligns with internal security policies. In this context, accountability is not only a defense measure but also a trust-building tool, reassuring supply chain partners, regulatory bodies, and insurers that data handling is transparent, monitored, and controlled.

A deeper layer of accountability can be achieved through the application of data provenance techniques, which trace the full history of digital objects as they move, transform, and are accessed across systems [20]. This method strengthens transparency by preserving contextual metadata, such as the source of data, sequence of modifications, and authorized points of access. In distributed environments like smart ports—where customs systems, cargo-handling platforms, and partner Application Programming Interfaces (APIs) interact in real time—provenance becomes critical for tracking responsibility across the data lifecycle. When disputes arise or investigations are launched, having a clear record of digital events significantly reduces ambiguity and facilitates quicker resolution. Additionally, these records support claim validation for cybersecurity insurance by showing that control measures were in place and that responses were timely and verifiable. Implementing automated provenance tracking across port workflows—such as electronic bills of lading, gate entry authentication, and remote crane operations—can substantially reinforce both operational integrity and legal defensibility.

13.5.2 Operationalizing Accountability: Roles, Responsibilities, and Structures in Ports

Accountability in port cybersecurity is not merely an abstract concept—it is implemented through clearly defined roles, structured responsibilities, and coordinated actions across specialized personnel. A dedicated port cybersecurity team (PCT) ensures that both operational technology (OT) and IT systems are safeguarded from cyber threats and that the port's digital infrastructure remains resilient.

Each member of this team holds specific responsibilities, reinforcing a culture of individual accountability while contributing to the collective cybersecurity posture of the port. The following roles are examples of how ports might structure their cybersecurity teams to promote effective protection. Depending on the port's size, complexity, and cybersecurity needs, the team may include positions such as:

- **CISO**: Oversees the port's cybersecurity strategy, aligns it with business goals, and leads incident response planning. Reports directly to senior leadership, ensuring strategic alignment.
- **Cybersecurity Manager**: Manages daily cybersecurity operations, policy enforcement, and coordination across departments, ensuring consistent implementation of controls.
- **Security Operations Center Analysts**: Monitor systems for cybersecurity threats, escalate incidents, and coordinate responses.
- **IT Security Specialists**: Safeguard IT systems using firewalls, intrusion detection, patch management, and regular audits.
- **OT Security Specialists**: Protect operational technologies like terminal systems, automated cranes, and SCADA platforms, ensuring continuity of port operations.
- **Incident Response Team**: Coordinates mitigation, investigation, and recovery efforts during cybersecurity incidents.
- **Risk and Compliance Officer**: Ensures regulatory compliance (e.g., IMO, ISPS Code, NIST, ISO/IEC 27001) and manages cybersecurity risks.
- **Cybersecurity Awareness and Training Coordinator**: Designs and leads training programs to promote secure behaviors, such as phishing simulations.
- **Third-Party Risk Manager**: Evaluates and ensures compliance of external vendors and contractors with internal security policies.

By formalizing these roles, ports can ensure that every level of the organization understands its contribution to overall cybersecurity accountability. In particular, the **Cybersecurity Manager** ensures day-to-day enforcement of security protocols, while the **Risk and Compliance Officer** integrates regulatory requirements into routine operations, minimizing non-compliance risks. Leadership is equally critical. The **CISO** and other executives set the tone from the top, modeling best practices and fostering a shared sense of responsibility.

Their support legitimizes the role of cybersecurity in organizational strategy and ensures that it receives appropriate resources and attention.

Training and awareness are essential components. Regular campaigns—organized by the **Cybersecurity Awareness and Training Coordinator**—ensure that all employees are aware of their responsibilities. Such programs help bridge the gap between technical policies and employee behavior, reinforcing accountability through education and real-world simulations. Finally, a robust reporting and escalation structure is essential. Security operations center (SOC) **Analysts** and the **Incident Response Team (IRT)** play a pivotal role in identifying, responding to, and documenting incidents. Transparent reporting channels empower employees to flag suspicious activity, while systematic incident management helps contain damage and improve future resilience. Meanwhile, the **Third-Party Risk Manager** ensures that accountability extends beyond internal operations to include contractors and vendors.

Through clearly assigned duties, coordinated team structures, and continuous reinforcement via leadership and training, ports can embed accountability into the fabric of their cybersecurity operations—turning a strategic principle into measurable and defensible practice.

13.6 Continuous Monitoring and Evaluating Cybersecurity Knowledge, Attitudes, and Behaviors

Maintaining a cyber-aware workforce requires more than one-time training efforts—it demands continuous evaluation of how personnel understand, internalize, and apply cybersecurity principles in real-world situations engaged [1, 3]. In port environments, where digital systems underpin essential activities such as cargo handling, logistics, and customs clearance, even a single lapse in employee awareness can lead to serious disruptions. For instance, a dockworker unknowingly connecting an unauthorized device or an administrative employee clicking on a phishing link may trigger consequences far beyond their immediate task. As such, efforts to monitor cybersecurity knowledge, attitudes, and behaviors (KAB) must be tailored to the operational realities of different roles within the port. When done properly, this approach strengthens overall resilience and helps close the gap between formal policy and practical implementation.

Evaluating knowledge retention is a foundational aspect of this process [21]. Rather than relying on occasional quizzes or static training sessions, ports should adopt flexible, role-specific assessments that track how well employees retain and apply cybersecurity concepts over time. Strategic leaders, for example, must stay informed about governance models, risk thresholds, and compliance obligations, while operational teams must demonstrate fluency in procedures like device control and threat identification. Tools such as adaptive learning modules, rotating scenario drills, and job-specific simulations allow for a more dynamic and relevant evaluation process. These tools can reveal blind spots in understanding and provide feedback loops that inform both training strategy and risk mitigation. Given the evolving threat landscape in maritime operations, this kind of targeted and ongoing knowledge monitoring ensures that all personnel stay equipped to handle emerging challenges.

Attitudes toward cybersecurity also influence how individuals respond to threats or follow procedures. In this context, "attitude" refers to one's willingness to engage with protocols, shaped by emotional reactions, perceived usefulness, and trust in institutional systems [22]. Anonymous attitude surveys can be used to measure sentiment across the workforce—tracking levels of concern, motivation, or skepticism regarding cybersecurity initiatives. These insights help leaders anticipate resistance, refine communication strategies, and adjust programs to sustain engagement. Importantly, such evaluations must be repeated regularly to identify shifting trends or early signs of disengagement. In dynamic port environments where personnel turnover, stress, or evolving technology can impact morale, attitude monitoring serves as a proactive tool to maintain alignment between values and behavior.

Behavioral monitoring complements attitude data by examining what employees actually do in practice—whether they report suspicious emails, follow device protocols, or engage appropriately during simulations. These real-time insights validate whether knowledge and attitude translate into secure actions. For instance, if behavior tracking shows repeated lapses in access control compliance, despite positive self-reported attitudes, it may signal the need for revised procedures or environmental changes. Tracking behavioral patterns over time also helps prioritize interventions where risks are highest. For port operators, this includes monitoring behaviors not only in office environments but also in field operations, where physical access controls and SCADA interfaces intersect with cybersecurity protocols.

Together, the continuous assessment of KAB forms an integrated framework for managing human-related cyber risks [21]. This feedback-driven approach allows port leadership to target specific gaps, adjust messaging, and adapt training programs based on real-time workforce needs. More than a compliance measure, it becomes a strategic tool—ensuring that awareness programs remain practical, relevant, and capable of evolving alongside threats. Ultimately, by embedding continuous KAB evaluation into the fabric of port operations, organizations can foster a culture of vigilance where cybersecurity is not only understood but acted upon consistently.

13.7 Empowering Port Employees to Enhance Cybersecurity

In the complex and high-risk setting of port operations, empowering employees—particularly frontline staff—has become essential to cybersecurity resilience. Workers such as crane operators, terminal crews, and logistics coordinators are often the first to detect irregular activity. Yet without the authority or confidence to act, these early warning signs may be overlooked. The following sections explain how ports can strengthen this critical first line of defense by building a workforce equipped to respond quickly and decisively to cyber threats.

13.7.1 The Role of Empowerment in Cybersecurity Resilience

Human error remains a leading cause of cyber incidents, often exploited through phishing, social engineering, or misconfigurations [2]. In port operations, where digital infrastructure underpins continuity, these vulnerabilities can cause widespread disruption. Empowering employees—especially frontline staff—forms a crucial line of defense by fostering engagement and responsibility.

Effective empowerment begins with fostering **awareness**. Employees must be well-informed about the types of cyber risks relevant to their roles, the potential consequences of those risks, and the best practices to prevent them. This awareness extends beyond general knowledge to include situational understanding, such as recognizing irregular digital behaviors during routine operations.

Empowerment also requires building **confidence**. Employees should feel capable of responding appropriately when they encounter suspicious activity. This includes knowing when and how to report incidents without hesitation or fear of negative repercussions. Confidence grows when training is practical, tools are accessible, and leadership demonstrates trust in employees' judgment.

A sense of **ownership** further strengthens the human layer of cybersecurity. When cybersecurity responsibilities are embedded into daily tasks and clearly communicated as part of the employee's role, individuals are more likely to take initiative. This personal connection to organizational security fosters vigilance and accountability in day-to-day operations.

Finally, **accountability** ensures that empowered behavior is sustained. This does not merely involve punitive measures for negligence, but rather a system of transparent expectations, constructive feedback, and positive reinforcement. When accountability is balanced with support, it motivates continuous learning and consistent adherence to security protocols.

By reinforcing these elements—awareness, confidence, ownership, and accountability—ports can bridge the gap between technical cybersecurity systems and human action. Empowerment, therefore, becomes a strategic enabler of resilience, transforming the workforce into a proactive and reliable component of port cybersecurity defense.

13.7.2 How Ports Empower Frontline Employees

Translating empowerment into practice requires targeted actions that integrate awareness, confidence, ownership, and accountability into daily routines. Ports can strengthen cybersecurity from the ground up by equipping frontline personnel with the knowledge, tools, and motivation to recognize and respond to cyber risks. The following five initiatives illustrate how this can be done effectively:

- **Interactive, Role-Specific Training:** Education forms the foundation of empowerment, but to be effective, training must go beyond passive instruction. Ports should deliver scenario-based exercises, phishing simulations, and operational role-specific workshops that mirror real challenges employees might face. These experiences help frontline staff build not just awareness of risks, but also the confidence to act. When training reflects practical situations and employees understand how their actions affect broader port security, it reinforces both ownership and commitment.
- **Gamification and Recognition:** Encouraging consistent engagement with cybersecurity can be challenging without positive reinforcement. Gamification—using points, badges, leaderboards, or team challenges—adds an element of motivation and keeps participation high. For example, a friendly competition to identify phishing emails can turn a mundane task into a shared achievement. Recognition programs further validate individual contributions, reinforcing the message that cybersecurity is a collective responsibility, not just an IT function. Over time, this builds a culture where accountability is normalized and rewarded.
- **Clear and Accessible Reporting Channels:** Even well-trained employees may hesitate to report suspicious activity if the process is unclear or intimidating. Ports must remove these barriers by making reporting tools simple, confidential, and easily available. Regular reminders, straightforward digital forms, and direct access to cybersecurity teams empower employees to report without second-guessing themselves. When reports are taken seriously and followed by visible action, trust grows—along with employees' confidence and sense of agency.
- **Intuitive Security Tools:** Empowerment depends on usability. Ports must provide frontline workers with tools that are functional, relevant, and aligned with their workflows. Simplified interfaces, real-time alerts, and automated prompts make it easier for personnel to detect and act on potential threats. For example, a dockworker alerted to unauthorized access should be able to respond without navigating complex systems. User-friendly tools help translate awareness into immediate action, supporting both confidence and operational ownership.
- **Ongoing Feedback and Adaptation:** Empowerment is not static—it must evolve with changing threats and workforce needs. Establishing two-way feedback mechanisms, such as surveys, debriefs, or informal discussions, allows employees to voice concerns, suggest improvements, and reflect on training. When ports respond to this feedback by adjusting tools, policies, or content, it signals respect for employees' insight and deepens their investment in security outcomes. This ongoing dialogue reinforces accountability, encourages learning, and positions employees as active contributors to the port's cybersecurity posture.

Together, these strategies ground the concept of empowerment in tangible, everyday practices. By embedding these approaches into port operations, organizations can ensure that their frontline personnel are not only prepared but fully engaged in safeguarding critical systems.

13.7.3 Responsibilities of Executive and Mid-Level Leadership in Empowering Employees

Employee empowerment in cybersecurity must be reinforced from the top. While frontline awareness and engagement are crucial, these efforts are most effective when supported by deliberate actions from executive and mid-level leaders. Leadership plays a defining role in shaping the conditions that make meaningful empowerment possible.

- **Executive Leadership:** At the highest level, empowerment begins with commitment. Executives establish the strategic importance of cybersecurity by embedding it into the port's core risk management agenda and aligning it with long-term operational goals. This includes allocating dedicated resources—such as budgets for training, modern security infrastructure, and staffing—to ensure employees have what they need to act effectively. Strategic policies, once issued, must be consistently reinforced through visible actions: endorsing internal awareness campaigns, publicly recognizing staff who model good cyber hygiene, and actively participating in incident response planning. When leadership is not only setting direction but also engaging in practice, it signals to the workforce that cybersecurity is a shared, top-down priority—not just a back-office function. This visibility fosters employee trust and motivation, encouraging initiative rather than mere compliance.
- **Mid-Level Leadership:** Managers and supervisors act as the bridge between executive vision and everyday operations. Their role is not only operational but also cultural. Mid-level leaders translate strategic goals into clear, context-specific actions—adapting training, setting expectations, and embedding secure behavior into daily workflows. Just as importantly, they foster environments where employees feel safe speaking up, even when unsure. This includes encouraging dialogue, responding to mistakes with learning rather than blame, and being present during daily challenges. By creating open channels for feedback and modeling secure practices themselves, mid-level leaders build credibility and reinforce the message that cybersecurity is everyone's job. When staff feel supported and trusted by their direct supervisors, they are far more likely to internalize cybersecurity responsibilities and act decisively in high-pressure situations.

Together, executive and mid-level leaders shape a security-aware workplace culture. Their sustained involvement not only improves operational readiness but also empowers employees with the confidence, clarity, and backing needed to serve as an effective front line in port cybersecurity.

13.7.4 Cultivating a Security-Conscious Port Culture

Empowerment efforts reach their full potential only when supported by a workplace culture that values and prioritizes cybersecurity. In the port environment, where digital systems and physical operations are closely interlinked, the development of a security-conscious culture is essential to sustaining resilience. Such a culture is shaped not by one-time initiatives but by consistent reinforcement of behaviors, values, and shared responsibilities across all levels of the workforce. When staff—from dockside workers to administrative and technical personnel—understand that their everyday actions influence the port's cyber risk posture, security becomes a lived practice rather than a policy requirement.

- **Peer Advocacy:** One powerful lever for cultural change is peer influence. By identifying and training respected employees within different units to serve as informal cybersecurity advocates, ports can spread awareness in a way that feels natural and credible. These peer advocates act as sounding boards, mentors, and role models, helping demystify cyber hygiene practices and normalize vigilance in daily routines. Unlike top-down mandates, peer-led reinforcement integrates security into the social fabric of operational teams. When colleagues see cybersecurity modeled by someone they trust, they are more likely to adopt similar behaviors, strengthening collective awareness and accountability.
- **Transparent Communication:** Cultural reinforcement also depends on how information is shared within the organization. Open, honest communication about cyber incidents, risks, and lessons learned builds trust and encourages reporting. When leaders and teams engage in dialogue—rather than silence or punishment—following a cyber event, employees feel safer raising concerns and more confident that their actions matter. Reducing the fear around mistakes, especially those made in good faith, helps shift reporting from an obligation to a norm. This is especially critical in high-pressure environments like ports, where delays in raising an issue can have serious cascading effects.
- **Balanced Accountability:** Establishing accountability is necessary for any culture of safety, but how it is framed makes the difference between fear and responsibility. A balanced approach recognizes the difference between willful negligence and honest error. If a mistake reveals gaps in training, unclear procedures, or excessive system complexity, the response should focus on identifying and correcting those gaps. Holding individuals accountable must be part of a broader learning cycle—one that encourages reflection, adaptation, and improvement. This approach reinforces trust and

encourages employees to engage rather than withdraw from cybersecurity practices.

A security-conscious culture is not separate from empowerment—it is the environment in which empowerment becomes sustainable. It allows awareness to flourish, encourages informed action, and supports collective responsibility. When combined with committed leadership, practical tools, and targeted training, such a culture turns cybersecurity from a compliance task into a shared mission. In a rapidly evolving threat landscape, ports that invest in cultural transformation are better positioned to detect, withstand, and recover from cyber disruptions—not only through technology, but through the vigilance and judgment of their people.

References

[1] C. Senarak, "Port Cybersecurity and Threat: A Structural Model for Prevention and Policy Development," *The Asian Journal of Shipping and Logistics*, vol. 37, no. 1, pp. 20–36, 2021.

[2] C. Senarak, "Port Cyberattacks from 2011 to 2023: A Literature Review and Discussion of Selected Cases," *Maritime Economics & Logistics*, vol. 26, no. 1, pp. 105–130, 2024.

[3] C. Senarak, "Cybersecurity Knowledge and Skills for Port Facility Security Officers of International Seaports: Perspectives of IT and Security Personnel," *The Asian Journal of Shipping and Logistics*, vol. 37, no. 4, pp. 345–360, 2021.

[4] C. Wang and H. Zhu, "Wrongdoing Monitor: A Graph-Based Behavioral Anomaly Detection in Cyber Security," *IEEE Transactions on Information Forensics and Security*, vol. 17, pp. 2703–2718, 2022.

[5] N. F. Syed, S. W. Shah, A. Shaghaghi, A. Anwar, Z. Baig and R. Doss, "Zero Trust Architecture (ZTA): A Comprehensive Survey," *IEEE Access*, vol. 10, pp. 57143–57179, 2022.

[6] V. Granova, A. Mashatan and O. Turetken, "Changing Hearts and Minds: The Role of Cybersecurity Champion Programs in Cybersecurity Culture," in HCII 2023. Lecture Notes in Computer Science, 2023.

[7] IAPH, "IAPH Cybersecurity Guidelines for Ports and Port Facilities," 2021. [Online]. Available: https://sustainableworldports.org/wp-content/uploads/IAPH-Cybersecurity-Guidelines-version-1_0.pdf.

[8] Harvard Kennedy School, "Transforming Cybersecurity Leadership through Senior Executive Fellows," 2025. [Online]. Available: www.hks.harvard.edu/educational-programs/executive-education/executive-education-alumni/executive-education-Transforming-Cybersecurity-Leadership.

[9] SANS, "SANS Cybersecurity Leadership Training," 2025. [Online]. Available: www.sans.org/cybersecurity-leadership/.

[10] MIT Sloan School of Management, "Cybersecurity for Leaders: Managing Risk in a Digital World," 2025. [Online]. Available: https://executive.mit.edu/course/cybersecurity-for-leaders/a056g00000URaaBAAT.html.

[11] NIST, "Cybersecurity Framework Workshops," 2025. [Online]. Available: www.nist.gov/cyberframework/cybersecurity-framework-workshops.

[12] MIT Sloan School of Management, "Cybersecurity for Managers: A Playbook," 2025. [Online]. Available: https://executive.mit.edu/course/cybersecurity-for-managers/a056g00000URaaIAAT.html.

[13] EC-Council, "Master Incident Handling in Cybersecurity," 2025. [Online]. Available: www.eccouncil.org/train-certify/ec-council-certified-incident-handler-ecih/.

[14] SANS, "ICS410: ICS/SCADA Security Essentials™," 2025. [Online]. Available: www.sans.org/cyber-security-courses/ics-scada-cyber-security-essentials/.

[15] Thailand National Cyber Academy, "Cybersecurity Foundation Course," 2025. [Online]. Available: www.thnca.or.th/our-services/ncsa-e-learning/basic-online/.

[16] Cisco Networking Academy, "CyberOps Associate," 2025. [Online]. Available: www.netacad.com/courses/cyberops-associate?courseLang=en-US.

[17] Lloyd's Register, "Maritime Cyber Security Awareness," 2025. [Online]. Available: www.lr.org/en/services/advisory/operational-services/maritime-training/understanding-rules-and-regulations/maritime-cyber-security-awareness/.

[18] Det Norske Veritas, "Cyber Security in the Maritime Industry," 2025. [Online]. Available: www.dnv.com/training/cyber-security-in-the-maritime-industry-96399/.

[19] M. Theoharidou, N. Papanikolaou, S. Pearson and D. Gritzalis, "Privacy Risk, Security, Accountability in the Cloud," in 5th International Conference on Cloud Computing Technology and Science, Bristol, UK, 2013.

[20] Y. S. Tan, R. K. Ko and G. Holmes, "Security and Data Accountability in Distributed Systems: A Provenance Survey," in 10th International Conference on High Performance Computing and Communications and 2013 IEEE International Conference on Embedded and Ubiquitous Computing, Zhangjiajie, China, 2013.

[21] T. O. Abrahams, O. A. Farayola, S. Kaggwa, P. U. Uwaoma, A. O. Hassan and S. O. Dawodu, "Cybersecurity Awareness and Education Programs: A Review of Employee Engagement and Accountability," *Computer Science & IT Research Journal*, vol. 5, no. 1, pp. 100–119, 2024.

[22] R. Bain, "An Attitude On Attitude Research," *American Journal of Sociology*, vol. 33, no. 6, pp. 940–957, 1928.

14 Collaborative Strategic Partnerships to Enhance Port Cybersecurity

14.1 Definition of Collaborative Strategic Partnerships

In today's interconnected industrial landscape—where resilience, innovation, and agility are critical—collaboration among organizations has shifted from being merely advantageous to fundamentally strategic. This is especially evident in complex environments such as seaports, where diverse actors—port authorities, terminal operators, logistics firms, customs bodies, and technology providers—must operate in close coordination across digital, operational, and regulatory dimensions [1]. To navigate shared challenges like cybersecurity threats, infrastructure upgrades, and digital transformation, many have turned to what are known as collaborative strategic partnerships CSPs [2].

CSPs are formal agreements between independent entities that commit to working together on areas of mutual strategic interest, while still maintaining their separate legal identities. These partnerships are characterized by joint decision-making, shared responsibility, and ongoing contributions—often in fields like technology, infrastructure, or security [2]. For example, in the port sector, this might take the form of a collaboration between a port authority and a tech firm to deploy smart infrastructure or among various stakeholders to create and enforce unified cybersecurity protocols.

Unlike short-term contracts or full-scale mergers, CSPs represent a structured yet flexible form of cooperation. Each partner contributes expertise, resources, or capabilities without giving up operational independence beyond the defined scope of the alliance. These arrangements are designed to achieve sustained, long-term benefits through coordinated but non-hierarchical interaction.

CSPs occupy a middle ground within a broader spectrum of organizational relationships. On one end are market-based exchanges—typified by transactional procurement of port services—where interactions are limited to pricing mechanisms and short-term goals [2]. On the other end are mergers and acquisitions, which consolidate control and integrate operations under a single authority. Between these extremes lie more collaborative structures: joint ventures, where entities co-create a new organization (e.g., a port and a shipping line jointly managing a terminal), and strategic cooperation agreements, where

DOI: 10.4324/9781003559320-14

organizations align on significant objectives—such as regulatory compliance or digitization—while retaining autonomy [2]. These hybrid forms, including CSPs, offer a balance of control, flexibility, and shared strategic focus.

14.2 Why Do Collaborative Strategic Partnerships Enhance Port Cybersecurity?

CSPs have become essential in addressing the increasing complexity and scale of cybersecurity challenges faced by ports. No single port can independently manage the full spectrum of technical, operational, and regulatory demands necessary for robust cyber defense. CSPs provide a practical means to combine complementary strengths, enabling ports to build more resilient and adaptive cybersecurity postures.

A primary driver behind forming CSPs in the cybersecurity realm is **access to specialized technologies and expertise**. Ports traditionally focus on cargo handling and logistics rather than cybersecurity innovation, meaning internal development of advanced defenses—such as artificial intelligence (AI)-driven anomaly detection, zero-trust models, or blockchain-based audit trails—is often beyond reach. By partnering with cybersecurity vendors and technology firms, ports gain timely entry to cutting-edge tools that would otherwise require significant time and resources to develop independently.

Beyond technology acquisition, CSPs enable **capacity building through knowledge exchange and skills development**. Cyber threats evolve rapidly, demanding ongoing training and preparedness exercises for port personnel. Partnerships facilitate joint workshops, scenario-based drills, and cross-organizational incident simulations that elevate staff readiness across departments. This shared learning cultivates a cyber-aware culture where security becomes an organizational priority rather than a niche concern. Such collective efforts improve compliance with international frameworks—ISO/IEC 27001, National Institute of Standards and Technology (NIST) Cybersecurity Framework, International Maritime Organization (IMO) MSC.428(98)—demonstrating a port's commitment to robust governance and reassuring stakeholders, including regulators and insurers.

Another significant advantage lies in **risk sharing and joint management of cyber incidents**. Complex projects like implementing digital twins or upgrading network infrastructure carry operational and financial risks that can be mitigated through collaborative approaches. For example, partnerships among port authorities, technology providers, and government agencies distribute responsibility and enable coordinated responses to security breaches, minimizing downtime and operational impact. The capacity to activate pre-agreed escalation protocols and communication channels in real time greatly enhances incident containment and recovery efforts.

CSPs also foster **real-time cyber threat intelligence (CTI) sharing**, an indispensable asset in today's threat landscape. By pooling information on attack patterns and vulnerabilities, partners gain broader situational awareness, improving early detection and proactive defense measures. This shared intelligence network strengthens predictive analytics and accelerates response times, as ports can draw on collective insights from technology vendors, shipping firms, and public security agencies. The synergy generated through these exchanges creates a force multiplier effect, allowing ports to confront emerging cyber risks more effectively than isolated efforts would permit.

Finally, strategic partnerships promote **continuous innovation and adaptation** in cybersecurity practices. By linking academic research, industry knowledge, and public policy support, CSPs shorten innovation cycles, enabling ports to pilot advanced solutions such as autonomous vehicle security or intelligent green port initiatives with greater confidence and speed [4]. Such collaborative innovation not only enhances cyber defenses but also aligns with broader goals of operational efficiency and environmental sustainability.

In sum, CSPs strengthen port cybersecurity by combining technological access, workforce development, shared risk management, intelligence sharing, and innovation acceleration. These elements, woven together through collaboration, create a more secure, resilient, and future-ready maritime ecosystem—one that can effectively respond to the dynamic cyber threats facing global ports.

14.3 Different Types of Collaboration for Port Managers to Consider

CSPs offer a broad spectrum of structural arrangements that ports can adopt to enhance cybersecurity resilience. Drawing from the typology of Todeva and Knoke (2005), this section selectively adapts several out of their 13 forms of CSPs to the port cybersecurity context [2]. Rather than listing every form in full, the focus is on those most relevant to port managers—based on the degree of coordination, resource sharing, and strategic control each offers. Each selected form is presented with its strengths, limitations, and suitability for various port scenarios.

Strategic cooperative agreements, R&D consortia, and joint ventures represent structured collaborations with varying degrees of intensity [2]. Strategic cooperative agreements are typically governed by contractual arrangements where ports and partners jointly define goals and share responsibility for outcomes. These are suitable for cybersecurity initiatives that require sustained collaboration—such as designing port-wide intrusion detection systems. Their advantage lies in balanced control and flexibility, but they demand ongoing coordination and mutual trust. R&D consortia, often seen in rapidly evolving fields, allow ports to collaborate with universities, technology developers, or maritime innovation hubs to advance cybersecurity tools. These arrangements promote shared learning and early innovation access, although they may suffer from conflicting interests or unclear intellectual property rights. Joint ventures involve a higher level of commitment, where ports co-invest with a cybersecurity firm to establish a dedicated entity for tasks like vulnerability assessment or secure port data management. While this approach ensures deeper integration and strategic alignment, it also involves higher legal, financial, and governance complexity.

Less intensive but still strategically valuable are licensing and equity investment models [2]. Licensing enables ports to legally adopt patented cybersecurity technologies—such as AI-based anomaly detection systems—without engaging in R&D or ownership. This approach offers quick implementation with minimal risk, though it can restrict customization or integration with port-specific infrastructure. Equity investments, by contrast, allow ports to acquire a financial stake in cybersecurity startups or service providers. This creates a channel for strategic influence and access to tailored solutions. However, it also introduces financial exposure and requires ports to evaluate the alignment between their operational objectives and those of the invested firms.

Industry standards groups and cooperatives represent more inclusive, community-based collaboration types [2]. Industry standards groups bring together ports, vendors, and regulators to develop and adopt shared cybersecurity protocols. Participation in such groups—especially those aligned with the IMO, International Association of Ports and Harbors (IAPH), or ISO/IEC 27001—can improve interoperability and demonstrate compliance readiness. However, consensus-driven processes may limit speed and responsiveness. Cooperatives provide a useful model for resource-constrained ports. By forming coalitions, ports can jointly invest in shared cybersecurity infrastructure such as security operations centers (SOCs) or cyber incident-reporting systems. The collective approach strengthens collective defense and makes sophisticated capabilities more accessible. The main drawback lies in ensuring equitable resource allocation and maintaining collaborative momentum among diverse members.

To support practical decision making, Figure 14.1 illustrates a strategic pathway for ports to engage in cybersecurity collaboration, arranged by increasing levels of collaboration intensity. The three scenarios—Scenario 1, Scenario 2, and Scenario 3—help port managers visualize distinct models based on cyber maturity, resource availability, and strategic ambition. Rather than representing fixed steps, these scenarios outline a flexible continuum of options. Ports may enter at any point, evolve gradually, or combine elements from multiple scenarios depending on their specific circumstances and goals.

- **Scenario 1** is designed for ports with limited resources or early-stage cybersecurity programs. These ports may find the greatest benefit in lower-intensity models such as cooperatives or participation in industry standards groups. These forms allow for cost-sharing, collective knowledge exchange, and improved baseline defenses without requiring deep structural commitments.
- **Scenario 2** suits ports with moderate cyber capabilities and a pressing need to adopt solutions quickly without entering long-term arrangements. Licensing agreements and participation in R&D consortia allow these ports to access advanced tools and innovation pipelines with lower risk. These

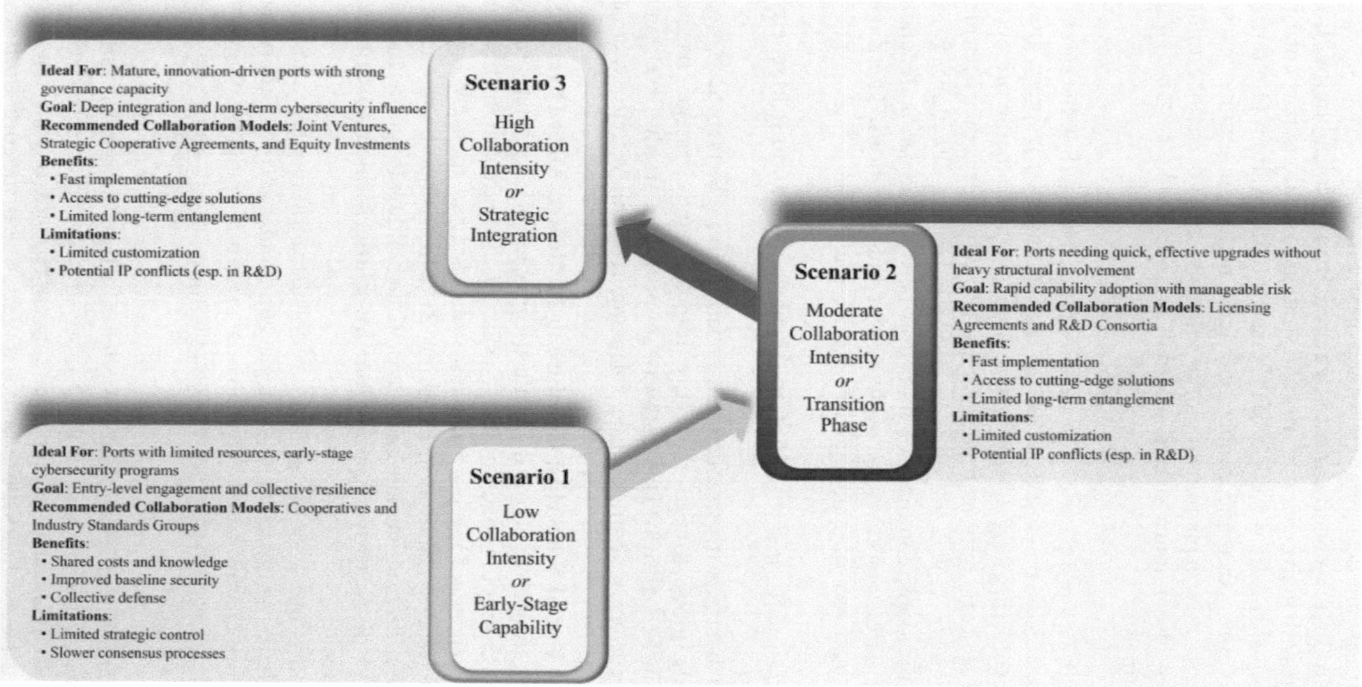

Figure 14.1 Strategic Collaboration Scenarios for Ports Arranged by Increasing Relationship Intensity.

arrangements are particularly effective for ports looking to strengthen their capabilities while retaining operational flexibility.

- **Scenario 3** represents the most integrated form of collaboration. It is ideal for ports with high cyber maturity and strategic ambitions, particularly those aiming to shape the direction of cybersecurity innovation. Options such as joint ventures, strategic cooperative agreements, and equity investments support long-term planning, tailored solutions, and governance influence—but they also require strong internal alignment and sustained resource commitments.

Although Figure 14.1 uses upward-pointing arrows to link the three collaboration scenarios—ranging from low to high intensity—the figure should not be seen as enforcing a rigid, step-by-step progression. Rather, it presents a flexible set of strategic options that ports can apply based on their specific operational contexts. Collaboration may unfold in various directions, with ports choosing to adopt, combine, or transition between scenarios depending on their capabilities, objectives, or evolving external conditions. The three main strategic directions for applying these models are:

- **Progression from Scenario 1 to Scenario 3: Building Maturity Step by Step**
  Ports may start with foundational collaboration efforts in Scenario 1 and gradually move toward the more intensive and strategic partnerships found in Scenario 3. This pathway supports the steady development of cybersecurity capabilities while balancing risk and resource demands at each stage.
- **Hybrid Use of Scenarios: Combining Models to Meet Diverse Needs**
  Ports often operate across different maturity levels in parallel. For instance, while engaging in broad knowledge sharing through an industry standards group (Scenario 1), a port may also test advanced tools through a time-limited R&D collaboration (Scenario 2). This blended approach enables ports to address immediate challenges while building longer-term readiness.
- **Selective or Adaptive Application: Matching Models to Context, not Sequence**
  Some ports may adopt high-intensity collaboration models from the outset if they have the capacity and strategic alignment to do so. Others may shift between scenarios based on changing priorities, budgets, or geopolitical factors. These scenarios are not stepping stones but tools—each valuable in its own right.

By framing these collaboration models as adaptable options rather than a fixed route, port managers can make more strategic and responsive decisions. Whether advancing step-by-step, blending approaches, or adapting as needed, the emphasis is on fit-for-purpose collaboration that supports both resilience and innovation.

14.4 The Cybersecurity Benefits of Collaborating with Government Agencies

Collaborating with government agencies provides ports with unique cybersecurity advantages. Key partners include the Cybersecurity and Infrastructure Security Agency (CISA) in the United States, the European Union Agency for Cybersecurity (ENISA), and the Cyber Security Agency of Singapore (CSA). These organizations offer valuable resources such as threat intelligence, regulatory guidance, incident response support, and strategic oversight that directly support ports within their jurisdictions. Additionally, through international cooperation and the sharing of best practices, their influence helps shape cybersecurity resilience in ports beyond their own countries. Through such partnerships, ports gain many cybersecurity benefits, as follows.

- **Regulatory and Policy Guidance:** Governments shape the cybersecurity rules and standards that ports must follow. Engaging early with these agencies helps ports stay ahead of compliance demands and align their security measures with national priorities. Advisors often tailor frameworks to maritime needs, helping ports reduce risks from non-compliance and boost their reputation as secure trade hubs. Early dialogue can also influence policymaking to reflect operational realities more effectively.
- **Threat Intelligence and Early Alerts:** Government cybersecurity centers aggregate information from diverse public and private networks, detecting emerging threats on a broad scale. Ports connected to these centers receive timely, sector-specific warnings about ransomware, phishing, and supply chain attacks—alerts often unavailable through commercial channels. Exercises led by governments allow ports to test detection and communication readiness before real incidents occur, reducing potential damage.
- **Coordinated Incident Response:** When cyber-attacks strike, government teams offer critical expertise and authority to assist in containment and recovery. They facilitate collaboration among ports, law enforcement, and intelligence agencies, ensuring swift, organized responses that minimize operational and reputational harm.
- **Access to Specialized Resources and Funding:** Governments often provide technical tools, training, and financial support to strengthen infrastructure security. Participation in such programs helps ports overcome resource limitations and accelerates the adoption of cutting-edge cybersecurity solutions.
- **Fostering a National Maritime Security Culture:** Government-led forums and task forces create platforms for knowledge sharing, standardization, and joint defense efforts. This collective approach strengthens not only individual ports but the entire maritime ecosystem, emphasizing cybersecurity as a shared responsibility essential to global trade security.

Several real-world cases illustrate how collaboration with government agencies significantly enhances port cybersecurity across regulatory, operational, and technical domains. For example, in the Netherlands, the Port of Amsterdam launched an extensive "Cybersecurity Programme" aimed at strengthening digital resilience across its port community [3]. Backed by the Dutch Ministry of Economic Affairs and Climate Policy through the Digital Trust Center, this initiative illustrates how government support can catalyze cross-sector collaboration. Two pivotal components were introduced: a centralized hotline for cyber incident reporting and the Cyber Resilient North Sea Canal Area Network (CYREN), which enables real-time intelligence sharing among port-region organizations [4]. The initiative has drawn participation from both public and private actors, fostering rapid response capabilities and a unified defense posture. As highlighted by Harbour Master Marleen van de Kerkhof, cyber incidents in port environments can trigger cascading operational disruptions. The Amsterdam example demonstrates how structured, government-enabled collaboration can establish trusted frameworks for coordinated cybersecurity that extend beyond individual operators.

14.5 The Cybersecurity Benefits of Collaborating with Shipping Lines and Other Users

Collaborating on cybersecurity with shipping lines and other commercial users is essential, as they are integral to the cybersecurity fabric of modern ports. The information technology (IT) and operational systems of these stakeholders—particularly shipping lines—are closely interconnected with port infrastructure, forming a complex digital ecosystem. In such a setup, a cyber vulnerability in one area can quickly ripple through the broader maritime supply chain. For example, the 2018 ransomware attack that initially targeted COSCO Shipping Lines' IT systems subsequently disrupted operations at COSCO-managed terminals, including those at the Port of Long Beach [5]. This incident highlights how cyber disruptions within a shipping line's systems can cascade into port operations, emphasizing the critical need for coordinated cybersecurity efforts.

Through close collaboration, ports and their commercial users can realize several cybersecurity benefits, including:

- **Improving Situational Awareness Through Real-Time Intelligence Sharing:** One of the most immediate gains from closer cooperation between ports and shipping lines is enhanced visibility into evolving threats. By sharing timely alerts—such as reports of phishing campaigns targeting vessel crews or indicators of compromise linked to onboard systems—stakeholders can improve their collective ability to detect and respond. Secure communication links, automated intelligence feeds, and joint cyber task forces all contribute to a shared awareness that helps identify and neutralize risks before they escalate.
- **Enabling Coordinated Cyber Incident Response:** A synchronized response is critical during a cyber incident. By establishing shared response

protocols and clearly defined communication pathways in advance, ports and shipping lines can react quickly and consistently when disruptions occur. This coordination reduces confusion, streamlines containment efforts, and helps restore normal operations with minimal delay. Defined roles and responsibilities are especially vital in complex environments where delays could cascade across global supply chains.

- **Promoting Consistent Cybersecurity Practices:** Collaborative efforts help standardize protective measures across different organizations. Joint training, phishing simulations, and harmonized authentication policies reduce the chances of human error—a leading cause of cyber breaches. This alignment ensures that both land-based and shipborne systems adhere to common security expectations, closing potential gaps that attackers might exploit between differently secured environments.
- **Driving Joint Innovation and Technology Adoption:** Working together enables ports and shipping companies to share costs and expertise when piloting emerging cybersecurity technologies. Whether deploying AI-driven anomaly detection, blockchain solutions for transparent logistics, or interoperable secure data platforms, this collaboration accelerates adoption. Shared technology strategies ensure interoperability and maximize the protective value of new tools across the maritime ecosystem.
- **Building Trust to Strengthen Collective Defense:** Long-term partnerships thrive on trust, especially when sensitive threat intelligence or vulnerability disclosures are involved. Open communication, shared objectives, and mutual respect form the basis of effective cooperation. When partners are confident in each other's intentions and discretion, they are more likely to unearth risks early, share lessons from incidents, and co-develop defensive strategies. Over time, this trust fosters a more resilient maritime security network.

Building on these collaborative principles, some ports have already taken proactive steps to formalize cybersecurity partnerships with key users. A notable example is the Port of Los Angeles, where institutional commitment and stakeholder coordination have produced tangible cybersecurity benefits. In April 2019, the port launched a cybersecurity working group that brought together shipping lines, terminal operators, rail carriers, and trucking firms to address shared digital threats [6]. The group fosters real-time exchange of threat intelligence, improving collective detection and response capabilities across the supply chain [6]. This initiative builds on the port's earlier investment in a Cyber Security Operations Center, established in 2014, and its ISO/IEC 27001 certification, which reflects a formal commitment to managing information security. Port officials emphasize that cyber risks affecting one link can quickly impact the entire logistics network. This case demonstrates how proactive coordination and institutional support can establish a unified defense posture in a highly interconnected maritime environment.

14.6 The Cybersecurity Benefits of Collaborating with Technology Providers

Technology providers—companies that design, develop, and implement cybersecurity tools and systems—are vital partners in strengthening port cybersecurity via delivering specialized tools, innovative solutions, and technical expertise necessary to address the unique challenges of maritime environments. Unlike managed security service providers who focus on ongoing monitoring and response, technology providers drive the development and integration of cutting-edge cybersecurity capabilities tailored to port operations, enabling ports to build resilient and future-ready digital infrastructures.

- **Access to Advanced Cybersecurity Technologies:** Technology providers lead innovation by developing state-of-the-art tools such as AI-driven threat detection, machine learning algorithms for behavioral anomaly identification, and blockchain solutions for secure data exchanges. These technologies enable ports to enhance protection across both IT systems and operational technology (OT)—including automated terminals, crane controllers, and traffic management systems—where cyber-attacks could significantly disrupt safety and efficiency. Collaborating with these providers gives ports early access to emerging security technologies that may be cost-prohibitive or require specialized expertise to implement independently.
- **Tailored and Integrated Security Solutions:** Ports operate complex environments that often combine legacy control systems with modern digital infrastructure and numerous external integrations. Technology providers specialize in designing customized cybersecurity architectures that align with these operational realities. This includes segmenting networks to isolate critical assets, hardening industrial control systems (ICS), and implementing zero-trust frameworks that require continuous verification of user and device access. These bespoke solutions facilitate secure modernization efforts while minimizing operational disruption, ensuring cybersecurity strategies support the port's specific logistical and strategic objectives.
- **In-Depth Vulnerability Assessments and Technical Expertise:** Technology providers bring deep knowledge in vulnerability assessment through advanced automated scanning and hands-on penetration testing. These assessments identify hidden weaknesses across software, hardware, and network components, including third-party systems like customs platforms or cargo-monitoring tools. By prioritizing risks based on severity and exploitability, providers offer actionable insights that help ports proactively address vulnerabilities and strengthen their overall security posture.
- **Enabling Proactive Cyber Defense and Automation:** Collaboration with technology vendors enables ports to move beyond reactive cybersecurity approaches by adopting automated defense mechanisms, such as security information and event management (SIEM) systems integrated with live threat intelligence. These platforms facilitate continuous monitoring,

rapid anomaly detection, and automated mitigation workflows that reduce response times. Additionally, providers support coordinated cybersecurity strategies across port tenants, contractors, and supply chain partners, enhancing collective resilience in a highly interconnected ecosystem.

- **Supporting Incident Response and Recovery with Specialized Tools:** In cybersecurity incidents, technology providers offer critical support through automation platforms like security orchestration, automation, and response (SOAR) systems that accelerate containment, forensic analysis, and system restoration. Their expertise ensures thorough post-incident reviews and continuous improvement of response protocols, helping ports recover swiftly while minimizing downtime and operational impact.

To illustrate how strategic partnerships can enhance port cybersecurity, consider the Port of Los Angeles's collaboration with IBM Security. In 2020, the port partnered with IBM to launch the Cyber Resilience Center (CRC), aimed at strengthening cyber defenses across its logistics network [7]. The CRC uses IBM's Cloud Pak for Security to unify data sources into a single dashboard, while SOAR automation streamlines incident response. IBM also provides X-Force Threat Intelligence and on-site personnel for continuous monitoring. The model fosters collaboration by involving tenants, vendors, and logistics providers, who share anonymized threat intelligence while retaining system control. This approach improves early-warning coordination and significantly reduces threat dwell time.

14.7 The Cybersecurity Benefits of Collaborating with MSSPs

Managed security service providers (MSSPs) are third-party firms that specialize in remotely managing an organization's cybersecurity operations. They play an essential role in enhancing port cybersecurity by delivering outsourced, continuous security operations tailored to the complex and evolving threat landscape facing maritime infrastructure. Unlike technology providers who primarily develop and supply cybersecurity tools and custom solutions, MSSPs focus on operating and managing security systems on behalf of ports, providing 24/7 threat monitoring, incident detection, and rapid response capabilities. By partnering with MSSPs, ports can leverage specialized expertise, advanced analytics, and continuous monitoring without the need to maintain costly internal cybersecurity teams. This collaboration supports many benefits as follows:

- **Continuous Monitoring and Rapid Threat Detection:** MSSPs operate SOCs that provide round-the-clock surveillance of port networks and systems. Through real-time analysis of security events, MSSPs detect anomalies, potential breaches, and emerging threats early, enabling immediate action before attacks escalate. For instance, the Port of Helsinki partnered with Netox to establish a dedicated SOC which delivers rapid incident resolution capabilities, reducing potential disruptions to port operations. Similarly, the Port of Tyne's collaboration with MSSPs integrates AI-powered threat detection within its private 5G network, ensuring continuous protection of critical assets.

- **Cost-Effective and Scalable Cybersecurity Services:** Building and operating an in-house SOC requires significant investment in skilled personnel, technology, and infrastructure—resources that many ports find challenging to sustain. MSSPs offer scalable service models that allow ports to tailor cybersecurity spending based on their operational size and risk profile. This flexibility enables ports to access expert security personnel, advanced monitoring tools, and threat intelligence feeds without large capital expenditures, optimizing cybersecurity budgets while maintaining robust defenses.
- **Advanced Threat Intelligence and AI-Driven Analytics:** MSSPs continuously collect and analyze global threat intelligence, leveraging AI and machine learning to identify new attack vectors and predict potential risks. This proactive approach empowers ports with actionable insights and automated alerts that facilitate swift threat hunting and mitigation. By staying ahead of evolving cyber threats, MSSPs help ports adapt their security posture dynamically and strengthen resilience across interconnected maritime networks.
- **Structured Incident Response and Recovery Support:** In the event of a cyber incident, MSSPs provide structured response frameworks that streamline containment, investigation, and remediation. Their expertise in coordinating response efforts reduces downtime and operational impact, ensuring rapid recovery aligned with international maritime cybersecurity regulations. The Port of Ashdod's partnership with Salvador Technologies exemplifies how MSSP-led recovery platforms can replace outdated manual procedures, accelerating restoration of control systems and operational technology after attacks.

While MSSPs provide scalable cybersecurity support, some leading maritime nations have adopted centralized, government-led approaches with similar strategic benefits. Singapore's Maritime and Port Authority (MPA) exemplifies this through its SOC, launched in May 2019 to protect critical maritime infrastructure [8]. Operating 24/7, the MSOC monitors digital activity across the port, detects anomalies, and coordinates responses via its integration with the Port Operations Control Centre. This centralized model improves situational awareness and enables rapid incident response. To complement this, the MPA partnered with the Singapore Shipping Association to deliver cybersecurity training for maritime personnel, strengthening both technical capacity and human readiness [8]. As MPA Chairman Niam Chiang Meng emphasized, safeguarding maritime infrastructure is essential amid rising cyber risks. The case demonstrates how state-driven investment in technology and workforce development can elevate cybersecurity maturity across an entire port ecosystem.

14.8 The Cybersecurity Benefits of Collaborating with Academic Institutions

Academic institutions—such as universities, technical colleges, and research centers—play a crucial role in advancing knowledge and developing solutions to real-world challenges through education, research, and innovation. In the context of port cybersecurity, these institutions serve as key partners in strengthening defenses through cutting-edge research, workforce development, and industry collaboration. By leveraging their expertise and innovation, ports can enhance their cybersecurity resilience and stay ahead of emerging threats. The following are the key benefits of such collaboration:

- **Research and Technological Innovation**: Universities are at the forefront of cybersecurity research, developing advanced threat detection systems, encryption techniques, and AI-driven security solutions. Ports can collaborate with academic researchers to integrate these technologies into their cybersecurity frameworks, enhancing protection against cyber threats targeting OT and IT systems.
- **Access to Skilled Cybersecurity Professionals**: Academic institutions provide ports with access to a highly trained talent pool specializing in network security, cyber forensics, and maritime cybersecurity. Through internships, research partnerships, and joint training programs, ports can attract cybersecurity specialists who bring fresh perspectives and technical expertise to help fortify port infrastructure against cyber threats.
- **Cybersecurity Awareness and Training Programs**: Universities play a critical role in developing cybersecurity awareness initiatives tailored to the maritime sector. By working with academic institutions, ports can implement comprehensive training programs and simulated cyber-attack exercises to educate employees on identifying and mitigating cyber risks. This is particularly important for port operators, IT personnel, and supply chain partners, as human error remains one of the leading causes of cybersecurity breaches.
- **Development of Industry Best Practices and Standards**: Many universities collaborate with government agencies, classification societies, and industry stakeholders to establish cybersecurity best practices specific to maritime and port operations. By engaging in these academia-industry partnerships, ports can ensure that their cybersecurity strategies align with global standards and remain adaptable to evolving cyber threats.
- **Joint Research and Threat Intelligence Collaboration**: Ports can participate in academic research projects focusing on real-world cybersecurity challenges, such as securing port automation systems, defending against ransomware attacks, and enhancing supply chain cybersecurity. These projects not only contribute to the advancement of maritime cybersecurity knowledge but also result in practical solutions that directly enhance port security protocols.

To demonstrate the cybersecurity benefits of collaborating with academic institutions, the following case studies highlight how ports and maritime authorities have partnered with universities and research centers to build cyber resilience. These collaborations foster innovation, expand talent pipelines, and support the development of specialized capabilities within port ecosystems. For instance, Singapore's MPA signed two MoUs to advance maritime cybersecurity through academic and industry alliances [9]. The first, with TalTech, SUTD, CR14, and SMI, focused on the Maritime Testbed of Shipboard Operational Technology (MariOT), enabling simulations of OT-based threats, joint research, and cyber drills. It also addressed AI risk, human factors, and faculty exchanges. The second MoU, with SSA, SIT, and SUTD, prioritized workforce development through co-designed OT curricula and mid-career training programs. Complementing these efforts, MPA launched the CyberSafe Scorecard (aligned with NIST Cybersecurity Framework (CSF)) and tested the pilot Maritime Cyber Assurance and Operations Centre via a tabletop exercise involving global stakeholders [9]. This case shows how sustained academic collaboration enhances both technological capacity and cyber workforce readiness in maritime environments.

14.9 The Cybersecurity Benefits of Collaborating with Classification Societies

Classification societies are independent organizations that develop and apply technical standards to the design, construction, and operation of ships and offshore structures. Traditionally focused on vessel safety and seaworthiness, their role has broadened in response to digital transformation across the maritime sector. Through their technical expertise, standardized guidelines, and independent oversight, these organizations help ports strengthen cyber defenses while navigating complex regulatory landscapes. Their role has expanded beyond physical vessel classification to include digital risk management and cybersecurity assurance, particularly as maritime operations become increasingly automated and interconnected. Strategic collaboration with classification societies provides ports with several cybersecurity benefits:

- **Integration of Industry Standards into Security Frameworks**: Classification societies develop structured cybersecurity guidelines that reflect current risks to information and operational technologies. By adopting these standards, ports can establish a consistent baseline for cyber hygiene and better protect digital assets, critical infrastructure, and operational continuity. These guidelines also provide a foundation for designing secure-by-default systems, especially relevant during new infrastructure development or digital transformation efforts.
- **Alignment with International Regulatory Expectations**: Ports are increasingly required to demonstrate compliance with cybersecurity-related regulations issued by global maritime bodies. Classification societies assist

by translating these requirements into actionable compliance strategies, offering certification schemes, and helping ports meet audit obligations. Their involvement can reduce exposure to legal penalties, operational disruptions, or reputational harm stemming from non-compliance.

- **Independent Audits and Vulnerability Assessments**: Through scheduled audits and targeted assessments, classification societies help ports identify weaknesses in cybersecurity postures—particularly in legacy systems or hybrid IT-OT environments. Their assessments often include recommendations grounded in best practices, threat intelligence, and lessons learned from across the maritime sector, giving port operators concrete guidance for reducing vulnerabilities.
- **Support in Incident Preparedness and Recovery**: When cybersecurity incidents occur, classification societies can act as technical advisors, guiding ports through containment, forensic investigation, and recovery efforts. Their frameworks emphasize structured response plans, clear escalation paths, and continuity strategies that minimize downtime and restore trust in operational integrity.
- **Reinforced Credibility and Stakeholder Confidence**: Association with a recognized classification society signals a port's commitment to high cybersecurity standards. This external validation enhances trust among shipping lines, insurers, regulators, and technology partners. It also contributes to improved risk profiles, potentially influencing favorable insurance terms and stakeholder engagement.

To illustrate how ports benefit from collaborating with classification societies on cybersecurity, consider the partnership between Singapore's MPA and the International Association of Classification Societies (IACS). Formalized through a Letter of Intent during the 33rd IMO Assembly in London, this collaboration focuses on harmonizing technical standards and unifying requirements for emerging maritime technologies—such as smart ships, digitalization, marine electrification, and alternative fuels [10]. The agreement fosters ongoing knowledge sharing and addresses industry challenges by aligning regulatory expectations and developing standardized guidelines. This strategic alignment supports safe technology deployment and enhances cyber resilience at Singapore's major transshipment hub. The case highlights how cooperation between port authorities and classification societies can drive innovation while protecting operational and environmental integrity.

References

[1] C. Senarak, "Shipping-Collaboration Model for the New Generation of Container Port in Innovation District: A Case of Eastern Economic Corridor," *The Asian Journal of Shipping and Logistics*, vol. 36, no. 2, pp. 65–77, 2020.

[2] E. Todeva and D. Knoke, "Strategic Alliances and Models of Collaboration," *Management Decision*, vol. 43, no. 1, pp. 123–148, 2005.

[3] Port of Amsterdam, "2018 Annual Report," 2018. [Online]. Available: www.portofamsterdam.com/sites/default/files/2020-06/annual-report-2018.pdf.

[4] Port Technology Team, "Amsterdam to Reinforce Cybersecurity Measures," 2019. [Online]. Available: www.porttechnology.org/news/amsterdam_to_reinforce_cybersecurity_measures/.

[5] C. Senarak, "Port Cyberattacks from 2011 to 2023: A Literature Review and Discussion of Selected Cases," *Maritime Economics & Logistics*, vol. 26, no. 1, pp. 105–130, 2024.

[6] C. SAN PEDRO, "Port Of Los Angeles Hosts Maritime Cross Sector Cybersecurity Roundtable," 2019. [Online]. Available: www.portoflosangeles.org/references/news_042519_cybersecurity.

[7] IBM, "IBM Works With Port of Los Angeles to Help Secure Maritime Supply Chain," 2020. [Online]. Available: https://newsroom.ibm.com/2020-12-07-IBM-Works-With-Port-of-Los-Angeles-to-Help-Secure-Maritime-Supply-Chain.

[8] Maritime and Port Authority of Singapore, "New 24/7 Maritime Cybersecurity Operations Centre to Boost Cyber Defence Readiness," 2019. [Online]. Available: www.mpa.gov.sg/media-centre/details/new-24-7-maritime-cybersecurity-operations-centre-to-boost-cyber-defence-readiness.

[9] Maritime and Port Authority of Singapore, "Collective Efforts to Strengthen Maritime Cybersecurity," 2024. [Online]. Available: www.mpa.gov.sg/media-centre/details/collective-efforts-to-strengthen-maritime-cybersecurity.

[10] IACS, "Collaboration between IACS and Singapore MPA," 2023. [Online]. Available: https://iacs.org.uk/news/collaboration-between-iacs-and-singapore-mpa.

15 Strategic Port Managers and Cybersecurity Team

15.1 Role of Port Managers in Ensuring the Port Cybersecurity and Resilience

15.1.1 Departmental Cybersecurity Roles of Port Managers

While earlier chapters have laid the foundation by presenting key cybersecurity and resilience principles—along with the vital contributions of mid-level and frontline personnel—this section shifts attention to the port managers who operate across departments. These individuals serve as crucial bridges between strategic intent and practical execution. Their role is not limited to supervising their teams; they actively translate high-level cybersecurity goals into concrete, daily actions that uphold security and resilience. With responsibilities spanning operations, information technology (IT), human resources, finance, customer relations, procurement, and more, their collaboration forms the backbone of a secure port ecosystem.

- **Port Operations Managers**: These managers are primarily responsible for overseeing the flow of goods, vessel docking, equipment handling, and warehouse activities. Their role centers on ensuring that the movement of cargo and coordination of logistics occur smoothly and safely. Within this operational mandate, they are well-positioned to embed cybersecurity into frontline procedures. For example, they can implement secure access controls at cargo-handling points, ensure terminal management systems are used in compliance with security protocols, and enforce safeguards to prevent data leaks from operational platforms. Their vigilance in detecting irregularities—such as delays tied to system malfunctions or signs of unauthorized access—allows them to act swiftly, initiating containment and escalation measures that protect both physical and digital assets.
- **IT and Security Managers**: At the core of their function is the maintenance and protection of the port's digital infrastructure, including servers, networks, and application systems. These managers are responsible for ensuring the availability, confidentiality, and integrity of critical digital platforms that support port services. Their role in cybersecurity is direct: they

DOI: 10.4324/9781003559320-15

coordinate patch updates, conduct penetration tests, and assess risks from external vendors and third-party systems. By aligning IT operations with broader security objectives, they ensure that technological upgrades and digital expansions enhance resilience without compromising workflow efficiency. They also provide necessary technical translations, enabling non-technical departments to understand and adhere to cybersecurity protocols.

- **Human Resources (HR) Managers**: The core responsibility of HR managers is to manage the recruitment, development, and well-being of personnel. Within this function, they influence cybersecurity resilience by shaping employee behavior and organizational culture. HR professionals can integrate cybersecurity into job descriptions, incorporate it into training programs, and include it in performance evaluations. Moreover, they help instill a sense of collective responsibility by fostering environments where reporting security concerns is encouraged rather than stigmatized. Their promotion of cyber awareness, especially among non-technical staff, helps reduce social engineering risks and builds what is often referred to as a "human firewall"—a proactive defense layer made up of informed personnel.
- **Finance and Accounting Managers**: Their primary duties involve managing the port's financial health, overseeing budgeting, transaction processing, and compliance with financial regulations. Due to the sensitive nature of financial data and platforms, these managers are at the forefront of safeguarding digital financial systems. They support cybersecurity by implementing secure payment gateways, monitoring for anomalies in transaction logs, and ensuring that systems used for billing, payroll, and vendor payments comply with data protection standards. In addition, they contribute to long-term resilience by assessing cyber risk in financial terms—deciding how to allocate resources to preventive technologies, insurance policies, and recovery planning based on potential impact and return on investment.
- **Sales and customer service relations (CSR) Managers**: Tasked with managing external communications, client engagement, and service quality, these managers uphold the port's reputation and ensure seamless interaction with customers. Their role in cybersecurity involves protecting customer data, securing digital platforms used for bookings and inquiries, and maintaining encrypted communication channels. In the event of a data breach, these managers lead the external communication effort—managing stakeholder expectations, guiding transparency measures, and restoring trust. Their preparedness and communication agility can significantly influence how a cyber incident is perceived externally and whether reputational damage can be contained.
- **Procurement Managers**: Procurement teams oversee the acquisition of goods, equipment, software, and services needed to support port operations. Their traditional focus on cost, quality, and delivery timelines now includes a growing responsibility to consider cybersecurity risks in the supply chain. By evaluating the cybersecurity maturity of vendors and incorporating specific clauses into procurement contracts, these managers act as gatekeepers,

preventing the introduction of vulnerabilities via third-party systems or hardware. They also contribute to long-term resilience by conducting periodic reviews of vendor performance and ensuring alignment with the port's overall cybersecurity policies.

15.1.2 Cross-Functional Collaboration for Cyber Resilience

Cyber threats rarely remain confined to one department. An attack that begins with a phishing email in HR can quickly disrupt cargo operations, financial systems, and beyond. This interconnectivity means no single team can protect the port alone. Cybersecurity and resilience depend on coordinated action across departments. Each manager contributes a vital perspective, and only through active collaboration can they identify vulnerabilities and build an effective defense. To support this, ports rely on structured mechanisms and practices that bring managers together and align their efforts across the organization.

- **Cybersecurity Committees:** Formal coordination structures, such as cybersecurity task forces or steering committees, enable cross-departmental alignment. Comprising representatives from IT, operations, HR, finance, procurement, and customer relations, these groups drive unified security strategies and ensure that response protocols are clearly defined and widely understood. Their purpose is not only to coordinate actions during incidents but also to establish a common direction that reinforces continuity and coherence across the organization.
- **Simulation-Based Preparedness:** Regular tabletop exercises and cybersecurity drills prepare departments to respond effectively to complex threats. In these scenarios, managers rehearse their roles during simulated attacks, exposing interdependencies and improving coordination. These exercises offer a practical space to test procedures, uncover communication breakdowns, and strengthen trust—critical assets in real-world crises.
- **Real-Time Communication:** Timely and accurate information sharing is central to coordinated defense. Many ports deploy secure internal platforms to distribute alerts, post incident updates, and manage response workflows. Standardizing language around threat levels and incident types ensures clarity and enables managers to act in unison rather than in disconnected silos.
- **Integrated Risk Reviews:** Collaboration also extends to routine decision making. During vendor evaluations or technology rollouts, departments contribute complementary expertise—IT vets cybersecurity controls, finance assesses value, HR ensures secure access, and operations evaluates practical impacts. This integrated approach minimizes oversights and supports a port-wide security framework.
- **Culture of Shared Accountability:** Finally, effective collaboration depends on a culture that values collective responsibility. When managers

view cybersecurity as a shared mission rather than a departmental burden, they contribute more openly to joint efforts. Leadership plays a key role in reinforcing this mindset by recognizing cross-functional success, encouraging transparency around vulnerabilities, and fostering a climate of trust.

Together, these practices form the foundation for collaborative cyber resilience. When departments coordinate closely—before, during, and after an incident—ports can respond more quickly, recover more smoothly, and prevent threats from spreading. Strengthening internal cooperation today also lays the groundwork for broader collaboration with external partners in the maritime ecosystem.

15.2 The Definition and Structure of the Port Cybersecurity Team (PCT)

15.2.1 Definition and General Structure of a Cybersecurity Team

A cybersecurity team is a coordinated unit of professionals organized to protect an organization's digital and physical assets from cyber threats through prevention, detection, response, and recovery [1]. These teams often operate within specialized subgroups—each with distinct roles but overlapping goals—to ensure layered and resilient protection. The team is typically structured into color-coded subteams, each specializing in specific defensive functions. Effective cybersecurity depends on collaboration among these color-coded teams, each contributing unique capabilities and perspectives [1]. The main subteams generally include:

- **Blue Team:** The core defenders responsible for protecting system integrity. They manage firewalls, monitor endpoints, and lead incident detection and response using established standards and frameworks like National Institute of Standards and Technology (NIST) and ISO 27001. Their goal is to maintain confidentiality, integrity, and availability of systems [2].
- **Red Team:** Authorized ethical hackers who simulate real-world attacks to identify security gaps. Using offensive tactics and frameworks such as MITRE ATT&CK, they help improve readiness by revealing vulnerabilities before adversaries exploit them [2].
- **Purple Team:** A collaborative blend of Red and Blue Teams working together to enhance defense tactics in real time. This synergy improves threat detection and response through shared insights and joint exercises [1].
- **White Team:** The governance body overseeing rules of engagement, compliance, and policy enforcement. They ensure that Red and Blue Teams operate within internal policies and regulatory frameworks, maintaining strategic alignment [1].
- **Green Team:** Focuses on operational efficiency by streamlining security processes and supporting ongoing program management. They ensure security operations run smoothly by applying frameworks like ITIL and COBIT [1].

- **Yellow Team:** Specializes in risk assessment and mitigation, analyzing vulnerabilities and their business impact. Their role includes developing strategies to reduce risk using forensic and vulnerability management standards [1].
- **Orange Team:** Responsible for physical security controls that protect infrastructure access points and critical facilities, ensuring that physical and digital security are integrated [1].
- **Gray Team:** Concentrates on insider threats and social engineering risks. They assess internal vulnerabilities by emulating covert adversaries to uncover weaknesses linked to human factors [1].
- **Black Team:** Conducts covert, advanced penetration tests mimicking sophisticated attackers. Their activities include deploying malware and zero-day exploits to evaluate and strengthen an organization's defenses beyond typical Red Team exercises [1].

While the cybersecurity team is primarily responsible for technical defense and operational tasks [1], it is important to distinguish it from the cybersecurity committee, which serves a distinct strategic and governance function within the organization. The committee—typically made up of managers from IT, operations, HR, finance, and customer relations—fulfills a strategic and governance role. It develops and oversees cybersecurity policies, ensures alignment with organizational goals, and fosters coordination among departments to manage cyber risks effectively.

15.2.2 Application to the Port Environment

In the port sector, cybersecurity must address both IT and operational technology (OT) systems critical to maritime logistics, cargo handling, and terminal operations. These environments face unique cyber-physical risks, making the case for a dedicated PCT—a structured, multidisciplinary unit tasked with defending the digital and physical layers of port infrastructure.

While many ports rely on general IT staff for cyber defense, few have formally structured cybersecurity teams comparable to those found in other critical infrastructure sectors. However, adopting elements of the color-coded team model described above can bring clarity, specialization, and resilience—particularly in ports advancing toward digital transformation or operating under national security obligations.

Rather than replicating every subteam in full, ports can adapt roles selectively based on operational needs:

- **Blue Team functions** may already be in place through firewall management, intrusion detection, and endpoint protection across terminal systems or crane automation platforms.
- **Red Team activities**—such as penetration testing of access controls or vessel IT interfaces—can be introduced through third-party specialists or exercises simulating maritime cyber threats.

- **Purple Team coordination** is especially valuable in port settings that support live simulations, enabling defenders and testers to refine responses together in real time.
- **White Team oversight** is essential in ports subject to international standards (e.g., International Maritime Organization (IMO) MSC.428(98)) or national critical infrastructure policies, ensuring compliance is embedded into operations.
- **Orange Team roles** can be formalized to secure physical access points, from surveillance systems at gates to biometric controls at ship-shore interfaces.
- **Gray and Black Team elements**, while less common in ports, may be relevant for high-risk terminals, involving insider threat modeling or adversary emulation by government-linked or red-teaming units.

It is important to note that this framework is not prescriptive. Not all ports require the full model, nor do these roles need to be internal. What matters is role clarity. In ports with a security operations centers (SOC), many of these functions already exist in practice. Formalizing them under a color-coded structure can enhance coordination, communication, and risk accountability.

Finally, cybersecurity in ports is not solely a technical task. Legal teams, operations managers, HR staff, and senior executives all play essential supporting roles. Their involvement ensures that cybersecurity practices are aligned with organizational behavior, regulatory compliance, and risk governance.

In summary, while not yet standard across the maritime domain, adopting a tailored and structured PCT—drawing from established cybersecurity frameworks—can strengthen a port's ability to manage digital risk. Flexibility in applying the model allows each port to scale its cyber capabilities in line with its infrastructure complexity and strategic role.

15.3 Roles of the PCT in the Cybersecurity Lifecycle

15.3.1 Functional Roles Across the Cybersecurity Lifecycle

Cyber threats in port environments span both digital and physical systems, affecting everything from cargo logistics to terminal safety. To manage these evolving risks, ports can align their cybersecurity approach with the NIST Cybersecurity Framework—a model the IMO has recommended for maritime application. This framework consists of five interdependent functions: **Identify, Protect, Detect, Respond, and Recover**. Each phase presents opportunities for the PCT to apply its expertise in a coordinated and structured way.

Figure 15.1 provides a visual overview of how these five cybersecurity functions correspond with the roles of key color-coded teams within the PCT. By mapping specific responsibilities to each stage of the lifecycle, ports can better understand how to organize their internal cybersecurity capabilities for both clarity and efficiency.

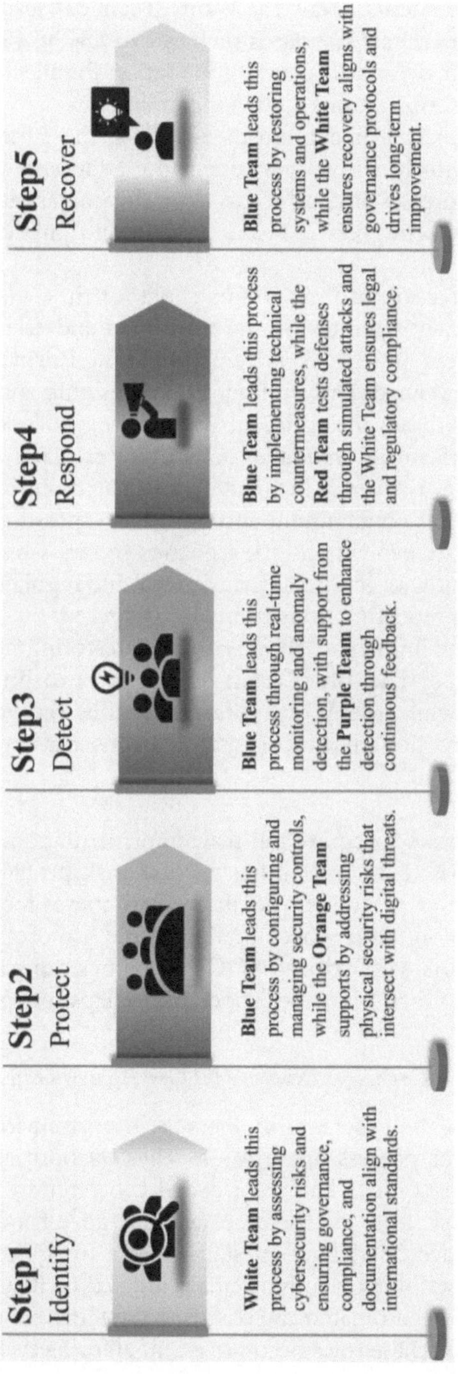

Figure 15.1 Cybersecurity Functions and Corresponding Team Responsibilities.

- **Identify**: The process begins with understanding the port's assets, risks, and compliance requirements. Here, the **White Team** can lead risk assessments and ensure policies reflect standards such as IMO MSC.428(98) and ISO/IEC 27001. Their oversight sets the foundation for all subsequent actions by clarifying roles, obligations, and vulnerabilities.
- **Protect**: To reduce the likelihood of incidents, the **Blue Team** manages cybersecurity controls across networks and endpoints. In parallel, the **Orange Team** addresses physical access to sensitive areas, such as data centers or terminal equipment rooms, ensuring cyber and physical safeguards are synchronized.
- **Detect**: Early detection of threats is essential for timely intervention. The **Blue Team** typically operates monitoring tools and security information and event management (SIEM) systems, while the **Purple Team** facilitates coordination between offensive (Red Team) insights and defensive strategies. In ports with advanced digital systems, this collaborative detection model can unearth subtle anomalies before they escalate.
- **Respond**: During a security incident, coordinated action is critical. The **Blue Team** executes containment and mitigation measures, while the **Red Team** may simulate evolving attack scenarios to stress-test responses. The **White Team** ensures all actions adhere to legal and regulatory expectations, particularly when reporting obligations are triggered.
- **Recover**: After the immediate threat subsides, restoring normal operations becomes the focus. The **Blue Team** leads efforts to bring systems back online securely, while the **White Team** evaluates recovery effectiveness, updates documentation, and incorporates lessons learned into governance protocols.

This structure does not require full-scale implementation. Ports may apply selected elements based on their infrastructure, risk profile, and regulatory environment. However, assigning roles in line with these lifecycle stages allows for better coordination, clearer accountability, and a more agile response to complex threats. Ports with existing SOC capabilities can particularly benefit by formalizing these functions to close operational gaps and improve resilience.

15.3.2 Organizational Capacity to Support the Cybersecurity Lifecycle

Effectively managing the cybersecurity lifecycle in port environments requires more than policies or process maturity—it relies on both a structured team model and skilled personnel. The color-coded cybersecurity team framework offers clear functional roles for defense, testing, governance, and recovery. However, without dedicated internal staff—such as engineers, analysts, and strategic leads—those functions often remain unfilled or fragmented. As ports increasingly depend on automated and connected systems, building internal capacity to operationalize these roles becomes essential for lifecycle-wide resilience.

Key organizational roles that can enable and reinforce the cybersecurity lifecycle include:

- **Chief Information Security Officer (CISO):** Serves as the senior executive responsible for shaping and overseeing the port's cybersecurity strategy, governance, and risk management [2]. The CISO ensures alignment between operational objectives and lifecycle functions, particularly in governance-heavy phases such as Identify and Recover.
- **Cybersecurity Manager or Team Leader:** Coordinates daily cybersecurity operations across departments, integrating technical efforts into broader port workflows. This role helps sustain lifecycle consistency by bridging protection, detection, and response phases.
- **Cybersecurity Engineers:** Deploy and maintain foundational technical defenses such as firewalls, encryption protocols, and access control mechanisms. Their work supports the Protect function by embedding security directly into digital infrastructure.
- **Cybersecurity Analysts:** Monitor systems continuously for threats, conduct risk assessments, and prioritize vulnerabilities. These functions underpin the Detect and Identify phases, enabling timely alerts and risk-informed decisions.
- **Incident Response Specialists and Handlers:** Lead mitigation efforts during active security incidents. Their forensic investigations, containment strategies, and collaboration across departments play a central role in the Respond and Recover phases.
- **SOC Team:** Acts as the real-time control hub for threat monitoring and rapid response. SOC teams sustain lifecycle continuity by ensuring round-the-clock visibility into both IT and OT environments.
- **Security Architects and Engineers:** Design scalable, secure infrastructure that supports evolving port technologies. Their work extends across the Protect, Detect, and Respond stages, incorporating modern defense strategies like zero-trust models and artificial intelligence (AI)-driven analytics.
- **Cybersecurity Consultants:** Provide external assessments and specialized support, such as penetration testing or compliance reviews. Consultants often assist with lifecycle functions in ports that lack in-house expertise or during transitions to smart port models.
- **Contracting Officer and Contracting Officer's Representative:** Ensure cybersecurity requirements are embedded in procurement contracts and vendor oversight [2]. Their input is especially critical in the Identify and Protect functions where supply chain security and third-party risk must be addressed early.
- **Legal Advisor for Cyber-Integrated Procurement:** Advises on regulatory compliance and legal safeguards during cybersecurity acquisitions [2]. This role contributes to lifecycle integrity by embedding enforceable obligations in vendor agreements and reducing legal risk across the lifecycle.

- **Risk Executive (Function):** Guides enterprise-level alignment between cyber risk and broader organizational tolerance. The Risk Executive plays a vital role in shaping risk-informed decisions across the Identify and Recover phases [2].
- **Port Cybersecurity/Facility Security Officer:** Expands the traditional International Ship and Port Facility Security (ISPS)-based Facility Security Officer role to include cyber-physical threats. This position helps ensure that digital threats are accounted for in both Protect and Respond lifecycle functions [3].

Establishing these roles is not just a technical upgrade—it is a foundational investment in operational resilience. As ports evolve through digital transformation or adopt smart port technologies, internal cybersecurity expertise will be essential to implementing and sustaining the full cybersecurity lifecycle. Embedding such roles into the port's structure ensures faster, coordinated threat responses, supports regulatory alignment, and integrates security into daily decision making and infrastructure development.

15.4 Strategic Collaboration and Communication in the PCT

Cybersecurity in ports is not solely driven by advanced tools or frameworks—it relies heavily on the strategic flow of information among professionals entrusted with protecting digital and physical infrastructure. Within the PCT, collaboration is not simply a matter of routine coordination; it is a deliberate, strategic process that supports real-time decision making, aligns operational priorities, and reinforces organizational resilience. In this context, both internal and external communication form the backbone of cybersecurity effectiveness.

Internally, the PCT must cultivate structured, timely, and role-specific communication mechanisms that allow specialized subteams—such as the Blue, Red, Purple, and White Teams—to work in concert. A clear communication framework ensures that the team's activities remain synchronized, particularly during high-pressure situations such as active incidents or coordinated drills [4]. This includes using daily briefings, color-coded dashboards, and structured reporting templates to streamline updates. Ports are encouraged to designate an internal coordination role to facilitate cross-team knowledge flow, ensuring that the intelligence gathered by one team—for example, anomaly detection by the Blue Team—is quickly shared with those handling containment or response. In practice, this could take the form of brief coordination stand-ups during elevated alert levels or the use of secure team channels where urgent updates are prioritized using subject tags such as "[ACTION REQUIRED]" or "[SITUATIONAL AWARENESS]."

Equally important is clarity on what types of information should be communicated across different cybersecurity functions. Each NIST function—Identify, Protect, Detect, Respond, and Recover—generates and requires different categories of data. For example, the asset inventory developed under the Identify function should inform vulnerability assessments and access controls under the Protect function. Similarly, logs from intrusion detection systems (Detect) must feed directly into incident response playbooks (Respond) and post-incident learning reports (Recover). Without disciplined sharing of such insights, ports risk operating in silos, which can delay response and amplify the impact of attacks. To avoid this, ports should establish a shared knowledge base accessible only to authorized team members, where key inputs such as recent threat indicators, containment measures, and recovery validations are regularly updated and version-controlled.

The methods and tools used to facilitate communication must also be aligned with the port's operational tempo and security requirements. While email may remain useful for formal reporting, it is often too slow and disjointed for dynamic cybersecurity operations. Ports are advised to adopt secure messaging platforms with role-specific channels, real-time alerting, and audit logging. These platforms can be integrated with the port's SIEM system to automatically push high-priority alerts to the relevant subteams. To minimize communication fatigue, structured communication protocols—such as message prioritization, shared action boards, and escalation checklists—should be applied consistently. Conducting periodic reviews of communication effectiveness, particularly after drills or real incidents, helps identify bottlenecks and fosters continuous improvement.

Beyond internal operations, the PCT must also maintain active and pre-defined lines of communication with external stakeholders [5]. These include national cybersecurity agencies, law enforcement, insurers, maritime regulators, port tenants, and critical vendors. The goal is not only to coordinate during incidents but also to align on preparedness and recovery strategies [5]. Communication breakdowns with external actors—such as delayed breach notifications or inconsistent status updates—can complicate incident handling and weaken trust. To mitigate this, ports should develop an external communications protocol that clearly assigns spokesperson roles, outlines reporting thresholds, and maps external contact points to specific scenarios. Establishing these protocols in advance allows the port to respond with speed and consistency when it matters most.

Finally, strategic communication must be embedded in the PCT's culture. It is not enough to have tools and plans in place—team members must also feel confident and empowered to share concerns, escalate incidents, and document lessons learned [6]. A culture of trust and transparency helps raise early warning signs, reduces the stigma around reporting errors, and promotes a learning-oriented posture. Port authorities should foster this environment through regular internal briefings, after-action reviews, and low-pressure simulation exercises that emphasize both technical coordination and interpersonal dynamics. As psychological safety improves, so too does the quality and timeliness of information sharing—a critical factor in any effective cybersecurity program.

15.5 Skillsets and Training for the PCT

Unlike middle managers or frontline operators—who require structured training to raise cybersecurity awareness and develop basic response capabilities—the PCT must master advanced, role-specific competencies. Their function extends beyond compliance and awareness; it involves active defense, offense, coordination, and oversight of cyber resilience in an environment characterized by complex technologies, critical infrastructure, and evolving threats. These professionals must understand not only information systems but also OT, port logistics, and maritime regulatory regimes. Their skillsets cannot be standardized or addressed through off-the-shelf programs. Instead, capability development must align with the functional structure emphasized in this book—centered on the Blue, Red, Purple, and White Teams. These core teams represent the foundational pillars of operational cybersecurity, each with distinct but interconnected responsibilities that demand specialized skills and continuous refinement.

15.5.1 Blue Team: Defensive Capabilities and Continuous Monitoring

The Blue Team forms the port's frontline cyber defense, charged with identifying, containing, and mitigating security incidents. Members are often security analysts, engineers, or SOC personnel tasked with maintaining a 24/7 defense posture. In the port context, this means safeguarding systems like terminal operating systems (TOSs), vessel traffic management services, and port-wide surveillance platforms.

To be effective, team members must master the following competencies:

- Threat detection through real-time log analysis and anomaly spotting.
- Secure network architecture, segmentation, and firewall management.
- Operation and tuning of SIEM systems.
- Patch management and vulnerability assessments in OT-heavy environments.

While general certifications such as CompTIA Security+ or Cisco CyberOps provide a foundation, true preparedness requires domain-specific, scenario-based training. Exercises should simulate port-specific threats, such as breaches via outdated crane control systems or compromises to smart container tracking. Familiarity with the port's physical and operational landscape further strengthens threat contextualization.

15.5.2 Red Team: Offensive Testing and Security Validation

The Red Team replicates adversarial tactics to discover weaknesses before real attackers do. Common roles include ethical hackers, penetration testers, and security consultants. Their job is not only to break into systems but to demonstrate how such intrusions can escalate into operational disruption.

Key skills required in the port setting include:

- Network and OT penetration testing using tools such as Metasploit or Burp Suite.
- Development of custom exploits targeting port-specific technologies.
- Physical intrusion and social engineering methods for restricted areas.
- Comprehensive reconnaissance and attack planning based on threat intelligence.

Certifications like Offensive Security Certified Professional or Certified Ethical Hacker serve as baseline credentials, but alone, they do not suffice. Real-world proficiency comes from training on maritime systems—such as compromising wireless networks controlling automated gates or spoofing radio-frequency identification (RFID)-based access cards. Red Team members must understand both the cyber and physical architecture of the port to mimic the tactics of sophisticated threat actors.

15.5.3 Purple Team: Collaborative Simulation and Validation

The Purple Team integrates the functions of Red and Blue, ensuring that defensive measures are continuously tested and improved through collaborative simulation. These professionals often emerge from either team and are adept at translating offensive tactics into actionable defense improvements.

Essential capabilities include:

- Running adversary emulations using frameworks like MITRE ATT&CK for industrial control systems (ICS).
- Designing full-spectrum cyber-attack scenarios, from initial breach to exfiltration.
- Mapping detection failures and recommending compensating security controls.
- Leading joint exercises with SOC staff, IT teams, and operational departments.

Training should go beyond lab simulations to include coordinated, full-cycle attack-defense drills using tools like Atomic Red Team or CALDERA. The effectiveness of the Purple Team hinges not just on technical mastery but also on their ability to foster collaboration across team boundaries and ensure lessons are operationalized.

15.5.4 White Team: Oversight, Ethics, and Strategic Alignment

The White Team occupies a unique space, ensuring that all cybersecurity operations adhere to legal, ethical, and strategic standards. This group includes cybersecurity managers, compliance officers, legal advisors, and risk governance professionals. Their scope includes everything from coordinating policy enforcement to managing external communications during incidents.

Required competencies include:

- Deep knowledge of regulatory frameworks such as ISO/IEC 27001, IMO MSC.428(98), ISPS Code, and MSC-FAL.1/Circ.3.
- Risk governance and audit capabilities.
- Crisis communication skills for interfacing with media, regulators, and stakeholders.
- Policy development, enforcement, and cross-functional alignment.

Traditional workshops on governance or compliance are insufficient. These professionals benefit more from regulatory engagement, scenario-based crisis exercises, and simulations that combine policy response with technical disruptions. Their leadership is critical during high-pressure events when decisions must balance legal mandates, reputational risks, and operational constraints.

15.5.5 Strategic Skill Development and Capability Building for Color-Coded Cybersecurity Teams

For ports implementing color-coded cybersecurity teams—such as Red, Blue, and Purple teams—skill development and capability sustainability must be treated as strategic priorities. These teams require specialized expertise that extends well beyond typical enterprise cybersecurity training, given the unique combination of IT systems, OT, physical cargo-handling equipment, and legacy maritime communication networks within port environments. Cybersecurity personnel must not only detect unusual network activities but also grasp the potential operational impacts on critical port assets like quay cranes, smart gates, and automatic identification systems. To support the effective implementation of these teams, three key strategies are recommended.

- **Forge Domain-Specific Training Partnerships:** To build such expertise, ports should establish partnerships with maritime-focused cybersecurity institutions or naval training centers. These collaborations provide access to specialized knowledge, bridging the gap between general cybersecurity skills and the complex requirements of maritime operations. Incorporating domain-relevant tools and datasets into training exercises not only improves technical proficiency but ensures that skills remain applicable in live port environments. Additionally, cross-training between cyber and physical security teams enhances coordination when responding to hybrid threats that span both digital and physical domains—an increasingly likely scenario in modern ports. Embedding cyber teams into the day-to-day rhythm of port operations further grounds their situational awareness, enabling more intuitive threat detection and faster, context-aware decision making.

- **Institutionalize Continuous Learning and Immersive Training:** Sustaining these capabilities requires more than initial training. As cyber threats evolve, continuous learning becomes essential to maintain readiness. By institutionalizing annual re-certifications, organizing cyber range exercises, and offering access to tailored threat intelligence platforms, ports ensure that their cyber teams remain agile and current. Environments such as digital twins provide risk-free, immersive simulations that mimic real-world attack scenarios, helping teams refine both their technical responses and decision making under pressure. These practices foster operational resilience, reduce error rates, and shorten recovery times when incidents occur.
- **Strengthen Talent Retention and Professional Growth:** Talent retention is equally crucial to long-term capability. Without consistent staffing, institutional knowledge and operational maturity suffer. Ports should therefore define clear career pathways and offer mentorship programs to support growth within the organization. Funding for advanced training and industry events not only keeps teams up to date but signals an organizational commitment to their development. Finally, recognizing cybersecurity as a core strategic function—on par with operations and logistics—and aligning incentives accordingly helps cultivate a culture of loyalty and professional pride, which is essential to protecting the intricate cyber-physical environment that underpins modern port operations.

15.6 Fostering All Strategies by the PCT

In the context of smart port development, the PCT should no longer be viewed as a reactive support unit. Instead, it ought to be recognized as a central figure in shaping and executing cybersecurity strategies across the organization. Modern ports function as digital ecosystems, increasingly dependent on interconnected IT, OT, and Internet of Things (IoT) systems to manage cargo, automate operations, and support decision making. As these systems grow more integrated and complex, dispersing cybersecurity responsibilities across multiple units risks undermining consistency and response coordination. To maintain resilience and operational coherence, ports may benefit from empowering their cybersecurity teams to oversee the design, coordination, and execution of all cybersecurity-related functions.

This expanded leadership role is not just operationally appropriate—it also carries financial rationale. In a smart port handling global trade and large-scale data flows, a single cyber incident can cause significant financial loss. Prolonged downtime, breached contracts, disrupted supply chains, and regulatory fines are common consequences. Placing the PCT at the core of cybersecurity efforts enhances the port's ability to detect threats early, respond swiftly, and invest strategically in risk prevention—ultimately reducing the severity of incidents and improving the port's insurance profile.

The unique operational vantage point of the PCT supports this expanded function. Situated at the crossroads of technical systems, risk governance, and business operations, the team interacts with real-time system diagnostics, threat intelligence feeds, and operational alerts. These insights, combined with their routine collaboration with departments such as IT, logistics, operations, and compliance—as well as with external parties like insurers and regulators—give the PCT both the situational awareness and strategic context needed to guide cybersecurity decisions that serve the port's broader objectives.

Several critical areas of cybersecurity management are particularly suited to be led or closely coordinated by the PCT:

- **Cyber Risk Governance and Policy Alignment**: The PCT can help ensure that cybersecurity protocols align with international standards such as ISO/IEC 27001 and MSC.428(98), while also reflecting the port's operational needs. Their guidance enables executive leadership to connect technical risks with broader strategic decisions.
- **Incident Response and Recovery Strategy**: Given their proximity to detection and monitoring systems, cybersecurity professionals are well-positioned to develop, test, and coordinate incident response plans. Their role extends into managing recovery efforts alongside OT engineers and emergency teams.
- **Third-Party and Supply Chain Cyber Risk Management**: As cyber threats increasingly target supply chains, cybersecurity teams can design frameworks to assess and manage third-party risks—integrating these into procurement and partnership protocols.
- **Cyber Awareness and Cultural Development**: Promoting a cybersecurity-aware culture requires ongoing engagement. The PCT can customize training and awareness campaigns to suit the needs of crane operators, IT staff, managers, and contractors.
- **Secure Deployment of Emerging Technologies**: In ports adopting AI, IoT, and blockchain systems, early involvement from cybersecurity personnel can help embed security into system design, reducing vulnerabilities before deployment.

To support this broadened scope, ports should consider adjusting where the cybersecurity team sits within the organizational structure. Rather than placing it solely under the IT department, the team could report directly to the Chief Information Officer (CIO) or port director. This adjustment enhances both visibility and influence, enabling cybersecurity perspectives to be included from the outset in digital transformation plans and infrastructure upgrades. Faster decision making, clearer strategic alignment, and stronger stakeholder confidence often follow from such elevation.

This approach not only improves technical outcomes but also supports long-term strategic goals. A cybersecurity team positioned as a core driver of resilience contributes to operational continuity, investor and insurer trust, and regulatory readiness. While this leadership model may not yet be widespread in academic literature, its logic reflects the structural and operational realities of modern ports. As digitalization deepens and threat landscapes evolve, anchoring cybersecurity within core strategic functions is not simply an ideal—it is becoming a competitive necessity.

References

[1] IT Minister, "Understanding Cybersecurity Teams," 2024. [Online]. Available: www.itminister.co.uk/blog/understanding-cybersecurity-teams/.

[2] J. Boyens, C. Paulsen, N. Bartol, R. Moorthy and S. Shankles, "Notional Supply Chain Risk Management Practices for Federal Information Systems," 2012. [Online]. Available: https://nvlpubs.nist.gov/nistpubs/ir/2012/NIST.IR.7622.pdf.

[3] C. Senarak, "Cybersecurity Knowledge and Skills for Port Facility Security Officers of International Seaports: Perspectives of IT and Security Personnel," *The Asian Journal of Shipping and Logistics*, vol. 37, no. 4, pp. 345–360, 2021.

[4] Z. Amos, "Why Collaboration Is Essential for Cybersecurity Teams," 2025. [Online]. Available: https://gca.isa.org/blog/why-collaboration-is-essential-for-cybersecurity-teams.

[5] C. Senarak, "Toward Sustainability and Digital Resilience: A Circular Economy Cybersecurity Framework for Seaports," *Cleaner Logistics and Supply Chain*, vol. 15, 100220, 2025.

[6] Capitol Technology University, "Why Collaboration is Essential for Cybersecurity Teams," 2024. [Online]. Available: www.captechu.edu/blog/importance-of-collaboration-for-cybersecurity-teams#:~:text=The%20Importance%20of%20Collaboration%20in%20Cybersecurity&text=This%20can%20be%20achieved%20by,and%20practiced%20by%20all%20employees.

Index